LATE MODERNISM

THE ARTS AND INTELLECTUAL LIFE
IN MODERN AMERICA

Casey Nelson Blake, Series Editor

Volumes in the series explore questions at the intersection of the history of expressive culture and the history of ideas in modern America. The series is meant as a bold intervention in two fields of cultural inquiry. It challenges scholars in American studies and cultural studies to move beyond sociological categories of analysis to consider the ideas that have informed and given form to artistic expression—whether architecture and the visual arts or music, dance, theater, and literature. The series also expands the domain of intellectual history by examining how artistic works, and aesthetic experience more generally, participate in the discussion of truth and value, civic purpose and personal meaning that have engaged scholars since the late nineteenth century.

LATE MODERNISM

ART, CULTURE, AND POLITICS IN COLD WAR AMERICA

Robert Genter

UNIVERSITY OF PENNSYLVANIA PRESS

PHILADELPHIA · OXFORD

Published by
University of Pennsylvania Press
Philadelphia, Pennsylvania 19104-4112
www.upenn.edu/pennpress

Printed in the United States of America
on acid-free paper
10 9 8 7 6 5 4 3 2 1

Library of Congress Cataloging-in-Publication Data

Genter, Robert.
Late modernism : art, culture, and politics in Cold War America / Robert Genter.
p. cm. — (The arts and intellectual life in modern America)
Includes bibliographical references (p.) and index.
ISBN 978-0-8122-4264-5 (hardcover : alk. paper)
1. Modernism (Art) —United States. 2. Arts, American—20th century. 3. Arts and society—United States—History—20th century. 4. Arts—Political aspects—United States—History—20th century. 5. United States—Intellectual life—20th century. I. Title.
NX504.G46 2010
700'.41120973—dc22 2010008114

To my father and to the memory of my mother

CONTENTS

INTRODUCTION

A Genealogy of Postwar American Modernism

In April 1949, the San Francisco Art Association held a three-day "Western Round Table on Modern Art," bringing together an eclectic group of artists, critics, and curators to discuss the state of modernism in America. Held at the San Francisco Museum of Art, the round table was designed "to bring a representation of the best informed opinion of the time to bear on questions about art today," with the goal of achieving progress "in the exposure of hidden assumptions, in the uprooting of obsolete ideas, and in the framing of new questions."[1] The boldness of this agenda was matched by the boldness of the participants, which included art historian Robert Goldwater, artists Marcel Duchamp and Mark Tobey, composer Arnold Schoenberg, and architect Frank Lloyd Wright. While the organizers of the conference tried to structure the discussion around specific themes such as the function of the artist, the roles of the critic and the collector, and the purpose of the museum, the participants, regardless of the topic, tended to return their comments to a statement made by Marcel Duchamp early in the proceedings in which he distinguished between "taste" and what he referred to as the "aesthetic echo." According to the famed artist and provocateur, taste simply referred to the commonplace "likes and dislikes" of the average consumer, while the aesthetic echo referred to the willingness to forgo the familiar for the mysterious or unknown. "While many people have taste," argued Duchamp, "only a few are equipped with aesthetic receptivity."[2] For Duchamp, the popular attacks against modern art in the postwar period signaled that most individuals lacked both the education and temperament to appreciate the work that he and his fellow artists were producing.

While not all participants were willing to echo Duchamp's unabashed elitism, most agreed that, because of the nature of mass society and mass culture, the goal of the modern artist was to carve out a realm to safeguard the work of art from the distorting hands of an ungrateful public. Modernism, in other words, needed safekeeping. One participant, however, grumbled numerous complaints against this consensus. Throughout the proceedings, literary critic Kenneth Burke, who had recently achieved academic fame for his 1945 book of literary criticism *A Grammar of Motives*, wondered aloud if his fellow discussants had not in fact distorted the project of art in general. A veteran of the avant-garde movements in Greenwich Village in the 1920s and 1930s and a poet and fiction writer in his own right, Burke had obvious modernist credentials. But he spent three days in San Francisco trying to convince his fellow artists and critics that they had gone astray in their aesthetic projects. Specifically, Burke took a stand against what he saw as the two opposed but equally untenable approaches to modern art. On the one hand, several commentators including Robert Goldwater argued that the artwork at its essence was an external manifestation of the artist's true being and therefore needed protection from the public at large. As Goldwater explained, the modern artist had to struggle to ensure that nothing disturbed "the integral expression of his own personality as he conceives it—be it dealers, be it patrons, be it the concept of society in general."[3] Modernism, according to such a definition, was the medium through which the artist discovered himself outside the concerns of the world at large. On the other hand, several commentators such as Marcel Duchamp and Frank Lloyd Wright argued that the work of art had little to do with the intentions or feelings of the artist and existed as an ontologically distinct statement in and of itself. "We don't emphasize enough that the work of art is independent of the artist," asserted Duchamp; "the work of art lives by itself, and the artist who happened to make it is like an irresponsible medium."[4] For Duchamp, the imperative was to shield the artwork from any interpretive or cognitive distortion, guaranteeing in some sense its sacredness. Although the two camps disagreed on the origins of the artwork, they agreed, as Arnold Schoenberg declared, that such work should "never bow to the taste of the mediocre."[5]

Burke cringed at such language, continuously interrupting his colleagues to question their claims and their motives. Of course Burke was not rejecting the project of modernism overall. He was just as committed as the others at the table to the belief that art at its essence was the privileged medium for disrupting the staid conventions of modern life and reenchanting what had become an awful, gray landscape. But Burke feared that his fellow artists and critics had let their antisocial, if not misanthropic, feelings interfere with the true purpose of art—persuasion. "Very well, the artist is expressing himself," exclaimed Burke, "but he must use some kind of language."[6] Throughout, Burke argued that an exclusive focus on separating the artist and the artwork from the consuming public was foolish, ignoring the fact that the goal of the artist was to persuade the spectator, listener, or reader. According to Burke, "there is always communication. . . . The communication is there the minute the painting is done" (27). Even worse, artists like Duchamp and Wright ignored the fundamental need for artistic statement in a confused modern age. According to Burke, the recent global catastrophes—from economic collapse to total war—had not only irreparably damaged the average individual but had destroyed the traditional vocabularies through which the world was understood. In such a vacuum, the artist had a responsibility to offer new forms of orientation, new ways of understanding modern experience, and new sites for communion. "That's why we should take modern expression so seriously," argued Burke, "because it is concerned with the basic motives of life, with the things over which men will lurk, and mull, and linger, and for which they will seek new statements" (28). Those scrambling to escape into the purity of the aesthetic realm, disconnected from the social landscape, had according to Burke forsaken the true task of the artist.

Burke's criticisms in the late 1940s predated what would become a larger revolt against the aesthetic and epistemological assumptions of modernism in the 1960s and 1970s, as a range of intellectuals and artists associated with the movement known as postmodernism criticized the project of modernism in the postwar period as too esoteric, too devoid of playfulness, and too disconnected from popular concerns. Of course Burke was no postmodernist. While he challenged the elitism and biases of those gathered together in San Francisco, Burke had not, as others eventually would, given up on the project of modernism. Instead, he argued that the project simply needed to be recast. According to Burke, modern artists could not remain content with isolating themselves from anything that hinted of the popular, vernacular, or commonplace in the name of individual purity. Such artists instead needed to begin the difficult project of unearthing the shared historical, cultural, and political traditions in which they lived and reorienting those traditions in ways that were not merely more equitable and just but also translatable and digestible to a skeptical audience. In other words, modern artists needed to stop focusing on simply expressing themselves and instead to begin *commu-*

nicating, using the methods available in the modern world, to those willing to listen. "Can't the artist create for a communication?" Burke wondered aloud; "certainly he is not talking to himself, is he?" (33). In other words, modern art according to Burke needed to recover its roots as a form of rhetoric.

Burke was part of a group of artists, writers, and intellectuals in the 1940s and 1950s that began critiquing modernism from the inside, so to speak, challenging the obvious elitism and sense of separation that had led so many artists to abnegate their responsibility to translate their visions to a consuming public. Throughout the postwar period, Burke and those who followed his lead like sociologists C. Wright Mills and Erving Goffman and novelist Ralph Ellison or mirrored his theoretical moves like sociologist David Riesman, Freudian revisionist Norman Brown, novelist James Baldwin, and artist Jasper Johns reformulated the project of modernism in the early Cold War, giving rise to the movement I refer to as *late modernism*. Unwilling to abandon the literary and cultural revolution begun in the late nineteenth and early twentieth centuries by their modernist predecessors, whose original goal was to explore new forms of consciousness and unearth new forms of perception in the hopes of transforming the world at large, late modernists argued not only that the nature of the aesthetic form needed to be rethought in an age of mass media but that the general assumptions about the nature of subjectivity needed to be updated. They reformulated aesthetics as a mode of symbolic action—a deliberate attempt to use the aesthetic form to challenge the choice of lens through which individuals made sense of the world around them and to persuade them that the visions offered by the artist were not merely more poetic but possibly more liberating. For late modernists, the spoken word, the written work, the musical refrain, and the abstract canvas were all calls to action on the part of the artist as rhetorician, that is, an artist who interweaved rational arguments, libidinal enticements, and poetic pleas in his works in order to produce a commitment or at least a response from the viewing audience. Modernists, in other words, needed to take communication, and everything connected to it, seriously. "For in this world, communication is never an absolute," proclaimed Burke, for "only angels communicate absolutely."[7] But Burke demanded that his fellow modernists at least try. In so doing, Burke and other late modernists ushered in a new form of cultural politics, one that did not simply point to the rise of postmodernism in the 1960s but that overcame the artistic limitations of those postwar modernists like the ones Burke encountered in San Francisco in the late 1940s. The future of modernism was up for grabs.

The Contours of American Modernism

In a 1967 essay, "The Culture of Modernism," Irving Howe, in troubled, almost exacerbated language, argued that the cultural sensibility of the Western avant-garde of the early twentieth century had reached an unfortunate end. The exhaustion of modernist literature, exemplified in the failure of current writers to match the enthusiasm or radicalism of their predecessors, was for Howe a key sign that modern society was able to assimilate any and every oppositional force. As Howe argued, "it seems greatly open to doubt whether by now, a few decades after World War II, there can still be located in the West a coherent and self-assured avant-garde."[8] In part, Howe blamed the failure of modernism on its practitioners who had either retreated into university classrooms or had turned to the trappings of authoritarian politics to address the ineffectiveness of art to enact real change. But more important, modernists recognized that the imperative to maintain a constant struggle against the reigning cultural landscape had become a source of exhaustion. The enthusiasm of the original "men of 1914"—T. S. Eliot, Ezra Pound, Wyndham Lewis, and the like—had lapsed over the decades, according to Howe, into the futile whining of Jack Kerouac and his compatriots racing across the American continent. The playfulness of the Beat Generation was for Howe merely a façade covering a larger existential despair over its inability to imagine any reconciliation between the self and the world, exemplified by the forlorn hero at the end of Kerouac's *On the Road* mournfully staring at the New Jersey landscape. "In modern America," explained Howe, "this problem often appears as a clash between a figure of consciousness who embodies the potential of the human and a society moving in an impersonal rhythm that is hostile or, what is perhaps worse, indifferent to that potential" (28). According to Howe, the incessant nihilism within modernist literature was a sign of this exhaustion.

Howe's essay was merely one of many eulogies written in the 1960s about the supposed end of modernism. In his 1965 introduction to his classic work of formalist criticism *Modern Poetry and the Tradition*, literary critic Cleanth Brooks asked the same question as Howe: "Has the revolution in poetry which began about the time of the First World War now exhausted itself?"[9] Both critics presented a narrative of decline, a story about the unraveling of modernism from its heyday in artistic circles in Paris and London in the 1920s to its disappearance by the 1960s. Howe saw this unraveling occurring through three historical stages. Modernism had burst onto the cultural scene in the nineteenth century as a reaction against bourgeois society, an aesthetic heroism emerging out of the remnants of the Romantic movement that challenged political, social, and religious norms through "a transcendental and orgiastic aggrandizement of matter and event in behalf of personal vitality."[10] This effort to delve into the depths of human consciousness to reveal the artifice of modern life—a theme Howe found in Walt Whitman, Arthur Rimbaud, and Charles Baudelaire—marked the ambitious attempt by early modernist practitioners to present a vision of man that ran counter to the gentility of late nineteenth-century society. But the experience of World War I and the collapse of the revolutionary movements in the aftermath gave rise to a chastened form of modernism found in the work of Virginia Woolf, Thomas Mann, and others, a modernism that began "to recoil from externality and now devotes itself . . . to a minute examination of its own inner dynamics: freedom, compulsion, caprice." This retreat to an extreme form of subjectivity, guarding against any social contamination, eventually proved to be an insurmountable problem. In its final stages after World War II, modernism abandoned its heroic claims, lapsing into a state of despair because of the perceived futility of art as a means of producing social change. At this point, "there occurs an emptying-out of the self, a revulsion from the wearisomeness of both individuality and psychological gain." Samuel Beckett, according to Howe, was the result.

My book picks up where Howe left off, charting a similar evolution of modernist practices but focusing specifically on the moment after World War II when the famed New York intellectual claimed that modernism had lost its noble purpose. In beginning my story at that moment, I want to challenge the declension narrative that Howe and others have presented and, in so doing, make a case for an invigorated "late modernism" that encompassed a wide range of artistic expression. Howe's essay in many ways reflected what was a widely acknowledged divide between defenders of a slightly more academic, and formalist version of *high modernism* and those practitioners of a supposedly irrational, perverse, and therefore immature form, which I term *romantic modernism*, associated with the members of the Beat Generation who had fled the university for the corrupt spaces of Times Square or the open road. Both sides accepted these caricatures. Literary critic Lionel Trilling, for instance, always stressed his distance from his former students Allen Ginsberg and Jack Kerouac, who, in turn, obsessively stressed their rejection of the staid modernism of their Columbia professor. Trilling openly challenged the "group of my students who have become excited over their discovery of the old animosity which Ezra Pound and William Carlos Williams bear to the iamb, and have come to feel that could they but break the iambic shackles, the whole of modern culture could find a true expression."[11] For Trilling, modernism had reached an impasse; for Ginsberg, modernism had only begun to change the world. This divide between teacher and student was nothing new in the history of modernism.[12] Since its inception, modernism had been divided against itself—between symbolism and surrealism, formalism and experimentalism, imagism and futurism, Ezra Pound and F. T. Marinetti, Pablo Picasso and Henri Matisse.[13]

In American intellectual circles after World War II, the tradition of high modernism reached its zenith, a form of modernist practice self-consciously determined to separate art from the detritus of daily existence. Arguing that the failure of religion to provide meaningful answers to a world continuously at war had rendered individual salvation problematic, high modernists believed that aesthetics was the only refuge in a disenchanted, chaotic landscape. High modernism originated in the 1920s in the poetry of T. S. Eliot, Ezra Pound, William Butler Yeats, and Rainer Maria Rilke and the novels of Virginia Woolf, Thomas Mann, and Marcel Proust but became the dominant version of modernism in the United States in the 1940s and 1950s, led in particular by the literary studies of the New Critics. Originating in the criticism of T. S. Eliot, William Empson, and I. A. Richards, the New Criticism was associated with the work of Allen Tate, John Crowe Ransom, Cleanth Brooks, and others, who turned modernism into a literary style and a pedagogical practice. Their defense of aesthetics as an autonomous practice separate from political and personal demands was echoed by a range of other critics throughout the early Cold War including Dwight Macdonald, Lionel Trilling, Philip Rahv, Clement Greenberg, and Theodor Adorno, all of whom turned to formalist modes of reading that treated the aesthetic object as an autonomous work disconnected from the distorting hand of mass society. For these high modernists, the work of art, either through the formal relationship of the painting's colors and designs or through the poem's internal tensions, presented a form of experience distinct from the banalities of everyday life. These critics officially institutionalized their brand of modernism in the 1950s, promoting a particular canon of writers and artists through established academic journals, publishing houses, university classrooms, popular magazines, and art galleries. Reflecting upon the threat of totalitarianism from abroad and the militarization of American society in the early Cold War, high modernists fought a desperate campaign to safeguard art as a distinct mode of knowledge separate from industrial growth.

Of course, modernists of all persuasions were committed to aesthetics as a form of disruption and disorientation, a process of making the familiar seem unfamiliar and the commonplace enchanted. But the institutionalization of high modernism, despite its commitment to challenging political orthodoxy and bourgeois values, was too conservative for an emerging group of artists in the 1950s who argued that the high modernist stress on aesthetics as a distinctive experience separate from everyday life had produced art that was isolated, overly intellectual, and cold and therefore irrelevant.[14] A range of new modernist practitioners—from Beat poets such as Allen Ginsberg, Jack Kerouac, and William Burroughs to writers such as Norman Mailer and Saul Bellow to abstract expressionists such as Jackson Pollock, Willem de Kooning, and Mark Rothko—argued, like many previous groups within the European avant-garde, that any commitment to aesthetics went hand-in-hand with a commitment to rejuvenating life. As Harold Rosenberg, the New York art critic whose 1952 essay "The American Action Painters" outlined this new commitment, said, "the new painting has broken down every distinction between art and life."[15] I refer to this motley group as romantic modernists because they were determined to return to what they saw as the original roots of modernism in the dissolution of Romanticism—to the writings of Henri Bergson and Friedrich Nietzsche, to the poetry of Arthur Rimbaud and Paul Verlaine, and to the disruptive techniques of André Breton and other European surrealists—as a way to translate life into art and vice versa. These artists, as they saw themselves, were returning to the moment in the late nineteenth century when Romanticism gave birth to modernism, that is, the moment in which aesthetics began to incorporate the metaphysical claims once generated by religion. As Cleanth Brooks explained in distinguishing between high and romantic modernism, "because the critical revolution that began some fifty years ago was essentially a reaction against Romanticism . . . and because the countermovements of the last fifteen years, including that of the Beatniks, have been essentially pro-Romantic, any attempt to set the revolution in a wider context will have to concern itself with Romanticism."[16] In part, these artists were frustrated with their lack of critical reception, arguing, as Jack Kerouac and Jackson Pollock both did throughout the 1950s, that they were producing modernist masterpieces unrecognized by their formalist counterparts. This frustration eventually translated into entirely new forms of modernist practice that operated through shock and immediacy and that incorporated spontaneous methods of production. Soon, the success of these romantic modernists produced in their high modernist counterparts endless stories about the contamination of modernism by arrogant bohemians and delinquent college dropouts.

In the end, however, neither mode of modernist practice was triumphant; as the traditional story goes, both high modernism and its precocious avant-garde challenger had their loftier claims punctured by the sudden rise of postmodernism in the 1960s. By the end of the decade, for instance, the playfulness of the soup can paintings of Andy Warhol had replaced Jackson Pollock's "drip" paintings as the emblem of American art. Critic Andrew Ross has observed in perhaps overstated language that "modernism ends when there are no places left to run to—the autonomy of art, the Romantic 'psyche,' poetic license, the bardic, magic, psychosis, suicide, and even silence."[17] Modernism in all its forms had seemingly relinquished its privileged status, a shocking transformation given its ubiquity only a few years prior. Indeed, modernism had appeared in the 1950s in endless forms—the action paintings of Willem de Kooning, the cultural reportage of *Partisan Review*, the Jamesian-inspired criticism of Dwight Macdonald, the aesthetic writings of Theodor Adorno, the spontaneous prose of Jack Kerouac, the color-field paintings of Mark Rothko, the projective verse of Charles Olson, and the Dadaist-inflected compositions of William Burroughs. The early Cold War was a moment of seemingly endless experimentation, craftsmanship, and innovation in American art. But the apparent displacement of both by the end of the 1960s—due to charges of elitism, to the reactionary politics of its practitioners such as Kerouac or Trilling who lambasted the student movement, and to the suicidal gestures of Pollock and Rothko—signaled a fundamental transition in American culture.

But we cannot act as if there was something linear or logical to the rise and fall of modernism, as if the complications inherent in the belief in the transformative potential of art inevitably meant that modernism in all its forms was destined to be eclipsed. Irving Howe himself, in a more honest moment, made a similar claim: "Modernism will not come to an end; its war chants will be repeated through the decades."[18] We must recognize instead the more complicated historical roots of modernism, thereby treating the transition to postmodernism less as a radical shift to a fundamentally new paradigm of literary and epistemological understanding and more as a complex, historically engaged challenge to the dominant strands of modernist practice.[19] Similarly, we need to move beyond the arbitrary divisions between high modernism and the avant-garde and between modernism and postmodernism, no longer treating these camps as the only possibilities of aesthetic and epistemological practice. In this spirit, I argue that this opposition between high and romantic modernism in the early Cold War was triangulated by another tradition, late modernism, which critiqued the theoretical assumptions of these other traditions and prefigured the movement toward postmodernism. Kenneth Burke's outburst at the round table in San Francisco in 1949 was an obvious example of this emerging trend. Indeed, there were a number of artists, writers, and critics from the 1950s who did not fit comfortably within any of the traditional modernist categories, artists such as Jasper Johns who challenged both the formalist aesthetics of Clement Greenberg and the overt expressionism of Jackson Pollock while also pointing the way toward the overt commercialism of Andy Warhol but without making the journey himself.

The title of my book therefore signifies both the chronological *lateness* of modernism in the 1960s, when such practices had supposedly run their course, and a demarcation of a viable modernist tradition in its own right, one that complicates the story that Howe and others have told over the years. Alongside the battle between high modernism and romantic modernism and between the intellectual elite and these bohemian upstarts was a third tradition that charted an entirely different course, one that leads to a fuller, more compelling explanation for the transition to postmodern aesthetics in the late twentieth century. In this, I am following the lead of critic Fredric Jameson, who argued years ago that cultural historians needed to introduce an intermediary concept between the demarcations of modernism and postmodernism, a space for those artists and writers who do not fit comfortably within any of the other established categories.[20] But unlike Jameson, who merely echoes Howe in linking late modernism to the last gasp of writers such as Samuel Beckett or Vladimir Nabokov, I want to posit a more complex version of late modernism, one that was able to offer a new and more flexible understanding of art and the aesthetic experience. If anything, the tradition of late modernism represented a *maturing* of modernism, an overcoming of the elitism that hampered high modernism and a rejection of the more mystical claims of romantic modernism. This tradition was best represented by Kenneth Burke, whose essays, reviews, and, more important, three major works from this period—*A Grammar of Motives*, *A Rhetoric of Motives*, and *The Rhetoric of Religion*—rethought the nature of modernism. Unlike high modernists who stressed the autonomy of the aesthetic object and unlike romantic modernists who treated art as a direct expression of a unique individual subject, Burke argued instead that the work was a rhetorical form, that is, an object that confronted and challenged the embedded assumptions within particular languages, discursive formations, and established motives. As I explore throughout this book, Burke and those who directly borrowed from his work such as C. Wright Mills, Erving Goffman, and Ralph Ellison or those who independently echoed his claims such as Norman Brown, David Riesman, James Baldwin, and Jasper Johns all treated art (as well as all discursive forms) as *persuasive* elements that intervened in and critiqued embedded assumptions of everyday life. These late modernists tried to open modernism by blending it with realism and rhetoric, treating art at its essence as a form of communication.

Of course late modernism did not represent any self-acknowledged group of compatriots any more than the earliest modernists considered themselves part of a unified movement. One can hardly imagine a cocktail conversation between Norman Brown, Jasper Johns, and Erving Goffman or, for that matter, one between T. S. Eliot, Virginia Woolf, and Friedrich Nietzsche. Obviously, any interpretive category is artificial at best, and I do not want to give the impression that these late modernists represented any sort of "school" in the traditional sense. But missing from the literature on art and culture after 1945 is any sense that there was a range of writers and artists who tried to find a language that did not partake of either the formalist visions of high modernism or the mystical visions of romantic modernism. For instance, the novelist Ralph Ellison spent years fighting against both alternatives. He repeatedly admitted that he had little patience for high modernist critics such as Lionel Trilling who limited the possibilities inherent within the aesthetic form by trying to divest art of any social or political attachments. "Fuck Trilling and his gang," Ellison wrote to his friend Albert Murray in 1957; "I know that a novel is simply hard to write, especially during this time when you can't take anything for granted anymore."[21] Similarly, Ellison had little respect for the bohemian denizens of New York, who included Norman Mailer, Jack Kerouac, Allen Ginsberg, and others, a modernist avant-garde pushing madness, despair, and sex. "Man, where did Norman Mailer and them—them—teenagers get that shit from," an exacerbated Ellison once asked; "that goddamned Mailer sounds like a degenerate" (211).

In contrast to these two dominant strands of modernist practice, Ellison centered his own project on what he referred to as "the enigma of aesthetic communication."[22] Unlike high modernists who focused on the artwork as a form disconnected from outside entanglements and romantic modernists who saw the artwork as a reflection of their own personalities, Ellison argued instead that the artwork was designed to address the complicated relationship between artist and audience, serving as a means to bridge social differences and to forge new connections between disparate individuals. The artwork in this sense did not skirt social communication, as many modernists would have it, but existed solely as a form of communication between the artist who offered his personal vision of redemption and an audience who "counters the artist's manipulation of forms with an attitude of antagonistic cooperation." In this way, the importance of any artwork was for Ellison its rhetorical nature, that is, the way in which it challenged the choice of cultural lens through which its audience made sense of the world. "By playing artfully upon the audience's sense of experience and form," explained Ellison, "the artist seeks to shape its emotions and perceptions to his vision, while it, in turn, simultaneously cooperates and resists, says yes no in an it-takes-two-to-tango binary response to his effort." In so doing, Ellison, like his other late modernist counterparts, offered an entirely new way of thinking about the nature of the modernist form, one that refused to shy away from the notion that art at its essence was a form of rhetoric, persuasion, and social communication.

But I want to guard against the assumption, despite what my terminology might suggest, that I am arguing that there was some sort of strict progression to modernist developments or that the eclipse of prior forms of modernism was inevitable. My category of late modernism instead is designed to open up our understanding of the possibilities inherent to the modernist movement overall, possibilities that often were grossly simplified or quickly brushed aside by postmodernist critics who have sometimes offered a less than nuanced account of their predecessors.[23] Indeed, the seeming shift from Jackson Pollock to Andy Warhol, from Jack Kerouac to Thomas Pynchon, and from Allen Tate to Paul de Man was anything but inevitable or absolute. Now that we have begun to rethink the nature of postmodernism after its heyday in the 1980s, absorbing its lessons and thinking through its implications, we can begin the task of forging new aesthetic practices that take into account the range of possibilities offered by the various forms of modernism and postmodernism available to us. In other words, I treat the development of modernism as a contested and continuous one that offers no easy solutions and no simple formulations. Thus, my book traces a combative debate between these three schools of modernist practice—high, romantic, and late modernism—and the divergent paths that such practices took throughout the 1950s and 1960s. In so doing, I suggest that the rethinking of the aesthetic form offered by Kenneth Burke, Jasper Johns, Ralph Ellison, and others might help us think through our own current impasse.

Modernism and the Cultural Politics of the Cold War

Of course these debates about modernist practices were not conducted in a vacuum. A cultural tradition predicated upon disrupting staid patterns of thought has always, despite claims from its formalist practitioners, maintained a close watch on political and economic developments. In this sense, the path of modernism in America after World War II was intimately connected to the larger political and cultural debates of the early Cold War. Whether it was Lionel Trilling fretting over the sexualization of American culture in the 1950s or Jack Kerouac lamenting the perceived decline in paternal authority in the wake of the feminist movement or Ralph Ellison reconsidering racial politics in the midst of the civil rights movement, modernists of all persuasions developed their particular aesthetic practices in relationship to the fluctuations of postwar society. But if anything drove modernism in the 1950s it was the larger fear over the threat of totalitarianism. No modernist—from Dwight Macdonald to William Burroughs to Kenneth Burke—wrote about the nature of society without explicitly referencing the threat from right-wing and left-wing authoritarian movements. Of course each group confronted totalitarian politics in different ways. High modernists such as Theodor Adorno, Lionel Trilling, Clement Greenberg, and others saw totalitarianism as an endemic part of the larger collapse of Western civilization and as a desperate psychological response to a world with no focus or direction. Unlike the originators of high modernism in the 1920s, those who wrote after the experience of World War II jettisoned the connection between aesthetic hierarchies and political ones that had led many modernists in the 1930s to turn to Fascism to realize their social visions. High modernism in the Cold War was almost by definition antiauthoritarian, exemplified by the litany of nonaesthetic concerns that appeared in works such as Theodor Adorno's *The Authoritarian Personality* and Lionel Trilling's *The Liberal Imagination*. High modernism had become a chastened form of modernism. But such practitioners held onto the belief that aesthetics as such, fundamentally disconnected from the contaminating hands of mass society, could disrupt the overtly rational norms of modern society.

I outline how this varied group of high modernists—Theodor Adorno, Allen Tate, Dwight Macdonald, Lionel Trilling, and others—confronted the problem of authoritarianism after World War II. The explicit goal of high modernism in America, besides institutionally defending the humanities in the face of the militarization of society in the early Cold War, was to carve out an image of man uncontaminated by the corrupting appeals of mass society. Promoting a political realism removed from the trappings of ideology, high modernists turned to Freudian psychology to rethink the grounding of the self, offering a new vision of man's personal autonomy and providing an almost antinomian defense of the individual. In so doing, high modernists like Adorno and Trilling echoed the anti-Communist sentiments of many Cold War liberals, presenting a chastened image of man in the modern age and oftentimes defending the excesses of the rising national security state in the 1950s as protection against the allure of group psychology. In many ways, then, high modernists became domesticated, forfeiting, as numerous challenging practitioners such as Kenneth Burke and Norman Mailer pointed out, the original antistatist, anticapitalist, and anarchic principles inherent to most forms of modernism. Thus, I trace the ever-increasing link between high modernists and the conservative politics of the early Cold War, a link that helps to explain the myriad challenges within modernist circles to their hegemony.

But of course the threat of totalitarianism drove most political discussions in the 1950s, even within other modernist circles. In contrast to their more austere counterparts, romantic modernists like painter Barnett Newman and novelists William Burroughs and Norman Mailer saw totalitarianism instead as a creeping social disease, one emanating from a decrepit American culture controlled by corporations, indistinguishable political parties, and government agencies. For romantic modernists, totalitarianism was, literally and metaphorically, a form of cancer infecting the body politic, a cancer that entered the individual's system in discrete psychological ways. By presenting such an encompassing definition of totalitarianism, these romantic modernists fretted over almost all of the socioeconomic changes in American life after 1945, lambasting everything from the decline of more rugged forms of masculinity in the wake of postindustrialism to the rise of modern advertising, the expansion of the federal government, and so on. In so doing, they offered a reactionary, libertarian form of politics, one that reflected their obsessive concern with the autonomy of self. They even saw totalitarian practices within the politics of high modernism itself; as William Burroughs once explained to Allen Ginsberg: "It's about time you wised up to Trilling. . . . He's got no orgones, no *mana*, no charge to him. Just soaks up your charge to keep the battery of his brain turning out crap for the *Partisan Review*."[24] All of the practices of romantic modernism—the action painting of New York art circles, the spontaneous poetics of Beat writers, and the philosophy of hip in the work of Norman Mailer—were part of a common effort to offer an image of man freed from the creeping disease of psychological control. Romantic modernists searched for an anchor point for individual identity in a world that had apparently reduced subjectivity to mere appearance. Such speculations on the metaphysical ranged from appropriations of Buddhist transcendentalism to discourses on a foundational *élan vital* or energy underlying artistic production. Through references to either mythology or metaphysics, the immediate was translated into the eternal, all in a desperate attempt to respiritualize the world by making the ordinary extraordinary.

However, not all modernists exhibited the paranoia found in disparate works such as William Burroughs's *Naked Lunch* or Theodor Adorno's *The Authoritarian Personality*. Although equally concerned with the problem of mass politics, late modernists were more willing to accept the disorder of the modern world without lapsing into the nostalgic visions of a prelapsarian moment that emerged from high modernist writings or without accepting the more mystical visions of romantic modernists. While most modernist practitioners such as Trilling, Adorno, and Burroughs fretted that the autonomous self was under siege from the contaminating influences of mass society and tried, albeit in different ways, to shore up individual subjectivity from noxious influences, late modernists such as C. Wright Mills and Kenneth Burke outlined the social, historical, and linguistic constitution of the self. In so doing, they promoted those more open and intersubjective forms of identity later associated with postmodernism.[25] These modernists were willing to view the self in a much more linear or horizontal fashion than their modernist counterparts who delved into the deeper depths of the self. This, if anything, was the common theme running through diverse texts such as David Riesman's *The Lonely Crowd*, Erving Goffman's *The Presentation of Self in Everyday Life*, and Ralph Ellison's *Invisible Man*. Late modernist practitioners offered a complex account of subject formation, one that dispensed with the overt essentialism of their counterparts and one that was willing to explore the liberating possibilities remaining in a world seemingly full of artifice, imitative practices, and social conformity.

From Kenneth Burke to James Baldwin to Jasper Johns, late modernists saw a complexity to human identity—a subject that was formed in and through its relations to others, to institutional forms, and to the political landscape.

Such late modernists argued that the self was neither fully whole nor autonomous but instead constituted through an endless parade of generalized and significant others—sometimes with overlapping agendas and sometimes with conflicting interests—that provided the context for self-identity. "What is our 'reality,'" argued Kenneth Burke, "but all this clutter of symbols about the past combined with whatever things we know mainly through maps, magazines, newspapers, and the like about the present?"[26] Like the postmodernist writers who came soon after them, late modernists saw the self as formed through a series of identificatory and linguistic practices. But unlike those postmodernists, Burke and others refused to believe that the self was reducible to the context in which it was situated. One can note the difficulty of this project by examining the odd terminology used by many late modernists—sociologist David Riesman referenced the *autonomous other-directed* personality, sociologist Erving Goffman spoke of the *presentation* of self in society, and Kenneth Burke described man as *homo rhetorician*. For all such writers, the self was not something given but something achieved through a delicate social, linguistic, and economic *performance*, a self that emerged from the landscape of everyday life and that tried to provide an account of its needs, desires, and possibilities. These late modernists provided a description of the self that included, however hesitant, language of the self as *subject*.

In this sense, my book is both a work of tradition building, in which I carve out an overlooked moment in American intellectual history, and a work of cultural history, in which I map these debates over modernism onto the cultural terrain of the early Cold War. In so doing, I chart the contentious debate between these three forms of modernism—high, romantic, and late—over the nature of art and the nature of the subject. In Part I, I analyze the rise and fall of high modernism, examining how a range of critics such as Lionel Trilling, Theodor Adorno, and Clement Greenberg tried to promote high art as a rejoinder to an American landscape dominated by science and technology and threatened by the specter of totalitarianism from abroad. As the Cold War progressed, these high modernists eventually forfeited their prior aesthetic commitments and turned to more conservative assumptions about social transformation. Throughout, I detail the response by several late modernists who critiqued the failed project of high modernism, exposing its biases and limitations. In Part II, I trace the development of romantic modernism, exemplified by the action painting of Jackson Pollock and Willem de Kooning and the spontaneous poetics of Jack Kerouac and Allen Ginsberg, an avant-garde that similarly critiqued the conservative politics of high modernism. Offering endless metaphysical speculations on the true grounding of being, these romantic modernists tried to salvage the self from a supposedly decrepit, authoritarian culture. Such wild speculations were at times quite cartoonish, and throughout Part II, I examine the rejoinder offered by late modernists to these compatriots as well, exposing the reactionary, if not retrograde, assumptions about identity lurking behind their aesthetic project. Finally, in Part III I summarize the theoretical and aesthetic project of late modernism, demonstrating not only the contribution of writers such as Kenneth Burke and Ralph Ellison to the postmodern turn of the 1960s and 1970s but their own independent reworking of modernism overall. Readers of course will object to certain characterizations of particular works or the pigeonholing of certain thinkers. This is endemic to any attempt at classification. But the refusal to make categorical distinctions leads, borrowing from a famous phrase, to the night in which all cows are black. As we begin to answer difficult questions such as "who comes after the subject," we might need to look backward to move forward.[27] Any post-postmodernist conceptualization of the self needs to recognize the social, political, and historical roots of this dilemma.

PART I

High Modernism in America

Self and Society in the Early Cold War

CHAPTER ONE

Science, Postmodernity, and the Rise of High Modernism

In July 1945 Vannevar Bush, director of the Office of Scientific Research and Development, submitted a presidential report titled *Science: The Endless Frontier* in which he detailed a plan for federal support of scientific research in peacetime. With a certain utopian flourish, Bush argued that "advances in science, when put to practical use mean more jobs, higher wages, shorter hours, more abundant crops, more leisure for recreation, for study, for learning how to live without the deadening drudgery which has been the burden of the common man for ages past."[1] Given the climate of a society transitioning to an uncertain peacetime order, Bush's arguments for a permanent collaboration between universities, corporations, and the military to conduct basic and applied research found a receptive audience. The technological achievements made by civilian scientists working under the auspices of the Office of Scientific Research and Development and the Manhattan Project had made federal officials very aware of the contributions to national strategic policy offered by scientific experts and generated considerable enthusiasm for extending large-scale, government-sponsored research into the postwar era, giving rise to what Alvin Weinberg, director of the Oak Ridge National Laboratory, termed "big science."[2] Indeed, by the end of hostilities with Japan, the "great science debate," as *Fortune* magazine described, had begun.[3] In obvious ways, the rise of Cold War tensions gave considerable urgency to the development of a working accommodation between scientists, military planners, and government officials, an accommodation that was formed through a series of protracted debates over the creation of the National Science Foundation in 1950, over the shortage of scientific manpower that reached a crisis point during the Korean War, and over the challenges that Soviet advancements presented after the famous launching of a Russian satellite in 1957. James Conant, in his 1947 retirement speech as president of the American Association for the Advancement of Science, summed up conventional wisdom in claiming that "every industrialized nation is dependent on applied science for the continuing welfare of its economy and, alas, for the military security of its frontiers and cities."[4] This dependence, argued Conant, meant science "will play a determining role in the outcome of affairs."

With considerable speed, the scientific establishment was institutionalized nationally within the Department of Defense, the National Aeronautics and Space Administration, the Department of Energy, and the National Science Foundation.[5] Various branches of the armed services, moreover, contributed funding for research into military equipment. For instance, the Office of Naval Research individually sponsored twelve hundred research projects at almost two hundred universities, and the Air Force Office of Scientific Research supported university research into guided missiles and aviation devices.[6] Programs across the country at places such as MIT and Stanford University were the beneficiaries of this funding, dramatically increasing research budgets. Besides their growing role as sites for scientific research, American universities also shouldered the burden of producing an adequate number of trained scientists and engineers, a responsibility that grew in importance as the Cold War lingered.[7] Graduate fellowships in the physical sciences were funded by several federal agencies including the Atomic Energy Commission and the National Science Foundation as well as by many defense contractors including IBM, General Electric, DuPont, and Westinghouse. But the outbreak of the Korean War proved that the supply of scientific talent did not match demand. Both during and after hostilities, the Office of Defense Mobilization issued regular warnings to the president, arguing that the current number of trained scientists and engineers "may well prove fatally inadequate to the great requirements of American leadership and security."[8] In response to a 1957 presidential committee on scientists and engineers, which encouraged the "marshaling" of the nation's "brainpower resources," President Eisenhower signed the National Defense Education Act of 1958, which provided federal assistance to states to improve education in math, science, and engineering and increased federal loans and fellowships for college students studying science.[9] Additionally, a number of curriculum reform movements in the late 1950s, including the Physical Science Study Committee, the Biological Sciences Curriculum Study, and the Chemical Education

Material Study, reshaped school programs in the hopes of garnering student interest.[10] By late 1958, the U.S. Office of Education enthusiastically reported that the nation's universities would confer one-third more bachelor degrees in the sciences than the previous year and that graduate programs in physics and engineering registered similar increases.[11]

As the sales of amateur microscopes, science kits, and telescopes escalated, American scientists achieved a corresponding elevation in their social standing. Mass-circulation magazines and television programs introduced the "wizards of the coming wonders," and several scientists, including J. Robert Oppenheimer with his ubiquitous porkpie hat, became national celebrities.[12] Many scientists were also swept into politics. When the Atomic Energy Commission was established in 1946, a civilian advisory committee was formed to serve as a scientific liaison to commission members. Even more directly, President Truman established the Science Advisory Committee within the Office of Defense Mobilization in 1951 to advise on national security policy, a committee whose original members were some of the most prominent American scientists including J. Robert Oppenheimer, James Conant, and James Killian. Despite their continuing rancor toward military officials over security regulations, postwar scientists received an inordinate amount of respect. Indeed, because they represented "the leaders of mankind's greatest inquiry into the mysteries of matter, of the earth, the universe, and of life itself," *Time* magazine named "fifteen scientists" including I. I. Rabi and Edward Teller the "men of the year" for 1960.[13] At the moment when science was "at the apogee of its power for good or evil," everyone in the United States including "statesmen and savants, builders and even priests" had become, according to the editors at *Time*, the "servants" of the modern scientist.

Of course American society as a whole had difficulty swallowing such a notion.[14] Warning that "the monuments of Big Science—the huge rockets, the high-energy accelerators, the high-flux research reactors" had become "the symbols of our time just as surely as Notre Dame is a symbol of a past age," Alvin Weinberg was just one of many commentators wondering if federal support of large-scale scientific research was a "marvel or menace."[15] By the time scientist and writer C. P. Snow delivered his famous 1959 lecture at Cambridge University in which he marked the mutual distrust between the "two cultures" of science and literature, intellectuals in America had already taken umbrage against scientists such as Snow for making disparaging remarks about the supposed failure of men of letters to offer anything more than "imbecile expressions of anti-social feelings."[16] For instance, in his response to the public debate that emerged after Snow's lecture, literary critic Lionel Trilling challenged Snow's promotion of "scientific philosopher-kings" to a position of power, noting that modern science, unlike literature, was incapable of "making a declaration about the qualities that life should have, about the qualities life does not have but should have."[17] As threats of impending nuclear disaster lingered in the air, many men of letters issued a similar defense of the humanities in the face of the militarization of American life.

The Challenge of High Modernism

Although modern science had become, as J. Robert Oppenheimer explained, part of "the common understanding," many postwar intellectuals such as Lionel Trilling worried about the implications, both political and psychological, of this intellectual shift, arguing that the scientific method was not the only framework for understanding the surrounding world.[18] Indeed, a conglomeration of artists, writers, and literary critics, both separately and in tandem, rethought the nature of aesthetics within this Cold War landscape, giving rise to the movement known as high modernism. Arguing that bourgeois society had failed in its emancipatory promises, that bureaucratic rationality had usurped the public sphere, and that the scientific method had morphed into a form of domination, high modernists went to great lengths to carve out aesthetics as the last vestige of prior utopian promises vanquished by recent atrocities. The constellation of intellectual traditions that composed the high modernist position in the 1940s and 1950s included the literary practices of the New Criticism, formulated in part by John Crowe Ransom, Allen Tate, and Cleanth Brooks; the cultural criticism of the New York intellectuals, including Dwight Macdonald, Lionel Trilling, Irving Howe, and Philip Rahv; the critical theory of the relocated Frankfurt school, centered on the work of Theodor Adorno, Max Horkheimer, Herbert Marcuse, and Erich Fromm; and the aesthetic writings of the art critic Clement Greenberg. At its core, high modernism was a defense of the humanities in the face of this rising enthusiasm for science and an argument for a disinterested and polite observance of the natural world in contrast to the aggressive hand of technology.

To many high modernists, the development of modern science went hand-in-hand with the rational administration of social life; for others, it marked the widespread acceptance of unimpeded capitalist growth as a social imperative. Members of the transplanted Institute for Social Research acknowledged both. Herbert Marcuse's *One-Dimensional Man* (1964), for instance, opened with an oft-repeated claim: "A comfortable, smooth, reasonable, democratic unfreedom prevails in advanced industrial civilization, a token of technical progress."[19] Packed with topical references to the military-industrial complex of the early Cold War, *One-Dimensional Man* was a vociferous critique of the intermingling of science, technology, and capitalist production, an indictment not only of the sacrifices demanded by American politicians but also of the historical trend of mechanization that characterized modern life. The footnotes in his book pointed to an earlier German text by Max Horkheimer and Theodor Adorno that had first outlined the Frankfurt school critique of modern industrial society. Written primarily while the two German scholars were living in southern California during the war, *Dialectic of Enlightenment* reflected the despondency of two Jewish émigrés coming to terms with the devastation in their homeland and with an American landscape that seemed, in Adorno's words, to "[display] capitalism in a state of almost complete purity."[20] Borrowing language from Nietzsche, Weber, and Marx, the two writers brushed aside the naïve belief that the technological advances ushered in by the Enlightenment were harbingers of a better tomorrow. Eighteenth-century proponents of the Enlightenment had promised that a commitment to the scientific method would bring emancipation from prerational forms of thought. In fact, the opposite was the case; the Enlightenment had produced unimaginable suffering. "Enlightenment," argued Horkheimer and Adorno, "dissolves the injustice of the old inequality—unmediated lordship and mastery—but at the same time perpetuates it in universal mediation, in the relation of any one existent to any other."[21] Reason, the guiding force of the Enlightenment, was seen as responsible for the domination of nature. Once envisioned as a benign tool for understanding the material world, reason had morphed into an insidious form, into an instrumental rationality that indiscriminately carved up and objectified a living reality. For Horkheimer and Adorno, instrumental rationality was reason stripped of any consideration for the qualitative differences between the objects to which it was applied and reason utilized without any acknowledgment of the ends to which it aimed. Everything in turn was reduced to an abstract equivalent. Even worse, instrumental rationality had reduced man, just as it had reduced nature, to an objective other, making him just as exchangeable as goods, services, and materials. The Enlightenment, in this sense, demanded sacrifice—both on the part of the natural world, which was stripped bare, and on the part of the masses, which produced and consumed the stale goods offered. For Horkheimer and Adorno, mastery over nature had led to mastery over man.

The lessons of *Dialectic of Enlightenment* were translated into an accessible language in Max Horkheimer's 1947 *Eclipse of Reason*, originally a series of lectures given at Columbia University. Continuing his melancholic view of recent history, Horkheimer argued that "the hopes of mankind" expressed in the revolutionary sentiments of the previous decades seemed "to be further from fulfillment today than they were even in the groping epochs when they were first formulated by humanists."[22] Reason, once seen as "a spiritual power living in each man," had morphed into merely an instrument to calculate the production and distribution of goods, bereft of the power to reflect upon the human condition as such. Horkheimer presented both pragmatism and positivism, which he considered to be the foundations of American thought, as successors to eighteenth-century Enlightenment philosophy, which had jettisoned its speculative promises by redefining technological progress as progress as a whole. According to Horkheimer, science had become the new theology. Although priding themselves on their open-mindedness, pragmatists and positivists were unwilling to interrogate the foundations—logic, intuition, experimentation—upon which their scientific methods were based. Consequently, according to Horkheimer, the nation's "official body of scientists" was "more independent of reason than the college of cardinals, since the latter must at least refer to the Gospels" (79). Monopolistic, dogmatic, and paradoxically uncritical, the modern scientist had paved the way for "an ever more rigid control in the institutions of an irrational world" (72), whether those institutions were part of a liberal society or a more authoritarian one.

Dwight Macdonald, the native-born high modernist whose theoretical position most closely paralleled that of the Frankfurt school, offered a similar critique in his 1946 manifesto *The Root Is Man*. In fact, Macdonald himself admitted that his work had much in common with "that remarkable group of historians of culture centering around Max Horkheimer's Institute for Social Research."[23] Macdonald's goal in that work was twofold. First, in the wake of American atrocities committed during the war, he leveled a vicious critique of scientific rationality and its cultist adherents, blaming them for the recent barbarism. In language comparable to that of Horkheimer and Adorno, Macdonald argued that the scientific method lacked the capacity to make "a qualitative discrimination about something which is by its very nature *not* reducible to uniform and hence measurable units."[24] Science was thus antithetical to morality. Second, he chastised contemporary radicals for failing to develop a political critique that did not partake of the language of historical progress or human engineering. Tying together the pragmatism of John

Dewey, the scientific materialism of Marxism, and the reformist politics of the New Deal under the rubric of scientific optimism, Macdonald chastised supposed radicals for their faith in the revolutionary potential of the working class and for their naïve belief in the supposed laws of historical progress. He also criticized contemporary radicals—from Communists to New Dealers to Progressives—for believing that centralized state power and applied scientific rationality were tools of social change. After the destruction in Japan, Macdonald wrote in the pages of *Politics* that "it seems fitting that The Bomb was not developed by any of the totalitarian powers . . . but by the two 'democracies,'" who continue to express "at least ideological respect to the humanitarian-democratic tradition."[25] The way forward seemed no way at all.

Macdonald was not the only American modernist to reach such conclusions. In many ways, his arguments in *The Root Is Man* were prefigured by the cultural criticism of John Crowe Ransom and Allen Tate (two of the early proponents of the form of textual analysis that became known as the New Criticism). Although both Ransom and Tate became influential literary critics, they began their careers through their association with the Fugitive group—a community of southern intellectuals who issued a series of proclamations throughout the 1930s lambasting industrialization, large-scale property holdings, and corporate control of the economy.[26] In particular, the Fugitive group, beginning with John Crowe Ransom's *The World's Body* (1938), criticized the growing dominance of scientific discourse in American life. According to Ransom and others, modern science had transformed curiosity into control, seeing the world as merely a collection of objects to be used and discarded and as reducible to a series of laws and measurements. Devoid of compassion, scientific rationality, as Ransom explained, had produced a "totalitarian state" in which its occupants were "not regarded as citizens," were deprived of their "inalienable rights to activities of their own," and were considered mere "functions" to the "effectiveness" of the state.[27] The goal of the New Criticism, as it developed as a form of literary practice, was to demonstrate that scientific discourse was not comprehensive of the whole range of cognitive possibilities. The language of science, according to Ransom, existed only on the level of symbols—words that operated in discourse as references to semantical objects. Such a use of language deprived "the world of actual objects" of any "qualitative density." Such a language also became a technique for control, as instrumental engagement with the world and with others became the only mode of apprehension.

The realization that scientific rationality had inexorably led to the gas chambers of Europe meant for many high modernists that the Enlightenment project, with its visions of inevitable progress, had been pregnant with barbarism from the start. The original project of modernity, as outlined in the late eighteenth century by the philosophers of the Enlightenment, developed under the belief that the autonomous development of the separate fields of science, moral law, and aesthetics according to their individual logic was the key to the rational development and enrichment of everyday life.[28] Beginning with Immanuel Kant's three critiques, in which the German thinker differentiated theoretical knowledge, practical reason, and aesthetic judgment, Enlightenment philosophers had gone to great lengths to liberate the critical rationality at play within each sphere from historical tradition and external authority. But as instrumental rationality gained primacy under the scientific-military alliance, high modernists argued that Enlightenment progress had turned into a nightmare. Vanquished from the public sphere, moral law and aesthetics seemed to have no place in a world run by scientists. Consequently, the characterization of the current situation as "post-modern" became commonplace.[29] Across academic disciplines, many intellectuals, even those uninterested in the project of high modernism, sensed that the project of modernity was over. In his 1959 book *The Sociological Imagination*, sociologist C. Wright Mills argued that Western society was "at the ending of what is called The Modern Age," soon to be "succeeded by a post-modern period."[30] According to Mills, "the ideological mark of The Fourth Epoch—that which sets it off from The Modern Age—is that the ideas of freedom and of reason have become moot; that increased rationality may not be assumed to make for increased freedom" (167). Management theorist Peter Drucker, in his own study of the early Cold War landscape, *Landmarks of Tomorrow*, also sensed a moment of passage. As Drucker explained, "we live in an age of transition, an age of overlap, in which the old 'modern' of yesterday no longer acts effectively but still provides means of expression, standards of expectations and tools of ordering, while the new, the 'post-modern,' still lacks definition, expression and tools but effectively controls our actions and their impact."[31] Similarly, in his 1957 introduction to *Mass Culture: The Popular Arts in America*, a collection of essays by a number of prominent postwar intellectuals, Bernard Rosenberg, too, invoked a sense of historical transformation: "In short, the postmodern world offers man everything or nothing. Any rational consideration of the probabilities leads to a fear that he will be overtaken by the social furies that already beset him."[32] For many, the promise of modernity appeared shattered.

The only solution for high modernists was to accept the splintering of art from its entanglement with political, economic, and scientific fields. If the separate movements of high modernism in the 1940s and 1950s amounted to anything, it was the defense of the humanities as a corrective to modern science. Dwight Macdonald's project, for instance, in *The Root Is Man* was to "define a sphere which is outside the reach of scientific investigation, and whose value judgments cannot be proved (though they can be demonstrated in appropriate and complete unscientific terms)."[33] For Macdonald, such a realm was "the traditional sphere of art and morality." He was echoed by Theodor Adorno who noted that "with the objectification of the world in the course of progressive demythologization, art and science have separated."[34] As such, aesthetics became for high modernists the only imaginable field through which the particular, the sensuous, and the contingent might be saved from the desiccated and desiccating methods of science and the only remaining habitat for intellectual engagement in which intuitions were not brutalized by concepts. The project of high modernism, then, was to protect the autonomy of art from outside impositions and to offer a form of experience—the aesthetic—that might mitigate the overbearing tendencies of modern life.

The Autonomy of the Aesthetic

To begin, high modernists charted the historical progression of art from its ritualistic uses to its isolation within a separate sphere of development at the end of modernity. Following in the footsteps of his friend Walter Benjamin, Theodor Adorno, for instance, noted the historical disintegration of the cultic function of art, which had once linked artistic production to the needs of religious and cultural institutions.[35] But after the subsequent revolutions in nineteenth-century Europe had severed the connection between artists and their courtly patrons and with "the authority of everything traditional irretrievably lost," artistic production became implicated with the rising bourgeois market society.[36] Freed from the bondage of church and state patrons but lacking monetary support, artists in the nineteenth and twentieth centuries were forced to align with the bourgeoisie and produce artworks for commodity circulation. Whereas premodern art had participated in religious and political life, modern art, in contrast, was a product of capitalist relations, which, having reduced all production to utility and exchange, had allowed aesthetics to develop autonomously. As Adorno explained, even though it railed against capitalist expansion, modern art "[owed] the historical unfolding of its productive forces" to "the advances of a civilizing rationality" (147). For the first time, artists were free to experiment with the formal properties of their respective mediums, a move evident in the litany of artistic styles in literature and painting in the late nineteenth and early twentieth centuries. But the problem for modern artists was to defend their newly won autonomy from their bourgeois consumers who often appropriated modern art for their own ideological commitments. Having experienced the power of the New York art market to determine not only the success of particular artists but also the development of specific artistic movements, Clement Greenberg, for instance, was very cognizant of the "umbilical cord of gold" that attached the avant-garde to the financial support of the "elite."[37] This defense of art as a singular discipline was a daunting proposition under such conditions.

Paradoxically, then, aesthetics became an autonomous discipline only when artworks became commodities, that is, only when market forces freed cultural production from serving any other purpose except exchange value. Socially, an artwork became autonomous by remaining "derivative, a mere agent of the law of value," forever tied in bad faith with "economic considerations."[38] Equally problematic was the recognition that the materials, designs, and schemas used by modern artists were contaminated by the historical context from which they were appropriated. Clement Greenberg, for example, connected the origins of Cubism not merely to the unresolved problems in Cezanne's picture planes but also to the "scientific outlook" of "the highest stage of industrial capitalism."[39] Consequently, "art's shame," as Adorno stated, was its closeness to "the existing pattern of material production" from which it tried to distinguish itself.[40] But since artworks now received their importance in relation to their exchange value because they had been freed from any overarching political, moral, or epistemic purpose, aesthetics was now ironically provided with a ready-made defense against any utilitarian subsumption. Modern artists did not have to provide any justification for the character of their works except through reference to the formal properties of their respective mediums. As pure, self-referential objects deprived of any standardized purpose, artworks retained an intrinsic autonomy through the unique organization of their materials and elements. "The more heavily the situation weighs upon it," Adorno explained, "the more firmly the work resists it by refusing to submit to anything heteronomous and constituting itself solely in accordance with its own laws."[41] This notion of form as the key marker of high modernist aesthetics was most fully developed in the literary practices of the New Critics. Reacting to the trends prevalent in American criticism throughout the early decades of the twentieth century, New Critics such as Allen Tate, John Crowe Ransom, and Cleanth Brooks went to great lengths to defend the aesthetic work as a unique source of meaning that was irreducible to historical, biographical, moral, or psychological explanations.[42] Calling for close readings and textual analysis to protect art from both propagandists and complacent readers, the New Critics argued that the modernist poem had no meaning or purpose extrinsic to its formal structure or to the poetic techniques with which it was constructed. In this way, aesthetics was safeguarded within its own space of development.

Officially announcing this new school of analysis in his 1941 book *The New Criticism*, John Crowe Ransom defined the poetic object as a unified structure of various elements, often contradictory and conflicting, held together by certain literary devices. Weaving together words, images, symbols, feelings, and rhythms into the "complex of meaning" that constituted the poem as a whole, the modernist poet attended to the "heterogeneity" of his elements while maintaining an overall "principle of assembly."[43] The New Critic who most thoroughly outlined the formal properties of modernist poetry was Cleanth Brooks, whose *Modern Poetry and the Tradition* (1939) and *The Well Wrought Urn* (1947) marked the theoretical culmination of the project begun by Tate and Ransom. Envisioning the modern poem as an unforced balancing of discordant attitudes and feelings such as pity and laughter, tenderness and frustration, and love and intellect, Brooks examined the use of four essential elements—paradox, wit, irony, and metaphor—that constituted the modernist poem. Paradox, for Brooks, was the juxtaposition of incongruous views in a given situation, such as the modernist refusal to suppress poetic references to the Christian in the celebration of the pagan. Similarly, wit was the ability to attend to the nuances of language, in particular, the refusal to privilege the denotative or dictionary meaning of words over the countless connotative meanings that might arise within the context of the poem itself. Irony was used, like wit, to temper or qualify a particular statement by offering a "reconcilement of opposite or discordant qualities."[44] The form most appropriate for these expressions of wit, paradox, and irony was of course metaphor, arguably the most important term for the New Critics. Given the poet's unwillingness to sacrifice the complexity of experience in the name of direct expression, metaphorical comparisons allowed for subtle shifts in tone, paradoxical attitudes, and pointed suggestions. As a structural component, metaphor also provided the context within which divergent images, words, and ideas gained meaning. Consequently, as Brooks argued, "comparison *is* the poem in a structural sense" (15). In this way, the form of the poem was not something that merely contained the poem's content; form was inseparable from the content by virtue of the subtle unity achieved. Therefore, since its meaning was not dependent upon any mimetic relation to the external world, the poem was the site of a distinct experience, wholly determined by the inner dialectic of its elements. Poetry, then, was similar to painting as "a pattern of resolved stresses," that is, as an ever-evolving matrix of "resolutions and balances and harmonizations" that submitted to no extrinsic standard or preconceived system (203).

Cleanth Brooks's reference to modernist painting marked the similarity between the formalism of the New Critics and the defense of abstract art offered by high modernist critics such as Clement Greenberg.[45] Modernism, for both Greenberg and Brooks, meant purity, self-definition, and self-criticism, that is, the willingness "to eliminate from the specific effects of each art any and every effect that might conceivably be borrowed from or by the medium of any other art."[46] In an endless series of reviews throughout the 1940s and 1950s, the famed New York art critic famously outlined the basics of abstract painting—its all-over composition, its flatness, and its optical effect—that marked its autonomy. Equally worried about the gross assimilation of art for political or entertainment purposes, Greenberg outlined the means by which modern artists assured "that the kind of experience they provided was valuable in its own right and not to be obtained from any other kind of activity." This involved a "radical reduction" of the medium itself.[47] Most important, abstract artists, according to Greenberg, had correctly jettisoned the imperative to represent external reality, an imperative that had once forced them to create "the illusion of a boxlike cavity" on their canvas to maintain the sense of three-dimensional space. But by preserving the "integrity of the picture plane," modern painters gradually sacrificed "verisimilitude" for the relentless experimentation with the effects of paint on the canvas. By abandoning representation and turning to abstraction as a guiding principle, modern artists now treated "every part of the canvas equivalent," creating all-over compositions woven "into a tight mesh whose principle of formal unity is contained and recapitulated in each thread, so that we find the essence of the whole work in every one of its parts."[48] Consequently, the aesthetic effect was "optical rather than pictorial," created through the "relations of color, shape, and line largely divorced from descriptive connotations."[49] Through the flatness and impenetrability of the picture plane, the abstract painting was a solid object, no longer a vehicle for transcendence nor a mirror for the outside world.

By clinging to a discussion of formal properties, high modernists placed the aesthetic object outside any discussion of artistic intention or audience reception. In his 1933 work *The Use of Poetry and the Use of Criticism*, T. S. Eliot laid the framework for such modernist reading practices by arguing that the enjoyment of poetry was contingent upon acceptance of the poem's fundamental separation from both the author and the reader. Eliot claimed that the "mature stage" of critical reading occurred "when we cease to identify ourselves with the poet we happen to be reading" and recognize that "the poem has its own existence, apart from us."[50] Critiquing most literary theories for reducing the aesthetic experience to merely a psychological or emotive state, John Crowe Ransom followed Eliot in defending the poetic object as "nothing short of a desperate ontological or metaphysical manoeuvre."[51] Consequently, Ransom directly challenged the "Humanists," who were using literary criticism to promote the "Aristotelian moral canon," and the "Proletarians," who appropriated literature for "the cause of loving-comradeship."[52] All attempts at mimetic representation, despite even the most politically progressive intentions, ushered in, as Theodor Adorno explained, an immediate accommodation to the world. Echoing Adorno's rejection of social realism, Ransom praised the German critic's willingness to provide a "special asylum of art" and to "[award] to it an *imperium in imperio*," thereby helping to move aesthetics away from the politics of "collectivism."[53]

In railing against any extra-aesthetic uses of art, whether for consumer gratification, for politics, or for profit, high modernists appropriated the aesthetic theory of Immanuel Kant to defend the passive, disinterested reception of art and the noncognitive dimension of the aesthetic experience. As John Ransom explained, modern criticism "leans again upon ontological analysis as it was meant to do by Kant."[54] Having set the agenda for modernity by distinguishing between the three spheres of intellectual and cultural development (science, morality, and art) and having, in his third critique on the nature of judgment, separated aesthetics from other realms of knowledge, the German philosopher had done "everything possible to prevent the confusion" between art and science.[55] Consequently, Clement Greenberg affectionately acknowledged Kant as "the first real Modernist" and argued that the philosopher's aesthetic ideas remained misunderstood by most critics.[56] The revolution in epistemology that Kant famously initiated in his first critique overthrew most forms of empiricism by showing that knowledge claims stemmed not from the character of the objects themselves but instead from the thinking subject. Noting that all experience was predicated on the ability of the knowing subject to subsume the perceptions it received under particular categories, Kant argued that the faculty of understanding contained those concepts necessary for categorizing perceptions and thereby making them meaningful. Similarly, the faculty of *judgment* was the capacity for subsuming perceptions under the rules provided by the concepts themselves. But Kant famously revised the role of judgment when he addressed the problem of aesthetics. In the case of particulars for which there was no corresponding universal given, judgment was forced to develop its own universal. Such reflective judgments, "obliged to ascend from the particular in nature to the universal," were not successful at locating a proper concept for the given material; consequently the act of judgment occurring in the absence of a given concept left the subject with only a nonconceptual awareness of order.[57] The elements of the individual aesthetic object might exhibit a coherence and unity, but the concept with which to judge such order was not given in advance. For Kant, there were no a priori rules or principles for making a judgment about a particular artistic object. Consequently, since such an object was not understandable by reference to any prior concepts, it existed for no predetermined purpose. Asserting its autonomy by virtue of the fact that there existed no predetermined concept with which to consume it, the object retained its beauty simply through its particular form. As Kant explained, "beauty is the form of the *purposiveness* of an object, so far as this is perceived in it *without any representation of a purpose*" (73). Aesthetics as such was now separate from the governing hand of science or morality. John Crowe Ransom noted that Kant had "carefully disengaged the artistic motive from 'pleasure' in the common sense; then from 'usefulness,' which would involve it in a labor for the sake of pleasure; then from the pursuit of the ethical good."[58] In a world governed by the exchange principle, the sheer uselessness of the modernist work revealed its contradictory position in society.

High modernists appropriated Kant's defense of the aesthetic work as a cognitively nonsubsumable object as a way to challenge the perceived encroachment of scientific discourse into everyday life. To counteract the ruthless domination of the particulars of life by the categorical claims of science, high modernists promoted the disinterested, purposeless, and humble reception of art. "The world of art," John Crowe Ransom asserted, "is the actual world which does not bear restriction; or at least defies the restrictiveness of science and offers enough fullness of content to give us the sense of the actual object."[59] For this reason, the New Critics waged their famous war against paraphrase. Arguing that the truth of the poem was the unique way in which the poet had worked out the various tensions—rhetorical, semantic, and philosophical—within it, the New Critics claimed that the meaning of the poem was not reducible to a series of propositions. Indeed, the "heresy of paraphrase" was the "violence" done to "the internal order of the poem itself" by believing the poem to be a verifiable, "logical conclusion."[60] Such Kantian residues appeared in the aesthetic modernism of Theodor Adorno as well. Arguing that modernist works were a special form of "knowledge" as "nonconceptual objects," Adorno claimed that the "total purposelessness" of the work "gives the lie to the totality of purposefulness in the world of domination, and only by virtue of this negation . . . has existing society up to now become aware of another that is possible."[61] High modernists, in this regard, set up a "dual theory of truth," contrasting the nonviolent synthesis of the particular and the universal within the modernist work as a "rival mode" of knowledge to the "functional" nature of science.[62] But fearing that their discussions of form seemed at times to echo rational discourse in an instrumental way, high modernists also argued that artists needed to be decidedly innovative, continuously breaking apart received traditions in an endless series of determinate negations. The modernist object needed to exhibit some form of confusion, distortion, or incalculable defect, something that challenged its formal brilliance in order to distinguish it from any simple piece of craftsmanship and to ensure the endless overturning of received tradition. Consequently, the poetic work was most successful when its language escaped "the subjective intention that occasioned the use of the word" and the musical piece was most successful when it temporarily shot beyond its structure with "a few superfluous notes or measures."[63] Modern artists avoided merely producing forms of consolation by refusing to create just pleasant or beautiful forms and by refusing to produce mere decoration. Art, if anything, was to resist such silly affirmations by revealing instead "what is ugliest and most distorted" through the disruption of conventions.[64]

Arguably the most famous analysis of the history of modernism as the dialectical unfolding of the advances and limitations of previous artistic traditions was Clement Greenberg's reading of the paintings of Jackson Pollock, and Greenberg's art criticism in large part was devoted to an analysis of the rise of abstract painting in the twentieth century as the inevitable evolution of this investigation into the formal properties of the medium. Beginning in the late nineteenth century with Paul Cezanne, who was, according to Greenberg, the "most copious source of what we know as modern art," contemporary painters dealt with the ambiguous position of art in bourgeois society.[65] Cezanne, in his mission to reaffirm the traditional Renaissance project of presenting "an ample and literal rendition of the illusion of the third dimension" (84), particularly in the face of Impressionism's failure to maintain pictorial depth in its exploration of color, ironically called attention to the surface of the canvas at the expense of maintaining the appearance of depth. In reducing his images to basic "masses and shapes" as a way to translate "the color method of the Impressionists" into solid brushstrokes, Cezanne inadvertently flattened his images, making "his backgrounds just as emphatic as the objects in the foreground."[66] This cunning of art history paved the way for Cubism, which furthered Cezanne's project by breaking up the pictorial object and its background into "little facet planes" through which "all space became one, neither 'positive' nor 'negative.'"[67] Paralleling this revolutionary development was the radical exploration of the Impressionist use of color by Henri Matisse, who, by stressing the intensity of color as a sheer surface manifestation, treated "the painted surface as something breathing and open."[68] In this way, the Cubists, by flattening the picture plane, and Matisse, by treating color as a solid form in and of itself, heralded the transition from figurative to nonfigurative painting, a project that, according to Greenberg's chronology, was completed by Jackson Pollock.

Clement Greenberg's adoration of the early work of Jackson Pollock was predicated on the artist's willingness to dispense with pristine images. In his 1945 review of Pollock's second one-man show at the Art of This Century, in which he praised the artist "as the strongest painter of his generation," Greenberg noted that Pollock was "not afraid to look ugly—all profoundly original art looks ugly at first."[69] Having criticized Picasso's later works in which the artist failed to transcend the boundaries of Cubist form by eliminating any moment of spontaneity, Greenberg celebrated Pollock's success in moving beyond Cubism with his famous "drip" paintings of the late 1940s. In a series of canvases, including *Full Fathom Five*, *Lavender Mist*, and *Autumn Rhythm*, Pollock pointed the way to the "formal essence" of painting by asserting the "ambiguous flatness" of the canvas, thereby allowing him to "control the oscillation between an emphatic physical surface and the suggestion of depth beneath it."[70] The optical impact of Pollock's style, with its subtle undulations, controlled chaos, vacillating layers of texture, and all-over composition, offered an aesthetic experience that freed the viewer from the heavy-handedness and didacticism of most art. Of course, Pollock's own understanding of his art, predicated, as we will see, on "romantic modernist" ideas of spontaneity and release, had little in common with Greenberg's formalism. But Greenberg's success in promoting his particular reading of Pollock's art demonstrated the success of high modernism overall.

Blending together the beautiful and the sublime and offering a form of experience in which the sensuous remained untrammeled, the high modernist artwork was seen as the privileged site for cultural rejuvenation. Ever more difficult and ever more hermetic, such works were reminders of the lost realm of the sensuous—those affections and inclinations that had been brushed aside by the impersonal, means-ends rationality of science—not by the mystical or sentimental examples of the Romantics but by merely maintaining a contradictory position in society.[71] In part, then, high modernists hoped that the aesthetic experience might teach the viewer to respect the transient and the ephemeral in and of itself without reference to abstractions. Clement Greenberg, reacting to the apparent cultural vacuum in America, expressed this sentiment most clearly: "I think a poor life is lived by any one who doesn't regularly take time out to stand and gaze, or sit and listen, or touch, or smell, or brood, without any further end in mind, simply for the satisfaction gotten from that which is gazed at, listened to, touched, smelled, or brooded upon."[72] Although each critic promoted slightly different modernist practitioners (Adorno favoring Arnold Schoenberg and Samuel Beckett, Clement Greenberg favoring Jackson Pollock and Henri Matisse, Lionel Trilling favoring Henry James and John Keats, and Cleanth Brooks favoring William Butler Yeats and T. S. Eliot), all argued that such art needed to figure within public life as prominently as science did. The distinctiveness of the modernist work—its formal autonomy and its unique assembly of materials—testified to the possibility or at least the illusion that the world might be different. Continuing the Fugitive critique of science, Cleanth Brooks argued that the tempering hand of modern art might serve as a fundamental corrective: "A diet of straight science, because science is power-knowledge, may contribute to *hubris*; whereas poetry . . . constantly reminds man that the thing described lies outside man's control, and thus rebukes *hubris*."[73] The problem, as Brooks realized, was finding adequate avenues in which the language of modernism might be translated. As federal funds flowed into universities for military research and scientists became national celebrities, high modernists waged a campaign within universities, publishing houses, and art galleries to defend the humanities as an antidote to modern science.

The Institutionalization of High Modernism

In January 1962 the *Saturday Evening Post* ran a front-page cover painted by Norman Rockwell, the popular commercial illustrator and artist. The image featured a wealthy-looking art collector, umbrella and hat in hand, intently pondering a large abstract canvas, unaware that Rockwell had made him the focus of attention. The editors of the magazine joined Rockwell in his playful joke, asking whether the man was "about to reach for his checkbook to buy a prize-winning work titled 'The Insubstance of Infinity'" or whether he was "imagining his teen-age daughter calling it 'Strictly from Blobsville.'"[74] Rockwell continued the joke in describing his experimentation with the Pollockesque-style canvas on the cover. According to Rockwell, he had recently attended a class in modern art techniques where he "learned a lot and loved it," although he did eventually tire of "waving a dripping brush" and had to invite the man painting the windows in his studio to help finish it. Sarcasm aside, Rockwell's commentary reflected the astounding success high modernism achieved in the 1940s and 1950s. Several legendary moments marked the ascendancy of high modernism. In 1944 director Alfred Barr facilitated the acquisition of Jackson Pollock's *She-Wolf* by the Museum of Modern Art, giving institutional recognition to the abstract expressionist movement and paving the way for the escalating "Pollock market" after the painter's untimely death.[75] The "picture boom," as *Art News* described, that followed the favorable economic climate after the war also advanced the cause of modern art.[76] In 1949, William Faulkner, praised for his insights into the psychological landscape of the human mind, was awarded the Nobel Prize in literature, helping to advance the reputation of the aging modernist writer. Similarly, despite considerable debate because of his political leanings, Ezra Pound won the Bollingen Prize in poetry that same year. In 1956 T. S. Eliot, whom Delmore Schwartz acknowledged as having his own "literary dictatorship," famously lectured to a crowd in Minneapolis, equaling, according to one account, "that of three hockey games."[77] Finally, in the most public moment of recognition, poet Robert Frost and abstract artist Mark Rothko were invited to the inauguration of John F. Kennedy in 1960, standing beside politicians, celebrities, and sports figures as representatives of American culture.

Despite such public exposure, appearing in photographs on the pages of countless mass-circulation magazines, high modernists recognized that their true cultural project rested elsewhere. The problem of modernism in the postwar era, as David Hollinger has argued, was neither a problem of authorship nor even of critical attention but a problem of readership.[78] Although experimental literary works were still in production and abstract paintings were filling gallery walls, the task in the 1940s was to *promote* modernism by gaining new financial support for artists and writers after the end of New Deal–sponsored federal subsidies, developing an educational curriculum to consolidate reading practices, and carving out avenues to translate modernist forms to an educated public. In 1946 Clement Greenberg, for instance, was troubled that "there exists in this country no self-assured, self-intelligible class of connoisseurs and amateurs of art with defined and independent tastes."[79] Culture required cultivation, literary education required educators, abstract painting needed gallery space and promotional support, and poetic production depended upon publishers and sales. Therefore, despite the seemingly ever-present elitism of high modernist rhetoric, many critics made deliberate efforts to carve out an intellectual milieu for modernist works. In his contribution to the 1952 *Partisan Review* symposium "Our Country and Our Culture," Lionel Trilling, for instance, encouraged the growth of a "new intellectual class" to counter the erosion of public tastes, and he asked his fellow men of letters to help "in the continuation of the traditional culture in the traditional forms."[80] Along with Jacques Barzun and W. H. Auden, Trilling served as a literary consultant for two book clubs, the Reader's Subscription and the Mid-Century Book Society, and wrote a number of introductions for the selected works.[81] Other high modernists, including many New York intellectuals, also took seriously this responsibility. Philip Rahv wrote several introductions to rereleases of works by Henry James, Franz Kafka, and Leo Tolstoy for Dial Press and the Modern Library, and William Phillips engaged in a similar project for English translations of the work of Fyodor Dostoevsky. Many other modernists including Allen Tate, Irving Howe, and Robert Penn Warren worked with major commercial publishers such as Henry Holt and Prentice Hall to publish collected volumes of writings by modernist writers. Likewise, Cleanth Brooks coedited four famous textbooks of literary criticism (*Understanding Poetry*, *Understanding Fiction*, *Understanding Drama*, and *An Approach to Literature*), and the success of those collections prompted countless other modernist critics to publish similar volumes, including the ubiquitous *Norton Anthology* collections. The most noteworthy pedagogical effort to introduce high modernism to a broad audience occurred in a series of

"Round Table" discussions in the pages of *Life* magazine.[82] Appropriating the idea from *Fortune* magazine, which had held a series of public discussions in the 1930s concerning the international economic situation, the editors of *Life*, under the instruction of Henry Luce himself, routinely gathered prominent intellectuals to discuss the state of American culture. The most famous was the 1948 "*Life* Round Table on Modern Art," featuring "fifteen distinguished critics and connoisseurs," including Meyer Schapiro, Clement Greenberg, Alfred Frankfurter, and H. W. Janson, all of whom attempted to translate high modernist art into an accessible vernacular. In fact, moderator Russell Davenport offered a suggestion on the problem of the "esthetic experience," telling the confused *Life* reader that when confronting a piece of abstract art "he should look devotedly at the picture, rather than at himself, or at any aspect of his environment," language borrowed directly from Clement Greenberg.[83]

Even more dramatically, high modernism was institutionalized in English classrooms across the country. The rise of the New Criticism was aided, as Gerald Graff has noted, by the explosion in undergraduate and graduate enrollments in the 1950s, caused in part by federal subsidies for war veterans to attend college and by a growing middle-class population whose employment prospects were linked to educational status.[84] As literary experts, New Critical practitioners gained cultural capital for their possession of a formal body of knowledge and a recondite professional vocabulary, and their success in shaping the nature of criticism was the result of the ease with which their reading practices were converted into a standardized teaching method. The codification of what John Crowe Ransom referred to as "Criticism, Inc., or Criticism, Ltd." was aided by the publication of Cleanth Brooks and Robert Penn Warren's *Understanding Poetry* (1938) and their *Understanding Fiction* (1943), two textbooks that disseminated the methods of the New Criticism into university classrooms. A number of academic journals devoted to New Critical reading practices appeared as well, including *Southern Review*, *Kenyon Review*, and *Sewanee Review*. New Critical practitioners also took over English departments at Yale, Princeton, and Cambridge, and independent poets such as Robert Lowell, Richard Wilbur, and Allen Tate found academic positions. John Crowe Ransom even obtained financial support from the Rockefeller Foundation for his School of English, a summer program at Kenyon College to educate English instructors on New Critical practices. Indeed, the New Criticism, as a commentator in the *Antioch Review* explained, "achieved for literature a superior status within the hierarchy of society's aspirations and values: the 'difficult' writer, the free writer, even if he is not read, has now come to be respected, and his societal role has at least a basis from which to develop toward some sort of leadership."[85]

Many of the literary critics associated with the New York intellectuals joined with the New Critics in promoting and canonizing modernist literature.[86] While critics such as Irving Howe had little patience for the aloof aestheticism of many of the New Critics, the similarities of both groups of modernist critics outweighed their differences. For Howe, both groups were "equally assertive in affirming their minority splendor, equally ideological in styles of thought."[87] Both groups were also interested in carving out an anti-bourgeois cultural stance that was unconnected to utopian politics or fellow traveling. Thus, despite a certain level of disagreement, it was "no wonder conflict melted into a gingerly friendship, plight calling to plight, ambition to ambition." Delmore Schwartz, Lionel Trilling, and Philip Rahv attended Ransom's summer program; Irving Howe readily used New Critical methods in the classroom when he taught at Brandeis University in the 1950s; and essays by Theodor Adorno, Philip Rahv, and William Phillips appeared in *Kenyon Review* while articles by Allen Tate and John Crowe Ransom were published in *Partisan Review*. More important, both groups were instrumental in promoting modernism as a literary form. Beginning with Edmund Wilson's *Axel's Castle* (1931) and continuing through Cleanth Brooks's *Modern Poetry and the Tradition* (1939) and Irving Howe's *The Idea of the Modern* (1967), these critics developed and expanded a canon of high modernist writers, a list that included T. S. Eliot, Thomas Mann, Franz Kafka, Ezra Pound, James Joyce, Fyodor Dostoevsky, William Butler Yeats, and a host of others.

Two modernist writers in particular, Henry James and William Faulkner, were promoted throughout the 1940s and 1950s as symbols of the American avant-garde. As Lawrence Schwartz has demonstrated, both the Fugitive critics and the New York intellectuals promoted Faulkner's writing in the 1940s through the publication of his collected works and through a series of flattering reviews and literary studies as a way to promote their own cultural agendas.[88] Gaining monetary assistance from the Humanities Division of the Rockefeller Foundation, which helped support several modernist journals in the 1940s such as *Kenyon Review*, *Sewanee Review*, and *Hudson Review*, they refashioned Faulkner into a literary iconoclast whose blend of traditional American sentiment with an innovative European writing style echoed their own humanist commitments. Faulkner, who was suffering financially from a lack of sales in the early 1940s, worked particularly well for this collection of modernist critics because he represented both the southern renaissance promoted by the New Critics and the existential anguish favored by the New York intellectuals. Similar cultural prestige was also placed upon the work of Henry James. In his 1941 introduction to James's collected short novels, Philip Rahv declared the novelist "among the two or three American writers" who was able "to invent and put to creative use the imaginative methods of the twentieth century."[89] Similarly, Dwight Macdonald's *The Root Is Man* (1946) celebrated James's critical temperament; Lionel Trilling's *The Liberal Imagination* (1950) contained numerous references to the modernist writer; and Irving Howe's *Politics and the Novel* (1957) included an essay on James. Several other works and collections by F. W. Dupree, F. R. Leavis, and F. O. Matthiessen also helped to solidify James's importance to American letters. Although the more revolutionary hopes embedded within high modernism were of course never realized, the surprising success that many critics had in disseminating these cultural forms, although in a contained fashion, contributed to a decisive cultural shift. Even though many still clung to their minority status, the cultural prestige of high modernism was solidified as the years wore on. Never one to admit that his job was done, Clement Greenberg even marked with dismay the change he had helped produce: "The avant-garde writer *gets ahead* now, and inside established channels: he obtains university or publishing or magazine jobs, finds it relatively easy to be published himself, is asked to lecture, participate in round tables, etc., writes introductions to the classics, and can even win the status of a public figure."[90] Unexpectedly, the culture in the United States had changed.

The ascendancy of high modernism, however, was not a total blessing for its proponents; indeed, the energetic and successful defense of the humanities in the face of the supposed vulgarities of modern science resulted in a considerable dilution of the critical and oppositional stance of highbrow culture. Four factors in particular distorted the high modernist project. The first was the limitations associated with professionalism. Obviously the institutionalization of the New Criticism contributed to its meteoric rise, but its classroom dissemination by second-rate interpreters effaced much of the sophistication and political critique offered by its original practitioners.[91] As a standardized teaching method, the New Criticism lost much of its critical edge. Writing in the pages of *Partisan Review*, Delmore Schwartz noted that as the New Criticism "[attached] literature to the university," the modernist canon became "merely a set of courses in the departments of English and comparative literature."[92] Even Lionel Trilling, the high modernist seemingly most attached to his professional identity, expressed his own concerns in a well-known short story, "Of This Time, of That Place," a semiautobiographical piece about a published poet and university professor whose encounter with a bohemian student precipitates his own anxieties about the demands that scholarship and decorum had forced upon him.[93] Trilling realized, as his friendship with many of the emerging Beat writers in the 1950s confirmed, that high modernism lived in part with a bad conscience.

Just as problematic was the fact that high modernism at times collapsed into mere elitism. The subtle theoretical position of Theodor Adorno and Clement Greenberg, for instance, was not matched by other promoters of high modernism such as Dwight Macdonald who lacked their sophisticated vocabulary with which to make aesthetic comparisons. Adorno's essays on music and poetry and Greenberg's commentaries on modern art were thoughtful discussions of these respective mediums. Macdonald's cultural criticism, however, was less a sustained analysis of artistic developments than an angry diatribe against "a too ready acceptance of the avant-garde by the public."[94] Having no notion or definition of the good, the beautiful, the sublime, or the transcendent and no understanding of the problem of form, Macdonald was unable to make convincing arguments about particular works of art. Claiming that high culture's major contribution was not its aesthetic practices per se but its "desperate effort . . . to erect again the barriers between the *cognoscenti* and the *ignoscenti* that had been breached by the rise of Masscult," Macdonald offered no explanation for his adoration of Pablo Picasso over Jackson Pollock or James Joyce's *A Portrait of the Artist as a Young Man* over his *Finnegan's Wake*.[95] Instead, as the numerous revisions of his famous essay "Masscult and Midcult" demonstrated, Macdonald offered only the restoration of "the cultural distinctions that have become increasingly blurred since the industrial revolution."[96] Consequently, his defense of high culture was easily lampooned by the middlebrow producers he chastised. Writing in *Harper's* magazine, editor Russell Lynes noted that the newest form of "snobbishness" in American society was no longer based upon wealth or family ties but on "high thinking," emblematic of those intellectuals determined to divide the country into castes based upon levels of cultural consumption: "All middlebrows, presumably, would have their radios taken away, be suspended from society until they had agreed to give up their subscriptions to the Book-of-the-Month, turned their color reproductions over to a Commission for the Dissolution of Middlebrow Taste, and renounced their affiliation with all educational and other cultural institutions whatsoever."[97] Appropriating Lynes's schema and his sarcasm, *Life* magazine presented photographic images of the three cultural types—one gazing at a Picasso, one enjoying a Grant Wood reproduction, and one ogling a calendar pinup—and provided a classification chart for readers to plot their own cultural tastes according to their preferences for specific reading material, clothes, furniture, games, and even salads.[98]

While such playful denunciations were mildly troubling, high modernists faced a third, and more difficult, problem. Their defense of modernist artworks as absolute commodities—their uselessness, their purposelessness, and their status as completely surplus labor—meant that such works were easily appropriated by bourgeois consumers for ulterior purposes. Willem de Kooning once proclaimed that "it is exactly in its uselessness that [art] is free," but he soon realized, like many of his fellow painters, that such freedom came at a price.[99] Feted within mass-market publications, abstract art was appropriated, as Harold Rosenberg explained, by "educational and profit-making enterprises" for use in "color reproductions, design adaptations, [and] human-interest stories."[100] For instance, Jackson Pollock's art dealer, Betty Parsons, allowed *Vogue* photographer Cecil Beaton to pose fashion models in front of the artist's abstract paintings for a magazine spread.[101] The photographs, which appeared in a 1951 issue, were one of many growing links among the fashion industry, modern advertising practices, and abstract art. Modernism also became decoration. Noting that "the blossoming of art galleries" had led to an "increasing interest" in private collections for the home, Betty Pepis, the home editor at the *New York Times*, offered a series of articles on proper display techniques for abstract art in the home, giving advice on proper framing, wall locations, lighting, and furniture arrangements.[102] Modern art was soon promoted in a number of advertisements as the perfect accessory for the modern home and as a symbol of cultural sophistication. Similarly, the editors at *Playboy* magazine refashioned the modern urban bachelor as a discriminating connoisseur of modern art and music. Modernism had become the latest form of conspicuous consumption.

Finally, in the ultimate moment of appropriation, high modernism was "borrowed" by politicians and intellectuals as a cultural tool in fighting the Cold War. Along with American symphonies, modern jazz, and Hollywood films, abstract art was one of many cultural exports federal agencies sent abroad as political propaganda in the 1950s.[103] Seemingly devoid of radical politics, antithetical to the social realism of the Popular Front era, outwardly universal while simultaneously very American, abstract expressionism became the perfect symbol of the intellectual, artistic, and personal freedom inherent to Western democracies and was seemingly antithetical to the oppressive cultures of totalitarian regimes. Unable to use federal funds directly because of negative publicity but determined to use abstract art as a symbol of American individualism in an ever-expanding cultural Cold War, the U.S. Information Agency and the CIA turned to anti-Communist supporters within the Museum of Modern Art for assistance. Under an expanded International Council branch, the Museum of Modern Art arranged a variety of exhibits of American art, including a major show of abstract expressionism titled "New American Painting" that traveled through European countries in 1958 and 1959. Former director Alfred Barr, in his catalogue introduction to the exhibition, reaffirmed the connection between the expressive freedom of abstract painters and the political freedom in Western countries: "They defiantly reject the conventional values of the society which surrounds them, but they are not politically engaged even though their paintings have been of freedom in a world in which freedom connotes a political attitude."[104] Despite the politics of many abstract artists such as Barnett Newman and Mark Rothko, which often ran counter to American foreign policy aims, the apolitical and purposeless nature of modernist works left them quite vulnerable.

Compromised, diluted, and appropriated, high modernism consequently suffered under its cultural success. By the end of the 1950s, literary critic Harry Levin considered it more than appropriate to ask in a *Massachusetts Review* article "what was modernism?" According to Levin, the success of the movement had tempered its original revolutionary impulse, so much so that "the *enfant terrible*" of the movement's early years had matured into "the elder statesman" of the mid-century scene.[105] Noting that the Institute of Modern Art in Boston had recently changed its name to the Institute of Contemporary Art and that a new apartment building in Manhattan had been christened the Picasso, Levin remarked that "we Americans have smoothly rounded some sort of cultural corner" (274) in which the bohemian had become fashionable, if not respectable. The official notice that the project of high modernism was in trouble was Lionel Trilling's well-known 1961 essay "On the Teaching of Modern Literature," written as a personal response to the introduction of a required course on modernist literature within the core curriculum at Columbia University. Noting the all-too-easy acceptance of the existential anguish of Kafka, Dostoevsky, and Nietzsche by his students, Trilling wondered if the contemporary adoration of such literature had merely resulted in "the socialization of the antisocial, or the acculturation of the anticultural, or the legitimization of the subversive."[106] Under such conditions, high modernism was open to severe criticism.

Beyond High Modernism

Two challenges to the hegemony of high modernism appeared in the 1940s and 1950s. The first was an appropriation of earlier and more spontaneous forms of artistic practice that attempted to overcome the rigid divide between art and life. The rise of *romantic modernism* began innocently enough in a Harlem apartment one summer evening in 1948 when a 22-year-old Columbia University undergraduate named Allen Ginsberg, lost and lonely in Morningside Heights, began to pleasure himself. A student of two renowned champions of high modernism, Lionel Trilling and Mark van Doren, Ginsberg had spent the previous academic year trying to come to terms with their austere visions. But after an evening of reading William Blake and masturbating in his bed, Ginsberg received his own visions. Absentmindedly glancing at Blake's poem "Ah! Sunflower," Ginsberg heard "a very deep earthen grave voice in the room," the voice of Blake himself telling Ginsberg that the young college student *was* the weary sunflower searching for spiritual redemption.[107] With this revelation came an increased sense of perception, a "sudden *visual* realization of the same awesome phenomenon," allowing Ginsberg to see through the façade of the world around him and to gain "a sense of cosmic consciousness, vibrations, understanding, awe, and wonder and surprise" (123). Floating away from his own body, peering past temporal existence, and achieving a form of bliss, Ginsberg promised himself to never abandon the experience: "Never deny the voice—no, never *forget* it, don't get lost mentally wandering in other spirit worlds or American or job worlds or advertising worlds or war worlds or earth worlds." Even more convinced of his visionary experience when the feeling again came over him later that week in the Columbia University bookstore, Ginsberg set out on a lifelong spiritual journey to convince others of their connection to this eternal consciousness.

Ginsberg's immediate response was to share this experience with his university professors. None were encouraging. As one of Ginsberg's biographers has described, "when Allen ran into the English department office, saying, 'I just saw the light!' Mark van Doren was the only professor who was sympathetic and asked him what he meant. Trilling and the others thought Allen had finally gone over the edge."[108] Even more troubling, Ginsberg had difficulty finding an adequate poetic voice of his own to translate his Blakean vision. Committed to the formal structure of poetry with its determined rhyme and syncopated meter and heavily borrowing motifs from his Romantic predecessors, Ginsberg merely produced straightforward, closed descriptions of his original experience. Eventually realizing that his Blakean vision was not simply about a spiritual reconciliation with the eternal but the transcendence of the quotidian *through* a deeper, more meaningful investigation of the world itself and encouraged by the example of William Carlos Williams, Ginsberg brought a new sense of openness into his poetry, rejecting his earlier focus on quatrains for a detailed examination of his immediate experience. As Ginsberg explained later in life, "after writing some very formalistic poetry, I decided I'd let loose whatever I wanted to let loose with and say what I really had on my mind and not write a poem, finally—break my own forms, break my own ideals, what I was supposed to be like as a poet and just write whatever I had in mind."[109] The difficulty, according to Ginsberg, was that in the late 1940s "the academic people were ignoring Williams and ignoring Pound and Louis Zukofsky and Mina Loy and Basil Bunting and most of the major rough writers of the Whitmanic, open form tradition in America" (93).

Unable to confront the horrors of the atomic age because of their commitment to "leaden verse" and because of their useless defense of the humanities as an academic subject, the New Critics, argued Ginsberg, ironically encouraged a false reconciliation with the Cold War landscape. As "consciousness within the academy was narrowing down, becoming more anxious and rigid," Ginsberg and his fellow Beat writers deliberately experimented with poetic form to reassert the fundamental connection between aesthetics and everyday life and thereby to transfigure the reified consciousness pervading American society. Determined to reassert man's fundamental spontaneity, physicality, and spiritual nature, Ginsberg chided formalist aesthetics: "Mind is shapely, Art is shapely, Meaning Mind practiced in spontaneity invents form in its own image and gets to Last Thoughts. Loose ghosts wailing for body try to invade the bodies of living man. I hear ghostly Academics in Limbo screeching about form."[110] Ginsberg's most acclaimed experimentation with open form was of course his 1955 poetic manifesto, *Howl*. Dispensing with any self-consciousness or fear, Ginsberg opened his poetic voice to the spontaneous, logically inconsistent, and unconscious thoughts that emerged from his contemplation of the world around him, what he once referred to as "prosaic realities mixed with emotional upsurges" (417). Ginsberg's mixture of visual imagery, conversational prose, pornographic details, and unapologetic anger was a direct rebuke to academic formalism and a forceful announcement that the official conception of modernism was open to challenge. "Poetry," as Ginsberg explained, "has been attacked by an ignorant & frightened bunch of bores who don't understand how it's made, & the trouble with these creeps is they wouldn't know Poetry if it came up and buggered them in broad daylight." Ginsberg's poetic project to merge art and life was also, as *Howl* famously demonstrated, a cultural and political challenge to the staid conformity and middle-class numbness he believed was spiritually destroying America. While he followed the New Critics in their concern with the political claims attached to poetry by both liberals and Communists and with their fight against the theoretical arrogance of science, which subordinated human existence to the strictures of categorical claims, Ginsberg, along with an emerging group of modernists who appropriated earlier and more open forms of artistic creation, instituted a cultural revolution of his own.

The other challenge to high modernism took a more conventional, if not more rigorous, approach in Kenneth Burke's 1945 masterpiece, *A Grammar of Motives*, a book that marked both the author's long struggle with the implications of formalist aesthetics and the emergence of *late modernism*. In this work, Burke questioned the efficacy and logic of high modernism, not in the name of metaphysics as Ginsberg would, but in the name of communication and rhetorical appeal. Equally disturbed by the will to power inherent within the rationalizing tendencies of modern science and technology, Burke too hoped that the aesthetic might serve as a counterbalance to the excesses of modernity. But he and those artists, writers, and critics who followed in his footsteps or paralleled the theoretical moves he made in that book were unwilling, on the one hand, to limit art to merely a disinterested, formal configuration of poetic elements separate from the interested hands of the artist and the audience and, on the other hand, to reduce art to the dreamlike, self-expressive activities of a poetic seeker in search of some form of holy communion. Burke would have little to do with either Lionel Trilling or Allen Ginsberg. Aesthetics, as Burke began to argue, was a very interested, very socially and communicatively grounded *act* in which the artist tried to construct a sense of self-identity from the crumbling landscape while simultaneously trying to appeal rhetorically to an often diverse and divisive audience. Burke's modernism, in this sense, dealt with the complicated dialectic between the intrinsic and the extrinsic, that is, between what the aesthetic act accomplished for the artist in relationship to the social, historical, familial, theological, and psychological grounds from which it emerged and what that act accomplished as a discordant, yet communicative, voice amid the chattering of the audience that consumed it. Art served, Burke asserted, as a form of reconciliation, identification, and courtship between the artist who produced it and the audience to whom it was addressed. Art, in other words, was a rhetorical act.

Burke did not develop his position on aesthetics very easily. In fact, he began his literary career as a committed participant in the Greenwich Village modernist circles in the 1920s and 1930s, having found the intellectual climate at Columbia University, where he pursued his undergraduate studies, a poor substitute for the rich literary culture downtown. Indeed, Burke's bohemian credentials were impeccable. A friend of William Carlos Williams, Malcolm Cowley, Hart Crane, and Alfred Steiglitz, and a contributor to a number of "little magazines" of artistic and political dissent including the *Masses*, *Secession*, *Broom*, the *Little Review*, and the *New Republic*, Burke emerged as "something of an aesthete" in the 1920s, once referring to himself "as 'a Flaubert.'"[111] His poetry, book reviews, and essays were published widely, and his 1924 collection of fiction, *The White Oxen and Other Stories*, placed him in the category of writer and critic. He was also editor in the 1920s of the literary journal *The Dial*, increasing his awareness of the modernist currents in poetry, painting, and theater in the international realm. His early career in the avant-garde was marked by the 1931 publication of a collection of essays, *Counter-Statement*, which tracked his development as a literary critic. Published the same year as Edmund Wilson's *Axel's Castle*, Burke's book helped introduce high modernist criticism to a broader American audience and announced his early allegiance to formalist circles.

Although he had already published *The White Oxen* in 1924 and had won the prestigious *Dial* Award in 1929 for his work as editorial assistant and literary critic, Burke did not fully enter the cultural debates over modernism until the appearance of *Counter-Statement*. A collection of eight essays ranging from literary studies of Andre Gide and Thomas Mann to theoretical discussions of literary methods, Burke's book was a celebration of the "antinomian" character of art and a commitment to the "purely aesthetic judgment" as distinct from "scientific criteria."[112] Like the New Critics who would follow his lead, Burke distinguished between art as "the psychology of information," which dealt with human existence only in generalities, and art as "the psychology of form," which was an "exercise of human propriety, the formulation of symbols which rigidify our sense of poise and rhythm" (42). According to Burke, there were five aspects to this psychology of form: syllogistic (the logical unraveling of elements or plot); qualitative (the preparation for the quality of a particular element through the quality of the preceding one); repetitive (the maintenance of one principle under new guises); conventional (the categorical expectancy associated with standard formal practices); and minor (the appearance of brief yet moving elements). Such forms were the basic "appeal" of any work of art, the "equipment" that enabled "the mind to follow processes amenable to it" (143). The subtle artistic use of formal elements created frustrations and expectations within the audience that demanded some sense of resolution. In "Lexicon Rhetoricae," Burke was willing to acknowledge that formal elements were integrated differently in each work of art according to the particular subject matter involved. He was also willing to acknowledge that the "perfection" of the aesthetic experience was continuously hampered by the "divergence in the ideologies of writer and reader" (178). Nonetheless, he was unwilling in this early book to consider "eloquence" anything but the formal properties of an artwork as they related to the particular content. Eloquence was jeopardized by the contingencies of history that distorted true "symbolic" interpretation, contingencies that included "variations in ideology," the "remoteness" of patterns of concern, the "degree of familiarity" with a pattern of experience, and the "divergence" of modes of existence (172). Due to particular vicissitudes, an antiquated symbolic configuration soon lost its eloquence and became merely "quaint." Consequently, Burke considered music the purest form of artistic expression because it was able to dispense with linguistic or verbal content in the name of structure by not relying on the "surprise" and "suspense" connected with imparting narrative "information." Indeed, because music was "fitted less than any other art for imparting information," its form could not "atrophy" and therefore was able to deal "minutely in frustrations and fulfillments of desire" (34). Eloquence as the subtle balance of formal elements and the minimization of extraneous content was for Burke the end of art and the essence of aesthetic appeal.

But Burke was not finished. If high modernists appropriated Kant to reflect on the productive side of aestheticism, Burke used the German philosopher to consider the consumptive side. In so doing, his early work brought the high modernist project full circle. Burke realized that to validate modernist goals he had to demonstrate that formalist elements were appreciable by the audience. In other words, he needed to prove that "though forms need not be prior to experience, they are certainly prior to the work of art exemplifying them" (141). He needed a theory of the subject, and Kant, not surprisingly, provided the answer. Kant of course had situated objective knowledge not in relationship to the natural world but in accordance with the thinking subject. Thus, as Burke explained, "we need but take [Plato's] universals out of heaven and situate them in the human mind (a process begun by Kant), making them not metaphysical, but psychological" (48). In borrowing from Kant's transcendental categories of apperception, Burke argued that the sense of contrast, comparison, expansion, and contraction needed for aesthetic enjoyment were formal categories within the mind, giving man "the potentiality of speech, art, mythology, and so on." Thus, art appealed to the "innate forms of the mind," "the germ-plasm of man." A transcendental aesthetic needed a transcendental subject, both of which took part in historical time but were not limited by it.

But by the time high modernism was institutionalized in American intellectual circles after World War II, Burke had already rejected many of his earlier statements. Beginning with his Depression-era works such as *Permanence and Change* (1935) and *Attitudes Toward History* (1937) and culminating in his Cold War-era works such as *A Grammar of Motives* (1945) and *A Rhetoric of Motives* (1950), Burke unearthed the political implications of high modernism and reenvisioned aesthetics, if not social theory in general, as a *symbolic act*, that is, as a deliberate attempt to destabilize the key symbols of authority residing in prevailing systems of thought, in notions of social and religious piety, and in the overall sense "of what properly goes with what."[113] Art, as such, was a way to gain and offer perspective, a form of critical discourse that used the force of the poetic to violate decorum, taste, and propriety by "merging things which common sense had divided and dividing things which common sense had merged" (113). In this way, aesthetics blended with the psychological, the sociological, the political, and the familial, all of those areas abandoned by high modernism. Borrowing from Aristotle, Freud, and Marx, Burke rejected his earlier search for transcendental forms of appeal and instead linked the efficacy of the aesthetic work to the artist's stylized and strategic resizing of an intractable situation in a way that appealed rhetorically to the social and linguistic communities of address. The artistic act was visionary, educational, confrontational, courting, and integrative, not through the artist's invocation of some spiritual or metaphysical principle as Ginsberg would have it but through the artist's use of comedy, burlesque, punning, incongruity, misnomer, and "verbal blasting." Art worked through its immersion into the social and temporal scene in which it was placed, not as a form of disinterested contemplation or a form of spiritual absolution but as a poetic solvent that dissolved the stale orientations littering the scene and that imagined new, and possibly more liberating, ones.

An example of Burke's "un-timeliness" was of course his participation in the 1949 "Western Round Table on Modern Art," discussed in the Introduction. Amid the clamor declaring "the work of art independent of the artist" and the painter uninterested in "the reaction of the public," Burke wondered aloud whether or not his high modernist counterparts had negated the efficacy of art in general.[114] Burke traced the root of the problem to the beginning of the nineteenth century when the study of aesthetics as a singular discipline emerged and theoreticians separated the poetic ("the work in itself, its kind, its properties, the internal relations among its parts, etc.") from the rhetorical ("the work's persuasiveness, its appeal").[115] Noting that this decision was the effect of the "specialized nature of our modern culture," Burke argued that the "systems of symbols," despite claims to the contrary, used by artists were not different in essence to those used by other specialists. "Each of these symbolic structures," continued Burke, "is an organized vocabulary which a man learns to manipulate for purposes of expression, discovery and communication" (36). Consequently, since there was no fundamental antithesis between art and rhetoric, there was no reason to keep reinforcing the solipsistic notion that the artist was merely "talking to himself" (33).

In a reversal of the argument of high modernism, Burke compared the disinterested stance of the formalist poet to the apolitical stance of the postwar scientist who reluctantly but thoroughly abdicated any responsibility for his role in furthering the advances of the Cold War state. While making claims about the purity and disinterested nature of basic research, the scientist refused to acknowledge that his specialized expertise, whether in chemical, biological, or physical research, was often swallowed up by larger military imperatives. Content with severing his role as a "technical expert" from his responsibility as a citizen, the "pure" scientist ignored the political purposes for which his discoveries were used. As Burke sarcastically noted, "the question of what the new force might mean, as released into a social texture emotionally and intellectually unfit to control it, or as surrendered to men whose *speciality* is *professional killing*—well, that is simply 'none of his business,' as specialist, however great may be his misgivings as father of a family, or as citizen of his nation and of the world."[116] Even those of "good will" associated with organizations such as the Federation of American Scientists, who clamored for international control of atomic energy, assumed that the inherent "morality of their speciality" would protect their discoveries from the ulterior motives of "fiends." Science, just like art, was never able to fully protect its autonomy. Formalist poets, like their formalist scientific counterparts, accepted modernity's severing of art and science from the sphere of moral development.

Or so it seemed. Burke also argued that claims for the purity of each branch of modernity were often merely a cover for motives hidden elsewhere. American critics who argued for the autonomy of scientific research, particularly in light of the pernicious use of science by Fascist countries during World War II, for instance, often used such arguments to overlook the growing relationship between research and development and the Cold War state. Burke argued that hidden behind the claims of high modernism were similar motives. For Burke, "although the cult of the 'imagination' is usually urged today by those who champion poetry as a field opposed to science, our investigations would suggest the ironic possibility that they exemplify an aspect of precisely the thinking they would reject" (223). Consequently, Burke turned high modernism on its head, arguing that the growing connection between the New Critics and the New York intellectuals and the emergence of an aggressive Cold War liberalism revealed the actual motives of Allen Tate, Lionel Trilling, and others. As he argued in *Rhetoric of Motives*, "whenever you find a doctrine of 'nonpolitical' esthetics affirmed with fervor, look for its politics."[117] Aesthetics, despite claims to the contrary, was nothing but interested. The tradition of late modernism of which Burke was a key figure began with this principle.

CHAPTER TWO

Reconsidering the Authoritarian Personality in America: The Sociological Challenge of David Riesman

In a 1961 revision of an *Art News* article, "New York Painting Only Yesterday," Clement Greenberg, reflective and triumphant, proclaimed that "someday it will have to be told how 'anti-Stalinism,' which started out more or less as 'Trotskyism,' turned into art for art's sake, and thereby cleared the way, heroically, for what was to come."[1] Greenberg's celebratory comparison between anti-Communism and modernist aesthetics validated Kenneth Burke's prescient claim that ulterior motives lurked behind the disinterested stance of high modernism. Indeed, besides their heroic attempt to defend the humanities in a world that had succumbed to the tools of instrumental reason, high modernists in the 1940s and 1950s fought a desperate struggle to salvage the individual from the trappings of modern authoritarian movements threatening the foundations of Western civilization. Although never engaging in the reactionary forms of nationalistic display like many of their intellectual compatriots, high modernists such as Lionel Trilling, Theodor Adorno, Max Horkheimer, Clement Greenberg, and Allen Tate echoed the rhetoric of many anti-Communist organizations. They also offered their theoretical perspectives to analyze not just the tremors of the Cold War landscape but, more important, the historical developments that had led so many of their fellow citizens on both sides of the Atlantic to abnegate their freedom for the illusionary dreams found in mass movements. High modernists joined with American sociologists, psychologists, and political scientists in dissecting the mental condition of those who had joined totalitarian organizations to determine if such ideologies had any widespread appeal in the United States. The result was a sustained investigation into the psyche of the American people, an investigation that supposedly revealed the frightening possibility that recent historical trends—ranging from economic catastrophe to postindustrialization—had given rise to the same pathological mental state that had plunged Europe into turmoil.

In this sense, the debates over modernist aesthetics that emerged in the 1940s and 1950s were not merely about formalist practices versus spontaneous poetics or disinterested contemplation versus rhetorical persuasion. Modernists of all stripes were swept up into this larger discussion about the threat that totalitarian ideologies posed to the American public. This debate, which was obviously not confined to modernist circles, was in fact about the fate of the self in an age of mass politics and mass culture—about whether or not the scale of political and economic institutions had usurped the critical capacities of the individual and had thereby paved the way for collectivism. Most high modernists answered in the affirmative; other modernists were less convinced. For instance, many romantic modernists such as Allen Ginsberg and Norman Mailer criticized high modernists for inciting a panic over the so-called authoritarian personality in America, a panic that they argued ironically reinforced the compulsive conformity about which Trilling, Adorno, and others were so worried. Similary, those artists and critics who composed the tradition of late modernism fretted over the almost compulsive anti-Communist stance of most high modernists. For instance, in a paper given to the American Committee for Cultural Freedom in 1951 titled "On the Limits of Totalitarian Power," sociologist David Riesman expressed reservations about the overreaction on the part of European commentators who, in their effort to warn the Western world about the appeal of mass movements, failed to understand how the complexities of modern society might mitigate against such movements instead of merely producing them. Speaking to an audience that included Hannah Arendt, Bruno Bettelheim, and Nathan Leites, Riesman suggested that such critics had overestimated the "psychological pressure" of totalitarian ideologies, particularly in the United States where such fanaticism had made little advance.[2] His argument was that liberal organizations such as the Committee for Cultural Freedom had done a much too efficient job of awakening their fellow citizens to the dangerous appeals of authoritarian ideologies, making everyone begin to "greatly overestimate the capacity of totalitarianism to restructure human personality" (415). In his paper, Riesman took to task writers from George Orwell to Aldous

Huxley to Theodor Adorno to Hannah Arendt, all of whom falsely assumed that the fragmentation of traditional social life had automatically produced broken personalities.

In many ways, Riesman offered the most famous discussion of the so-called American character in the 1950s, a discussion that centered on the critical capacities of ordinary citizens to resist the allure of political movements and to challenge the pressures of social conformity. His 1950 best-selling book *The Lonely Crowd: A Study of the Changing American Character* was just one of many books published by critics that detailed how postwar social and economic changes had unsettled the lives, expectations, and outlooks of most Americans. But unlike high modernists such as Theodor Adorno or Lionel Trilling, who saw nothing but confusion and uncertainty in the eyes of ordinary citizens in an age of mass politics and mass culture, Riesman saw a new American character that, while still beset by many of the same psychological hang-ups as past generations, had developed a more flexible personality structure. This American character possessed the capacity for positive adjustment and mutability, traits that not only helped individuals escape the lure of political movements but also pointed to a more open form of selfhood than that imagined by other critics. According to Riesman, high modernist critics, who held fast to a notion of "psychological integration," had underestimated "the amount of disintegration and inconsistency of response that an individual can stand" (424). In response, he called for "a more robust view of man's potentialities, not only for evil, about which we have heard and learned so much, not only for heroism, about which we have also learned, but also for sheer unheroic cussed resistance to totalitarian efforts to make a new man of him" (425). In this sense, debates over modernist aesthetics were also about the nature of identity in modern America. In *The Lonely Crowd*, Riesman, like other late modernists, offered an entirely different vision of man's capabilities and capacities for change.

Discovering the Authoritarian Personality

In a 1954 *Saturday Review* article on Allan Valentine's *The Age of Conformity*, William Barrett, the associate editor of *Partisan Review*, argued that Valentine's indictment of the authoritarian tendencies within American life was "nothing new." For Barrett, "there could hardly be a subject that has been so thoroughly scoured and picked apart by this time by journalists, sociologists, pundits, and assorted visiting firemen from foreign shores."[3] Indeed, the firemen from abroad to whom Barrett referred helped to shift discussions dramatically within the United States about a general breakdown of Western society. Growing fears about the concentration of power within the United States had of course already appeared in diverse works such as James Burnham's *The Managerial Revolution* (1941), Peter Drucker's *Future of Industrial Man* (1942), and Dwight Macdonald's *The Root Is Man* (1946), but the emigration of prominent European intellectuals who had firsthand experience of totalitarianism added a certain gravitas to the American debate. From psychologists such as Erik Erikson, Wilhelm Reich, and Bruno Bettelheim to writers such as André Malraux, George Orwell, and Arthur Koestler to critics such as Hannah Arendt, Paul Tillich, and Franz Neumann, arriving European intellectuals taught a horrifying lesson to their American listeners, and their concerns were quickly translated into the pages of *Partisan Review*, *Commentary*, *New Republic*, *Encounter*, and *Politics*. As fanaticism, nationalism, and ethnic and racial intolerance swept through Europe, chastised American and emigrant European intellectuals surveyed the landscape of the United States for evidence of such burning embers.

The book that first attempted to explain the rise of totalitarianism in the heart of civilized Western Europe and the book that first implored American intellectuals to begin fretting over the situation in their own country was Erich Fromm's *Escape from Freedom* (1941). A practicing psychoanalyst and former member of the Institute for Social Research, Fromm emigrated from Germany in 1933 and established himself as a penetrating critic of the socioeconomic conditions that had produced fascism. Blending psychoanalysis and empirical studies, Fromm linked recent historical changes in capitalism to the widespread psychological malaise affecting the millions of Europeans who were willing to sacrifice themselves to the authoritarian state. The breadth of his historical perspective accounted for the appeal of his book as did his trenchant depiction of the loneliness of the modern individual, who, according to Fromm, had begun, in a tragic reversal of history, to bemoan the litany of freedoms provided by Western civilization. Borrowing themes from Max Weber and Karl Marx, Fromm sketched the historical emergence of the modern individual: the development of the capitalist market system had freed the individual from bondage and servitude; the rise of Protestantism had challenged the authority of the church; and the French and American revolutions in the eighteenth century had ushered in civil and political liberties. Freed from the "primary ties" of family, church, and caste found in medieval society, the individual had emerged upon the world's stage, "independent, self-reliant, and critical," liberated from the "old enemies of freedom" in the name of self-discovery.[4] But this sense of freedom, cautioned Fromm, was illusionary and ignored the "new enemies of a different nature."[5] In fact, the individual now needed to confront the "*inner* restraints, compulsions, and fears" that arose with the collapse of "*outer* restraints." Free to determine his way within the democratic state, the individual had been deprived of any markers for a positive sense of freedom, leaving him "more isolated, alone, and afraid" (104). Overwhelmed by the bureaucratic indifference of modern organizations, the modern individual came to consider the demands of freedom too burdensome. Unable to withstand the feelings of "isolation and powerlessness," the individual tried to "escape from freedom" (133). Under such conditions, the modern individual, according to Fromm, had developed sadomasochistic impulses. This "burden of freedom" was overcome by forgoing "the independence of one's own individual self" and masochistically fusing "with somebody or something" (140) in order to acquire the strength the individual lacked. These "masochistic strivings" were satisfied by subordination to a "bigger and more powerful whole" whether in the form of "a person, an institution, God, the nation, conscience, or a psychic compulsion" (154). According to Fromm, this new "authoritarian character" took pleasure in submission to state authority and joy in the willful destruction of others as scapegoats for the individual's own powerless condition.

Fromm's book had an immediate impact. Most, if not all, discussions of totalitarianism in the United States were filtered through his analytic lens. Fromm's discussion of the sadomasochistic structure of the modern personality was appropriated, for instance, into psychologist Abraham Maslow's oft-cited 1943 *Journal of Social Psychology* article "The Authoritarian Character Structure," which was the culmination of his five-year study of authoritarian beliefs in America. Social scientists, such as Harold Lasswell, Hadley Cantril, and William Kornhauser, all of whom conducted extended investigations into political pathologies, borrowed from Fromm's speculative framework. The book, however, that most readily translated Fromm's analytic framework into an American vernacular was Arthur Schlesinger's 1949 book *The Vital Center: The Politics of Freedom*. He argued, with a certain Eliotic inflection, that modern America, with "its quota of lonely and frustrated people, craving social, intellectual and even sexual fulfillment they cannot obtain in existing society," had become a breeding ground for individuals who "*want* to be disciplined."[6] According to Schlesinger, the impersonality of American society had forced the individual to find "outlets for the impulses of sadism and masochism" (54). For most of these critics, three factors in particular seemed to be producing the sadomasochistic character that Fromm had analyzed. The first was the economic turmoil of the Great Depression. The effect of the unemployment crisis of the previous decades was a tremendous amount of uncertainty and confusion, effects that seemed to linger into the 1950s when the surprising postwar abundance should have mitigated such anxieties. For example, contributors to Daniel Bell's *The New American Right* (1955) noted that the hysteria surrounding the threat of Communist subversion in the United States, which had produced the demagoguery of Joseph McCarthy, was linked to a perpetual "status anxiety" on the part of a rising lower middle class fretting that international events might disrupt its recent socioeconomic gains.

The second factor supposedly producing this sadomasochistic personality was the gradual disappearance of early industrial society of the late nineteenth century. The apparent completion of the industrial revolution through advanced automation and computer-based technology had prompted the transition in the 1950s from a goods-producing to a service-centered economy, as labor was slowly removed from the production process and transferred to clerical, technical, professional, and managerial positions. In 1962, sociologist Daniel Bell detailed this transition in a talk titled "The Post-Industrial Society," which he gave at the Columbia University Seminar on Technology and Social Change. Arguing that the major institutions of American society were now "a vast new array of conglomerations of universities, research institutes, [and] research corporations," Bell presented a vision of social life turned upside down, as the "exponential growth" of scientific research had made it "more and more difficult" on the "cultural level of society" to develop "terms for expressing what is occurring in the realm of science and in life itself."[7] The public imagination was stirred by this shift, as the American worker symbolically transformed from the brawny, muscular industrial laborer from the turn of the century into the weak, conformist white-collar worker of the 1950s. The representations of "manly work," as Barbara Melosh has shown, that dominated the state-sponsored art of the New Deal in the 1930s were erased by caricatures such as those found in sociologist William Whyte's 1956 work *The Organization Man* of the "unmanly arts of persuasion" of professional life.[8] No longer engaging in the harsh physical demands of productive labor, the middle-class male of the new corporate order bore little relation to his ancestors. According to Whyte, the replacement of the nineteenth-century Protestant ethic of "individual initiative and imagination" by the social ethic of cooperative group dynamics within the corporate world had made "morally legitimate the pressures of society against the individual."[9]

This transition from a goods-producing to a service-centered economy had, according to most critics, produced an intolerable cultural asphyxiation, the third factor producing an authoritarian character. In this sense, the modernist defense of high culture was not merely a reaction to the unsettling prominence of scientific language in everyday life; it was also a challenge to the degradation of intellectual life by the culture industry. In a series of highly influential essays including Clement Greenberg's "Avant-Garde and Kitsch," Dwight Macdonald's "A Theory of Popular Culture," and Theodor Adorno's "On Popular Music" and "How to Look at Television," high modernists noted the psychologically damaging effects of the standardization of consumer goods on American society. The steady flow of cheap cultural goods not only competed with the artifacts of high culture for audience attention but also had led to the degradation of the intellectual faculties of most consumers. Inundated with standardized slogans, the modern individual had fallen prey to a culture industry that had produced a form of psychological dependency in the consumer who masochistically subjected himself to its pleasures in the same fashion as "the prisoner who loves his cell because he has been left nothing else to love."[10] Consequently, the individual was unable to discriminate not only between the relative merits of consumer goods but between politicians supposedly speaking in his interests and economic structures supposedly operating for his benefit. Even the most sophisticated minds were unable to comprehend "the complexities of a highly organized and institutionalized society" in the "plain terms of consistency and reason."[11] The tools of sophisticated discrimination and contemplation were expelled from the minds of mass consumers in the name of profit and social control.

All of these concerns were funneled into the most comprehensive study of the irrational nature of the modern individual, *The Authoritarian Personality*, a collaborative investigation commissioned by the American Jewish Committee and authored by Theodor Adorno, Else Frenkel-Brunswik, Daniel Levinson, and R. Nevitt Sanford. The project was initiated in 1944 after Max Horkheimer was appointed head of the Department of Scientific Research for the American Jewish Committee and helped to launch a five-volume study on modern anti-Semitism titled Studies in Prejudice.[12] Because of its experimentation with depth psychology and projective testing, *The Authoritarian Personality* became the definitive postwar study of modern prejudice. Initially restricted to a small sampling of female students at the University of California, the study was expanded to include an examination of the psychological dispositions of middle-class professionals, psychiatric patients at a California clinic, working-class men and women in local unions, members of parent-teacher associations, church groups, women's clubs, inmates at the San

Quentin State Prison, female public school teachers and social workers, and students at the University of Oregon and George Washington University.

Finding themselves "in perfect agreement with the description of the authoritarian character given by Fromm and Maslow," Adorno and his collaborators argued that the increasing isolation of the modern individual had become a breeding ground for compulsive conformity.[13] Rejecting the assumption that latent authoritarian tendencies were apparent only in overt action or consciously stated opinions, the authors turned to psychology to investigate those "established patterns of hope and aspirations, fears and anxieties that dispose [individuals] to certain beliefs and make them resistant to others" (10). Most influential was the development of the famous F-scale, an attitudinal scale that measured the presence of "antidemocratic tendencies at the personality level" (223). Through a series of clinical interviews, thematic apperception tests, and detailed questionnaires, the F-scale was supposedly able to measure the authoritarian potential of individuals according to a series of traits that included a rigid adherence to conventional values, a submissive attitude toward authorities, and an overly aggressive reaction to outsiders. Although these traits were not comprehensive of "*all* the features of this personality pattern," they did, according to the book's authors, form "a more or less enduring structure in the person that renders him receptive to antidemocratic propaganda" (228). Such receptivity was linked to the psychological weakening of the individual. The apparent causes were numerous, including widespread ignorance about the current economic and political situation and a growing inability to balance the conflicting psychic demands of internal and external forces. This last conclusion became the dominant paradigm for most discussions of authoritarianism. As the study explained, "weakness in the ego is expressed in the inability to build up a consistent and enduring set of moral values within the personality; and it is the state of affairs, apparently, that makes it necessary for the individual to seek some organizing and coordinating agency outside of himself" (234). Thus, ego weakness was marked by several character traits, including an opposition to introspection, a prejudiced use of stereotypes, and a revulsion against individual weakness.

Reactions in the United States to the study were overwhelmingly positive. In his 1950 *Commentary* review, Nathan Glazer praised the Studies in Prejudice series (and *The Authoritarian Personality* in particular) for making scientific research into the subject of prejudice "immeasurably richer" through the analytic methods employed.[14] Even Paul Lazarsfeld, who had personal difficulties with Adorno when the two worked together on Lazarsfeld's Radio

Research Project at Princeton University in the late 1930s, praised the methodological achievements of the study. But due to the long delay in publication, the abiding criticism of the book when published in 1950 was its failure to consider the problem of left-wing authoritarianism. For instance, Edward Shils, in his contribution to a 1954 review, *Studies in the Scope and Method of "The Authoritarian Personality,"* argued that the recent upsetting of the traditional left-right political dichotomy by both "Fascism and Bolshevism" exposed the limitations of Adorno's study.[15] Of course Adorno, in his more interpretive discussions of character typology, had already noticed this similarity. As he explained, the Berkeley study revealed a number of "'rigid' low scorers" who were involved extensively in "some progressive movement" and who exhibited "features of compulsiveness, even of paranoid obsession" that "could hardly be distinguished from some of our high extremes."[16] In fact, Adorno, more than other contributors, often elided the distinction between left-wing and right-wing versions of the authoritarian personality.

Indeed, by the time Cold War anxieties emerged after the Potsdam conference in 1945, the theoretical differences between Fascism and Communism were not easily translatable. The movement of American intellectuals, including many high modernists, from Stalinism to Trotskyism to liberal anti-Communism, particularly in the wake of the Nazi-Soviet pact of 1939, has been well documented.[17] In 1949, the anti-Communist organization Americans for Intellectual Freedom famously picketed the Cultural and Scientific Conference for World Peace, arguing that the conference was merely a façade for pro-Communist organizers. Inspired by the demonstrations and encouraged by anti-Communist intellectuals living in Europe, the Americans for Intellectual Freedom directly led to a much more prominent organization. Founded in 1951, the American Committee for Cultural Freedom, an affiliate of the Congress for Cultural Freedom that had been formed the previous year in Berlin, united the various strains of liberal anti-Communism in the United States, counting intellectuals such as Arthur Schlesinger, Jr., Daniel Bell, James Burnham, Norman Thomas, and Diana Trilling as members. Although the high modernists who joined the American Committee for Cultural Freedom approached the cause of anti-Communism in different ways (Clement Greenberg leading a direct campaign against fellow travelers at the *Nation*, Lionel Trilling reluctantly supporting investigations into Communist academics at Columbia University, and Allen Tate occasionally writing anti-Communist polemics), all of them saw Communism and Fascism as merely two variants of the same affliction. Even Theodor Adorno and Max Horkheimer, seeing the sources of both ideologies in the regressive tendencies of the Enlightenment, adopted a form of liberal anti-Communism when they returned to Germany in the early 1950s, and both, like their intellectual companions in America, warned against political subversion in their own country.[18]

Consequently, American critics appropriated the analytic lens of their German counterparts and applied it to the problem of Communism, painting a disturbing portrait of American society as psychologically weak and therefore particularly vulnerable to political infestation. Since the writers of *The Authoritarian Personality* openly admitted that they had not given Communism "any special attention," a host of other social scientists rushed to fill in the gaps.[19] For instance, psychologist Milton Rokeach, in his book *The Open and Closed Mind*, extended the F-scale to measure not simply intolerance but also "dogmatism and opinionation," two traits supposedly shared by Communists and Fascists.[20] Examples of this shift in perspective were ubiquitous in American intellectual circles. Beginning in 1953, an anti-Communist liberal organization, The Fund for the Republic, sponsored a scholarly series titled "Communism in American Life." Most of the volumes, including Theodore Draper's *Roots of American Communism* (1957), Robert Iverson's *The Communists and the Schools* (1959), and Nathan Glazer's *The Social Basis of American Communism* (1961), detailed the influence of the Communist Party in the preceding decades and warned about the irrational allure of authoritarianism. What united these works, along with other independent studies including Irving Howe and Lewis Coser's *The American Communist Party: A Critical History* (1957) and Daniel Bell's *Marxian Socialism in the United States* (1952), was the common belief that party members were driven by an "orgiastic chiliasm."[21] As Daniel Bell noted, the problem was "explaining the tremendous emotional hold that communism has on tens of thousands of persons" (186). Claiming that the answer rested on "a mythopoeic and psychological level," Bell argued that party ideology provided a "set of satisfactions" for the average Communist, including a sense of "'purpose' in a world where most people's energies are dissipated in a set of violent but aimless quests" (187).

Most of these speculative arguments concerning the threat posed by Communism were based upon myriad social scientific investigations conducted throughout the 1950s into the psychology of party members, research that borrowed heavily from the analytic methods of *The Authoritarian Personality*.[22] Such studies broadened the scope of *The Authoritarian Personality* by considering the effects of class position, educational level, cultural sophistication, voting behavior, and family background on ideological receptivity and by extending the analytic samples to include not just middle-class Californians but almost every possible racial, ethnic, religious, and class group in the country, an almost absurd extension that led Paul Lazarsfeld to suggest jokingly that only "contributors of money to the Boy Scout movement" had not yet been studied.[23] The most notable of these works was a 1954 investigation, *The Appeals of Communism*, conducted by political scientist Gabriel Almond of the Center of International Studies at Princeton University. After interviewing hundreds of party members, Almond concluded that party recruits exhibited a certain "neurotic susceptibility" to Communist indoctrination, caused by deep psychological feelings of inadequacy that resulted in a willingness to merge with "the *corpus mysticum* of the party."[24] Irving Howe, in his and Lewis Coser's history of the Communist Party, pointed to Almond's findings to demonstrate that most recent party members had weak psychological constitutions. Arguing that "ego strength and weakness are grounded in historical contexts," Howe noted that the current feelings of alienation had led to "caesaristic identification" with party authorities as compensation for individual lack.[25] The Communist Party as such was a haven for neurotics. Indeed, this was the lesson learned, as Howe and Almond argued, from the myriad confessions written by former Communist Party members who tried to explain the appeals of Communism in relationship to their own individual lives. Testimony from ex-Communists and undercover federal agents—Richard Wright's *Black Boy* (1945), Louis Budenz's *This Is My Story* (1947), and Elizabeth Bentley's *Out of Bondage* (1951)—offered firsthand accounts of the supposedly masochistic strivings of party members. Even more influential was Whittaker Chambers's *Witness* (1952), the most famous account of life inside the Communist underground, which received considerable critical attention from the New York intellectuals. Although most commentators, including William Phillips, Arthur Schlesinger, Jr., and Irving Howe, disagreed with his political and religious beliefs, all noted that Chambers had offered a window onto "the appeals of communism," explaining why a man "with no friends, no social ties, no church, no community" stumbled into fanaticism.[26]

High Modernism and the Problem of Ego Autonomy

High modernists such as Allen Tate, Lionel Trilling, and Theodor Adorno appropriated these social, historical, and autobiographical arguments to show that the main psychological condition of most individuals after World War II was a demonstrable ego weakness. The widespread appearance of the authoritarian personality proved that the ego, resting precariously between the compulsions of the superego and the atavistic impulses of the id, was neither as transparent nor as stable as modern psychology presupposed. As Max Horkheimer explained in *Eclipse of Reason*, "the individual subject of reason tends to become a shrunken ego, captive of an evanescent present, forgetting the use of the intellectual functions by which he was once able to transcend his actual position in reality."[27] Deafened by the "giant loud-speaker of industrial culture," the individual was left merely "echoing, repeating, [and] imitating his surroundings" until, in a final abdication of responsibility, he ended "adapting himself to all the powerful groups to which he eventually belongs" (141). In such a world, mimicry had become the only form of survival and the primary form of submission. High modernists followed Freud in viewing man's ego as nothing more than a "poor creature" subservient to three separate masters—the external world, the impulses of the id, and the disciplinary superego. In *The Ego and the Id*, Freud had posited the ego as merely a vicissitude of the drives, that is, as the result of the transformation of object-libido into narcissistic-libido. In the name of self-preservation, the original libidinal cathexis with the primary love object was severed and this lost relationship was internalized through the formation of the ego that served as a substitute for the external object. But the ego, whose tasks included the rational ordering of experience, was often overwhelmed by the incomprehensibility of modern life. Having no independent source of its own, the ego only too often considered itself "deserted by all protecting forces" and allowed itself to perish.[28] Under such conditions, submissiveness became the predominant character trait. High modernists agreed with Freud that the ego was merely a secondary formation, noting, as Lionel Trilling asserted, that "mind came into being when the sensations and emotions were checked by external resistance or by conflict with each other."[29] As such, the ego almost exclusively served defensive functions that were too often abandoned. In his 1951 essay "William Dean Howells and the Roots of Modern Taste," Trilling argued that the lure of totalitarianism rested in the "irresistible temptation" to yield the self to the forces of grandeur.[30] Trilling rooted this problem in the willingness of party members to abandon lived reality with its attendant class dynamics for an imagined Communist society where the "spirit" was capable of "making its own terms" (214). Individual psychology, which had once served the function of reason, had given way to group psychology, making the ego merely a historical relic.

Even worse, the individual was now defenseless against intrapsychic tensions. Freud's warning in *Civilization and Its Discontents* had taught high modernists about the psychological significance of the death instinct. In his later works, Freud had postulated that the fundamental drive for pleasure inherent to man's nature was balanced by a corresponding drive to return to a state of inertia or even nonexistence. But given the vicissitudes of the drives, this death instinct often morphed into an impulse for aggression. In a 1944 conference titled "Psychiatric Symposium on Anti-Semitism," held at the University of California at Berkeley, Theodor Adorno joined a number of psychologists including Ernst Simmel, Gordon Allport, and R. Nevitt Sanford in an attempt to delineate "the most powerful energy" threatening mankind—"the human instinct of destruction hidden within the unconscious and *emanating hatred* from there."[31] Other high modernists, including Lionel Trilling, issued similar warnings, arguing that the "impulse toward charismatic power" originated in "not only the threat to being which comes from without but also the seduction to non-being which establishes itself within."[32] With such an understanding came a radical revision of traditional images of human nature. Most famously, Reinhold Niebuhr and Dwight Macdonald urged their fellow New York intellectuals to dispense with seemingly naïve and overly optimistic attitudes about human behavior, arguing that there was "evil as well as good at the base of human nature."[33] In contrast to the images of man's perfectibility offered by Progressives and radicals, many European and American intellectuals pointed to the bloodshed of the twentieth century in their defense of Freud's theories.

Although high modernists argued that the ego needed to remain resistant to the excessive demands of the reality principle and to the dark impulses of the id, they also worried about the damaging effects of the ego's own projective fantasies. Consequently, high modernists originally constructed a notion of ego autonomy only to dismantle it. In *The Ego and the Id*, Freud had argued that the ego suffered in both its futile attempt to disguise the id's inherent conflict with reality by transforming itself into the object of choice and its futile attempt to satisfy the overbearing demands of the superego by covering over the gap between itself and its ideal. Consequently, according to Freud, the ego "only too often" became "sycophantic, opportunist and lying" in the midst of this impossible situation.[34] Following Freud's logic, Adorno worried that the narcissistic tendencies of the ego encouraged the individual to apprehend reality in terms of its own projective fantasies. Having no independent source of its own, the ego was inherently fragile, an instability that often resulted in either its negation or its irrational and unyielding rigidity. Because the "id's libido quantum" was "so much larger than that of the ego" and therefore "always bound to regain the upper hand," the ego often distorted the nature of external reality in a pathological and hallucinatory manner to disguise the id's inherent conflict with the reality principle.[35] Violence was the only foreseeable outcome. The weakened ego was no longer able to restrain "the aggressive wishes which originate from the id," and consequently the ego projected those wishes onto the outside world as "evil intentions," paving the way for the seemingly justified domination of a hostile world in the name of "self-defense."[36] In this sense, the domineering character of Enlightenment thought stemmed from the ego's own narcissism. As Horkheimer and Adorno explained in the pages of *Dialectic of Enlightenment*, "objectifying (like sick) thought contains the despotism of the subjective purpose which is hostile to the thing and forgets the thing itself, thus committing the mental act of violence which is later put into practice" (193). Unable to project anything but "its own unhappiness," the ego gave into the most destructive urges.

Other high modernists issued similar warnings about the domineering tendencies of the ego. In a 1952 lecture, "The Man of Letters in the Modern World," given at the International Exposition of the Arts in Paris, which was sponsored by the Congress for Cultural Freedom, Allen Tate presented "the man of letters" with the formidable task of recreating "the image of man" in an age of "mass control."[37] Tate traced the recent enslavement of mankind by the forces of terror to Descartes's philosophical separation of mind from body and rationality from desire, an intellectual revolution that isolated man from his true nature. Echoing Horkheimer and Adorno's critique of the Enlightenment, Tate argued that the historical era of the Cartesian ego had culminated with the specter of totalitarianism. The violent dissection of the realm of nature in the name of rationality had morphed into the violent dissection of mankind in the name of social betterment and expert planning. With a naïve belief in the rational mind's infallibility, the so-called enlightened subject had separated "means from ends, action from sensibility, matter from mind, society from the individual, religion from moral agency, love from lust, poetry from thought, communion from experience, and mankind in the community from men in the crowd" (13). According to Tate, too many individuals in the modern age refused to temper their own intellects with a sense of humility and were unwilling to accept a life lived with contradiction.

This of course was the basis for the high modernist critique of fellow travelers, Progressives, and party members, those who had tied "the liberal imagination" to the demands of political movements. Lionel Trilling's vitriolic attack on the ideological posturing of Communists, for instance, was in response to his larger fear that the individual, in the name of moral righteousness, was trying to impose upon his fellow men "a similarity which would be himself" and was trying to negate "their differences from one another" as a cure for his own confusions.[38] As a literary example, Trilling pointed to Henry James's *The Princess Casamassima* as an "incomparable representation of the spiritual circumstances of our civilization" (176). James's novel tells the tale of Hyacinth Robinson, the poor illegitimate son of a French seamstress and an English nobleman, who becomes involved in a number of revolutionary anarchist groups but who begins, through his relationship with an Italian aristocrat, Princess Casamassima, to question the usefulness of violent action. According to Trilling, Hyacinth learns that revolutionary passion is by its very nature "guilty," arising not from some empathetic "response to human misery" but from a need for "certainty" (171). Conversely, the Princess, because of her guilt over her privileged position, befriends Paul Muniment, a working-class companion of Hyacinth, and commits herself to revolutionary activity. The Princess, for Trilling, is "the very embodiment of the modern will," one that clings to its own sense of virtue but that "hates itself" and hates the complexity of the world in which it lives, a will that "longs for an absolute humanity" (176) without differences. Political action wrapped in ideology was, for Trilling, nothing more than a veneer for "the impulses to revenge and to dominance" (171).

In this sense, high modernists established a nearly impossible project for themselves—safeguarding the highly unstable autonomy of the ego from the domineering force of the drives and from the repressive authority of the superego while simultaneously muting the narcissistic tendencies of the ego itself. The fact that the latent aggressiveness inherent within each psychic component had apparently been so easily captured by the nihilistic philosophies of the twentieth century testified to the intractability of the problem. In his 1951 essay "The Poet as Hero: Keats in His Letters," Trilling referenced the "mature masculinity" of John Keats as a model for a life in which such psychic tensions were held in delicate balance.[39] Keats was a man and a hero before he was a poet, "the last image of health" before the "sickness of Europe began to be apparent" (258). Keats balanced the conflicting forces, internal and external, that threatened to overpower him, matching his passion for friendship and community with his enjoyment of solitude, taking pleasure in "the sensory, the sensuous, and the sensual" but exhibiting "probity" in the face of life's complications. Moreover, Keats had tempered the sadistic impulses of the death instinct not by ignoring "the problem of evil" but by confronting it in all its manifestations. Keats recognized the tragic consequences of "passivity" and "melancholy," those impulses seeking to return the individual to a state of inertia, or worse, a state of nothingness. Keats's countered this drive to "surrender to the passive, unconscious life" with an affirmation of "the active principle," but he also remained keenly aware that any such "masculine energy" needed to be assuaged by a "diligent indolence" (243). The mature self, as Trilling explained, was endowed with Keats's "negative capability," the intellectual power to find answers not in "a formula of any kind, not a piece of rationality" but rather in "a way of being and of acting" (251). This "negative capability," according to Trilling, was dependent upon a certain personal strength, found in a self that was "certain of its existence" and that could do "without the armor of systematic certainties" (249).

Other high modernists found similar intellectual heroes. In his portrait of Thomas Mann, with whom he had collaborated when the two were in exile in southern California during the early 1940s, Theodor Adorno described a man living "in a world of high-handed and self-centered people" who knew that "the only better alternative" was to "loosen the bonds of identity and not become rigid," an artist with "two extremely different handwritings," one of "heaviness" and one of "involuntary starts," and a man whose rhythm of life was "not continuity but rather an oscillation" between the extremes of "rigidity and illumination."[40] The modernist hero of Dwight Macdonald's *The Root Is Man* was a slightly more distant figure—the American modernist Henry James, who possessed the maturity to recognize the "imperfections" of "present knowledge."[41] Willing to accept the "tragic limitations of human existence," James, according to Macdonald, taught the importance of moderation, exhibiting a life lived "with contradictions" and "skepticism" (145). Similarly, Clement Greenberg, years after Jackson Pollock's death, claimed that the artist had possessed "what Keats called Negative Capability: he could be doubtful and uncertain without becoming bewildered—that is, in what concerned his art."[42] Of course, since Pollock was not able to maintain such a temperament in his personal life and since he was, much to the chagrin of Greenberg, an acknowledged Stalinist for most of his life, high modernists like Greenberg had difficulty in translating this negative capability to the general public as an antidote to antidemocratic sentiments.

Modernist Aesthetics and the Tempering of the Self

Some Cold War intellectuals, most notably Sidney Hook, placed considerable faith in progressive education to reinforce liberal tolerance. Even Max Horkheimer, in one of his more optimistic moments, argued that irrational politics stemmed from a "lack of enlightenment."[43] In his contribution to a United Nations–supported investigation into the "tensions that cause war," Horkheimer observed that "the task of those engaged in education on all levels, from the high school history class to the mass media of communication, was to see to it that the experiences of the last war of aggression, which came very close to success, become deeply engraved in the minds of all people" (241). This was also the conclusion of *Life* magazine's 1948 "Round Table on the Pursuit of Happiness," featuring "eighteen prominent Americans" including Edmund Walsh, Sidney Hook, and Erich Fromm, all of whom concluded that "editors, educators, the clergy and various individuals and institutions immediately concerned with the enlightenment of the people" needed to help stem the tide of dread threatening democratic society.[44] Of course pedagogical indoctrination was not very appealing to many high modernists who were quite skeptical of the nation's educational system. The other solutions offered by social scientists—mandatory therapy sessions for suspected political deviants and compulsory physical activity to sublimate aggression—were similarly untenable to those who worried about the pressures of conformity. Instead, the danger of identity thinking, argued many high modernists, might also be tempered by the aesthetic experience provided by modern art. As an order of knowledge and a cognitive experience separate from the instrumental world of science, the realm of art, even more than progressive education, supposedly softened the hostile tendencies of the ego. For instance, Lionel Trilling argued that the "negative capability" taught through the experience of art emancipated the individual from the compulsive need to grasp reality in a strictly cognitive manner. The "practical usefulness" of the novel, according to Trilling, arose from its "unremitting work" in forcing the individual "to put his own motives under examination, suggesting that reality is not as his conventional education has led him to see it."[45] Modernist art, according to Trilling, presented a direct challenge to utopian illusions and moral crusading in the name of maturity, sobriety, and skepticism.

Of course high modernists described the tempering nature of art in different ways. In his essay "The Sense of the Past," Trilling defended the modernist canon for the "historical sense" it provided readers, serving as a quelling agent for the will's innate aggression.[46] Trilling argued that the literary work functioned as a form of estrangement because it opened a window to a moment of reality no longer recoverable and no longer understandable. In contrast to liberals and Communists who sought redemption in forthcoming utopias, Trilling turned to the past. This sense of history provided a moment beyond ideology—"without the sense of the past we might be more certain, less weighted down and apprehensive" (185). Naturally, Trilling was not promoting some antiquarian impulse. To acknowledge the "pastness" of a work of art, he argued, was to acknowledge it as a "thing we can never wholly understand." Aggressive contemplation was retarded by "the mystery, the unreachable part" of the artwork that was irreducible to "ideological or subjective distortion" (180). Any particular meaning derived from a historically distinct piece of literature was therefore incomplete. For Trilling, "we ought to have it fully in mind that our abstraction is not perfectly equivalent to the infinite complication of events from which we have abstracted" (189). This "historical sense" provided by art counted as "one of the aesthetic and critical faculties" that aided the individual in escaping his own subjective "abstractions" (188).

Like Trilling, Theodor Adorno argued that if totalitarian ideologies strove to awaken the primal aggression of man, modern art might serve to temper that impulse. But in contrast to Trilling, Adorno described the reception of the aesthetic object as a form of mimesis. He reformulated the concept to refer not to the imitative reproduction of nature but to the spectator's role in the consumption of the aesthetic object.[47] In order to avoid the reductive translation of the artwork by preformed categories of thought, the spectator needed, according to Adorno, to imitate or mimic the movements within the object itself. The spectator was to trace mentally the internal dynamics of the work, following the contours of the painterly strokes, the trajectories of the musical refrain, and the rhythmic articulations of the poetic verse. In other words, the spectator did "not understand a work of art" when it was translated "into concepts" but rather when the spectator was "immersed in its immanent movement," that is, when the work was "recomposed by the ear in accordance with its own logic, repainted by the eye, when the linguistic sensorium speaks along with it."[48] The aesthetic experience was receptive and sensuous, offering a form of knowing separate from conceptual domination. Since the spectator did "not actually think" but instead made himself "into an arena for intellectual experience, without unraveling it," the aesthetic experience produced a momentary hesitation in the individual and a sense of wonderment, effects that served to loosen the rigidity of the individual ego.[49]

The spectator of course was not entirely passive. The aesthetic experience required active effort—an attentiveness to artistic detail and a knowledge of previous artistic traditions. High modernism was nothing if not deeply intellectual. But the experience of high art was not reducible to an understanding of technique; indeed, the works themselves produced their own standard of judgment to which the spectator submitted. As Adorno argued, "the ability to see works of art from the inside . . . is probably the only form in which aesthetics is still possible."[50] This aesthetic experience avoided both the complete loss of self associated with total immersion in the object and the domination of it associated with cognitive manipulation. Mimesis taught the spectator to respect the otherness of the other by momentarily relaxing the need to grasp and repress and by momentarily suspending the cognitive for a form of perception much closer to the erotic. As such, the aesthetic experience "may contain the potential to counteract the deterioration of human capacities—what would be called 'ego weakness' in current psychological terminology" (102). Adorno was not alone in his speculations; his reconsideration of mimesis as the elemental principle of aesthetics was in fact prefigured by the New Critics. For example, in his 1938 essay, "The Mimetic Principle," John Crowe Ransom argued that "the doctrine of mimesis" was "the best foundation for any aesthetic."[51] Mimesis, according to Ransom, aimed for "a kind of cognition" that "grows increasingly difficult for us in practical life"—the ability to carefully attend to the particularities of the aesthetic object by "[tracing] its configurations, colors, planes, [and] objects" in the spirit of an erotic "love" that ran counter to the motives of "power," "appetite," or "greed" (206). As such, the aesthetic experience taught patience and respect, loosening the borders of the ego but without loosening the destructive tendencies of the drives or the hostile forces of the superego.

In this way, the aesthetic experience became the antidote to the compulsions of the liberal imagination and pointed to a form of identity that was less petrified—a mature and nonrepressive ego with a more intimate relationship to itself and to the natural world. The aesthetic experience, at least one that was uninvolved in persuasion or propaganda, was a way to sway the boundaries of the ego and force the subject to abandon itself, if only for a moment, to the irreducible particularity of the art object. This experience helped to transform a self that was hopelessly and aggressively trapped within its own immediacy into a self that was attentive to the variegated nature of reality. Aesthetic contemplation also prodded the return of the sensuous from its repression by the ego and the superego. Naturally, such a return served neither as a form of orgasmic release nor as a means for simple enjoyment. Instead, it provided a release from the compulsive nature of the ego and a general openness to the individual's lost archaic impulses. Moreover, it served to channel desire in and through the aesthetic object so that such desire was neither captured by the glittering appeals of the culture industry nor funneled into mass politics. Modern art taught the spectator to "not become stupid, not to be lulled to sleep, not to go along" but also not to dominate and not to coerce.[52] Of course, since the current landscape had fallen into the hands of administrators, any reconciliation of the self with the larger world was impossible. The fundamental divisions within modernity prevented any such reconciliation, leaving individual subjectivity mediated only by a relationship to the aesthetic sphere. This notion of a nonrepressive ego autonomy became for high modernists the best solution for dealing with the aggression of the self produced paradoxically by its exhaustion.

The Challenge of David Riesman

Thus, despite the rigor of its theoretical formulations, high modernism seemed to breathe desperation—over the apparent liquidation of the subject, over the failures of prewar and postwar social movements, and over the creeping tide of totalitarianism. As Clement Greenberg observed, "the present age as much as any in history lacks an operative notion, a viable concept of the human being—a lack that is one of the 'still centers' around which the crisis of our times revolves."[53] Consequently, utopian speculations were found in high modernist discourse in a strictly negative way. The reconstitution of ego autonomy through the tempering impulse of modernist art was a benign response to an intractable situation. Adorno himself admitted his frustrations in his 1951 memoir, *Minima Moralia*: "In face of the totalitarian unison with which the eradication of difference is proclaimed as a purpose in itself, even part of the social force of liberation may have temporarily withdrawn to the individual sphere. If critical theory lingers there, it is only with a bad conscience."[54] Since any reconciliation of the individual with his surroundings seemed more and more improbable as the years passed, high modernists could only conceive of art as the last vestige of reason against the domineering tendencies of technological rationality. In their frustration, as we will see in the following chapter, high modernists turned from their original adversarial stance and began to accept the more conservative assumptions of orthodox psychoanalysis, a move that deeply impacted their political critique.

Other social critics, however, were not convinced that this high modernist vision was accurate and searched for alternatives to the notion of a nonrepressive ego identity that discovered itself only in the aesthetic realm. A range of other modernists came forth in the postwar period to challenge this argument about a fundamental weakness in the American character. One of the most forceful of these late modernist critics was sociologist David Riesman, whose 1950 book *The Lonely Crowd: A Study in the Changing American Character* became a key marker of this shift in perspective. Riesman, however, was an unlikely candidate to challenge the hegemony of high modernism.[55] In fact, his relationship with many of the New York intellectuals and many members of the Frankfurt school contributed to his early pessimism about American society. For instance, Riesman, having been introduced to Hannah Arendt through Daniel Bell, befriended the German intellectual and began a correspondence with her while she was completing work on *The Origins of Totalitarianism* in the late 1940s. Riesman read versions of Arendt's book in manuscript form, and the two exchanged opinions on "the terror, the liquidation, [and] the atomization," as he put it in a letter in 1949, that characterized life under totalitarianism.[56] Riesman was quite laudatory in his remarks to Arendt, expressing to her in the same letter "how stimulating it is to confront your own understanding of what is going on and to find myself at every point, with negligible qualifications, in agreement." Indeed, Riesman was "overwhelmed" by the historical scope and sweeping grandeur of Arendt's manuscript, and he told her in the summer of 1949 that her book had inspired him to rename his own manuscript "Passionless Existence in America."[57] Riesman's enthusiasm was also reflected in his 1951 *Commentary* review in which he praised Arendt's "extraordinarily penetrating book" into the "fanatical ideals" motivating totalitarian movements.[58] But Riesman's review was slightly more critical than his letters to Arendt had been two years prior; by then, Riesman was not wholly convinced of her argument. First, he questioned Arendt's causal claims, arguing, for instance, that her attempt to locate the origins of Hitler's maniacal drive toward European occupation in the expansionist tendencies of Lord Cromer and the British Empire in nineteenth-century Egypt was much too overdrawn. More important, Riesman argued that her book tended to "overinterpret" totalitarianism by making it appear "consistently fanatical" and by ignoring the "more or less accidental concatenations of bureaucratic forces, slip-ups, careerisms, as explanatory factors" (397). Riesman's growing hesitations in respect to Arendt's book signaled in some measure his own confusion over theories that supposedly explained the appeal of totalitarian movements.

This was not the first time Riesman challenged such theories. In fact, Riesman had used the same argument previously in his review of *The Tensions That Cause War*, a collection of essays stemming from a 1948 UNESCO conference in which a number of intellectuals, including Max Horkheimer and

Hadley Cantril, debated the usefulness of the social sciences in dissipating psychological insecurities. Despite his appreciation of such efforts, Riesman chided the essayists for their overestimation of the efficacy of social scientific tools and for their enthusiasm for "the clichés of conventional Marxism" and "the clichés of the psychological approach."[59] Pointing to the determinism within Horkheimer's argument, which delineated man "as the prisoner of industrialism, standardization, and mass culture" (521), Riesman encouraged the UNESCO participants to broaden their understanding of man's resiliency. Horkheimer had argued that the problem with modern forms of identity was the "*personae* phenomenon," a concept he borrowed from psychologist Gordon Allport, who had noted the dispersion of the modern subject into a "set of masks." The collapse of an "integrated ego" had forced the individual to become "one person in the barber shop, another in an interview situation; a tender husband and father at home and a hard-boiled, hard-driving businessman from nine to five."[60] In contrast, Riesman stressed the flexibility of the modern personality, that is, the ability to function as "split personalities," which signaled a level of maturity and resistance. According to Riesman, instead of "cutting men down to the size of categories," intellectuals needed to allow them "to play the multiplicity of roles, with the multiplicity of emotional responses, that we constantly show ourselves capable of."[61] Unwilling to hold fast to the image of ego autonomy offered by high modernists, Riesman searched for an alternative that better expressed the dialectical relationship between self and society.

The book that emerged from Riesman's confrontation with the high modernist investigation into the modern authoritarian personality was his hugely successful 1950 study of the American character *The Lonely Crowd*, a book that would sell by the thousands and that would eventually place the well-known author on the September 1954 cover of *Time* magazine. An almost accidental sociologist, Riesman was an unlikely candidate to write such an influential study. The project, which one reviewer referred to as "the *Catcher in the Rye* of sociology," began in 1947 when Riesman received a two-year research appointment at the Committee on National Policy at Yale University in which he planned, with the help of sociologist Nathan Glazer, to study the relationship between political opinion and mass communication.[62] Preliminary information was culled from interviews conducted by the National Opinion Research Center, interviews sociologist C. Wright Mills had done for his book *White Collar: The American Middle Classes*, Glazer's studies at the Bureau of Applied Social Research at Columbia University, and interviews Riesman's research assistants conducted at a boarding school in New Haven. Originally interested in the causes of political apathy among American voters, Riesman broadened his focus to include the relationship between political behavior and changing character structures in modern society. From this sampling, Riesman categorized his interview subjects according to their mode of social conformity, originally labeling the two most prominent as conscience-directed and other-directed. In this sense, his book fit in with the larger trend within American sociology that measured the link between politics and personality in light of the horrific scene overseas.

Indeed, *The Lonely Crowd* was inspired much more by the Studies in Prejudice series than Riesman originally acknowledged. Despite the myriad references to Alexis de Tocqueville and Thorstein Veblen, Riesman was just as interested in the problem of political deviance as he was in theories concerning national character; as he admitted years later, he and his collaborators had worked "in the vein of *Escape from Freedom* and of the research tradition that led to *The Authoritarian Personality*."[63] For instance, the interview guides used by Riesman and his researchers were modeled in part on those used by Adorno and his colleagues, although Riesman shied away from their projective testing methods (Rorschach and thematic apperception tests) and used conventional interview practices. Riesman was also well versed in the recent theoretical attempts to merge psychoanalysis with more conventional sociological approaches, a project inaugurated by Sigmund Freud in *Group Psychology and the Analysis of the Ego* and continued in more contemporaneous works such as Harold Lasswell's *Psychopathology and Politics*. Like many such works, Riesman's book drew heavily upon individual case studies of social behavior. In total, Riesman and his colleagues gathered 180 interviews between February and July 1948 for their study. Respondents included Harlem residents at the Neighborhood Center for Black Organization, students at a vocational trade school in Connecticut, residents of a small, middle-class Vermont community, teenagers at a progressive school in California, and graduate students in medical and academic programs at several major universities, as well as a number of single interviews from professional actors, missionaries, small farmers, and manufacturers. Twenty-one of Riesman's interviews were later collected, along with his lengthy interpretations of the political orientation of each interview subject, in *Faces in the Crowd: Individual Studies in Character and Politics*, his 1952 addendum to *The Lonely Crowd* in which Riesman further explained his interview and research methods.

Although Riesman envisioned his work as less clinical and more historical than *The Authoritarian Personality*, he was deeply influenced, like Adorno and his colleagues, by the theoretical path opened up by the work of Erich Fromm. In fact, Riesman had engaged in what he termed "conversational" analysis with Fromm in the 1940s after Riesman's mother, an analysand of Karen Horney, encouraged him to visit the German psychoanalyst so she might have someone with whom to converse about the nature of therapy.[64] In particular, Riesman was influenced by the theoretical perspective of *Escape from Freedom* and, more directly, by an unpublished study of the political attitudes of German workers in the 1930s in which Fromm had attempted to measure their authoritarian tendencies through an analysis of their responses to a series of open-ended questions about work, morality, and politics. Through a statistical analysis of their responses to an elaborate questionnaire, Fromm hoped to uncover discrepancies between the consciously held political ideas of German workers, who routinely voted for left-wing political parties, and the unconsciously held parochial attitudes making them more and more sympathetic to Fascist ideas. For Riesman, Fromm's perspective offered a version of "psychoanalytic social psychology" that was not merely derivative of Freud's methods but an extension as well (574). While undergoing therapy, Riesman also had the opportunity to attend seminars held by social psychologist Harry Stack Sullivan at the William Alanson White Institute and lectures by Ernst Schachtel and Fromm at the New School for Social Research.

Borrowing themes from Karl Marx, Max Weber, J. J. Bachofer, and Georg Simmel, Fromm had repudiated theories about man's character that focused on one particular structural factor or that tended to project onto the past conditions found in the present. Instead, Fromm treated man's character—his behavior, his social attitudes, his aesthetic preferences, his morality, and so on—as the product of shared traits within a given society during the course of its development. Character, according to Fromm, was formed neither by the vicissitudes of any particular phase of libidinal development nor by the activation of physiologically conditioned drives within a self-contained psychic structure. Instead, character was formed by man's interaction with the world around him, as his existential need to overcome feelings of finitude and helplessness forced his adaptation to the prevailing social, political, and economic institutions in which he found himself. Echoing the work of Harry Stack Sullivan, Karen Horney, Abram Kardiner, and other social psychologists and anthropologists, Fromm revised the Freudian conception of man's development. For Freud, character traits such as parsimony and stubbornness were the result of disruptions to man's instinctual development during the teleological activation of a particular erogenous zone; for Fromm, such traits were imposed upon man by the specific characterological requirements demanded by a specific society. As such, the formation of an anal character structure was a process determined by a particular form of economic relations that prioritized those traits and a process reinforced by institutional, religious, and familial training. For Fromm, "character . . . is the specific form in which human energy is shaped by the dynamic adaptation of human needs to the particular mode of existence of a given society."[65] Character, in this sense, was an orientation toward the world, a learned assemblage of traits, attitudes, and reactions and an internalization of external norms and expectations.

By abandoning Freud's theory of ontogenetic development, Fromm was able to trace the rise and fall of particular character structures as the result of large-scale historical changes in political, economic, and religious regimes. The channeling of human energy in the name of socialization was quite different under feudalism, for instance, where a learned "receptive orientation" had made individuals passive, dependent, and loyal to the religious and political authorities to which they willingly submitted themselves than under early capitalism, where a learned "hoarding orientation" had encouraged individuals to gain pleasure from the ruthless acquisition of property and goods under new market relations, all at the expense of devotion to outside authority. As Fromm explained, such orientations formed "the essential nucleus of the character structure of most members of a group which has developed as the result of the basic experiences and mode of life common to that group" (277). Political difficulties like those that plagued Europe in the twentieth century stemmed from a lag between changes in economic conditions and outdated character traits from the previous order. Normal psychic dispositions, such as a craving for aggressiveness and ruthlessness in the economic realm, were stunted by a bureaucratic order that interfered with such pursuits. Consequently, the ensuing frustration was transferred from the economic realm to the political, which explained, according to Fromm, the Fascist impulses within the German lower middle classes.

Riesman was quite persuaded by Fromm's successful integration of psychoanalytic categories with traditional historical and sociological arguments, and the perspective Fromm offered became the starting point for Riesman's book. As he described, "*The Lonely Crowd* did not move outward from individuals towards society, but rather the other way around; we started with society and with particular historical developments within society."[66] Paralleling Fromm's description of the emergence of the individual from the bonds of primary ties with the onset of capitalist expansion, Riesman charted the historical development of an inner-directed character structure—the self-sufficient and pioneering individual of early capitalism whose adherence to an ethic of work and productive labor marked the self-discipline needed to confront an ever-expanding and unpredictable environment. In an age of historically new roles and opportunities, the old mechanism of conformity based upon a specific body of social customs and traditions began to collapse and was replaced by a set of behavioral norms and internalized controls instilled by parental authorities, a "psychological gyroscope" that helped the individual commit to his chosen goal or career in the face of social pressures. Reflecting in part Freud's description of the introjection of parental authority and the subsequent development of "the watchful superego as a socializing agency," Riesman noted that "the drive instilled in the child is to *live up to ideals* and to test his ability to be on his own by continuous experiments in self-mastery—instead of by following tradition."[67] Embodied in the pioneering spirit of the frontiersmen of American expansion, the inner-directed man confronted the intractability of the world around him through the driving sense of purpose instilled at an early age. Work or productive labor had become the central element in man's conception of himself, property became a sign of his independence, and discipline became a marker of his self-mastery.

But with the transition from an economy based upon production, manufacturing, and thrift to one based upon consumption, service, and abundance, a subsequent characterological change had occurred. Borrowing from Fromm's description of the "marketing orientation," in which the personal values of adaptation and sociability marked an economic regime based upon the salability of goods and services, Riesman described the shift to an "other-directed" character structure in which the source of direction or discipline was no longer provided by the internalized "gyroscope" derived from parental authority but by the demands and commands of contemporaries, peer groups, and social authorities. Forced to become more self-aware of the opinions of others and abandoned by parents whose authority had little say in a consumer-driven, people-oriented, and interpersonal world, the other-directed person was forced to find a "source of direction" from "either those known to him or those with whom he is indirectly acquainted, through friends and through the mass media" (21). Ever sensitive to the expectations of his peers and trained to pattern his desires on the models offered by the mass media, this new character type developed a sensitive "radar screen" to navigate the ever-shifting judgments of value and worth in an endless search for respect, admiration, and acknowledgment.

Besides his descriptive typology, Riesman added a "non-historical" dimension to his analysis and provided categories with which to describe the difficult relationship between the individual and the characterological requirements demanded by a particular social structure, noting that there were great disparities in and a wide variety of modes of reconciliation with such pressures. Recognizing that "social character [was] not all of character," Riesman detailed three "universal types" of reconciliation between the individual and the dominant social character: the first was a relatively painless conformity to such personality requirements that Riesman termed "adjusted"; the second was a refusal to reconcile with those demands that he referred to as "anomic"; and the third was a mature capacity to decide whether or not to conform to behavioral demands that he termed "autonomous" (241). Riesman knew from the biographical detail his research interviews unearthed and from Fromm's own work that there was never a clear fit between characterological demands and actual individual behavior. Character types, in this sense, were not ontological categories; instead, they were merely abstractions for understanding the general pattern of assimilation and socialization within a given period. In reality, individuals dealt with the demands for conformity in different ways, and Riesman's empirical evidence pointed to anomic and adjusted inner-directed personalities as well as anomic and adjusted other-directed ones. Guiding his study, however, was the assumption that such personalities might also become *autonomous*, that is, they might also possess a reflective capacity for choosing whether or not to conform to a given characterological requirement. In the *Time* magazine profile of his work, the editors offered Riesman himself as the prime example of "an autonomous man," someone who "mingled" the best ideas of the social sciences and the humanities together and someone who "has tried hard not to bore anybody—or to be bored."[68] Readers were left to decide on the implications of such a perspective.

Published at the nadir of a certain level of national self-analysis, Riesman's book was quickly linked to the myriad studies that criticized the bureaucratization of American life through recourse to heraldic images of an inner-directed world washed away. Noting his references to Max Weber, Erich Fromm, and other prognosticators of social decline, most early reviewers depicted Riesman as a humanist critic of "'groupism' and the zeitgeist."[69] Although magazines such as the *Nation* took him to task for his supposed contribution to the rise of "the new cocktail-and-breezeway Bohemia," most found his analysis an astute portrait of the ubiquitous malaise under postindustrialism.[70] Consequently, many high modernists assumed that Riesman shared their critique. For instance, in his review of *The Lonely Crowd*, Lionel Trilling praised Riesman for avoiding the "jargonistic" and "platitudinous" language of modern sociology and for producing "a work of literature in the old comprehensive sense of the word according to which Hume's essays are literature, or Gibbon's history, or Tocqueville's *Democracy in America*."[71] Like the great novels of the past that engaged in "the investigation and criticism of morals and manners," Riesman's book, according to Trilling, explored the subtle shifts within American culture by exposing what was occurring in the nation's factories, schools, families, movie theaters, political parties, and courthouses. Noting that Riesman had detailed contemporary "morals and manners" more thoroughly than any other sociologist, Trilling saw *The Lonely Crowd* as a compelling rejoinder to the current preeminence of "affability, blandness, [and] lively sensitivity to the opinion of the group" as forms of social adjustment. Trilling asserted that "it is still inner-direction that must seem the more fully human, even in its excess" (97), and he argued that Riesman himself, however hesitantly, echoed such a preference. Autonomy for Trilling meant individualism, and he praised Riesman for salvaging the word from its pejorative and bland uses.

Despite such praise, Riesman spent years after the original publication of his book trying to correct the misunderstanding that he had outlined a tragic historical decline. In several interviews and a number of new prefaces to the book, Riesman argued that "the authors of *The Lonely Crowd* [were] not conservatives harking back to a rugged individualism that was once a radical Emersonian ideal."[72] In fact, he directly challenged two misreadings. First, despite even some ambivalence of his own, Riesman railed against "the panic doctrine" present in many high modernist works and in the pages of many social science journals that the country was "on the road to fascism."[73] While he appreciated Adorno's inventive combination of psychological and sociological categories, he resisted "the research assumption that authoritarianism is the main problem facing American society today."[74] Most of his hesitancy stemmed from the unexpected findings in his interview materials. Not surprisingly, Riesman discovered several interview subjects who bore a strong resemblance to the ego-weakened, authoritarian personalities found in Adorno's study, including, for instance, Robert Gibbons, a seventeen-year-old student at a Connecticut trade school whose growing feelings of alienation and declining economic status bore a similarity to the "status-threatened youths in Weimer Germany who were early recruits to Nazism."[75] Abandoned by his father, a middle-class office manager, and forced to work part-time to support his mother, Gibbons was unable to relate to his working-class associates and unable to find a proper outlet for his pent-up aggression, choosing instead to vent his frustrations within the political arena by scapegoating foreigners. According to Riesman, Gibbons had never gained the ability to overcome his sense of powerlessness either by relating to others in a healthy way or by using the elements of consumer culture to prop up his identity. Instead, Gibbons remained suspended between the other-directed world of his fellow classmates and the inner-directed environment of his middle-class upbringing, a suspension that Riesman believed might lead to self-destruction or to reactionary political attachments. But Riesman hesitated to pass such judgment, claiming that "all this is not enough to permit a prediction that Gibbons will become a fascist rather than remaining, as he now is, a 'clinical' case" (220). Indeed, Riesman was much more generous toward his interview subjects than Adorno and his colleagues were to theirs.

In fact, Riesman pointed to Gibbons's classmate Joseph Pizzeri as a counterexample. An eighteen-year-old son of Italian immigrants, Pizzeri had learned to cope with his declining social status without resorting to compensatory feelings of superiority over others or repressed frustration. According to Riesman, Pizzeri had found a way to adapt to the traditional values of hard work and obedience without reference to the compulsive need for inner-directed self-improvement or for other-directed social acceptance. As Riesman argued, despite his apparent fixation within the oral stage of personality development (which was expressed by his overattachment to primary groups), Pizzeri did "not at all resemble the sado-masochistic type described by Fromm in *Escape from Freedom* (or the anti-democratic, authoritarian personality described by Frenkel-Brunswik and Sanford)" (163). Whereas Fromm saw orality exclusively in terms of sadistic ingestion, self-aggrandizement, and exploitation, Riesman noted that an oral disposition might also mark a form of receptivity, openness, amiability, and generosity, traits that helped Pizzeri maintain a stable relationship with those around him. In fact, Riesman noted that despite Pizzeri's tendency toward submissiveness he did not answer in the affirmative any of the questions posed to him that Adorno and his researchers deemed typical of authoritarian personalities. Such examples made Riesman quite wary of holding fast to psychoanalytic categories as explanatory tools.

Riesman's difficulties with the assumptions embedded in the social scientific perspective on authoritarian behavior was also evident in his analysis of Walter Poster, a sociology graduate student at Princeton University and the son of Jewish immigrant parents in Minnesota. Poster was, according to Riesman, an example of a character type that did not fall easily under his typology, a person who was neither emphatically inner-directed nor other-directed and who was neither clearly destined for an anomic outlook nor an adjusted one. Instead, Poster, as Riesman originally explained, was a prime example of the rebellious and resentful personality whose ambivalence toward his family had resulted in a pathological projection of his anger from his parents to society as a whole. Echoing Harold Lasswell's claims in *Psychopathology and Politics* and Adorno's findings in *The Authoritarian Personality*, Riesman argued that Poster was an example of how "affects arising in the personal sphere are displaced upon the public sphere and rationalized in terms of the general good" (529). Unable to assert himself against parental expectations, Poster was unable to define his own identity in any meaningful way, choosing instead to give into his "sado-masochistic tendencies" by sacrificing himself in the name of the larger public good to radical politics. As Riesman explained, "at odds with his father, his solution was to run away from himself and to choose one of the totalitarian political positions which is hostile to the cultivation of the individual self, namely Stalinism" (530). As such, Poster used the party apparatus to escape from his family's authority without ever engaging in any form of self-realization or self-emergence, marking him as neither inner-directed nor other-directed.

However, sensitive to the accusation that his own bias against Poster's political opinions might have clouded his judgment concerning the young man's character and maturity, Riesman soon believed that his claims regarding Poster's political fate were too hasty and decided to interview him again four months later. Much to his surprise, Poster, despite Riesman's belief that his unsettled psychological state would keep Poster "thrashing about" for a prolonged period, had in fact become more "at peace with himself" by ending his "ambivalence" and "animus" toward his family and accepting their "warmth and positive feeling" (544). Equally surprising was that such a resolution to his family turmoil had also resulted in the "sharpening" of Poster's political position, enabling him to formulate a much more coherent and consistent critique of American society and strengthening his commitment to the Communist cause. As Riesman explained in his revised discussion, Poster's case history was "an example of how radical political views may in certain situations be less directly related to the family pattern of emotions than in the picture portrayed by Lasswell and taken as the starting point of my original analysis." Consequently, Riesman cautioned against the tendency within books such as Eric Hoffer's *The True Believer* or Milton Rokeach's *The Open and the Closed Mind* to regard any form of political allegiance as a form of fanaticism; if anything, Riesman believed that there was something slightly odd, if not pathological, about those who exhibited no rudimentary political attachment. Unlike Harold Lasswell or Lionel Trilling, Riesman refused to consider politics merely "the dumping ground" for private emotional or familial troubles. For him, studies of the authoritarian personality did "not carry us far" in understanding the outlooks, personalities, and political orientations of most, if not all, Americans.[76] Consequently, *Faces in the Crowd* was full of hesitations, corrections, and open admissions of speculation, something Riesman found missing in *The Authoritarian Personality*.

The second misreading of his book that Riesman challenged was the tendency of hasty readers to equate the rise of other-directedness with everything fundamentally amiss in American culture. Riesman always fretted that the irony and speculation with which he wrote was misinterpreted as nostalgia for an inner-directed world steadily disappearing and as a mockery of the contemporary, other-directed society quickly emerging. In fact, his typology referred only to the mechanisms of conformity, internal and external, that directed individual behavior and not to the actual content or political orientation of any particular character type. All three types, tradition-directed, inner-directed, and other-directed, possessed the capacity for adjusted, anomic, and autonomous behavior. As Riesman explained, "the achievement of autonomy presents quite different problems when it has to be won against a background of inner-direction or of other-direction."[77] In fact, he argued that other-directed personalities, continuously attuned to an everyday world of social expectations and demands, possessed a greater sensitivity to others and a greater capacity for understanding individual development. Unlike Erich Fromm, Riesman believed that the loss of the primary ties of blood, soil, and nation allowed for forms of relatedness, care, and compassion missing from earlier forms of social organization and that the weakening of inner-directed restrictions helped to expand everyday notions of the good life. Indeed, Riesman was quite befuddled by reviewers who marked the book as a tragic tale: "Not that Americans today are more conformist—that has always been a profound misinterpretation; and it is not that today's Americans are peculiar in wanting to impress others or be liked by them; people generally did and do. The difference lies in a greater resonance with others, a heightened self-consciousness about relations to people, and a widening of the circle of people with whom one wants to feel in touch."[78] The other-directed self, in this sense, was more responsible and more responsive to the demands for recognition, affection, and love from others within the community of action. Such a self was present to others, for others, and with others in a way that previous character types were not.

Consequently, where high modernists saw only confusion, dread, and uncertainty as the life-denying consequences of recent social changes, Riesman saw mobility, flexibility, and openness as the life-affirming possibilities. As he explained, "Aldous Huxley's acidly brilliant vision in *Brave New World* that advancing mechanization and organization require a graded retrogression in personality development may metaphorically describe what has happened to some people and some cultures, but it is no less true that standardization in machinery (once the earlier, more ferocious stages of industrialization are over) allows us greater rather than less variety in character structure."[79] Riesman knew that character types were never a perfect fit; indeed, he seemed more interested in the ways in which individuals struggled and squirmed beneath the roles they had been assigned to play. Character was not destiny, the individual was not merely a replica of a particular social role, and personality was not reducible to a particular stage of psychological development. Willing to experiment with alternative roles in an endless struggle for autonomy, the other-directed personality was more self-aware and more self-conscious than his predecessors and therefore more able "to recognize and respect his own feelings, his own potentialities, [and] his own limitations."[80] Although the other-directed personality was intruded upon by myriad visages and voices throughout the day, Riesman argued that social interaction was simultaneously threatening and benign, something to fret about and something to enjoy. Agreeing with his high modernist companions that the self was already constituted before it was self-constituted, he also argued that the self gained purpose, direction, and meaning through involvement with the projects of others and through face-to-face interactions with members of various peer groups.

In this sense, Riesman's formulation of identity bore little resemblance to high modernist notions of aesthetic self-formation. In a series of articles published in early volumes of *American Quarterly*, including "Listening to Popular Music," which he had begun in 1947 but did not finish until after the publication of *The Lonely Crowd*, and "Movies and Audiences," which he coauthored with his wife, Evelyn, Riesman challenged the disdain with which highbrow critics dissected America's cultural landscape.[81] Rejecting arguments that the culture industry completely manipulated passive audiences, Riesman criticized high modernists for their failure to address the reception side of cultural consumption and for their inability to appreciate how the divisions of class, race, gender, and religion affected the ways in which the interpretation of goods took place. Borrowing from the findings of Paul Lazarsfeld and his fellow researchers at the Bureau of Applied Social Research, which demonstrated that the meaning and content digested by consumers from mass media was often translated, distorted, or inverted by local opinion leaders and local settings, Riesman argued that "the same or virtually the same popular culture materials" were utilized by American audiences "in radically different ways and for radically different purposes," and consequently "it may then appear that it is the audience which manipulates the product (and hence the producer), no less than the other way around."[82] For instance, in his 1950 article "Listening to Popular Music," Riesman challenged Theodor Adorno's argument in "On Radio Music" concerning stereotyped listening habits and called for not merely an analysis of the content of popular music but an investigation into the actual audiences who consumed such cultural forms. As Riesman explained, "the danger exists then of assuming that the *other* audience, the audience one does not converse with, is more passive, more manipulated, more vulgar in taste, than may be the case." He pointed to the abrupt shifts in popular music tastes over the years as examples of the music industry reacting to, instead of directing, consumer demands. Riesman distinguished between majority tastes (those who digested popular music uncritically and used it primarily for social purposes such as camaraderie or personal distinction) and minority tastes (those who rebelled against commercialized forms through the development of sophisticated standards of listening). Consequently, he encouraged researchers to examine not only the sites in which music and other cultural goods were consumed but the particular character structure of the individual who used these goods for divergent purposes. As he observed, "we cannot simply ask 'who listens to what?' before we find out who 'who' is and what 'what' is by means of a psychological and content analysis which will give us a better appreciation of the manifold uses, the plasticity of music for its variegated audiences" (193).

In this sense, Riesman was much more encouraged by the often idiosyncratic ways in which commodities were endowed with meaning and argued that the advantage other-directed personalities had over their inner-directed predecessors was precisely in the ways in which cultural consumption allowed for a rapid expansion of forms of identification. He challenged the tendency to divide leisure activities between active and passive forms, in particular, the tendency to promote "craftsmanlike leisure" activities as a way to recover the lost value of craft skill and to denounce the passive consumption of movies, popular music, novels, and magazines. Arguing that it was silly to try to convert a bobby-soxer into a craft hobbiest, Riesman believed that it was "a blind alley for the other-directed man to try to adapt his styles in leisure to those which grew out of an earlier character and an earlier social situation."[83] In contrast to what he considered the "puritan" critique of mass culture, Riesman argued that the "great variety" of cultural products made possible by the standardization of the production process allowed for liberation from imposed characterological conformity. Riesman pointed in particular to Hollywood films as "liberating" agents—"even the fan who imitates the casual manner of Humphrey Bogart or the fearless energetic pride of Katharine Hepburn may in the process be emancipating himself or herself from a narrow-minded peer-group" (291). Where high modernists saw standardization, conformity, and manipulation Riesman saw complexity, discovery, and liberation. Of course Riesman was neither promoting anti-intellectualism nor espousing populist rhetoric; indeed, his defense of popular culture bore little resemblance to the uncritical democratization of popular tastes associated with certain forms of postmodernism in the 1960s. Instead, Riesman was trying to move beyond the simplistic dichotomy between elitism and populism, choosing instead to portray American culture not en masse but as divided into a series of audiences and tastes. This was the challenge he posed in his contribution to a *Partisan Review* symposium, "America and the Intellectuals." He sensed within the highbrow rejection of American culture resentment against the success of the project of high modernism. As more and more members of the upper-class and middle-class strata became cultural aficionados themselves, intellectuals such as Dwight Macdonald and Clement Greenberg began to "[fear] the shifts in middlebrow taste which might leave [them] in the position of liking something also liked by a *New Yorker* or *Harper's* audience."[84] Lingering battles over literary and artistic canons were, according to Riesman, merely signs of confusion on the part of high modernists over the surprising popularization of such works.

Riesman's reservations about highbrow elitism and his refusal to underestimate the strength of the American character in the face of authoritarianism meant that his understanding of individual autonomy was very different from his high modernist counterparts. Part of his project was not merely to delineate a change in the American character but to offer a vision of an other-directed personality that had achieved a certain level of autonomy. Despite the contradiction in the notion of an autonomous other-directed self, Riesman believed such a personality served as an alternative to high modernist visions of a nonrepressive ego identity. In fact, the most surprising part of *Faces in the Crowd* was his portrait of Isabelle Sutherland, a thirty-two-year-old divorcee who Riesman argued was the closest of his twenty-one interview subjects to achieving some form of autonomy. Having struggled against the "sternly inner-directed voices of her parents and the other-directed voices of her peer group," Sutherland had simultaneously overcome both the residing fear of dependence imparted by her parents and the residing fear of independence caused by her relations with others.[85] Exhibiting expressions of intimacy and candor, Sutherland bore little relation to the "mature masculinity" of those heroes of high modernism such as Thomas Mann or Jackson Pollock. Sutherland was far from a cultural aesthete, concerned neither with having advanced tastes nor with using her leisure time for "escape, information, and enrichment of vision" (591). Although her enjoyment of competitive sports and comedy programs on the radio were "not the pastimes of a person of profound originality or passionate preoccupation with the arts," Sutherland had achieved a certain level of self-awareness and "psychic sensitivity" (592).

According to Riesman, the willingness of the high modernist self to give itself over to the aesthetic object, that is, to overcome its own compulsions by letting itself merge with the otherness of the contemplated work, was not matched by a similar willingness to mitigate the dangerously compulsive search for self-identity through reconciliation with others in an interpersonal realm. Indeed, the nonrepressive ego identity for which high modernists searched was only located within the aesthetic, not social, realm. Mimesis as an aesthetic principle was always safeguarded against mimicry as a social one. For Riesman, however, it was impossible to escape the presence of others, whether such a presence was merely a passing glance on the street, a polite command at the workplace, or an abrasive order by a local authority. "Moving as we do," Riesman argued, "against an ever-changing natural and urban landscape, we are very conscious of the people who fill the social space around us."[86] More important, encounters with others were not necessarily self-effacing or self-destructive and community did not necessarily entail conformity; instead, such encounters were often self-changing and self-constituting. As Riesman explained, the autonomous other-directed self was "aware of the possibility he might change, that there are many roles open to him, roles other people have taken in history or in his milieu . . . [and] this taking the role of the other leads to becoming aware of actual differences and potential similarities between the other and the self."[87] For him, the self was neither impervious to forms of difference or alterity nor wholly determined by the opinions forced upon it. Indeed, the autonomous other-directed person lived in the precarious point between active self-determination or sovereignty and pure passivity or subordination.

Consequently, Riesman's invocation of "autonomy" was simply his refusal to dispense with any vocabulary of self or subject. The autonomous other-directed self was, however fragile, a unified self, a self that displayed a certain constancy in its actions, promises, and commitments. Riesman borrowed language from George Herbert Mead to describe the "chameleon-like quality" that characterized the autonomous other-directed personality: "we are each of us an entire stock company, as well as prompter for all the parts."[88] Such a self was able to link past actions, present concerns, and future plans into a personal sense of identity but one that developed within the context of the life plans, expectations, and needs of others. "The autonomous person," Riesman noted, "differs from the anomic in that he can exercise some choice over the structuring of his experience; if he conforms it is not compulsively and if he deviates it is not unknowingly."[89] Self-identity or ego identity did not entail simply the maintenance of a proper relation of the self to itself but also the maintenance of the self's relation to others from which it drew support. As Riesman argued, "depriving [man] of the sociability his character has come to crave will not make him autonomous, but only anomic—resembling in this the cruelty of depriving the addict of liquor or drugs by sudden incarceration" (277). Riesman was unwilling to abandon the quotidian—the everyday acts of speaking, listening, acting, and working. In this way, autonomy marked nothing more and nothing less than the emergence of the self from a panoply of identificatory ties.

In this way, Riesman helped to point the way past high modernism. Although just as committed to anti-Communism as his counterparts and just as worried about the specter of conformity, Riesman refused to give into the almost antinomian perspective of high modernism. He simply refused to believe that the aesthetic sphere was the only site for self-identity and refused to believe that the self could constitute itself independently of any relations with others or any acknowledgment of other egos. The autonomous other-directed personality discovered itself and constituted itself in relation to others, as a being situated within a specific community with specific norms and specific forms of etiquette. Of course, he "did not assume that an individual would be the replica of his social role, but rather that there might be great tension between an individual's search for fulfillment and the demands of the institutions in which he had a part, or from which he felt alienated."[90] But the autonomous other-directed personality acknowledged and accepted that its psychic life was continuously infiltrated by the other and recognized that identification with others was a way of expounding the boundaries of the ego. High modernism, despite its lofty ambitions, had obvious limitations. Answers outside the aesthetic sphere were necessary.

CHAPTER THREE

Psychoanalysis and the Debate over the Democratic Personality: Norman Brown's Freudian Revisions

In his 1955 book *Freud and the Crisis of Our Culture*, Lionel Trilling, enthusiastic but slightly concerned, noted that psychoanalysis had surprisingly become "an integral part of our modern intellectual apparatus."[1] Pointing to the use of Freudian ideas in every part of American culture, from Broadway plays to literary criticism, Trilling argued that a revolution had occurred in "the cultural situation of our country" (13). But Trilling hoped that Americans, recently thumbing through Freud's writings, would understand the true importance of his findings—that psychoanalysis was instrumental in helping to liberate the individual from excessive entanglements with and demands from the culture at large. Trilling's enthusiasm for the ideas of Freud reflected of course a larger shift within American intellectual history, as sociologists, historians, and anthropologists hurried to find new theoretical sources during the Cold War that were untainted by the language of dialectical materialism. Equally important, as we have seen, American intellectuals struggled to find a paradigm through which to view the rise of totalitarianism, a political upheaval that seemed to have psychological sources not necessarily contained by the problem of class struggle. Consequently, as William Barrett's "firemen from abroad" arrived in America and issued warnings about mass politics, a large number of practicing European psychoanalysts arrived with them, transforming psychology, if not the culture as a whole.[2] Almost two hundred psychoanalysts from Austria, Germany, and France, including such notable figures as Otto Fenichel, Theodor Reik, Franz Alexander, and Helene Deutsch, came during the war and helped to found psychoanalytic institutes in Los Angeles, Chicago, and New York. These refugee psychoanalysts offered a theoretical perspective with which not only to understand the psychological makeup of those individuals who fell prey to totalitarian ideologies but also to devise forms of therapeutic assistance to help such damaged personalities.

Psychoanalysis of course was nothing new to high modernists like Trilling. Modernism, in all of its manifestations, had been deeply influenced by the language of psychoanalysis, and Freud's *The Interpretation of Dreams* was, in many ways, the first modernist text. But as is evident by the language of Theodor Adorno's *The Authoritarian Personality* and Lionel Trilling's *The Liberal Imagination*, high modernists appropriated Freud's concepts not merely to examine the nature of dream life or the contours of the unconscious but to understand how mass society had ravaged the individual psyche. As the specter of totalitarianism seemed to reach the shores of America under the auspices of late capitalism, high modernists reluctantly revised their original suggestion that a strong ego was an autocratic one and joined with their colleagues in the psychoanalytic profession in trying to fashion an image of a democratic personality capable of escaping the psychopathologies of the modern age. Many soon came to recognize the folly in promoting the aesthetic experience as the only cure for social ills. As one of Adorno's commentators has noted, "the less optimistic Adorno becomes about the possibility of revolutionary or even progressive collective practice, the more important the elements of resistance offered by the strong ego becomes to him."[3] Aesthetic mimesis soon seemed to be a naïve response to an intractable situation. Thus, worried about the apparent weakness of the modern personality, high modernists like Adorno and Trilling participated in a larger national discussion about identity formation. In so doing, they eventually dropped their exclusive focus on aesthetic mimesis and offered a normative vision of a properly functioning Oedipal identity as the framework for a healthy democratic personality, an image that was a reversal and retraction of their original adversarial stance and a marker of their emerging conservatism. In an ironic shift, high modernists began to mimic the reactionary language of the larger culture of the 1950s, bemoaning the loss of family ties, the rise in juvenile delinquency, and the growing sexual experimentation of the decade.

Other modernists were quite quick to pounce on this shift within the theory of high modernism, arguing that Adorno, Trilling, and others had negated the critical project of modernism by clinging to the conservative assumptions of orthodox psychoanalysis. Modernists of all persuasions participated in this larger debate about the importance of Freud's ideas to the liberation of the self. For instance, many romantic modernists, unwilling to believe that an autonomous ego was a sign of mental health, turned to the theories of the psychoanalyst Wilhelm Reich, who argued, in contrast to high modernists, that the ego itself was the site of control and conformity. In so doing, romantic modernists, as we will see in Chapter 4, prioritized the id over the ego, desire over rationality, and the imaginary over the symbolic. Their goal was to turn conventional psychoanalysis on its head. Many late modernists, similarly unwilling to defend the project of high modernism, also offered their own interpretation of Freud and challenged the conservative assumptions embedded within the notion of a strong Oedipal identity. But late modernists were unwilling to follow the mystical path of romantic modernists, arguing instead that the goal of psychoanalysis should be the reclamation of the self with the surrounding world and not the compulsive drive for autonomy and separation. For example, the psychoanalyst Norman Brown offered, in his 1959 manifesto *Life Against Death: The Psychoanalytical Meaning of History*, a fundamental rethinking of conventional Freudian thought. Refusing to believe in either the image of a strong ego forged through the Oedipus complex (pace Theodor Adorno and Lionel Trilling) or the image of an ego washed away by a flood of libidinal desire (pace Allen Ginsberg), Brown promoted, in a manner similar to David Riesman and others, an image of an open, flexible ego, one more attuned to its embeddedness in the social realm and to its connection to the human body. "What orthodox psychoanalysis has in fact done," argued Brown, "is to reintroduce the soul-body dualism in its own new lingo, by hypostatizing the 'ego' into a substantial essence which by means of 'defense mechanisms' continues to do battle against the 'id.'"[4] Afraid of the limitless possibilities of the human body and afraid of any contamination by others, high modernists, following traditional psychoanalysis, had unfortunately sealed off the self. Consequently, they had forfeited, according to Brown, any possibility for more open and therefore less repressed personal relations. As Brown explained, "if psychoanalysis believes that with magic, words and autoplastic ego-modifications it can escape the universal neurosis, it develops a private psychosis instead" (156). By clinging to certain outdated ideas of Freud (including conservative assumptions about gender and sexuality), high modernists had become not only domesticated but also highly reactionary. The most obvious example, according to Brown, was their almost compulsive promotion of the so-called democratic personality, a project that not only revealed the pernicious influence of psychoanalysis in American culture but that also revealed the ironic alignment between high modernism and the national security state.

The Golden Age of Psychoanalysis

In 1955, *Newsweek* declared that "the U.S. is without a doubt the most psychologically oriented, or psychiatrically oriented nation in the world" and noted that the almost compulsive search for mental health "now goes on in the nation's art, in its schools, in its pillows, even in its religion."[5] America's recent "Freud obsession," as one European commentator explained, was quite remarkable given the resistance, if not outright dismissal, Freud received almost fifty years prior when he delivered a series of public lectures at Clark University in 1909.[6] But the bullets of World War II quickly changed the professional status of psychoanalysis.[7] Government officials were very much aware that the treatment of veterans with psychiatric disabilities from the previous conflict had cost approximately one billion dollars. To combat this, a detailed screening process was established by the Selective Service System that weeded out roughly 12 percent of the fifteen million men examined for apparent psychological handicaps, a process that was aided by the roughly one-third of all available psychiatrists who volunteered at the 108 military induction centers.[8] Screening of course was the first step; as the Army distributed more than nine million copies of *Psychology for the Fighting Man* to anxious soldiers, psychiatrists were attached to military divisions to advise in the treatment of patients. In his 1948 survey *Psychiatry in a Troubled World*, Dr. William Menninger, chief consultant in neuropsychiatry to the surgeon general, detailed the endless psychological disorders therapists encountered in wartime patients and praised them for their help in winning the war.[9]

After the end of hostilities, the psychoanalytic profession vaulted into public discourse on this wave of enthusiasm. Those psychiatrists who had practiced in wartime service noted that the high rate of soldiers who suffered from psychological breakdown demonstrated that mental illness was a serious health problem. For instance, Air Force psychiatrists Roy Grinker and John Spiegel of the Don Cesar Convalescent Hospital in St. Petersburg, Florida, argued that their experiences during the war were the perfect training "for the understanding of the psychology and psychopathology of people under the stresses of ordinary civilian life."[10] In 1946, William Menninger and a number of other members of the American Psychiatric Association formed the Group for the Advancement of Psychiatry, a pressure organization that called for a more prominent role for psychiatrists in promoting positive forms of mental health. As Menninger explained in the pages of the *New York Times*, psychoanalysis "has contributed enormously to the understanding of normal behavior, and hence serves as the only logical basis for preventive psychiatry—a valid mental hygiene."[11] Federal officials who had witnessed the efficacy of psychoanalysis in promoting the war effort were more than willing to enlist the aid of psychiatrists in confronting similar problems in civilian life. Indeed, the signing of the National Mental Health Act in 1946 marked the official beginning of the "romance of American psychology." Promoted by Congressman J. Percy Priest and Senator Claude Pepper, the National Mental Health Act dramatically increased funding for research into the etiology of mental disorders.[12] Given the widely reported cases of mental breakdown in the military, little convincing was needed to prove that the American public was vulnerable to psychological illness. In 1946, for instance, *Time* magazine argued that "about 8,000,000 U.S. citizens" were "neurotic or worse," and nearly ten years later *Newsweek* placed the number at ten million.[13] In response, countless psychoanalysts including Dr. George Stevenson of the National Association for Mental Health and Dr. Marie Nyswander of the National Addiction Research Project appeared in the pages of national magazines to "remake ideas about psychiatry."[14] Similar articles also helped to transform the stoic, European analyst into a benevolent, native-born therapist, making treatment seem more ordinary.[15] A number of Hollywood films also portrayed psychoanalysis in a positive light, featuring sensitive therapists helping troubled characters find balance (*Lady in the Dark* [1944], *Spellbound* [1945], and *The Three Faces of Eve* [1957]) or using psychoanalytic themes to explain the behavior of characters (*Rebel Without a Cause* [1955] and *The Seven Year Itch* [1955]). In fact, the most popular book in postwar America, Dr. Benjamin Spock's *Common Sense Book of Baby and Child Care* (1946), translated Freudian ideas into an accessible vernacular. By the 1950s psychoanalysis had reached what historian Nathan Hale refers to as its "golden age" in the United States.[16]

Building the Democratic Personality

In a 1949 *New York Times* article, Dr. Franz Alexander, the director of the Institute of Psychoanalysis in Chicago, argued, in what had become conventional wisdom, that the tools of psychoanalysis were paramount in an age of atomic warfare: "We have harnessed the forces of nature, but we now face the consequences of our failure to harness the emotional forces of man."[17] For the multitude of American intellectuals who appropriated Freudian ideas in the 1940s, psychoanalysis became not only the most popular vocabulary with which to diagnose personal ills but also the favorite tool with which to correct the deficiencies in the modern personality produced by a turbulent global order.[18] Consequently, a debate emerged in American intellectual circles about the character of the democratic personality, that is, the type of psychological makeup appropriate for the healthy functioning of democratic institutions and the type of personality adaptable to the demands that freedom entailed. As Lawrence Frank, one of the leading proponents of child development research, explained, "freedom for the personality may be viewed as the crucial issue of a democratic society, for which we must seek to develop individuals who can accept all the inhibitions and requirements necessary to group life without distortions and coercive, affective reactions."[19] Consequently, countless psychiatrists offered their theoretical perspectives to social science researchers, producing myriad studies of racial and ethnic intolerance, deviant sexuality, psychopathic behavior, criminality, and delinquency—anything that threatened the democratic polity. A wide range of American social scientists, including those associated with the Studies in Prejudice series, detailed the nature of a democratic character structure and outlined the context in which such a character structure might be fostered.

Three separate but related groups of intellectuals contributed to this discourse. The first were those investigators connected with the "culture and personality" school of anthropology. Two intellectual trends converged in the 1940s to produce this field of anthropological research.[20] The first emerged out of a series of seminars held by psychoanalyst Abram Kardiner at the New York Psychoanalytic Institute in 1936 and later moved to the anthropology department at Columbia University, which were designed to integrate Freudian theory with anthropological research. Centered on the concept of a "basic personality structure," Kardiner's work stressed the importance of early child-rearing practices such as toilet training and weaning on personality formation and how such "primary institutions" like the family impacted later adaptation to the "secondary institutions" of the socioeconomic realm.[21] Kardiner's studies of the cultures of the Trobriand Islanders, the Zuni Pueblo, and the Kwakiutl in such works as *The Individual and His Society* (1939) and *The Psychological Frontiers of Society* (1945) gave inspiration to the second trend of the culture and personality school—the rise of national character studies developed in the work of Margaret Mead, Ruth Benedict, and Geoffrey Gorer. Influenced by Kardiner's claim that the similarity of early childhood experiences produced a definable personality structure, American anthropologists dissected the national character of those countries involved in World War II. Written with the help of funding from the Office of War Information and the Office of Strategic Services, works such as Mead's *And Keep Your Powder Dry: An Anthropologist Looks at America* (1942), Benedict's *The Chrysanthemum and the Sword: Patterns of Japanese Culture* (1946), and Gorer's *The People of Great Russia* (1949) were not only cross-cultural analyses of the impact of economic and social instability on strife-ridden societies but also warnings about the larger problem of mental health in an uncertain age.

The national character studies produced by American anthropologists bore a strong similarity, at least in terms of intent, to the social character studies offered by humanistic psychologists such as Erich Fromm and Abraham Maslow, the second group of intellectuals concerned with fostering a democratic personality. Although less connected institutionally, humanistic psychologists found a wide reading audience for their defense of what Fromm referred to as the "core" part of man's personality. Indeed, Fromm's depiction of man's character structure was not merely an attempt to describe the authoritarian personality but also an attempt to imagine a democratic one. Paralleling Freud's conception of the genital character, Fromm offered the image of a "productive" character orientation that avoided the pitfalls of the widespread marketing orientation and one that realized its own potentialities through rational self-control: "Mental health, in the humanistic sense, is characterized . . . by a sense of identity based on one's experience of self as the subject and agent of one's powers."[22] Fromm's redefining of the problem of freedom was echoed by the more therapeutically inclined work of Abraham Maslow. An admirer of the work of Karen Horney and Ruth Benedict, Maslow emphasized man's capacity for free choice, introspection, and self-actualization, brushing aside the more pessimistic language of behavioral psychology. In works such as *Motivation and Personality* (1954) and *Toward a Psychology of Being* (1962), Maslow linked this process of self-actualization to the formation of a "democratic character structure," one with the capacity for "spontaneity" and "openness," and he pointed to historical figures such as Abraham Lincoln and Albert Einstein as examples of self-actualized individuals and as counterpoints to the reactionary individuals in mass society.[23]

In many ways, these psychological and anthropological perspectives on the democratic character were all prefigured by the political theory of Harold Lasswell, whose use of psychoanalysis transformed traditional understandings of political behavior. An analysand of Theodor Reik in Berlin in the 1920s, Lasswell was one of the first social scientists to merge psychology and anthropology with the study of political behavior. In *Psychopathology and Politics* (1930), he made explicit what he saw as the irrational basis of mass politics. After examining psychiatric records at state hospitals in Baltimore, Philadelphia, and Washington, D.C., Lasswell argued that political beliefs were nothing more than the unconscious projections of personal turmoil onto the public sphere. "Political movements," asserted Lasswell, "derive their vitality from the displacement of private affects upon public objects."[24] Calling for a "politics of prevention," Lasswell pressed for a prominent role for psychiatrists in alleviating the collective insecurities of the American polity. His arguments in *World Politics and Personal Insecurity* (1935) and *Power and Personality* (1948) deeply influenced social scientists studying the problem of political deviance in American society, shaping the arguments in Gabriel Almond's *Appeals of Communism* (1954), Gordon Allport's *The Nature of Prejudice* (1954), and Hadley Cantril's *Politics of Despair* (1958).

Much of the interdisciplinary perspective offered by these three fields of study was funneled into the theoretical conclusions of Theodor Adorno's *The Authoritarian Personality* and into the language of high modernism in general. Given his refusal to envision any unmediated reconciliation with the world as a whole, Adorno was obliged, however reluctantly, to retain some normative vision of an autonomous character structure. Consequently, despite his criticisms of overly simplified conceptions of ego autonomy, Adorno and his colleagues eventually accepted the commonplace notion that the only foundation for the democratic personality was a well-integrated ego, in what was a major shift in the stance of high modernism.[25] The reason was mostly political. First, Adorno admitted that his experience in America had shaken his faith in the redemptive powers of art. "In America," explained Adorno, "I was liberated from a certain naïve belief in culture and attained the capacity to see culture from the outside."[26] Second, chastened by recent events in Europe and anxious to gain some perspective on the forces shaping man's personality, Adorno was forced to overcome his trepidations about American sociology. Thus, despite his initial reservations about the empirical work of American social scientists when he began working on *The Authoritarian Personality*, Adorno found such work "the most fruitful thing" he encountered in America and defended such analytic tools to his compatriots in Frankfurt when he returned home (358). In many ways, then, the analytic framework of *The Authoritarian Personality* was a composite of these trends in American sociology. Appropriating the use of Rorschach tests as developed in the field work of Abram Kardiner, borrowing from the political psychology of Harold Lasswell, and committing themselves to the vision of an integrated personality as presented by Erich Fromm, Adorno and his colleagues fashioned an analytic perspective to study political deviance that borrowed heavily from mainstream psychology.

What emerged from this discourse was a normative vision of a democratic personality capable of resisting the pathological deviations threatening the Western world. The "genuine liberal," as Adorno described, was an emotionally secure individual capable of weathering frustrations without producing an unraveling of ego integration. Three traits in particular characterized this personality. First, the genuine liberal had "a strong sense of personal autonomy and independence."[27] Although maintaining a positive relationship with family members and friends, the democratic character resisted any interference with personal beliefs and avoided any sentimental bonds with others that hinted of excessive attachment. Autonomy, however, did not mean a belligerent nonconformity; the authors of *The Authoritarian Personality* were not trying to produce rebels or delinquents. In fact, such figures, despite the bravado with which they stood against society, were classic examples of the authoritarian personality in development. The democratic personality simply lacked any compulsive identification with others. Second, the genuine liberal expressed a tolerance for marginalized groups. Such a personality felt no compulsion to bolster his integrity by projecting his insecurities onto outsiders. Instead of resorting to stereotypes or racial markers in dealing with others, the genuine liberal ignored such differences, expressing "views with regard to minorities" that were guided "by the idea of the individual" (781). Third, the democratic personality exhibited a healthy ego strength, expressed by a sense of responsibility and an ability to postpone libidinal gratification. The genuine liberal, as one contributor explained, was very close "to the psychoanalytic ideal, representing a balance of superego, ego and id," possessing the ability to stop from immediately gratifying every id impulse but also able to avoid the compulsive repression of those impulses by indulging in more benign forms of release.[28]

Of course, the real problem was determining why the democratic personality was increasingly harder to cultivate. Studies of totalitarianism by Erich Fromm and others sketched rather vague historical analyses but did not explain why some individuals were susceptible to nihilistic philosophies and others were not. As Lionel Trilling explained in *Freud and the Crisis of Our Culture*, the founder of psychoanalysis was a prominent example of an individual who was reared in an authoritarian culture but who escaped such pernicious influences. Unwilling to reduce the answer merely to economic self-interest, the authors of *The Authoritarian Personality* focused instead upon the specific conditions under which the individual personality was formed, that is, upon the early process of socialization within the family that directed the satisfaction of unconscious desires toward particular modes of gratification. Consequently, the writers "leaned most heavily upon Freud" in examining "the major influences upon personality development that arise in the course of child training as carried forward in a setting of family life."[29] Although unwilling to jettison the sociological conditions under which the family developed, Adorno and his colleagues turned to Freudian psychology to grasp the most formative aspects of individual development. In this way, *The Authoritarian Personality* bore a striking similarity to the psychoanalytic framework of Abram Kardiner's *The Psychological Frontiers of Society* and Harold Lasswell's *Psychopathology and Politics*.

Following Freud, Adorno and his colleagues argued that the successful resolution of the Oedipus complex was the only means by which the individual psyche could be fortified against the irrational nature of modern life.[30] Although he had tended to restrain himself from offering any normative conception of individual development, Freud himself had argued in *Inhibitions, Symptoms, and Anxiety* (1926) that "mental health very much depends on the superego's being normally developed."[31] As a "special psychic agency," the superego emerged as "the heir of the Oedipus complex," that is, as the result of the child's internalization of paternal authority caused by the severing of attachment to the mother under the threat of castration by the father. Identifying with the father as representative of the laws of society, the child gained the capacity for reasoned judgment that the father embodied. "In earlier times," explained Max Horkheimer, "a loving imitation of the self-reliant, prudent man, devoted to his duty, was the source of moral autonomy in the individual."[32] The internalization of the character traits of the father gave the son a basis for identity separate from extrafamilial pressures and a basis for moral judgment separate from external authority. A strong Oedipal identity also helped to guard against any regression to the immature, if not pathological, pre-Oedipal, maternal world. In this sense, a well-functioning superego guarded against any identification with other subjects or the internalization of other personal relations by the ego deemed dangerous. Although Adorno was never quite comfortable with the equation between the internalization of paternal authority and ego autonomy, he considered that paradox more digestible than the all too obvious equation between the dissolution of the subject and the rise of group psychology. Consequently, he and the other authors of *The Authoritarian Personality* portrayed a functioning Oedipal identity as the most tangible source of opposition to any false reconciliation with the outside world. High modernism had become domesticated.

The Family, Youth Culture, and the Specter of Homosexuality

The problem for high modernists, however, was that recent socioeconomic changes had damaged the framework of the traditional bourgeois family. The "obsolescence of the Freudian concept of man," as Herbert Marcuse declared in a 1963 address to the American Political Science Association, was directly connected to the decline in the status of the father.[33] With the rise of large, bureaucratic organizations, the modern father, whether the proletarian figure of the working-class family or the salaried bureaucrat of the middle-class home, was no longer an independent economic agent and no longer an identifiable personality. Socially and economically castrated, such fathers had little guidance to offer their sons. As Max Horkehimer described, "the socially conditioned weakness of the father, which is not disproved by his occasional outbreaks of masculinity, prevents the child's real identification with him."[34] Given that the father was no longer "the powerful figure" he was once pictured to be, the internalization of his authority was no longer the normative condition. Instead, the son turned outside the family for images of stronger paternal figures. Of course, the members of the Frankfurt school were not the only ones to note the eclipse of the modern family. As historian Elaine May has demonstrated, the social and economic dislocations caused by the Great Depression and World War II led to rising concerns about the stability of the American family.[35] Immediately after the war and prior to the surprising explosion in birth rates during the 1950s, intellectuals flooded the mass media to declare "the American family in trouble."[36]

Naturally, as most recognized, this did not mean that paternal discipline had disappeared. For the authors of *The Authoritarian Personality*, it simply meant that the traditional father-son relationship had become perverted. Psychoanalyst Erik Erikson had demonstrated to Adorno that the modern father, due to his thwarted status aspirations and declining purchasing power, compensated by asserting himself against his son.[37] The result was a tremendous distortion of the internalization process. Authority was reduced to the obsessive enforcement of rules, an enforcement that was both incomprehensible and overwhelming to the son. Consequently, the superego remained externalized, posited in punitive external agencies and expressed by the rigid adherence to conventional values. The result, as Adorno explained, was "a sadomasochistic resolution of the Oedipus complex."[38] An uncritical acceptance of authority led to the masochistic enjoyment of obedience. But the corresponding unconscious resentment of the father produced deep-rooted anger that was externalized as sadistic aggression against outsiders. "Ambivalence is all-pervasive," said Adorno, "being evidenced mainly by the simultaneity of blind belief in authority and readiness to attack those who are deemed weak and who are socially acceptable as 'victims.'" The result was an unresolved Oedipal complex in which unconscious libidinal impulses remained ego-alien and the superego remained externalized while the ego remained powerless to manage any such conflicts.

Even worse, the end of internalization caused by the collapse of the modern family left libidinal impulses defenseless against manipulation by the culture industry. Due to the requirements of reproduction, the family as an institution still survived, albeit as a caricature of what it once was, but its functions had been eclipsed. In his contribution to a 1949 collection of essays by sociologists and psychologists on the "function and destiny" of the family, Max Horkheimer detailed the weakening of familial bonds. "Today," argued Horkheimer, "the father tends to be directly replaced by collective entities, the school class, the sports team, the club, the state."[39] With the father no longer a model of authority in the traditional sense, the ego was refashioned according to the models of identification offered by mass media. In a 1954 essay, "How to Look at Television," published in the *Quarterly of Film, Radio, and Television*, Theodor Adorno drew an explicit connection between the rise of mass culture, the unraveling of a highly integrated ego, and the collapse of the bourgeois family. All of the psychological characteristics attached to proper internalization—"concentration, intellectual effort, and erudition"—were "lowered" by the ubiquitous "'message' of adjustment and unreflecting obedience" issued from the loudspeaker of the culture industry.[40] Of course high modernists like Adorno or Horkheimer were not the only ones to make this claim. In fact, most social scientists linked the problems of mass culture to the apparent distortions in the socialization of American children. In a group of works including journalist Vance Packard's 1957 best-seller *The Hidden Persuaders* and psychologist Fredric Wertham's 1954 best-seller *The*

Seduction of the Innocent, critics argued that with traditional modes of character formation vanishing, mass culture was able to simultaneously unleash the destructive impulses of the id and the submissive demands of the superego. In this way, Adorno echoed the more conservative claims of psychiatrists such as Wertham. "This, convincingly enough," explained Adorno, "may be the nucleus of truth in the old-fashioned arguments against all kinds of mass media for inciting criminality in the audience" (170).

For writers like Packard, Wertham, and Adorno, the clearest sign that the functions of the family had been eclipsed by the luring hand of mass culture was the oft-noted postwar transformation in adolescent development patterns marked by the birth of the American teenager. As historian Grace Palladino has noted, a series of socioeconomic changes in the 1940s, including the expansion of educational opportunities and the tremendous market explosion of the postwar years, gave rise to a new type of adolescent possessing an identity separate from the family and armed with a newfound purchasing power, a group that journalists soon "dubbed 'teeners,' 'teensters,' and in 1941, 'teenagers.'"[41] As mass-circulation magazines such as *Life*, *Ladies' Home Journal*, and *Collier's* introduced readers to the ever-shifting trends adopted, as one journalist estimated, by the nation's "18,000,000 teen-agers," numerous social scientists offered warnings about what sociologist Edgar Friedenberg described as "the vanishing adolescent."[42] Recognizing that the rise of the teenager had less to do with any spontaneous self-recognition on the part of adolescents and more to do with the promotional activities of magazine publishers and movie producers, Friedenberg was one of many critics who marked high-school students as naïve consumers of age-related merchandise. Dwight Macdonald's musings on popular culture, for instance, were best expressed in a series of articles he wrote for the *New Yorker* on the youth marketer Eugene Gilbert, founder of a commercial research firm that studied teenage buying habits.[43] In his 1957 book *Advertising and Marketing to Young People*, Gilbert urged businesses to take advantage of the vast purchasing power of the teenage market. Gilbert had helped, as Macdonald quickly argued, to "make the teenagers class-conscious: the more they find advertising directed at them qua teenagers, and the more they are polled on their peculiar tastes and interests, the more their sense of themselves as a special group is enhanced."[44] For Macdonald, the insularity of youth culture and the clique-like devotion to consumer trends were signs that adolescent development had been overtaken by mass culture.

As the Department of Justice and the U.S. Children's Bureau confronted the problem of juvenile delinquency and as the U.S. Senate held hearings to investigate the impact of comic books and Hollywood films on young adults, notable social scientists such as Bruno Bettelheim and Robert Jay Lifton conducted research into the psychological makeup of American teenagers.[45] One of the more widely cited examples was a fifteen-year study conducted by researchers at Purdue University, work that resulted in the 1957 report *The American Teenager*, written by H. H. Remmers and D. H. Radler. Their findings confirmed the worst fears. The transition from a "parent-oriented" to a "peer-oriented" direction marked a decline in the "dignity and integrity of the individual" and a corresponding decline in "the standards and values of his parents."[46] Similar findings were echoed in other published research reports such as Grace and Fred Hechinger's *Teen-Age Tyranny* and Robert Havighurst's *Dilemmas of Youth*. But delinquency was not the worst problem; as the authors of *The American Teenager* explained, "the typical teenager shows an alarming disposition to reject some democratic belief . . . and to accept many authoritarian and totalitarian beliefs and values in their place" (198). As Dwight Macdonald, who referenced such studies in his *New Yorker* articles, explained, "the Second World War was more destructive of family life than the First had been," sweeping more fathers into military service and more mothers into war industries, a trend that did not substantively change after 1945.[47] Consequently, the teenager was becoming "more and more independent of his parents," leading to a generation of children more susceptible to extrafamilial forces such as advertising agencies, juvenile gangs, and, even worse, political movements.

Dwight Macdonald, however, was not the only high modernist to worry about the nation's youth. Theodor Adorno, in collaboration with psychologist Else Frenkel-Brunswik, had in fact begun an independent study of the behavior of children from a range of socioeconomic backgrounds, a project that was to serve as an empirical analysis of the more speculative claims found in *The Authoritarian Personality*. Adorno was always sensitive to "the *genetic* dimension" that produced an authoritarian character structure, and he considered the pilot study he began with Frenkel-Brunswik an integral part of the Berkeley project overall.[48] An émigré from the University of Vienna, Frenkel-Brunswik had already commenced investigations into the political predisposition of children while she was a researcher at the Institute of Child Welfare at the University of California. Her studies, which coalesced in two important articles, "A Study of Prejudice in Children" and "Intolerance of Ambiguity as an Emotional and Perceptual Personality Variable," were eventually folded into Horkheimer's research project. After work on *The Authoritarian Personality* was completed and after Adorno had returned to Frankfurt, Frenkel-Brunswik undertook this empirical investigation into the causes of prejudice in children.[49] Pointing to the economic cleavages that had torn apart the modern family, Frenkel-Brunswik argued that the narrow personality susceptible to authoritarian movements was the product of a familial environment that resorted to traumatic, if not overwhelming, discipline to ensure adolescent submission. Generally found in families that had been socially and economically marginalized, such strong expectations of conformity failed to produce any meaningful identification with parents, and consequently, with such strong castration anxiety never producing an internalized conscience, "children's personalities tend to fall into patterns similar to those observed in the adults described in *The Authoritarian Personality*."[50] Thus, Frenkel-Brunswik argued, in what soon became conventional wisdom, that families with more affectionate relationships that allowed for the proper internalization of paternal authority were more conducive to producing unprejudiced children.

This notion that lingering hostility toward the father had produced masochistic obedience to external authority and sadistic aggression toward outsiders contributed to an intellectual shift in theories concerning family structure. Reviewing Frenkel-Brunswik's findings, Theodor Adorno noted with surprise that "precisely the 'good', i.e. conventional, children are *freer* from aggression and therefore from one of the most fundamental aspects of the authoritarian personality."[51] Of course others had already formulated a similar claim. As historian William Graebner has noted, many child-rearing experts such as Lawrence Frank, Kurt Lewin, and Erik Erikson outlined a "'democratic' model of child rearing" in the 1940s that stressed the importance of permissiveness in parenting to ward off the child's innate potential for aggression.[52] In works such as Nathan Ackerman's *The Psychodynamics of Family Life* (1958) and Virginia Satir's *Conjoint Family Therapy* (1964), family-therapy activists connected the rise of authoritarian discipline in the home to the "rising tide of mental contagion."[53] By the end of the 1950s, traditional child-rearing manuals such as John Watson's *Psychological Care of Infant and Child* (1928), which stressed the scientific upbringing of children, were replaced by books such as Benjamin Spock's *Common Sense Book of Baby and Child Care* (1946), which stressed permissive child and parent relations.[54] Of course, therapists were not the only ones convinced by this research. In an intellectual nod to these new child-rearing manuals, Lionel Trilling argued, for example, that "the remarkable firmness" in his hero John Keats was the result of "the indulgence of his childhood" and the absence of any "vigorous and strictly disciplinary training."[55] Because he was "happily indulged as a child," Keats was able to dispense with the "childish joys" of the pre-Oedipal stage. Proper Oedipal identity was produced, as Trilling believed, not by an authoritarian household that instilled strict discipline but by a more compassionate family that balanced any anxiety produced by the necessary castration complex with offers of love. Following the logic of many social scientists, Trilling argued that a well-functioning superego was less "the surrogate of society" and more "a sanction beyond the culture," that is, a source of individual autonomy against the dictates of mass society.[56] But given the socioeconomic collapse of most primary institutions, this autonomy was becoming anachronistic. "In a society like ours," explained Trilling, "which . . . tends to be seductive rather than coercive, the individual's old defenses against the domination of the culture become weaker and weaker. The influence of the family deteriorates and is replaced by the influence of the school" (49). In this way, Trilling followed Adorno and Horkheimer in envisioning the family as the proper horizon for psychological growth and, despite a certain recalcitrance, was forced to agree with family therapists about the vicissitudes of child development. High modernism, in this sense, lost some of its adversarial quality.

Such a myopic commitment to a traditional Oedipal form of identity accounted for some of the reactionary positions adopted by a number of high modernists, in particular, their demonization of homosexuality. Indeed, this concern about the link between youth culture and authoritarianism, which was an endemic part of early Cold War culture, was triangulated by a similar concern about the relationship between political and sexual deviance. The collapse of the Oedipal subject in a postpatriarchal world was marked, according to Adorno, by the emergence of a late capitalist landscape in which all sense of difference had been jettisoned, a world, that is, marked by the replacement of the bourgeois subject as the emblematic symbol of autonomous subjectivity by the figure of the homosexual as the emblematic symbol of mass politics. As he explained in the pages of *Minima Moralia*, "totalitarianism and homosexuality belong together."[57] The connection Adorno drew between reactionary politics and sexual perversion was, as many historians have recently noted, an endemic part of the language of the early Cold War. Evidenced most famously by the U.S. Senate's 1950 investigation into "the employment of homosexuals and other sex perverts in government," right-wing politicians joined with many anti-Communist liberals to castigate homosexuals for their supposed threat to national security, arguing that homosexuals lacked the moral rectitude to resist Communist ideology. Triggered in part by the rise of substantive homosexual communities in many urban areas and by the publication of Alfred Kinsey's *Sexual Behavior in the Human Male,* which documented widespread homosexual activity, this anxiety over the "sex pervert, whether a homosexual, an exhibitionist, or even a dangerous sadist," was everywhere.[58] Deviance in the early Cold War had political, social, and sexual connotations, wrapped together into the figures of the authoritarian personality, the juvenile delinquent, the psychopath, the rebel, and the homosexual, all of whom supposedly suffered from deviations from normative family upbringing and all of whom threatened the body politic.

By the time *Life* magazine had introduced its readers to the "'gay' world" of urban culture, social scientists had already launched investigations into the causes of sexual deviance, labeling homosexuality a neurotic disease that was neither an inherited trait nor a glandular problem, as previously argued, but a psychological disorder caused by failed identification patterns.[59] The largest of the many postwar investigations into homosexuality was conducted by the Research Committee of the New York School of Medical Psychoanalysis. Authored by Irving Bieber, *Homosexuality: A Psychoanalytic Study* (1962) established the psychoanalytic community's official position on sexual deviance. Following his predecessors, Bieber argued that "the development of personality disorders in a child is almost always evidence of the pervasive effects of parental psychopathology."[60] As a psychological disorder, homosexuality was no exception. The classic family pattern that produced homosexuality in children was a mother who exhibited "close-binding-intimate qualities" toward her child and a father who exhibited "detachment and hostility" toward his son over "sexual competitiveness" with the mother, a pattern that was tragic for Oedipal development (46, 112). Unable to identify properly with his father and jealously guarded from outside heterosexual relations by a protective mother, such a child pathologically turned to homosexuality as an outlet for his frustrations.

Many high modernists concurred with the findings of American social scientists, arguing, as Max Horkheimer did, that there existed "a deep-rooted affinity between homosexuality, authoritarianism, and the present decay of the family."[61] In fact, most studies of the authoritarian personality including Erich Fromm's *Escape from Freedom*, Gabriel Almond's *The Appeal of Communism*, and Harold Lasswell's *The Democratic Character* made explicit the connection between political and sexual deviance, and many, in their denouncement of Kinsey's attempt to normalize same-sex preferences, pointed to this research. Lionel Trilling, for instance, was one of the first to bristle at Kinsey's book. Unwilling to normalize deviant sexual behavior simply because such behavior was reflected in the natural world, Trilling argued that sexuality was never reducible merely to the physical act but also intertwined, as Freud had explained, with psychic phenomena. In particular, Kinsey failed, according to Trilling, to accept the commonplace notion that same-sex attraction was "evidence of a 'psychopathic personality'" even though a litany of studies proved him wrong. As Trilling explained, "their opinion of the etiology of homosexuality as lying in some warp—as our culture judges it—of the psychic structure has not, I believe, changed. And I think that they would say that the condition that produced homosexuality also produce other character traits on which judgment could be passed."[62] Despite his lingering hostility toward mainstream psychology, Trilling reiterated traditional claims concerning the link between political and sexual deviance.

Theodor Adorno, however, was the high modernist who made most explicit the connection between homosexuality and authoritarianism. Both in the pages of *The Authoritarian Personality* and in his own cultural criticism, Adorno portrayed homosexuality as the product of a narcissistic object choice caused by the failure of proper psychological development.[63] Of course Freud himself had always wavered on the problem of "inversion."[64] His most repeated theory concerning its psychological origins, however, was that homosexuality arose from an improper resolution of the Oedipus complex. The child's emergence from the narcissistic stages of the pre-Oedipal period was predicated upon the threat of castration by the father. However, when such castration anxiety was too strong, the child regressed from the achievements of the phallic stage back into the oral and anal stages of the pre-Oedipal period. Unable to identify with the father and unable to maintain the pre-Oedipal relationship with the mother, the child, in a stunning reversal, began to identify with the mother, assuming her submissive position in relation to the patriarchal order. This feminine position adopted by the son was pathological for two reasons. First, desperate for some love from his father, the child identified with the mother and therefore began to love men in the same way she did in hopes of attracting the father. Second, the homosexual object choice made by the child was also a pathological attempt to ward off castration anxiety. By choosing a same-sex partner who resembled his own self prior to the intervention of the father, the child was able to maintain the illusion of wholeness. Consequently, this attachment was exclusively narcissistic, that is, merely the projection of the child's own self (what he once was and soon hoped to be) onto his partner in the name of self-defense.

Borrowing Freud's etiology, Adorno saw within the figure of the homosexual the psychological makeup of the authoritarian personality. First, due to the failure to identify properly with the father, the homosexual never gained any sense of normative gender identity and consequently lacked an overall ability to perceive social distinctions. "That large sensitivity to difference," explained Adorno, "which is the hallmark of the truly humane develops out of the most powerful experience of difference, that of the sexes."[65] The homosexual, for Adorno, was hopelessly confined within his own immediacy. "Homosexuals," argued Adorno, "exhibit a certain experiential colour-blindness, an incapacity to apprehend individuality; women are, in the double sense, 'all the same' to them." Second, and more important, the assumption by homosexuals of what Adorno saw as a fundamentally passive position represented a breeding ground for authoritarian submission, albeit in a rather convoluted fashion. Although homosexual desire was a product of overwhelming castration anxiety, such desire had to be repudiated because of the continuing presence of that authority. According to Adorno, "the forbidden action which is converted into aggression is generally homosexual in nature. Through fear of castration, obedience to the father is taken to the extreme of an anticipation of castration in conscious emotional approximation to the nature of a small girl, and actual hatred of the father is suppressed."[66] Having identified with the passive position of the opposite-sex parent, the homosexual developed a masochistic form of desire that, under repression, found a form of release in authoritarian politics. "In paranoia," said Adorno, "this hatred [for the father] leads to a castration wish as a generalized urge to destruction." Desire for the same-sex object was renounced through submission to the authoritarian leader, even though both positions were passive and feminine. But in repressing homosexual urges, the authoritarian follower participated in the leader's power and made up for his own inadequacy. A fundamental passivity was disguised as a vigorous activity. "He-men are thus, in their own constitution," explained Adorno, "what film-plots usually present them to be, masochists. At the root of their sadism is a lie, and only as liars do they truly become sadists, agents of repression. This lie, however, is nothing other than repressed homosexuality presenting itself as the only approved form of heterosexuality."[67] Authoritarianism, in this sense, was an outlet for repressed homosexuality. Thus, in the figure of the homosexual, Adorno saw the perfect example of the "post-psychological, de-individualized social atom" that characterized the sadomasochistic follower of authoritarian movements.[68]

Paternal Authority and the Lost Moment in High Modernism

The difference, however, between Adorno, Trilling, and other high modernists and the litany of therapists, sociologists, and political scientists who shared their assumptions about proper Oedipal identity was that the latter assumed that the rehabilitation of the family through proper child-rearing instruction would cure the ills of delinquency, homosexuality, and political deviance while high modernists, with their strong disinclination to pass over such affairs to administrators, were much more pessimistic. For instance, anthropologist Margaret Mead argued that "administrative and guidance officers in the schools and colleges" had the capability of contributing "to the formation of a type of personality which will be effective in a democratic society."[69] Worried about the effects of social engineering, Max Horkheimer, on the other hand, was less convinced. "The popular confidence which today is placed in mental cures and theories," argued Horkheimer, "transcends by far the sound expectations responsible psychology can fulfill."[70] Under the specter of advanced industrial society, high modernists could do little more than mourn the passing of the nineteenth-century bourgeois family and the economic conditions that had supported it. Consequently, the celebration of high modernist art found in works such as Allen Tate's *Reason in Madness* (1941), Cleanth Brooks's *The Well Wrought Urn* (1947), and Theodor Adorno's *Minima Moralia* (1951) went hand-in-hand with the romanticization of the simple market society of early nineteenth-century capitalism, that is, the era of the self-mastering individual, the small producer, and the independent bourgeois family. The historical transition from laissez-faire capitalism to administered corporate capitalism had unearthed the economic grounds for autonomous subjectivity, which, as Horkheimer and Adorno explained in *Dialectic of Enlightenment*, had existed as a historical reality during the "short intermezzo of liberalism."[71] No longer defined by feudal ties, the early bourgeois individual had pursued his self-interest within the realm of civil society, unimpeded except by the constraints of formal law and the strength of individual initiative. It was a moment of simple commodity circulation, when value was limited by the work placed into production and when the skills of craftsmanship "encouraged independent thinking."[72] The autonomy of the ego in this sense was determined by material existence; the ego "extended and contracted as the prospects of economic self-sufficiency and productive ownership extend and contract from generation to generation," until the moment in which the ego passed "from the dispossessed bourgeoisie to the totalitarian cartel-lords."[73]

In the character of the self-mastering, propertied bourgeois individual, high modernists had found the exemplar of the autonomous personality deemed lost. Prior to the appearance of large bureaucratic organizations, the "independent entrepreneur," with his "much-vaunted independence," possessed a "strong yet sober ego" that had developed in response to the "challenges of an acquisitive world" and to the demands of his dependent family members that "transcended his immediate needs" (140). More important, the autonomous individual was not merely the "middle-class proprietor" but also the paterfamilias of the early bourgeois household—a household that had once served as the "landed cell of society" because of its isolation from the corrupting influence of market relations (107). Tragically, the ravaging hand of industrialization had destroyed this socioeconomic realm, leaving most high modernists haunted by images of this prelapsarian past. Horkheimer and Adorno's defense of early nineteenth-century market society in *Dialectic of Enlightenment* was echoed by the social criticism of the New Critics, particularly those writers such as Allen Tate, John Crowe Ransom, and Robert Penn Warren who participated in the agrarian movement of the Fugitive group of the 1930s. In books such as *I'll Take My Stand* (1930) and *Who Owns America?* (1936), this collection of southern writers protested the expansion of industrial capitalism into all spheres of life, which erased the socioeconomic conditions sustaining the propertied individual.[74] Allen Tate openly admitted his nostalgia, claiming that "a forward-looking radicalism is a contradiction; it aims at rearranging the foliage."[75] Similarly, Dwight Macdonald's disenchantment with contemporary politics produced nostalgia for preindustrial forms of society. In a series of memoirs titled "Politics Past," which were published in *Encounter* in 1957, Macdonald bid farewell to his earlier political commitments, retreating from his original Trotskyism and equating democratic politics with small-scale property ownership.[76] Of course even during the heyday of *Politics* in 1944, Macdonald had argued that "the United States between Jefferson's decisive popular victory in 1800 over Hamilton's aristocratic big-money party and the Civil War was as thoroughly democratic a nation as Western history had seen since the

Greek city states."[77] The way forward for Macdonald, as it was for Allen Tate, was the way backward.

Beyond Oedipal Identity: Identification and Desire in the Work of Norman Brown

The conservatism of high modernism was of course not very palatable to modernists of other persuasions who had little interest in reinstating benign paternal power as a way to cure the ills of modern life. Indeed, those artists and writers who constituted the tradition of romantic modernism had, as we will see in Part II, little respect for this defense of Oedipal identity as the only healthy foundation for subjectivity. They were of course not the only ones to oppose this claim. Many late modernists followed suit and offered their own critique of traditional Freudian psychoanalysis and spoke out against such obvious homophobia. In his introduction to Edgar Friedenberg's *The Vanishing Adolescent*, for instance, David Riesman lambasted left-wing intellectuals and right-wing politicians for perpetuating an environment "aggressively hostile to male homosexuality."[78] Riesman argued that "the resulting panic fear of homosexuality tends to make many adult males overreact to adolescent boys and young men, sometimes treating them as vicarious bearers of their own suppressed energies and aims, and almost always communicating to them their own anxiety and lack of clarity of role." Such anxiety, according to Riesman, stemmed from unrecognized feelings of loss and envy associated with this rigid separation of the self from others. In other words, the linkage between sexual object choice, gender identification, and autonomous development elaborated in the psychoanalytic drama of individual maturation was, for Riesman, not merely an unattainable ideal but an artificial construct that reinforced traditional dichotomies between masculinity and femininity, activity and passivity, and individuality and dependency. For Riesman, privileging identification with the father as a fortification against the return of the repressed maternal realm was a limited view of man's "psychic mobility" and "fluidity of identification," a view that unfortunately concretized gender and sexual differences.[79] "I do not think," argued Riesman, "these nuances of difference should be used to force either men or women into a statistically normative mold—men should no more be confined to abstractions than women to the earthy and concrete."[80] In so doing, Riesman challenged the equation between homosexuality and psychopathology that marked postwar psychology.

More generally, Riesman refused to believe that homosexuality was an arrested form of development because he refused to believe that a strong Oedipal identity was the only nonpathological form of identity. In many ways, Riesman's historical analysis of the shift from the inner-directed character of late nineteenth-century industrial society to the other-directed personality of mid-twentieth-century postindustrial order also demarked this transition in the socialization process from the bourgeois father as the model of authority to the peer group as the frame of orientation. Riesman offered two reasons to avoid the high modernist description of this transformation as a story of decline. First, Riesman recognized that the nostalgia inherent within the work of Theodor Adorno and Allen Tate offered no legitimate answers to a culture confronting this historical transformation. "To suggest," argued Riesman, "to newer, more other-directed people that they should return to the pastimes of their presumably rural grandparents does not usually make sense."[81] Second, and more important, Riesman disagreed with the psychoanalytic claim that a strong ego was produced solely by the Oedipal complex. In a series of articles published in *Psychiatry*, Riesman reconsidered Freud's surprising integration into the American social sciences. Challenging the Freudian claim that there was a fixed form of mental health, Riesman argued that Freud had "succeeded in imposing on a later generation a mortgage of reactionary and constricting ideas."[82] In particular, Riesman saw Freud's elevation of an Oedipal identity to a psychoanalytic ideal as a result of his late nineteenth-century bourgeois background, a background that stressed the fixed boundaries of class and nation over and against wider social interaction. "There is," explained Riesman, "something romantic and parochial in Freud's image of the ideal of man as one who goes directly at what he wants, including sexual objects, without getting lost in the toils and discontents of thought."[83] Riesman countered the extremes of Freudian psychoanalysis with the interpersonal psychology of Harry Stack Sullivan, one of the founders of the William Alanson White Institute and one of the first to turn away from traditional psychoanalysis and toward a discussion of the interactive character of personality formation. According to Riesman, "Sullivan's very emphasis on interpersonal relations—the view of the world which sees it as composed of people while paying less attention to the world of interpersonal ideals or of things, of objects in nature—may itself in my opinion be taken as a symptom of the shift towards other-direction."[84] Unlike Freud, Sullivan argued that there were other conceivable subject positions besides a simple polarity between internalized paternal authority and unreflective conformity.

Challenging the conventional notion that pre-Oedipal attachments were simply sources of oral fantasies of engulfment, Riesman argued that autonomy was not antithetical to relatedness and that individuality was not antithetical to openness. The key question therefore was not how the ego could purge itself of internal tensions and defend its boundaries from outside attachments but how the ego could integrate this material into a more differentiated yet structured form. As Riesman explained, "'genital maturity' means for Freud lesser rather than greater complexity and differentiation of emotions."[85] That was why Freud fit in "with the current vogue of the 'tough guy.'"[86] Vigilantly warding off any attachment to the other was, according to Riesman, a form of weakness, not a form of strength. "Feelings of identification with other," argued Riesman, "are quite consistent with a strong feeling of individuality and personal value."[87] Riesman's unwillingness to accept the arguments of *The Authoritarian Personality* signified his unwillingness to link the formation of a democratic (and therefore heterosexual) personality to a strong Oedipal identity. "Yet we wonder in reading this book," speculated Riesman, "whether the authors, had they had access in their sample to seventeenth-century Puritans in New England, would have regarded them as authoritarian and, if so, how they would explain the rise of political democracy in just such a setting."[88] For Riesman, political behavior, like sexual behavior, was much more complicated than Adorno and his colleagues had allowed.

Riesman's invective against the psychoanalytic assumptions embedded within high modernism was an effort, using a broad historical scope and analysis, at formulating a vision of subjectivity not bounded by such parochialism. But the modernist writer who grappled with the theoretical implications of psychoanalysis and Oedipal discourse on the most direct level was Norman Brown, whose radical reinterpretation of Freud in the late 1950s was a rebuke to the conservative impulse of high modernism. His background, however, did not necessarily point to his later cultural radicalism. Brown was born on September 25, 1913, in Mexico after his father had moved there to "make his fortune as a mining engineer," but the family relocated to England so Brown and his sister could receive a more traditional education.[89] After obtaining his bachelor's degree in classical philology from Oxford University, Brown made "the most decisive gesture" in his life and moved to America in 1936. Originally believing in the ideology of American exceptionalism, Brown claimed his decision was prompted by the "lack of cultural and intellectual space" in England. America meant, for Brown, "the possibility of open space, of clearing away the rubbish of the past." Continuing his education,

Brown received a doctorate from the University of Wisconsin and obtained a teaching position as professor of languages at Nebraska Wesleyan University in 1942. After Brown's academic career was briefly interrupted by wartime service in the Office of Strategic Services, he took a position in 1946 as professor of classics at Wesleyan University. Brown, whom *Time* magazine would later refer to as an advocate for "the complete abolition of 20th-century civilization," began his career as a traditional classical scholar.[90] Like many others at that time, Brown's study of classical mythology was deeply influenced by the language of Marxism. For instance, in his first work, *Hermes the Thief: The Evolution of a Myth* (1947), Brown argued that the "cult of Hermes" that arose in the ninth century B.C. reflected the maturing of a "new and commercial civilization" and its inevitable conflict with a decaying aristocracy.[91] Brown's reduction of classical mythology to a product of class struggle continued in his 1953 work on Hesiod's *Theogony*, which Brown saw as testifying to "the emergence of conflict between classes" at the start of the "Iron Age."[92] Indeed, Brown admitted that his early work represented his "emotional and ideological involvement in the hopes and dreams of the Left."[93]

Two events, however, forced Brown to abandon not only his Marxist analytic lens but also his studies of classical mythology and to launch what *Esquire* magazine referred to as "a shattering, mind-changing, revolutionary attack on The System."[94] First, the failure of traditional American radicalism in the postwar period, marked in particular by the resounding defeat of Henry Wallace in the 1948 presidential campaign, forced Brown to re-evaluate his stance on traditional politics and Marxist thought in general. Brown's "disillusionment with that election" led him to conclude that "there was something seriously wrong with the premises and understandings of human nature and society" with which he had been operating.[95] Like many American intellectuals, including many modernists, Brown recognized that traditional arguments about either the revolutionary potential of the working class or the inevitability of social progress made little sense. Second, like other scholars who had witnessed "the holocaustic self-destruction" of recent years, Brown discovered in the writings of Freud an analytic lens with which to explain the irrational and aggressive nature of man. As Brown explained, "it is a shattering experience for anyone seriously committed to the Western traditions of morality and rationality to take a steadfast, unflinching look at what Freud has to say."[96] In a world of gas chambers and atomic weapons, Freud's pessimism in *Group Psychology and the Analysis of the Ego* was much more understandable and persuasive than progressive visions. But unlike most postwar therapists and many high modernists, Brown refused to reduce Freud's ideas to simplistic notions of mental health and mental rehabilitation. Brown instead saw something much more optimistic and liberating within psychoanalysis. Encouraged by the slew of postwar books on Freudian theory and in particular by the examples set by Herbert Marcuse and Wilhelm Reich, both of whom helped him to understand that psychoanalysis was not merely a science of therapeutic adjustment but a radical reinterpretation of man's potentialities, Brown offered his influential reappraisal of Freudian thought in his 1959 book *Life Against Death: The Psychoanalytic Meaning of History*.

Originally titled "The Life and Death of the Body: Psychoanalytical Eschatology," Brown's book was "addressed to all who are ready to call into question old assumptions and to entertain new possibilities" (xvii). For Brown, the ease with which both sides in the Cold War had trampled the hopes and potential of the working class, either by false promises of economic abundance or by sheer military force, had revealed the emptiness of both liberalism and Marxism. Brown's turn to Freud was driven by the sense felt among him and his contemporaries that the age of modernity was over, and that therefore a new language was needed to address the complexities of a postmodern landscape. As he explained, "the signs that since 1945 human history has entered a new phase can be seen on every side—not only in politics, but also in art, in philosophy, in religion."[97] Two effects followed from this rupture in history: first, the traditional utopian visions that had played such an influential role in radical politics had to be reevaluated, and second, the language with which man used to discuss art, mortality, religion, and politics had to be updated to fit the new historical circumstances. Consequently, Brown, like many other postwar intellectuals, turned to psychoanalysis. Reading Freud helped Brown to rethink the nature of man in two ways. First, Brown argued, echoing the language of Horkheimer and Adorno's *Dialectic of Enlightenment* and Dwight Macdonald's *The Root Is Man*, that recent events confirmed Freud's pessimistic view of human nature. Second, Brown pointed to the successful use of psychoanalysis in the anthropological and sociological studies of Erich Fromm, Margaret Mead, and others to dissect man's character. For Brown, Freud had successfully challenged both the Enlightenment view of man as an essentially rational, thinking being and the Marxist view of man as an essentially laboring being. Instead, Freud had unearthed those unconscious wishful impulses that rested behind the rational, secondary processes found in political deliberation, intellectual reasoning, and productive work. "The essence of man," argued Brown, "consists, not, as Descartes maintained, in thinking, but in desiring," a claim that rested at the heart of Freud's project.[98]

But Brown was not convinced by the conservative interpretations of Freud offered by the psychoanalytic community in the 1950s. The domestication of Freud by family therapists, ego psychologists, and even many high modernists had, according to Brown, robbed psychoanalysis of its radical interpretation of man's behavior and of its utopian promises. Believing that the vicissitudes of desire had been too easily manipulated by the persuasive appeal of mass culture and mass politics, high modernists had in turn focused obsessively on the means to harness, if not eliminate, desire itself. Their fear of the force of man's desire had made them cling to an Oedipal form of identity in which desire was sublimated through work and constrained by familial taboos. In contrast, Brown argued that American intellectuals needed to return to the more utopian arguments in Freud's work. Moreover, the strict focus by such analysts on child-rearing practices, proper family structures, and normative developmental patterns ignored Freud's later metapsychological musings on the life and death instincts and therefore ignored his larger critique of civilization's foundations. In their struggle to safeguard the autonomy of the self from corrosive influences, high modernists had forfeited any real discussion of the radical transformation of society itself, a transformation that might mitigate some of the more destructive influences of present-day society. Instead, high modernists fixated upon banal ideas about child development and proper family structures. As Brown explained, "those psychoanalytically minded anthropologists who attempt to explain the varieties of culture from the variable actualities of infant-rearing practices are chasing a will-o'-the-wisp" (171). Theories of social adjustment reflected not only the conservative political stance of such analysts but also a foreshortening of Freud's insights into the nature of desire and sexual pleasure. "When the neo-Freudians lose sight of the body," argued Brown, "they abandon the scientific criticism of society, and either preach social adjustment or else fall back on their own private prejudices in favor of the 'democratic personality' or the 'self-actualizing personality' or whatever" (144). Indeed, what was missing from the work of Adorno or Trilling, for example, was any discussion of the importance of the body itself—as the conduit of desire and as the site of personal identity. The self, in the language of high modernism, often seemed merely an abstraction. In their attempt to dissect the nature of the authoritarian and democratic personalities, American psychoanalysts had exposed their own intellectual limitations.

In large measure, then, Brown directed his intellectual assault on the high modernist claim that the classic Oedipal pattern of development was the only way to produce healthy and autonomous personalities. In a stunning reversal, Brown argued that Oedipal identity actually represented a foreshortening of man's potentialities. As he repeatedly explained, "the pattern of normal adult sexuality (in Freud's terminology, genital organization) is a tyranny of one component in infantile sexuality, a tyranny which suppresses some of the other components altogether and subordinates the rest to itself" (27). In contrast to most psychoanalysts, Brown argued that Oedipal identity was no less pathological than other subject positions; in fact, it was even more a distortion of man's nature than most positions. As he asserted, "the path of instinctual renunciation" demanded by the paternal order was "the path of sickness and self-destruction" (57). Brown began by arguing that the Oedipal pattern of development originated not merely from some culturally imposed sanction but from man's inevitable flight from death itself. According to Brown, Freud was correct in recognizing two fundamentally opposing instincts within man—the life instinct or Eros, which sought to preserve and enrich life through the formation of ever-greater unities, and the death instinct, which sought a complete reduction of tension and the return to an organic state of rest. High modernists were correct in taking Freud's metapsychology seriously. But for Brown, proper human existence demanded acceptance and recognition of both and not the current instinctual ambivalence and polarity. Because of their resounding fear of the death instinct, high modernists never clearly discussed its true source and never acknowledged how the life instinct might mitigate its destructiveness.

In response, Brown offered an alternative explanation. According to him, the incapacity to accept death was generated by an overwhelming anxiety that developed during childhood, caused in part by the trauma of birth itself and by separation from the nurturing mother. The feeling of omnipotence generated during childhood, originating in the disavowal of dependence on the mother for nourishment and protection, was traumatically negated by the child's eventual confrontation with the reality principle. "Anxiety," as Brown maintained, "is a response to experiences of separateness, individuality, and death" (115). Eventually recognizing that a wholesale dismissal of reality was impossible, the child chose instead to flee from death by fleeing from the maternal realm and seeking shelter in the paternal world. Oedipal development was simultaneously a flight from the mother, from infantile sexuality, and from the fact of death, all of which seemed overwhelming. According to Brown, "the special concentration of libido in the genital region, in the infantile phallic phase and in the adult genital organization, is engendered by the regressive death instinct, and represents the residue of the human incapacity to accept death, separation, and individuality" (116). The flight to the father, therefore, was not necessarily a progressive development but instead appeared more as a reactionary one.

For Brown, two effects resulted from the assumption of the Oedipal position. First, the child succumbed to a tremendous castration complex originating both from the recognition of the mother's supposed lack and from the threat of punishment handed down by the father. The castration complex ensured the separation of the child from the mother; however, the harshness of the separation did little to stop the flight from death that had driven the child from the mother in the first place. Instead, the child declared his ultimate independence and separation from any corrupting influences outside of himself. Indeed, "the castration complex establishes as absolute the dualism of the self and the other, the dualism which infantile narcissism had sought to overcome" (129). The result was an immense withdrawal of libido from the world in the name of autonomy. The seemingly independent individual of Oedipal development was therefore nothing more than an individual trying to escape the fact of death by trying to escape the body itself. The body from the high modernist perspective was the site of corruption and cultural entanglement. The end result of the Oedipal project was "narcissistic inflation," that is, the grandiose dream of complete autonomy supposedly generated by the internalization of paternal authority. "The Oedipal project," explained Brown, "is the quest to conquer death by becoming father of oneself" (120). Any notion of fusion, unity, or reciprocity was eliminated in the name of rational self-control and self-reliance. Three results followed. First, the death instinct was transformed into the aggressive manipulation of the outside world simply because the Oedipal position failed to mitigate the drive toward death. The Oedipal subject tried to escape this drive toward self-destruction by clinging to external embodiments of himself—to the property he controlled, to those objects his labor created, and to the monuments he constructed. Almost compulsively, the Oedipal subject tried to reconstruct the world in his own image. Second, dependence on others was denied in the name of separation. Any form of community, togetherness, or relatedness outside the bourgeois family was seen as a capitulation to the forces of collectivism and control. Third, the body as a whole was desexualized through the genital organization of the libido. The assumption of the Oedipal position required the foreshortening of those pre-Oedipal zones of desire that marked infantile development; as such, the body was divested of most of its sites of gratification. As Brown explained, "the morbid death instinct, already transformed into a principle of denial, blossoms after the castration complex into a principle of self-denial and denial of one's own body" (129). In this sense, man's flight from death was in reality a flight from himself.

According to Brown, the propertied, autonomous individual of early capitalism so heralded by high modernists was the prime example of the limitations of Oedipal identity. The internalization of paternal authority, which was deemed the pathway to individuation, was in reality a defensive structure. "Through the institution of the super-ego," said Brown, "the parents are internalized and man finally succeeds in becoming father of himself, but at the cost of becoming his own child and keeping his ego infantile" (129). The productive, craft-driven work of the propertied individual of early capitalism was originally seen as the proper objectification of man's inner energy, and his completed work was seen as a reflection of his abilities and imaginative potential. Such labor contained a world-constitutive function in which man transformed an initially hostile environment into a world of permanent objects. In reality, according to Brown, such labor acted as a form of sublimation in which the fact of death was repressed through an escape from the body. For Brown, the desexualization of the body produced by the Oedipal moment led to man's fundamental disembodiment: man restricted the potentialities of his body through labor; he subordinated fore pleasure to end pleasure; and his essence passed into property. A whole host of dualisms was then produced—an almost compulsive drive toward activity was used to defend against the dangers of passivity, a belligerent defense of the individual in the name of autonomy was to guard against any corruption from society or from others, the mind and abstract thought were prioritized and separated from the sordid, earthly body, and so on. Consequently, "involuted Eros and involuted aggression constitute the 'autonomous self' or what passes for individuality in the human species." The rational, self-directed individual of the Oedipal position was merely a mirage. If anything, Brown wanted to remind high modernists that the body was always libidinally invested.

The second effect of the Oedipal project was a repudiation of any opposite-sex identification, thereby establishing rigid divides among gender and sexual identities. The demotion of homosexuality to a pathology by orthodox psychoanalysts was merely the most obvious example of this widespread "restriction of the erotic potentialities of the human body" (27). The

Oedipal project made the attainment of masculinity an imperative for male children and linked such an attainment to the formation of heterosexual desire. In defense against castration anxiety, the child attributed passivity and therefore death to the maternal realm and aligned activity with the paternal sphere. Strict gender divisions resulted, an obvious distortion of what Freud saw as the fundamentally bisexual nature of infantile sexuality. Femininity was linked with passivity, subordination, and masochism; masculinity was equated with activity, independence, and aggression. Brown argued that "the dualism of masculine-feminine is merely the transposition into genital terms of the dualism of activity and passivity; and activity and passivity represent unstable fusions of Eros and Death at war with each other" (132). Divisions in sexuality were also a product of such dualisms. The normative outcome of the Oedipus complex was predicated upon the mutually exclusive opposition between desire and identification, that is, between possessive love for the mother on the one hand and the internalization of the attributes of the father on the other hand. Orthodox psychoanalysts assumed that the desire for one sex was maintained only through a corresponding identification with the other sex. "In each sex," said Brown, "it is the attitude belonging to the opposite sex which succumbs to repression. In each sex the unconscious does not accept the repression but wants to recover the bisexuality of childhood." In adopting the Oedipal position, the child overcame the complicated nature of infantile sexuality and channeled his desire into a strict division between object choice for the opposite sex and rivaled identification with the same sex. "Hence, measured by the standard of the unconscious and of childhood," argued Brown, "the sexual differentiation of the adult libido, as presupposed in genital organization and the human family—masculine aggressiveness and feminine passivity—is a loss of sexual completeness." Heterosexuality was linked with masculine aggression, and homosexuality was linked with feminine masochism.

As a way around the limitations of Oedipal thinking, Brown turned to the work of ego psychologists who had, following the lead of Anna Freud and Melanie Klein, begun to examine the complexities of the pre-Oedipal moment. "The clue," explained Brown, "not only to normal adult sexuality but to our whole repressed and hidden ultimate essence lies in infantile sexuality" (30). Part of Brown's project in *Life Against Death* was to reevaluate the traditional understanding of narcissism, which Freud had described as the pre-Oedipal stage that existed between autoeroticism and object-choice in which the child took his own body as his object of desire. Freud's theory of narcissism, in which the child refused to acknowledge any attachment to outside objects with the exception of those that reflected his own sense of self or sense of what he wanted to be, was influential in helping orthodox psychoanalysts criticize homosexuality as a failed form of development. The homosexual object choice was a narcissistic one because such a choice was presumably molded on the child's own image of himself. Instead of turning his desire to the mother, whose importance for the child's survival should have made her the first object choice, the narcissistic child turned his desire to the father who reflected the child's own sense of self. Desire for the mother and identification with the father transformed into desire for the father and identification with the mother. The importance of the Oedipal position was to safeguard against this slippage. But as Brown argued, "Freud's distinction between identification and object-choice, or between narcissistic and anaclitic object-choice, does not survive close examination" (42). Freud himself, in his more speculative moments, had argued this as well. Freud recognized a negative Oedipal moment in which the child identified with the parent of the opposite sex and desired the parent of the same sex. Such a discovery demonstrated the complexity and fundamental oscillation of desire and identification. The rigidness of the Oedipal moment represented a foreshortening of the complexity of infantile sexuality. As Brown explained, Freud "is unable to maintain consistently the correlation of identification with love of the father and object-choice with love the mother, and has to speak of anaclitic relations with the father and identifications with the mother." The instability of identity arose from the capacity to desire and to identify with the father and with the mother simultaneously, that is, to exist at the crossroads of the positive and negative Oedipus complex. Identification often led to object love and vice versa; or more accurately, any distinction made between identification and desire was artificial at best. "Close examination of Freud's own premises and arguments," explained Brown, "suggests that there is only one loving relationship to objects in the world, a relation of being-one-with-the-world which, though closer to Freud's narcissistic relation (identification), is also at the root of his other category of possessive love (object-choice)." All of the divisions that plagued the Oedipal position were therefore artificial and ignored the commensurability of identification and desire.

By returning to the pre-Oedipal moment, Brown hoped to resuscitate the human body and provide an image of psychical corporeality ignored by most psychoanalysts and most high modernists. For Brown, the Oedipal moment was linked with feelings of resentment, anxiety, and loss; the pre-Oedipal moment avoided the tyranny of genital sexuality and restored the fullness of the body itself. In contrast to Oedipal identity, which sublimated desire in the name of work, pre-Oedipal identity remained in touch with myriad possibilities for the gratification of the body. "Infantile sexuality," explained Brown, "is the pursuit of pleasure obtained through the activity of any and all organs of the human body" (30). The resurrection of the body that Brown promoted was connected to the resurrection of previously repressed and tabooed zones of sexual pleasure. Indeed, Brown refused to privilege certain bodily organs or zones; as he explained, with the dismantling of the pressures of Oedipal development, "the human body would become polymorphously perverse, delighting in that full life of all the body which it now fears" (308). Such a body was not bound by the exclusivity of fixed gender or sexual identities. The oscillation between identification and desire inherent in the pre-Oedipal moment represented for Brown the true nature of the human body. "Our repressed desires are not just for delight," he argued, "but specifically for delight in the fulfillment of the life of our own bodies" (31). Sexuality was, for Brown, not the complex unfolding of innate psychosexual stages; instead, sexuality was a fluid process. The polarity produced by the Oedipal position was only abrogated by the reaffirmation of this prior moment of bisexual identification. "Deeper than the problem of the relation between the sexes," asserted Brown, "is the problem of the reunification of the sexes in the self" (134). Eroticization, in this sense, was not bound by one strict object choice.

However, Brown was not trying to dissolve the fortifications of the ego and release the self into a flood of libidinal desire. Unlike romantic modernists such as Allen Ginsberg or Jackson Pollock who, as we will see in Chapter 4, were determined to liberate desire in every imaginable way and who saw the ego as the site of repression, Brown, in *Life Against Death*, refused to follow their simplification of Freud. He remained committed to the notion that the ego, as a precipitate of the cathexis of the id, was essential in maintaining a sense of wholeness and individuality. As he explained, "the path to that ultimate reunification of ego and body is not a dissolution but a strengthening of the human ego" (292). Indeed, Brown offered an image of the ego as open and receptive, not closed and autarkic. Brown distinguished between an Apollonian ego, that is, one modeled on the Greek god of rationality and order, and a Dionysian ego, that is, one based on the Greek god of wine and ecstasy. "While the Apollonian ego is the ego of genital organization," explained Brown, "the Dionysian ego would be once more a body-ego and would not have to be dissolved in body-rapture" (176). In so doing, Brown was reviving

Freud's conception of a bodily ego. In *The Ego and the Id*, Freud had elaborated the interrelation between man's psychic interiority and his bodily exteriority, arguing that the ego was formed through libidinal investment in parts of the body. As such, the ego was less an autonomous entity or realm and more a permeable envelope marking both the subtle boundary between interior and exterior and the continual assimilation with and attachment to loved objects. Indeed, the ego was always constituted by its relationship to the others around it. Through the vicissitudes of desire and identification, the individual self was formed through its erotic attachment to others. "The expansion of the self," said Brown, "in which human perfection consists, is at the same time the expansion of the active life of the human body, unifying our body with other bodies in the world in active interaction" (48). Oedipal identity did little to help bridge the gap between the individual and those around him; if anything, the internalization of paternal authority was based upon a fundamental separation from others. Like David Riesman, Brown rejected the high modernist notion of a self and a body that was identical to itself; there was no way and no legitimate reason to purge the self of any identification with or erotic attachment to others. Instead, the key was to return to the body as the site of subjectivity. "With such a transfigured body," argued Brown, "the human ego becomes once more what it was designed to be in the first place, a body-ego and the surface of a body, sensing that communication between body and body which is life" (292). In language reminiscent of Riesman's discussion of an autonomous other-directed personality, Brown's vision of a resuscitated bodily ego linked his late modernist reading of Freud to the theoretical challenge presented by the famed sociologist.

The Vicissitudes of Modernism

In May 1960, Brown gave an infamous oration to the Columbia University chapter of Phi Beta Kappa. Later published in *Harper's* magazine under the title "Apocalypse: The Place of Mystery in the Life of the Mind," Brown's speech signaled another dramatic shift in his thinking. This astounding transformation culminated in the 1966 publication of *Love's Body*, a work composed of ambiguous, poetic aphorisms in the vein of Nietzsche that linked Freudian and Kleinian psychoanalysis to Blakean romanticism and to Christian and Buddhist doctrine. Such language was in stark contrast to the theoretical outlook of his book on Freud. As Brown explained to an interviewer, he felt "when writing *Love's Body* some kind of obligation to undo what I had done in *Life Against Death*."[99] Brown was now less interested in opening the individual ego to outside forces and more concerned with abolishing the ego as such. The sense of connection and interaction that characterized his notion of a Dionysian or bodily ego was transformed into an image of communion in which the ego was dissolved through its absorption into the body of the world itself. Individualism in this sense became the problem. According to Brown, "souls, personalities, and egos are masks, specters, concealing our unity as body."[100] In openly turning from psychoanalysis to mysticism, Brown abandoned any notion of political transformation for what he referred to as poetic radicalism. As he explained, "the meaning of love's body turned out to be different from that anticipated by the author of *Life Against Death*—much more poetical, much less political."[101] Any artificial construction that hinted of sublimation had to be overturned. Brown's utopia was beyond the limits of language, logic, and time itself. Such a utopia was to be constructed neither by man nor by the individual human body but by Nietzsche's superman, that figure with "supernatural powers" who had learned to dispense with man's "crutches" and had discovered the "power of walking."[102] Written during the explosion in cultural radicalism that marked the 1960s as a decade, *Love's Body* did little more than confirm, in aphorisms derived from academic citations, the mystical visions a young Allen Ginsberg had had at Columbia University years prior. Brown's invitation by Phi Beta Kappa to present his poetic vision at Columbia (a university that had once spurred Ginsberg's own Blakean dreams) signaled how entrenched and widespread Ginsberg's reformulation of modernism had become. Norman Brown was merely the latest convert to this cultural movement.

PART II

The Revolt of Romantic Modernism

Beatniks, Action Painters, and Reichians

CHAPTER FOUR

A Question of Character: The Dramaturgy of Erving Goffman and C. Wright Mills

In William Burroughs's 1952 novel *Queer*, the narrator, William Lee, travels from Mexico City to South America in search of a plant called yage, which, as Lee explains, is used by Russian leaders "to induce states of automatic and ultimately, of course, thought control."[1] Noting that officials in the United States are experimenting with similar drugs, Lee fantasizes about the power to control the mind of another: "Think of it: thought control. Take anyone apart and rebuild to your taste. Anything about somebody bugs you, you say, 'Yage! I want that routine took clear out of his mind'" (89). Seeing little difference in the political practices of the two superpowers, both of which have instituted psychological control through the mechanisms of state power, Lee argues that his own desire to "schlup" or possess those around him marks him as the Ugly American—maniacal and possessive. Throughout the novel, Lee's sexual desire for Eugene Allerton, a former member of the Counter-Intelligence Corps and currently Lee's indifferent lover, parallels what Burroughs saw as the aggressive seduction of the individual by the national political machine. Indeed, *Queer* was one of many meditations Burroughs wrote on the social engineering of hapless masses. As Lee explains to his friend: "Automatic obedience, synthetic schizophrenia, mass-produced to order. That is the Russian dream, and America is not far behind. The bureaucrats of both countries want the same thing: Control" (91). As the language of psychoanalysis became part of the American vernacular, Burroughs wondered aloud whether or not his fellow citizens had merely accepted another form of conditioning.

Burroughs's invectives against state control set the tone for the other dominant modernist tradition in the early Cold War, that group of Beat poets, abstract expressionists, and purveyors of hipsterism who reacted to the hegemony of high modernism by returning to the origins of modernist practices in the late nineteenth century when artists and writers began peeling away the metaphysical and transcendental claims found in religion and applying them to art. I refer to this group of avant-garde writers, artists, and critics as *romantic modernists* for their inspired return to the original roots of modernism in Romanticism, a project designed to convert art into life and vice versa. Ranging from the action painting of Jackson Pollock and Willem de Kooning to the color-field painting of Mark Rothko and Barnett Newman, the art criticism of Harold Rosenberg, the spontaneous poetry of Jack Kerouac and Allen Ginsberg, and the fiction of Norman Mailer and William Burroughs, this tradition of romantic modernism transformed American art and literature by injecting new forms of experimentation, spontaneity, and expressionism into artistic practices. But more important, their aesthetic project was designed to liberate the individual from the stultifying conditions of modern life. Portraying modern man as castrated by the bureaucratic nature of American society, these romantic modernists argued that totalitarianism, in the form of mass media and mass politics, had crept into Western society. But unlike their high modernist counterparts who turned to Freudian notions of proper ego autonomy to safeguard the mental health of the individual, romantic modernists argued instead that the ego itself was the site of psychological control. Borrowing from the psychoanalytic work of Wilhelm Reich and Robert Lindner, writers such as Burroughs and Mailer argued that the ego was an artificial construction that originated from the hostile repression of man's libidinal impulses, a regression that emanated from an endless list of familial and social taboos. Consequently, the ego was merely a defense mechanism or characterological prison holding in check man's true desires and not the source of autonomy as Theodor Adorno and Lionel Trilling, among others, claimed. Indeed, unlike high modernists who privileged reason over desire and mind over the body, romantic modernists inverted this hierarchy, seeking instead to liberate man from the artificial trappings of character.

In this sense, the main argument within modernist circles in the early Cold War was about the actual sources of the self. In their criticisms of high modernism, David Riesman and Kenneth Burke, for instance, echoed the concerns of romantic modernists in worrying not only about the limitations of formalist aesthetics but also about the conservatism within high modernism. As we have seen, Burke, Riesman, and others similarly criticized their high modernist counterparts for clinging to orthodox notions of Oedipal identity as the only means to safeguard the self. But unlike abstract expressionists and purveyors of hipsterism, late modernists refused to abandon any notion of the individual ego, choosing instead to offer a more open and flexible image of the self, one that gained its coherency from its identification and attachment to others. In this way, late modernists refused to accept the artificial divisions between reason and desire, mind and body, and masculinity and femininity that their fellow modernists constructed. Instead, as we saw in the work of Norman Brown, late modernists tried to transcend these divisions, offering an image of a bodily ego that had overcome the taboos on libidinal expression but that maintained a sense of wholeness and relatedness. Indeed, the strongest critics of the tradition of romantic modernism were the sociologists Erving Goffman and C. Wright Mills, both of whom, borrowing from the work of Kenneth Burke, used the language of dramatism and characterological development to offer a fuller image of man's possibilities. In viewing man through the lens of the theatrical stage, Goffman and Mills, albeit in different ways, portrayed the individual self not merely as a conduit for desire but as a being existing in a variety of social institutions, playing a variety of prescribed roles, and struggling to gain coherence in the face of forces acting upon him. As C. Wright Mills said in *The Sociological Imagination*, "we cannot adequately understand 'man' as an isolated biological creature, as a bundle of reflexes or a set of instincts. . . . Whatever else he may be, man is a social and an historical actor who must be understood, if at all, in close and intricate interplay with social and historical structures."[2] As romantic modernists like William Burroughs and Norman Mailer railed against all of the institutions entrapping and distorting man's desire, late modernists like Mills and Goffman argued for a more complex understanding of the various roles, responsibilities, and relationships in which modern man found himself. In the early Cold War, the debates over modernism were in many ways a debate about character.

Brainwashing and Mental Manipulation in the Cold War

In 1951, soon after Chinese troops crossed the Yalu River and turned the United Nations–led police action in North Korea into a major conflagration, Harold Martin, an editor at the *Saturday Evening Post*, published an account of the capture and indoctrination of eighteen marines by Chinese authorities, describing how "They Tried to Make Our Marines Love Stalin."[3] Martin's article, which depicted the use of torture and hypnosis by the Chinese, was one of many accounts of the indoctrination methods used upon captured American soldiers. When a series of public broadcasts in 1952 and 1953, in which American prisoners of war confessed that the U.S. military had used germ warfare on North Korean troops, reached the American public, the nation went into a panic about the sinister act of "brainwashing."[4] Such fears were officially confirmed in April 1953 at a prearmistice exchange of prisoners, referred to as "Little Switch," when 149 released American soldiers told of the systematic attempt by their Chinese captors to convert them to Communism. These fears reached a climax in September 1953 when the last American prisoners of war returned from Korea, upon which the American public learned that 21 captured soldiers had decided not to come home. As ex-prisoners were marshaled to a "de-brainwashing" facility at the Valley Forge Army Hospital, *Newsweek* wondered aloud, "Washed Brains of POWs: Can They Be Rewashed?"[5] These worries over the apparent susceptibility of seemingly strong-willed American soldiers to Chinese propaganda were part of a much larger anxiety concerning the use of advanced psychological techniques by Communist infiltrators to gain possession of American minds. As the search for political deviants went on in the nation's classrooms, laboratories, and federal offices, national publications reported on the development of Russian hypnotic practices at the "headquarters" of this new war on the mind at the "Presidium of the Soviet Academy of Sciences in Moscow."[6] Similarly, a number of scholarly books including Edward Hunter's *Brainwashing in Red China* (1951), Nathan Leites's *Ritual of Liquidation* (1954), and William Sargant's *Battle for the Mind* (1957) detailed Russian experiments to condition man's reflexes and convert him to Communist ideology.

In the "TNT age of brainwashing," totalitarianism, once envisioned as the usurpation of political control by military means, was now seen as the subtle, discreet enslavement of the individual through the use of hypnosis, Pavlovian psychology, and subliminal manipulation.[7] More insidious and more threatening, totalitarianism was no longer considered merely an outside threat but an internal, psychological one as well.[8] The fullest discussion of thought control practices came from Dr. Joost Meerloo, a professor of psychology at Columbia University and the New School for Social Research. In his 1956 book *The Rape of the Mind*, Meerloo coined the term *menticide* to describe not just the process of "mind-killing" performed by Communist psychologists on American soldiers but also the widespread pressures placed on the human psyche by modern technological changes.[9] Exploring both Pavlovian psychology and Freudian theory, Meerloo suggested that Communist brainwashing techniques were not an "oriental" aberration but part of modern life as a whole. According to Meerloo, "the mechanization of modern life has already influenced man to become more passive and to adjust himself to ready-made conformity. No longer does man think in personal values. . . . He thinks more and more in the values brought to him by mass media" (96). When he testified at the Navy court of inquiry of Colonel Frank Schwable, one of the germ warfare confessors from the Korean War, telling the court that no individual, regardless of how strong willed, could have withstood Communist brainwashing techniques, Meerloo noted the inability of most Americans to resist the "hypnotic" techniques employed by Madison Avenue executives.[10] The "rape of the mind," according to Meerloo, occurred everyday.

Romantic Modernism and the Specter of Totalitarianism

Within this national debate over brainwashing, many romantic modernists offered their own diagnosis of the mental health of American citizens. Echoing the concerns of Theodor Adorno and Lionel Trilling, these modernists similarly worried about the threat of mass politics. In part, the theory of totalitarianism sketched out by romantic modernists in the 1950s was borrowed from their high modernist counterparts. For instance, psychoanalyst Robert Lindner, whose work shaped the language of many romantic modernists, applied Erich Fromm's theory to his clinical practice. Working as the chief psychiatrist at the federal penitentiary in Lewisburg, Pennsylvania, Lindner was fascinated by the increasing number of highly neurotic Communist Party members he found in prison. In best-selling books such as *Rebel Without a Cause* (1944), *Prescription for Rebellion* (1952), *The Fifty-Minute Hour* (1956), and *Must You Conform?* (1956), Lindner, whose sardonic wit marked him, as his friend Norman Mailer explained, "almost alone among analysts in his sustained argument that the healthy man was a rebel," mounted a sustained investigation of the authoritarian personality.[11] Borrowing his language from Fromm, Lindner argued that the "tremendous appeal" of Communism stemmed from the loss of any "protective orientational framework" through which the individual might confront "the terrifying outside environment."[12] Lindner's reiteration of the high modernist understanding of totalitarianism was echoed by another influential romantic modernist, Harold Rosenberg. A contributor to *Symposium*, *New Masses*, and *Partisan Review* in the 1930s and a champion of the Communist Party in a number of poems and essays early in his life, Rosenberg eventually broke with the Stalinist movement and became a contributor to Irving Howe's magazine *Dissent*, critiquing both the utopianism of the party and the arrogance of anti-Communist liberals.[13] In this sense, Rosenberg's famous promotion of more existential, spontaneous forms of modernism in essays such as "The American Action Painters" was in response to both the reactionary formalism of high modernism *and* the regimented structure of the Communist Party. Detailing his experience with the party apparatus in his essay "The Heroes of Marxist Science," Rosenberg argued that the "deeper temptation" that made seemingly rational individuals submit to the "intense process of self-transformation" was the belief, adopted in the face of the "poverty and injustice" of recent years, that the "hardness" of the party would "rescue mankind from catastrophe."[14] Unlike Lindner, however, Rosenberg hesitated to reduce the appeal of Communism to individual psychological weakness. In contrast to most studies of political deviance, Rosenberg stressed the "purposefully constructed" character of the Communist Party member. Arguing that the posturing of most members (that "mixture of smugness, boredom, and absent-mindedness" [182]) was merely a disciplinary formation imposed by party officials, Rosenberg portrayed the Communist less as a neurotic, weak-willed utopian and more as a manipulated, molded character.

In this way, romantic modernists recast totalitarianism not as a vast military machine storming through society and instituting a police state but as a plague seeping through the open and accessible pores of the national body. Totalitarianism, according to romantic modernists, was not the exclusive project of one political party; instead, it was symptomatic of any tendency toward social or psychological control, whether through the repressive actions of right-wing demagogues, the rhetoric of anti-Communist liberals, or the propaganda pamphlets of the Communist Party. As Norman Mailer explained, "totalitarianism has come to America with no concentration camps and no need for them, no political parties and no desire for new parties, no, totalitarianism has slipped into the body cells and psyche of each of us."[15] The spread of totalitarianism was evident in all spheres of American life—the normative language of the psychoanalyst, the surveillance tools of the FBI, the artificial pleasures of the culture industry, the inescapable presence of mass media, the faceless façeades of corporate offices, and the redundant rhetoric of left-wing proselytizers. Defined as the insidious attack on the integrity of the body, totalitarianism according to Mailer was the result of indecision, inactivity, and stasis, a deadening of the individual body not agile enough to escape penetration by noxious influences. Totalitarianism, in the favorite metaphor of romantic modernists, was a form of cancer. To Mailer, "featureless, symptomless diseases like virus and colds and the ubiquitous cancer are the appropriate metaphor of all those political forces like the FBI, or like the liberalism of the Democratic Party, which are historically faceless" (7). Totalitarianism was embodied in General Edward Cummings, the reactionary military leader of *The Naked and the Dead* who perpetuates the militarization of American society; in Leroy Hollingsworth, the blond-haired, blue-eyed midwesterner of *Barbary Shore* who exemplifies the brutal violence hidden in the soul of middle America; and in Barney Kelly, the ruthless power broker of *An American Dream*, who represents the conspiratorial power of the police, the CIA, the Mafia, and the media. Totalitarianism was a "*Geist*, spirit," a tasteless manifestation with many forms ranging from the FBI to SANE: "People on your own side are just as likely to be totalitarian as people on the other side" (126).

The romantic modernist most worried about the parasitic control of the individual by psychological conditioning was of course William Burroughs, whose collection of fiction from the 1950s and 1960s was an extended meditation on state power. No longer associated with one particular political program, authoritarianism was perceived as a much more threatening system of control. As Burroughs explained in a letter to Allen Ginsberg during the writing of *Naked Lunch*, "brainwashing, thought control, etc. is the vilest form of crime against the person of another," the ultimate "confusion of ethics and legality" that had paved the way for the "monstrosities" of "Nazism and Communism."[16] Power was no longer based upon brute force or explicit subjugation; instead, modern domination was exercised through mental coercion. In the "Mayan Caper" episode from his 1961 novel *The Soft Machine*, Burroughs speculated on the origins of such control.[17] For him, the Mayan civilization, whose archaeological remains he had studied while living in Mexico, marked the historical beginning of this subjugation of the masses by the state. Utilizing only a minimal police force, the Mayan priests manipulated the peasant masses, whose lives were dependent upon a fragile agricultural economy, by controlling the ceremonial calendar that detailed the proper schedule for crop planting and harvesting and that linked these events to an elaborate series of religious ceremonies. According to Burroughs, "the ancient Mayans possessed one of the most precise and hermetic control calendars ever used on this planet, a calendar that in effect controlled what the populace did, thought, and felt on any given day."[18] Even the narrator of the novel, when he travels back in time to investigate the origins of Mayan civilization, feels "the crushing weight of evil insect control forcing my thoughts and feelings into prearranged molds, squeezing my spirit in a soft invisible vise" (89).

Burroughs updated this historical allegory for the technological age in his science-fiction trilogy about a planetary invasion by parasitic organisms called the Nova Mob who use sex, drug addiction, and advertising to instill control. The power of the Nova Mob, according to Burroughs, was viral—a form of possession in which the infecting agent occupied a weakened host who never realized that any bodily penetration had actually occurred. The virus waited "for a point of intersection," eventually infiltrating the body in "some ugly noxious or disgusting act," eating away the human tissue, and replacing it with "exact copies of itself" until the host became a "program empty body."[19] The control systems of the Nova Mob were coordinated by transnational corporate organizations such as the fictional Trak system, which Burroughs detailed in the fourth routine of *The Soft Machine*. Maintaining its own news agency ("the Trak Service"), its own military force ("the Trak police"), and its own advertising system ("the Trak Sex and Dream Utilities"), the corporation retained control through the "habit-forming" commodities forced upon a dependent population, "perfect" products that possessed a "precise molecular affinity for its client of predilection" (42–43). Perception and taste as such were fashioned by outside forces. As the narrator of *Nova Express* explains, "the scanning pattern we accept as 'reality' has been imposed by the controlling power on this planet, a power primarily oriented towards total control" (53).

Burroughs connected his concerns about psychological control to the Cold War landscape most explicitly in *Naked Lunch*, a Pavlovian nightmare world of advanced brainwashing techniques, subliminal conditioning, and manipulative advertising. Although lacking any narrative arch, the story involves the descent of the narrator-protagonist Will Lee, desperate to evade the authorities, into the dystopian underworld of Interzone. Described as a "vast hive" of activity humming with "sex and commerce," Interzone is a "single, vast building" representative of the pornographic, drug-addicted, and authoritarian bent of modern capitalist society.[20] As Lee soon discovers, Interzone is under siege from three conspiratorial parties seeking control: the Liquefactionists (representative of the Fascist desire to reduce individual bodies to "liquid" [75]); the Senders (representative of the left-wing authoritarian desire to control "physical movements, mental processes, emotional reactions and *apparent* sensory impressions" [147]); and the Divisionists (representative of the leveling tendencies of Western democracies that proliferate by growing "exact replicas of themselves" [149]). These three cannibalistic parties are aided by a number of nefarious technicians. The most notorious is Dr. Benway, who is "an expert on all phases of interrogation, brainwashing, and control" (20). As director of the Reconditioning Center of Freeland, Benway realizes that aggressive force only precipitates resistance, and therefore he uses an endless list of techniques including hypnotism, electroshock therapy, psychoanalysis, and various drugs to convince "subjects" that they "deserve *any* treatment" because "there is something (never specified) horribly wrong" with them (21).

As with many romantic modernists, Burroughs's paranoia ran deep. He envisioned an inevitable future where scientists installed radio antennas in the brains of all citizens at birth to control behavior and to "make certain thoughts impossible" (80), a fear shared by his fellow Beat writers. For instance, Jack Kerouac, despite his often pastoral view of America, often echoed Burroughs's concerns about state power. "It's Communists destroying everybody," Kerouac wrote in *Big Sur*; "systematic individuals are poisoned till finally they'll have everybody, this madness changes you completely and in the morning you no longer have the same mind. . . . It's the brainwash drug."[21] More emphatically, Allen Ginsberg detailed his personal experience with institutional control. He of course was traumatized by the continued institutionalization of his mother, Naomi Ginsberg, who suffered from epilepsy and paranoia and who received countless treatments, including electroshock therapy, while living in a state mental hospital. More directly, Ginsberg himself was institutionalized in 1949 in the Columbia Psychiatric Institute after having been arrested for his connection to a robbery committed by his friend Herbert Huncke, an experience that he referenced in his poetic manifesto, "Howl." Stridently libertarian and slightly misanthropic, most romantic modernists like Ginsberg and Kerouac saw little difference between the police state in Soviet Russia and the capitalist state in America. As Ginsberg expressed in his journal, "O Capitalist & Communists you shd get in bed with me / bring your pencils & notebooks / lie there snorting out revolutions and epidemics famines and excess grain production."[22] In response, many romantic modernists adopted anarchism as an alternative. Anarchism, like modernism in general, spoke to the dream of life lived outside the dictates of state control and cultural decay, both maintaining *la promesse de bonheur* in the face of revolutionary failures. After supporting Henry Wallace's Progressive Party in 1948 and espousing "revolutionary socialism" in his 1951 novel *Barbary Shore*, Norman Mailer, for instance, abandoned organized politics, except for a less than serious run for New York mayor in 1960, and espoused an anticapitalist, anti-Stalinist, decentralized anarchism.[23] But the critic Paul Goodman, whose writings appeared in a litany of "little magazines" in the 1940s and 1950s, offered the strongest defense of anarchism as a political principle. In his 1946 work *The May Pamphlet*, Goodman presented a vision of a decentralized libertarian society, one in direct contrast to modern America. As an intellectual defense of his position, Goodman pointed to the psychoanalytic theory of Wilhelm Reich, whose "main points were anarchist points," as scientific evidence that man in his natural state was a benign being.[24]

The Reichian Tradition in America

Goodman's reference to Wilhelm Reich reflected the importance of the Austrian psychoanalyst to the development of romantic modernism. Although remembered mostly for his metaphysical speculations at the end of his career and for his persecution by the Food and Drug Administration and subsequent incarceration in 1956 for violating a court injunction, Reich was one of the key figures in translating psychiatric practices into sexual politics. His arrival at the New School for Social Research in New York in 1939 marked Reich's introduction to American intellectual life, and in a series of books published in the late 1920s and 1930s including *Character Analysis* and *The Function of the Orgasm*, Reich merged psychoanalytic thought with Marxist theory and strongly influenced Erich Fromm's *Escape from Freedom*, Theodor Adorno's *The Authoritarian Personality*, and Norman O. Brown's *Life Against Death*. A psychoanalytic deviant who was expelled from both the German Communist Party and the International Psychoanalytical Association, Reich stunned American intellectuals with his frank defense of uninhibited sexuality and his scientific experiments with what he believed was the energy source of all living organisms. Indeed, the "strange case" of Wilhelm Reich became a matter of public importance in the early Cold War. The *New Republic* openly wondered in 1947 why a "deviant" such as Reich, who had begun "to collect a cult of no little influence," had not been denounced by every major psychoanalytic association.[25] Even *Newsweek* offered its own puzzled interpretation of the "Reich cult," that "strange mutation" in the psychoanalytic movement that resulted in Reich's imprisonment in a federal penitentiary for contempt of court after the Food and Drug Administration had banned the transportation of the analyst's infamous "orgone accumulators" across state lines.[26] When Reich died of a heart attack in 1957, his assistants at the Orgone Institute Research Laboratory in Maine aided in the circulation of his books, ensuring for their martyr a lasting influence, particularly with romantic modernists such as William Burroughs, Norman Mailer, and Saul Bellow who enthusiastically incorporated Reich's theories into their fiction.

Reich's radical revision of Freud began with his rejection of ego autonomy as the sign of a healthy personality. In a series of works including *The Function of the Orgasm* and *Character Analysis*, Reich challenged orthodox psychoanalysis by vehemently defending the therapeutic importance of liberating man's instinctual energy. Unlike Freud, who had posited a "primary biological destructiveness" within man, Reich argued that at the heart of man's personality rested the spontaneous currents of the libido, that "biological core" of man that gave him "depth, natural sociality and sexuality."[27] According to Reich, the unconscious that Freud had discovered was in reality a construction resulting from social and familial repression of man's basic instincts, a repression that converted the benevolent impulses of the id into "sadism, avarice, lasciviousness, envy, [and] perversion of all kinds" (233), characteristics that Freud had mistakenly assumed were an inherent part of human nature. Such perversions were held in check by social norms, which converted the energy of the unconscious into the artificial structure of the ego, that "mask of self-control, compulsive insincere politeness, and pseudo-sociality" (233). Unlike high modernists who saw the ego as the site of rationality, Reich saw man's ego as a defensive outer shell. Threatened by instinctual energies from the biological core and imperiled by social restrictions on the release of such energies, the ego constructed an elaborate defense. Spontaneous feelings were stifled and converted into neurotic physical characteristics. Accumulated resistances to these impulses were translated into stereotypical expressions, posture, and physical demeanors, what Reich referred to as man's *character*. As such, "the psychoanalysis of these various characteristics proves that they are merely various forms of an armoring of the ego against the dangers of the outside world and the repressed instinctual demands of the id."[28] Character therefore was nothing but a disease. "Etiologically," asserted Reich, "there is just as much anxiety behind the excessive politeness of one person as there is behind the gruff and occasionally brutal reaction of another." Man's character was developed first in relationship to the prohibitions issued by the family during early childhood and solidified in response to the demands of religious, educational, and economic institutions. In this sense, character was a defensive mechanism that blocked awareness of the actual repressive nature of modern society. This was particularly true, according to Reich, in relation to authoritarian regimes on both the left and right that prayed upon submissive, sexually repressed, and self-destructive individuals. The ego in this sense was not the basis for autonomy; it was merely the outcome of the internalization of behavioral norms and the cause of the current cultural malaise. The goal of Reichian therapy, therefore, was the loosening of man's character armoring or muscular rigidity, a process Reich referred to as vegetotherapy, which combined chiropractic techniques, breathing exercises, and yoga.

Similarly believing that man's character was a perversion of his true desires, romantic modernists were drawn to Reich's assault on the ego and followed him in defining any characterological manifestation as an "emotional plague" (508). Novelist Saul Bellow was one of many enthusiasts. Bellow was introduced to Reichian theory in the early 1950s through his colleague at New York University, Isaac Rosenfeld, whose own introduction to the writings of the Austrian psychoanalyst had come through his bohemian companions in Greenwich Village. After a visit in 1951 to the Orgone Energy Laboratory in Forest Hills, Queens, Bellow was recommended to an orthodox Reichian analyst, Dr. Chester Raphael, with whom Bellow underwent therapy for two years.[29] The author soon incorporated Reichian theory into his fiction as well, most famously in his 1956 novella *Seize the Day*.[30] The story details the life of Tommy Wilhelm, a middle-aged, financially unsuccessful Jewish man recently separated from his wife and children. Brooding upon his lifetime of countless mishaps, Wilhelm is little more than a damaged personality, representative of one of the many caricatures of white-collar workers dominating postwar American fiction. More important, he is also representative of the armored personality that Reich railed against. Wilhelm is described as a "large, odd, excited, fleshy blond, abrupt personality" (39) whose "entire chest" aches as though it was "tightly tied with ropes" (56). Named after the Austrian psychoanalyst, Wilhelm eventually begins to dispense with the trappings of his suffocating world, becoming unwilling to reconcile with "the great, great crowd, the inexhaustible current of millions of every race and kind pouring out, pressing round" (55). He is helped in this project by Dr. Tamkin, a disguised Reichian therapist, who teaches Wilhelm the difference between a life lived in harmony with one's natural impulses and one lived in the interests of "the social life" (70). Through his incessant prodding of Wilhelm's character armor, Tamkin releases the pent-up forces within his reluctant patient. The surrender of his character armoring at the sight of an unknown person's funeral leads to his final emotional release, as "the source of all tears had suddenly sprung open within him, black, deep, and hot, and they were pouring out and convulsed his body, bending his stubborn head, bowing his shoulders, twisting his face, crippling the very hands with which he held the handkerchief" (118).

Translations of Reichian theory more rebellious than Bellow's *Seize the Day* were soon incorporated into American fiction, including the work of Norman Mailer. Admitting that "if I were ever to look for an analyst I would be inclined to get me to a Reichian," Mailer used the analyst's work to rethink man's nature.[31] His 1964 novel *An American Dream*, for instance, details the pathetic life of Stephen Rojack, an ex-Army lieutenant and current professor of existential psychology, who is burdened by his artificial life. Rojack is an actor with multiple roles, a man of "separate parts" that do not cohere—"a college professor, television performer, marginal socialite, author."[32] He is also a dependent husband whose marriage represents "the armature of my ego" and whose impending divorce from his castrating wife Deborah is about to "topple" him "like clay."[33] As the novel opens, Rojack is suffering through a friend's cocktail party, artificially speaking in "a sort of boozed Connecticut gentry voice" that was "the product of living with Deborah's near-English lilts" (11). Suicidal, Rojack vomits off the balcony and hastily leaves the party "before my new disease takes another step" (14). Over time, Rojack is able to strip away his character armoring, descending into the second layer of his personality—that unconscious arena of repressed desires that have been, according to Reich, converted into sadism and violence and that ultimately lead Rojack to the vicious murder of his wife. As the "sensation of not belonging to myself" (176) dissipates and he emerges "no longer a person, a character, a man of habits" (55), Rojack descends even further into his unconscious self, past the lasciviousness that had produced his murderous rage and into the biological core of his being, a transformation precipitated by his newfound love for a nightclub singer. Through her tenderness, Rojack learns to come "up from my body rather than down from my mind" (128), the key theme in Reichian therapy. For Mailer and Bellow, the goal of any revolutionary project was the characterological release associated with the dismantling of man's ego.

Other romantic modernists, even without reference to Reich's theories, made similar claims about the artificiality of man's ego. In a 1963 *New York Times* essay, "Missing Persons," Harold Rosenberg detailed what he saw as the constructed character of modern man, that "psychically alienated citizen" who was "entirely present in the flesh" but, owing to the "jelly of unreality" in which he lived, had been "sequestered" by a binding "web of routines."[34] In several essays including "From Play Acting to Self" and "Character Change and Drama," Rosenberg noted the ways in which modern institutions artificially produced a normative character structure in man. For instance, the legal apparatus, according to Rosenberg, reduced the complexity of the life of the individual to a demarcated series of acts "done in particular instances" by visualizing him "as a kind of actor with a role whom the court has located in the situational system of the legal code."[35] Drawing an implicit connection between the language of the courtroom and the language of the stage, Rosenberg compared the judge to the dramatist, both of whom left aside the "personalities" of the characters they manipulated by "determining in advance that [the individual's] emotions, his thoughts, and his gestures should correspond with and earn in every respect the fate prepared for him" (139). Very few heroic personalities (Rosenberg pointed to Shakespeare's Hamlet and Dostoevsky's Father Zossima of *The Brothers Karamazov*) transcended the dramatic identity imposed upon them. Consequently, in contrast to representations of "the human individual as an actor," Rosenberg chose instead the "organic point of view"—the "biological or historical organism-concept" that depicted man as "an egg with an ancestry, developing, changing its form, maturing; later, degenerating, dying, decaying, again changing its form" (135). The biological, in this sense, was antithetical to character.

Orgone Energy and the Fate of the Self

Rosenberg's reference to the biological reflected the need for romantic modernists to find an ontological foundation for subjectivity uncontaminated by modern culture. Once again, Wilhelm Reich pointed the way. If character was nothing but an artifice, the goal of therapeutic treatment, according to Reich, was the unregulated flow of the libidinal energy. Described as a "crazy Bergsonian," Reich radically reinterpreted the French philosopher's notion of an *élan vital* as a tangible entity.[36] Dispensing with any mechanistic understanding of the body, Reich depicted the libido as a physiological force, not simply as an abstraction signifying sexual instincts as Freud's successors had done. Reich always remained biologically oriented in the face of orthodox attempts to psychologize the physiological. Comparing the libido to an electrical current, Reich conducted a series of experiments in the 1930s that resulted in his discovery of a primordial cosmic energy that supposedly constituted the essence of all living things—the orgone. This energy was the tangible source of the libido and the power behind all creation. According to Reich, "orgone energy is demonstrable visually, thermically, and electroscopically, in the soil, in the atmosphere, and in plant and animal organisms."[37] Orgone energy was blue or blue-gray in color, ubiquitous and harmonic, present in organic beings, in the sky, and in celestial systems. In his 1948 work *The Cancer Biopathy*, Reich introduced his experiments with an orgone accumulator, a large metal box lined with wool or wood, big enough for a person to enter, into which orgone energy was dispersed. This energy was designed to restore an individual's "biopsychic motility" by dissolving muscular rigidity.[38]

Many romantic modernists followed Reich in portraying man as a bioelectric substance that needed to accumulate more energy to survive. In his bravado-filled 1957 *Dissent* article "The White Negro," in which he announced the birth of the hipster, Norman Mailer translated existentialism into a self-described American vernacular in order to "set out on that uncharted journey into the rebellious imperatives of the self."[39] Declaring Reich one of his intellectual guides, Mailer marked the hipster as a response to "overcivilized man," a philosophical psychopath who had dismantled the "character" of his own "frustrations" (341). The goal of the hipster was the spontaneous release of man's primordial "energy," an image of man not as "a static character" but as a "network of forces" (349). According to Mailer, the hipster had insight into the psychological "defeats" that "attack the body and imprison one's energy until one is jailed in the prison air of other people's habits, other people's defeats, boredom, quiet desperation, and muted icy self-destroying rage" (339). In language borrowed from Reich, Mailer argued that the cultural imperative was to create a new nervous system, one that overthrew the "dead weight of the institutions of the past" that had imprisoned the individual's "reflexes and rhythms." He even constructed his own version of the orgone accumulator in his New York apartment, a large, carpet-lined box that he used to engage in a form of primal screaming designed to release his character armor.[40]

But the most avid enthusiasts of Reich were the members of the Beat Generation, that cadre of romantic modernists dedicated to upturning man's cauldron of libidinal impulses. Allen Ginsberg had the most direct contact with Reich, writing to the analyst in his Queens office in 1948 concerning treatment for the poet's burgeoning homosexual impulses.[41] The analyst's assistant recommended an orthodox Reichian, Dr. Allan Cott, who eventually treated Ginsberg in his Newark office for a few years on a twice-weekly basis. Likewise, Jack Kerouac took to the psychoanalyst's work in the late 1940s at the prodding of William Burroughs, an event Kerouac detailed in *On the Road* when Old Bull Lee suggests to Sal Paradise to step into his orgone accumulator to "put some juice in your bones."[42] Indeed, William Burroughs praised Reich as "the only man in the analysis line who is on that beam," and with the help of his friend Kells Elvin constructed an eight-foot-high orgone accumulator, a device Burroughs continuously revisited throughout his life in his battle against drug addiction.[43] Burroughs also incorporated Reich's theories into his fiction. In his first novel, *Junky*, in which he mapped the underground world of drugs and addiction, Burroughs offered an emotional account of the "suffering of the nervous system, of flesh and viscera, and cells" of "narcotics addicts."[44] In a chapter originally removed when the book was first published in 1953, Burroughs, through his reading of Reich's *The Cancer Biopathy*, equated junk with the negation of life—the disruption of the flow of orgone energy by the artificial excitations produced by addiction. Junk was a "cellular equation" of "life measured out in eyedroppers of morphine solution," a world of addiction in which "orgones, life force—that we all have to score for all the time" were withdrawn and "death and rot" flooded in (88). Orgone theory was also a part of Burroughs's revolutionary project. In *Nova Express*, Burroughs translated his notion of junk infecting orgone energy into a mythological narrative of a planetary invasion by an alien mob. The ultimate goal of the Nova Mob, led by the double entity called Mr. Bradly Mr. Martin, is the absorption of mankind's orgone energy. Resistance occurs through a rigorous training program, which Burroughs details in the chapter "Smorbrot," where cadet K9 withdraws from the biological and psychological addiction of Nova control through his immersion in the "blue light" of an orgone accumulator.[45] This notion of death infecting orgone energy was not, according to Burroughs, limited to science fiction. In fact, the notion of totalitarianism as a form of cancer expressed by both Burroughs and Mailer was derived from their reading of Reich's *The Cancer Biopathy* in which he detailed how character armoring produced cancerous mutations in healthy human cells.

From the Biological to the Dramaturgical

Reich was not the only thinker to ground an ontological principle of freedom within the biological, and the Freudian language distilled by the Austrian psychoanalyst also found defenders in high modernist circles as well. In his 1955 work *Freud and the Crisis of Our Culture*, Lionel Trilling returned to Freud, in a manner similar to Reich, to assert that there was a part of the human self that remained impervious to the imperatives of culture. According to Trilling, "Freud's emphasis on biology" helped to demonstrate that "there is a hard, irreducible stubborn core of biological urgency, and biological necessity, and biological reason, which culture cannot reach and which reserves the right, which sooner or later it will exercise, to judge the culture and resist and revise it."[46] Trilling's comments, especially after he chastised "literary intellectuals" who only "gossiped" about Reich but refused to produce "a considered critical examination of what he says" (289), sounded remarkably like the speculations of the Austrian psychoanalyst. Other high modernists followed suit, including Dwight Macdonald, who visited Isaac Rosenfeld's apartment on Hester Street to experiment with his accumulator.[47] Although never a devotee, Macdonald's attempt in *The Root Is Man* to find a metabiological principle upon which to ground his defense of man's "vital core" paralleled Reich's own conclusions. Of course American intellectuals did not have to search through the mystical writings of Wilhelm Reich for a secure definition of selfhood. In a 1956 essay, "The Instinct of Rebellion," psychoanalyst Robert Lindner reaffirmed the importance of the physiological to the psychological. Lindner challenged those "Freudian revisionists" such as David Riesman who showed "contempt for biology" and who committed the "Marxian error" of relating "psychic phenomena" to "the relations, productive or otherwise, of men."[48] Arguing for a radical redefinition of the concept, Lindner defended man's instincts as an "indispensable principle of psychology" and linked such instincts to rebellion as "a fundamental attribute of mankind" (123).

But even before postwar modernists began exploring man's biological frame, Kenneth Burke had searched for the same type of ontological security many would soon find in the writings of Wilhelm Reich. In *Permanence and Change: An Anatomy of Purpose* (1935), one of the transitional books in his canon marking a momentary point of rest between the high modernism of *Counter-Statement* and the dramaturgical leanings of *A Grammar of Motives*, Burke confronted the "Babel of orientations" emanating from newspapers, lecture halls, religious sermons, and congressional addresses, orientations that were desperately trying to explain the apparent collapse of the capitalist order. Worried that the "cataclysmic shifts in the organization of the nation under war, prosperous peace, and depression" had dislodged any shared orientation, Burke sought a way to avoid the "individualization" of patterns of response that were leading to chaos.[49] In the midst of such change, Burke hoped to uncover permanence in the findings of biologists and neurologists.

Underneath the vagaries of historical circumstance, argued Burke, rested a consistency to man's actions; as he explained, "the fact that man's neurological structure has remained pretty much of a constant through all the shifts of his environment would justify us in looking for permanence beneath the differences" (159). In doing so, he located the question of eloquence (so pivotal in his first book) not simply in the psychological but in the biological. Beyond present incapacities were one course of human satisfaction and one form of biological motivation continuously reemerging from any given historical texture—the norms of communication and cooperation. Metaphysics, defined as the investigation into the nature of the universe, was replaced by metabiology, defined as the search for the organic imperatives motivating human life. In this sense, "each biological organism has 'purposes' intrinsic to its nature (a specific nature which aims at some kinds of 'good' rather than others)" (168). Burke viewed man not as a machine but as an organism endowed with the capacity to overcome "a world of contingencies" in the name of biological communion. While such claims were notably muted and quite vague, *Permanence and Change* was marked by Burke's desire to overcome this collective insecurity through reference to a beleaguered ontology.

But Burke's strength as a critic was his willingness to interrogate continuously the assumptions embedded in his work, and by the time he had published *A Grammar of Motives*, he had backed away from such essentialism. Like David Riesman, who worried that investigations into the intrinsic character of man might myopically neglect what was extrinsic, Burke moved from vague notions of metabiology to studies of social interaction, an intellectual shift characteristic of many late modernists. In his 1954 prologue to the second edition of *Permanence and Change*, Burke criticized his "somewhat Gauguinesque" tendency to ignore "social motives as such" and noted that "human kinds of domination and subjection must decidedly never be reduced to the strictly 'natural' or 'biological'" (li). Consequently, he engaged upon his famous *Motivorum* project—a planned, three-volume investigation into "what is involved, when we say what people are doing and why they are doing it."[50] Beginning with *A Grammar of Motives*, Burke argued that any search for some essence to man's character buried underneath historical debris was a flawed venture. Positing some metaphysical force as the wellspring of human action was, according to Burke, a gross simplification of man's potential. For Burke, such attempts to get at the substance of a thing in this fashion fell into an intractable paradox. Although the word substance was used "to designate what some thing or agent intrinsically *is*," etymologically the word defined "something that stands beneath or supports the person or thing" (22). Continuing with the pun, Burke argued that any definition claiming to define man's substance ironically did nothing but reveal what man was *not*. As he explained, "though used to designate something *within* the thing, *intrinsic* to it, the word etymologically refers to something *outside* the thing, *extrinsic* to it" (23). For instance, in their desire to valorize the inherent dignity of man outside of imposed character structures, romantic modernists ended up dissolving man into the natural world. Orgone energy as the substance of man told something about nature but nothing about man himself.

In response, Burke took the opposite approach and searched for a heuristic tool to make sense of the endless ambiguity of human action. Accepting the "*inevitable paradox of definition*," Burke chose instead to locate the individual within the panoply of "generating principles" in order to understand the constraining context in which the individual operated. Correcting his argument from *Permanence and Change*, Burke argued that the "search for the intrinsic" in terms of "'instincts,' 'drives,' [and] 'urges'" as "motivational springs" needed to be balanced with a "dialectical counterpart" in order "to see beyond these peculiarly 'intrinsic' motives to 'extrinsic' or 'scenic' motives" (49). Instead of such gross essentializing, Burke offered a dramaturgical approach that was committed to proportionalizing. Claiming that there were a multitude of ways of accounting for individual motivations, Burke argued that "human relations should be analyzed with respect to the leads discovered by a study of drama."[51] For Burke, the self was less an expression of some private, inner substance and more an effect of the interweaving of a multitude of identifications, the product of an elaborate drama in which the individual was assigned a part to play. "People are neither animals nor machines (to be analyzed by the migration of metaphors from biology or mechanics), but actors and acters," all of whom "establish identity by relation to groups" (311). To understand the field in which the subject emerged, Burke offered his famous "pentad" of terms (act, scene, agent, agency, and purpose) with which to understand human motivation. For Burke, *act* referenced the event that took place; *scene* referred to the situation in which the act occurred; *agent* was the person who performed the act; *agency* named the means or instruments utilized; and *purpose* explained the motivation behind the act. Too many philosophical schools of thought clung to one term within the pentad, reducing the diversity of human life to one component. Marxism, for instance, stressed the agent as the motivating force, reducing human action to the interplay of class forces. Darwinism, conversely, focused only on the scenic background in which the struggle for survival took place. Too many philosophies were trapped within a particular scheme and were unable to address the complexities of man, his motivations, his actions, and his purposes. Any reference, for instance, to a particular actor or agent had to acknowledge the scene in which the actor was located, the agency or means at his disposal, the particular act he was undertaking, and his overall purpose or motive. One term always had to be counterbalanced by another; dramatism in this sense had to replace metaphysics. In turning to this new language, Burke offered a new analytic tool for those modernists who followed him.

Erving Goffman and the Performative Self

An early translator of Burke's work was the sociologist Erving Goffman, whose idiosyncratic analysis of social interaction borrowed heavily from the conceptual apparatus of *A Grammar of Motives*. Like most writers who came of scholarly age in the 1950s, Goffman was preoccupied with the fate of the self in the midst of an increasingly militarized Cold War landscape and spent considerable energy criticizing the institutional control of everyday life in America. Like William Burroughs, Goffman filled his works with sympathetic portrayals of prison inmates and stigmatized individuals. For instance, in *Asylums*, his 1961 field study of the lives of mental patients at St. Elizabeths Hospital in Washington, D.C., Goffman investigated the nature of "total institutions," those highly administered places of "residence and work" where "like-situated individuals" were subjected to an "enclosed, formally administered round of life."[52] Exemplified by prisons, psychiatric hospitals, military barracks, and boarding schools, the total institution was the most insidious example of the ubiquitous modern organizational structures that were disciplining mankind. By stripping the individual of any privacy and by instilling an institutional identity controlled by staff members, total institutions had led to "the gradual establishment of the body as a serviceable possession" (340). Such an institutional identity was centered on a documented case history, which was filled with discrediting information culled from interviews with authorities, family members, and the patient himself and which was designed "to show the ways in which the patient is 'sick' and the reasons why it was right to commit him and is right currently to keep him committed" (155). Although *Asylums* bore a similarity to William Burroughs's *Naked Lunch*, Goffman's book also focused on the multitude of ways that institutionalized individuals escaped the "official selves" forced upon them, not by stepping into orgone accumulators but by forging a new sense of self-identity from the fragments of their lives. Goffman, much like Kenneth Burke, criticized the high modernist obsession with mental health while simultaneously refusing to engage in the more metaphysical speculations about orgone energy offered by romantic modernists.

In many ways, Goffman's intellectual career paralleled Burke's own—both scholars working at the margins of their respective disciplines due to the eclectic nature of their scholarship and to their perspicacious writing styles. In fact, Burke taught a seminar at the University of Chicago in 1947 and, according to one account, Goffman was the only participant who understood his sense of humor.[53] But unlike Burke, Goffman had a more traditional intellectual upbringing. A Canadian-born graduate of the sociology department at the University of Chicago, Goffman achieved early academic success with the 1959 publication of *The Presentation of Self in Everyday Life*, his dramaturgically inspired study of social interaction based upon his eighteen-month observation of community life on the Shetland Isles off the coast of Scotland.[54] Prior to his tenured position at the University of California, Goffman also served as a visiting scientist for the Laboratory of Socio-Environmental Studies at the National Institute of Mental Health in Bethesda, Maryland. His three-year position was combined with a year of fieldwork at St. Elizabeths Hospital, an experience that shaped his portrayal of institutional life in *Asylums* (1961) and *Stigma* (1963). His work—an odd combination of Durkheimian concepts and pragmatist idioms—placed him at a distance from traditional sociology. Equally unique was Goffman's research methodology, which included studies of island communities, mental hospitals, department stores, and sporting events through his personal immersion into these worlds. Similarly, Goffman included in his work many discussions of prostitutes, drug addicts, physically deformed people, and racial minorities, offering a glimpse into the other side of American life that had been fictionalized by Beat writers but not yet examined by the sociological profession.

More important, Goffman formulated a new vocabulary to address the exigencies of modern life without recourse to what he saw as outdated doctrine. Consequently, Goffman helped to lead what Clifford Geertz has referred to as "the reconfiguration of social thought" in the 1950s through the introduction of literary analogies to the social sciences, a "constructional, genuinely dramaturgical" language that crossed disciplinary boundaries.[55] In this sense, Goffman was one of the first theorists to grapple with the defining characteristics of the postmodern condition—performativity, artifice, and role-playing. In fact, Goffman referred to his early books as investigations into "our general dramaturgical rules and inclinations for conducting action."[56] If the individual worker was no longer defined by his relation to the mode of production but instead to the role he played within an organization, then a dramaturgical language was much more appropriate for understanding modern life. He even described *The Presentation of Self in Everyday Life* as a "sort of handbook" for the type of "social life that is organized within the physical confines of a building or plant."[57] Goffman's use of terms such as *performance team*, *front* and *back regions*, and *role segregation* represented the influx of service terms into everyday discourse, and his book found a place on the shelf next to the works of Vance Packard, David Riesman, William Whyte, Daniel Bell, and C. Wright Mills as an early study of postindustrialism. But for all his criticisms of middle-class propriety, Goffman never engaged in the polemical attacks on the "organization man" that most critics did. For him, the key problem was survival and this was a practical concern. In many ways, then, Goffman was an inheritor of past sociological traditions and a precursor to later postmodern ones.

Beginning with *The Presentation of Self in Everyday Life*, Goffman confronted the long-standing Hobbesian problem of maintaining social order. In a world of crowds, the possibilities for disorder were ubiquitous, and Goffman spent considerable time analyzing the norms of social interaction that came into effect whenever someone entered into the presence of others. For Goffman, rules of propriety governed most action—the officious language used in businesses, the etiquette customs practiced in restaurants, and the verbal cues offered during telephone conversations. In a number of books including *Encounters* (1961), *Behavior in Public Places* (1963), and *Interaction Ritual* (1967), Goffman offered a taxonomy of rules of deportment that governed those well-orchestrated moments of social interaction, moments that shared much in common, at least in terms of their staging, with theatrical productions. Accordingly, Goffman argued that the self was best construed as a *character*, similar to those inhabiting novels and plays, and he described social interaction through the metaphor of a staged drama. Following "the language of Kenneth Burke," Goffman claimed that "doing is being," and he translated Burke's pentad of terms into theatrical imagery.[58] In *The Presentation of Self in Everyday Life*, Goffman argued that all social encounters—from public displays such as political conventions and sporting events to smaller affairs such as classroom activities to intimate engagements between individuals meeting on city streets—were comparable, at least in terms of dynamic structure, to staged theatrical productions. The Burkean *purpose* of any face-to-face interaction was the successful resolution of such encounters through an agreement by participants to maintain "the definition of the situation" that they collectively acknowledged.[59] Consequently, the *act* that took place under such encounters was similar to a "performance" in which the individual *actor*, using a variety of verbal and visual techniques, enacted a particular role and participated in a particular scene. In this sense, social interaction, according to Goffman, was a desperate attempt by the individual to "guide and control" impressions formed of him and to "control the conduct of others, especially in their responsive treatment of him" (3). Such interaction was also predicated upon a defined *scene* or region in which the performance took place. But since such "collective representations" were very fragile, subject to fraud, and dependent upon the proper setting and manner of the participants, a collection of devices or *agencies* including props, performance signs, informal cues, and other "staging devices" were utilized for "creating a scene" (210). Unlike actual theatrical productions, however, everyday performances did not have directors, and social actors were given meager directions for the roles to be played. But given the "dramaturgical loyalty" to commit to a collective situation, most performances maintained a modicum of success.

For Goffman, then, the self was constituted within this dramatic economy of interaction—responding to the actions and demands of others within a particular scene and operating against a backdrop of customs that guided etiquette. In other words, the performance led to the self-constitution of the subject, not vice versa. As Goffman explained, the self "is a product of a scene that comes off, and is not a cause of it" (252). Through his rewriting of Burke's dramaturgy, Goffman brushed aside all metaphysical speculations that viewed the self as a posited entity and instead descended into concrete, everyday experience to watch the subject struggle to emerge. Appeals to a changeless, biological core were not merely disingenuous speculations but avoidances of the deeper problem of self-identity. The self, according to Goffman, emerged; it was not found. He argued that "when the individual withdraws from a situated self he does not draw into some psychological world that he creates himself but rather acts in the name of some other socially created identity."[60] But misreadings of Goffman's books abounded, particularly among romantic modernists such as Saul Bellow, who appropriated the sociologist's work for their own critical perspective. Echoing Goffman's language, Bellow argued that "most men in their self-presentation to the world settle upon a few simple attributes and create a surface easy to characterize and to understand." This "presentation" of the self was supposedly in direct contrast to "their real, complex existence" hidden elsewhere.[61] In actuality, Goffman had little patience for such "individualistic modes of thought" that dwelled upon notions of "characterological weaknesses" supposedly generated "within the deep recesses of the individual personality."[62] In direct contrast, Goffman argued that "it might be better to start from outside the individual and work inward than to start inside the individual and work out." Thus, Goffman did not ask *what* the self was but *who* the self was. For him, the self was not simply "an organic thing" situated in a "specific location" but a "dramatic effect arising diffusely from a scene that is presented" (253). In other words, Goffman did not search for a subject that was simply identical with itself but a subject that emerged from the vicissitudes of everyday life. But since there were a multitude of social settings in everyday life, the individual was allowed "to imagine or play out simultaneously other kinds of performances attesting to other realities" (207). Stages were plural, roles were multiple, and opportunities were ever present.

Consequently, Goffman's late modernist voice was much weaker than the bravado of the hipster or the Reichian self. Such a voice had to be responsive to the performances and evaluations of others. In a 1956 article, "Embarrassment and Social Organization," Goffman noted the emotional demands that interaction placed upon the individual.[63] For Goffman, the performative self cried, became flushed with embarrassment, laughed at personal failings, and became mentally ill; in other words, the self was all too human. In contrast to many misreadings, Goffman never innocently believed in ironic detachment or mere playfulness.[64] Self-identity was an existential struggle, and he had little patience for hollowed-out impression manipulators. In fact, Goffman expressed scorn for the disingenuous attempts by "New York hipsters" at "'making' a situation," that is, for exploiting "matters by intentionally tampering with the frame, introducing at their expense references and acts which are difficult to manage."[65] Goffman cited as an example of such dishonesty the work of Chandler Brossard, in particular his novel *Who Walk in Darkness?* which Norman Mailer noted as the foundational text in the birth of the hipster. True to his Durkheimian background, Goffman argued that ceremonial rules still had relevance in a postindustrial order in which interaction was diverse, plural, and brief. In any situation in which an individual made "an implicit or explicit claim to be a person of a particular kind," that individual made a "moral demand" upon others to honor his own "definitional" claim.[66] In two early essays, "The Nature of Deference and Demeanor" and "Alienation from Interaction," Goffman noted the importance for social interaction of "avoidance rituals" in which the individual kept "at a distance" from others to not violate the "ideal sphere" around each person, and "presentational rituals," in which the individual acknowledged the sanctity of others.[67] Thus, the interaction order was a fundamentally moral one despite the bumps and bruises incurred along the way.

But realizing that harmony could easily dissolve into discord, Goffman always treated the self with a certain amount of admitted sacredness, and the sometimes tragic tone of his writing bristled with resentment over the institutional domination of the individual. In particular, his experience working at the National Institute for Mental Health made him seriously question claims about proper mental health bandied about by psychiatrists and family therapists. Goffman argued that "the enlightened psychiatric approach" moralistically defined any "situational impropriety," whether political or sexual, as "psychotic behavior," and he realized that notions about proper ego autonomy were often forms of social control.[68] "If the psychiatric faction is to impress upon [the patient] its views about his personal make-up," explained Goffman, "then they must be able to show in detail how their version of his past and their version of his character hold up much better than his own."[69] If anything, such institutional control led to the mortification of the individual self. Goffman referred to "personal identity" as the documented record of an individual's "biographical life line," those representative markers stored "in the personnel files of an organization" that anchored an individual "as an object for biography."[70] Goffman recognized that informational records such as fingerprints, social security numbers, photographs, registration cards, and drivers' licenses created a record of individual actions. Serving as an "identity peg," these records created "a single continuous record of social facts" to which "other biographical facts" might be attached (56–57). In some sense, the story of an individual's life was already narrated from a third-person perspective. In fact, an individual's personal identity "can arise even before he is born and continue after he has been buried, existing, then, at times when the individual himself can have no feelings at all, let alone feelings of identity" (106). In *Asylums*, Goffman noted the difficulty patients had in maintaining any form of self-identity while leading "an enclosed, formally administered round of life."[71] The "moral career of the mental patient" began when institutional authorities stripped the inmate of his everyday routines and physical props that supported his identity outside the facility and substituted an institutionally sanctioned one constructed around a "case history" of inappropriate behaviors. This case history, then, served as an officially sanctioned identity for the patient, one that he neither constructed himself nor continued to narrate. The patient soon came to learn that the self was "not a fortress" but "a small open city" that could easily be occupied "by the enemy" (165). Thus, the subject could not escape the normative demands placed upon it because, for Goffman, there were no flights of fancy.

In this way, the self was first and foremost, despite what Reich argued, a character—whether one in a familial drama, a neighborhood performance, or an organizational setting. But because the "segregative tendencies as regards role are strong," coherence was at times unmanageable.[72] Other times the "enemy" was just too strong. But subjectivity, for Goffman, was not so easily brushed aside. The individual's personal and social identities were mediated by an "'ego' or 'felt' identity," what he referred to as the desperate attempt to maintain "continuity and character" in the face of "various social experiences" and various social roles.[73] Such "self identity" was achieved only by tying together the various portraits and profiles the individual inhabited. Like David Riesman, Goffman struggled to find a vocabulary with which to assert simultaneously the social nature of the self as well as its autonomy. Goffman realized social theory could not dispense with a notion of the subject. Self-identity or self-constitution was an imperative. For Goffman, the individual was "a kind of holding company for a set of not relevantly connected roles," and the key problem was developing a perspective "to find out how the individual runs this holding company."[74] Thus he argued that an individual's autobiography was separate from his institutional biography, although both partook of the same materials. As Goffman put it, "the individual constructs his image of himself out of the same materials from which others first construct a social and personal identification of him, but he exercises important liberties in regard to what he fashions."[75] The self, then, was an achievement—a desperate attempt to maintain self-identity across a multiplicity of roles, institutional settings, and social positions.

Like Riesman, Goffman argued that the drama of everyday life was constituted from the individual's mimetic involvement with others and from a pregiven context with established rules and requirements. The individual, in this sense, was thrown into a world of language, traditions, and laws not of his own making. By definition, the self was other-directed. But this temporalization and spatialization of the self was not, according to Goffman, a threat to self-identity; it was its precondition. As he explained, it was only "against something that the self can emerge."[76] Like Riesman, Goffman argued that autonomy was achieved neither by dismantling the strictures of the ego (as the Reichians would have it) nor by fixating on the vigilant defense of the ego against dangerous influences (as high modernists argued) but by integrating roles, attachments, and relationships into a differentiated and ever fluid whole. A developing sense of inwardness, in other words, was a synthetic process arising from a panoply of identificatory ties and performance roles. "Individuals," said Goffman, "are almost always free to modulate what they are required to do, being free, thus, to give way to the wider constraints of their multiple self-identifications."[77] Thus, the individual was a composite of "various identificatory demands" assigned to him, a "juggler and synthesizer" who made the disparate moments in his life continuous (139). Goffman knew that identity was neither a static entity nor a timeless substance but something that flowed in and through time. For him, it was impossible to specify the self independently of any mimetic involvement with others—those communities into which the subject was born, given a role to play, and taught proper forms of response. The key question was how each individual performer made his own what had been offered to him. In this sense, the optimism buried within Goffman's coy prose was quite similar to other critics like Burke and Riesman who shared his perspective—the continuing belief that even without the metaphysical support so sought after by William Burroughs and Norman Mailer the psychical birth of the individual was still possible. According to this dramaturgical perspective, the self was nothing more and nothing less than the emplotment of an individual history through a series of institutional, social, and personal actions, a portrait "pieced together from the expressive implications of the full flow of events in an undertaking."[78]

C. Wright Mills and the Writing of the Self

Goffman, however, was not the only postwar critic to translate Burke's dramaturgical perspective into a unique sociological vision. C. Wright Mills, the persistent gadfly in the sociology department at Columbia University until his untimely death in 1962, appropriated Burke's work on dramaturgy and linked it to a radical critique of American society at the onset of the Cold War. Like Erving Goffman, Mills was unclassifiable as an academic, rejecting the frameworks of positivism, Parsonian structuralism, and statistical analysis that marked American sociology. Instead, Mills borrowed from a wide range of thinkers—George Herbert Mead, Max Weber, Sigmund Freud, and Kenneth Burke—to fashion a perspective that investigated the intricate relationship between individual actors and the institutional realms in which they operated and that examined the various levels of personal resistance or resignation endemic to any system of power relations. In such classic works as *The Power Elite* (1956) and *The Causes of World War Three* (1958), Mills emerged as somewhat of a radical iconoclast untouched by the ideological battles in left-wing circles in the 1930s over international Communism, who made only one brief effort to court the working class in *The New Men of Power* (1948), and as a relentless critic of American military expansion who took to task his colleagues for their inability to stake out an alternative to Cold War liberalism. But Mills was much more than a maverick public intellectual. Despite the jargon of his admirers and despite some of his own boasting, Mills was deeply committed to refashioning American social sciences and offered a complex understanding of human agency similar to that offered by Riesman, Goffman, and others. While he has always been labeled a "lone-wolf writer," Mills was in fact an eclectic, almost burlesque, thinker who struggled with his own sense of identity.[79] Among other things that have escaped his supporters, Mills was fascinated by American films, wanted to ditch sociology and write poetry, began a travelogue for *Esquire* magazine about his 1956 adventures in Europe, wrote a "play-novel-movie-script" called "Unmailed Letters to a Fey Tiger," and was a respectful sympathizer with the Quaker Fellowship of Reconciliation.[80]

Never simply a pamphleteer, Mills remained faithful to the intellectual background he garnered while an undergraduate at the University of Texas and a sociology graduate student at the University of Wisconsin. Steeped in the sociology of Karl Mannheim and the pragmatism of John Dewey, Mills very quickly plunged into an investigation of the social nature of man's character.[81] Although he eagerly read the work of Theodor Adorno and Max Horkheimer, Mills retained enough of the social-psychological perspective of American pragmatism to resist what he saw as their rigid understanding of man's psychic character. For instance, in a 1945 memorandum to an editor at Oxford University Press concerning Max Horkheimer's then-titled *Twilight of Reason*, Mills defended the tradition of American pragmatism from what he saw as Horkheimer's depiction of its "nominalist" character: "*But* frankly, I don't see any evidence that Horkheimer has really gotten hold of pragmatism except (1) in a rather vulgar form and (2) in the later pronouncements of the *Partisan Review* writers whom he belatedly attacks."[82] In this sense, Mills shared with Erving Goffman a frustration with theories of ego autonomy bandied about by high modernists. In a 1943 study of dozens of textbooks on the problem of social pathology, Mills bristled over such conservative assumptions. In language later echoed by Goffman in *Asylums*, Mills argued that "the concept [of the maladjusted], as well as that of the 'normal,' is usually left empty of concrete, social content; or its content, is in effect, a propaganda for conformity to those norms and traits ideally associated with small-town, middle-class *milieux*."[83] Mills had little use for the studies of political deviance that would reach a climax with *The Authoritarian Personality*. But he also had little patience for what he saw as the naïve perspective of romantic modernists who latched onto the work of Wilhelm Reich. Instead, Mills began to sketch out a much more complicated understanding of man's character in a work he coauthored with his former teacher Hans Gerth. Unfortunately, *Character and Social Structure* has received only cursory treatment from intellectual historians interested in Mills's work. The references to motivation, role-playing, and character in *The Sociological Imagination* were, according to Mills, only the "barest" summaries of his more "detailed discussion" in *Character and Social Structure.*[84] This wide-ranging book was a fusion of sociology and psychology, of Max Weber, George Herbert Mead, and Sigmund Freud, a fusion that Mills tried to maintain, sometimes unsuccessfully, throughout all of his writings.

Character and Social Structure was an effort to rethink the nature of personality formation in ways that echoed the perspective offered by Kenneth Burke. Like him, Mills refused to take comfort in metaphysical speculations about human identity. He rejected the litany of failed attempts by psychologists to pinpoint some universal constant or some immutable biological element that would overcome the relativity of human nature. As he explained in *The Sociological Imagination*, "the human variety is such that no 'elemental' psychologies, no theory of 'instincts,' no principles of 'basic human nature' of which we know, enables us to account for the enormous human variety of types of individuals" (164). In this light, Wilhelm Reich offered a limited view of man's potentials. The biological was merely a constraint upon action, not a determinant of it. Reich was an example of modern writers who attempted "to show that the ethical choice he would impose upon his patients and readers had biological roots in the patient" and therefore "can pretend to himself and to his public that he is simply releasing the patient to live out his true self."[85] In response, Mills stressed the need to "drop this metaphysical accent on the biological" and to begin tackling the complicated problem of "why and how human conduct takes a specific direction."[86] Intentionality was in part explainable by reference to unsocialized drives but was not understandable without knowledge of how meaning was imparted onto actions. For Mills, the key problem was determining how feelings became emotions, sensations became perceptions, and impulses became purposes. Nothing implicit within the individual's psychic structure explained how a particular impulse was translated into a socially directed purpose. Thus Mills chose to view human action in interpersonal terms, as action that was "informed by awareness of other actors and directly oriented to their expectations and to anticipations of their behavior" (10). Like Erving Goffman, Mills appropriated the notion of role-playing, one of the "metaphors of poets and philosophers," to describe human conduct.

In this sense, Mills was interested in the *whole* of man, not merely his biological traits or his physiological structure. Whereas Reich and his followers tried to get beyond man's character armoring, Mills began and ended his discussion of man with this notion. Mills had little use for subject-centered philosophies that paid little attention to man's social backdrop. The "cult of alienation" that pervaded most American criticism was, according to Mills, "a lament and a form of collapse into self-indulgence."[87] Man's character structure, argued Mills, was not an artificial construct to be removed by immersion in an orgone accumulator but was in fact the essence of man's being. Such a character structure was a complicated integration of man's individual psychic structure with the pattern of desires and expectations instilled by his personal upbringing and the various social roles he inhabited over his lifetime. As Mills explained, "man as a *person* (from the Latin *persona*, meaning 'mask') is composed of the specific roles which he enacts and of the effects of enacting those roles upon his self."[88] Of course, the individual played myriad and often contradictory roles stemming from separate familial, economic, and political orders. "One person may play many different roles," noted Mills, "and each of these roles may be a segment of the different institutions and interpersonal situations in which the person moves" (12). Such divergent roles had profoundly different effects upon man's character structure. According to Mills, "the meanings which the person incorporates from his expected roles are thus linked to his gestures, produce changes in his body, and influence the feelings of which he is aware" (63). Such meanings were influenced by the presence of others with whom the individual interacted and to whom he reported. Man's self-image, as Mills explained, "develops and changes as the person, through his social experiences, becomes aware of the expectations and appraisals of others" (84). Borrowing a concept from George Herbert Mead, Mills argued that the image of the self built by the individual was directly related to those "significant others" with whom he interacted—those compatriots who acted as a reflective mirror with which the individual evaluated himself. "The attitudes of significant others toward the person," explained Mills, "leave their mark upon his self-image; they form a residue from social experience which he may re-experience and use in evaluating his own self-image" (95). In this way, the self was permeated by the presence of others—an unstable balance constructed through the integration of various social roles and normative expectations.

Consequently, self-consciousness was possible, according to Mills, only by becoming critically aware of the narratives—familial, institutional, political, and economic—in which the individual was embedded. Identity was composed of an uncomfortable mixture of stories inherited from family members, historical traditions, mass culture, literature and poetry, and religious institutions. Every spoken word had a history loaded with ideological assumptions. However, the problem, as Burke had already pointed out and as Mills was quick to reiterate, was that the traditional vocabularies that had long guided action in the United States had become obsolete. According to Burke, "our vast reversals from year to year in economic status, our cataclysmic shifts in organization of the nation under war . . . all such factors make for the *individualization* of one's typical, or recurrent, patterns of stimuli, as against their highly *socialized* or *universalized* character during a period of relative stability."[89] Mills recognized that this disorientation of which Burke spoke was even more widespread, albeit in a different way, in the "postmodern" world of the 1950s. According to Mills, "the uneasiness, the malaise of our time, is due to this root fact: in our politics and economy, in family life and religion—in practically every sphere of our existence—the certainties of the eighteenth and nineteenth centuries have disintegrated or been destroyed and, at the same time, no new sanctions or justifications for the new routines we live, and must live, have taken hold."[90] This was precisely his concern in *White Collar*, his 1951 study of the rise of the new professional middle class. The shift from goods to services, from production to distribution, and from craftsmanship to salesmanship that characterized postindustrialism troubled Mills because he recognized that the speed with which this shift took place had made obsolete traditional motives guiding work and success. While the blue-collar worker morphed into the white-collar bureaucrat, most in America, including Dwight Macdonald and Theodor Adorno, continued to mouth the language of rugged individualism that had legitimized small-market relations. Such an ideology, which presented "The American as a single type of ingenious farmer-artisan," had little resonance in a world of office workers and sales personnel (xiv).

Consequently, Mills famously described white-collar workers as "rear-guarders" not because he felt they were inherently reactionary but because they were offered no alternatives. As he argued in *The Sociological Imagination*, individuals "want orienting values too, and suitable ways of feeling and styles of emotion" but "do not readily find these in the literature today."[91] In this sense, Mills wrote *White Collar* less as an attempt to satirize the new professional classes and more as an attempt to communicate with them, characterizing the work as "everybody's book . . . for in truth, who is not a little man?"[92] But most readers missed the point. Dwight Macdonald, for instance, lashed out at Mills in the January 1952 issue of *Partisan Review*. For Macdonald, "the chief trouble with the book, certainly what makes it hard to read, is the style which is inexpressive and monotonous in a vigorous kind of way."[93] Mills was deeply hurt by the review, and he searched for advice from other colleagues. In a letter to David Riesman, Mills lamented that "nobody, except a few friends, seem to get hold of what I really intended to do with this book."[94] Consequently, *White Collar* was a failure in several ways—the book sold poorly, was overargued, and failed to address racial and ethnic differences. After its publication, Mills received many inquiries from white-collar workers asking for suggestions on improving their lives. One response from Mills to a reader was to "start a White Collar Center in your home town."[95] Such a center would focus on employee complaints, allowing white-collar workers to stop worrying about their "loss of status" and instead to begin to "think politically." Although such words might seem helpful on paper, Mills knew in reality that they were marginally useful—to his readers and to himself. Mills was quite open about the fact that his attempt to translate the existential into the political was part of his own search for a stable identity. In this sense, *White Collar* was in part autobiographical. Mills was admittedly "the son of a white collar man who traveled all the time," his father working for years as an insurance broker.[96] While he was struggling with the book, Mills's uneasiness intensified—"then you worry that everything you write about 'the new little man' isn't about anybody at all but your own God damn self" (138). His personal letters and diaries reveal a man troubled by his inability to offer any substantial answers. At his worst, Mills made banal remarks about the craftsmanship ideal as the essence of man's being, which was a benign answer to the complicated problem of subject formation. But Mills was determined to overcome the divisions between history and biography that obscured any understanding of the world. In this sense, his sociological project was best exemplified in an unfinished manuscript entitled "Contacting the Enemy: Tovarich, Written to an Imaginary Soviet Colleague," a series of unpublished letters to an unspecified Soviet intellectual named after the Russian word for comrade.

Mills began writing to his imaginary friend in 1956 during an extended trip to Europe, where he served as a Fulbright lecturer at the University of Copenhagen. As he explained in one of his letters, he originally planned to write a "Letter to Europeans" in which he would not only explain how Europe appeared to an American but offer a word of thanks to those who were kind enough to help him during his travels. But his attempt to articulate his understanding of the nationalist squabbles holding back European progress always failed, and instead, Mills found himself compulsively writing to his as-yet-unmet friend. Envisioned less as a political tract, Mills's letters to his Soviet counterpart were more an attempt at "conversation" for the two supposed adversaries to "make our own separate peace" (221). But more important, Mills hoped that his letters, centered mostly on his own daily routine, would function as a conversational form of autobiography in which Mills could come to terms with himself while simultaneously coming to terms with the larger world. In this sense, Mills's Tovarich letters were the unpublished testimony of a man in dialogue with himself. His letters were admittedly a form of "self scrutiny," which Mills confessed was "an old American habit" formed in response to a national lack of "the kind of ready-made identity many Europeans seem to have" (222). Writing the self in this fashion was for Mills a revelatory act in which the disparate acts of his life could be gathered together and also a confessional act in which his drive for self-knowledge helped to reveal his past mistakes and prior ideological confusions. As Mills explained to his Russian friend, "the facts will come out, so far as I know then, but it is not altogether pleasant or easy to confront some of them" (26). Tovarich, in this sense, simultaneously served for Mills as a reader and a confessant. "Let us talk to one another 'naively,'" Mills asked Tovarich, "each telling as honestly as he can, who he might be and how he thinks he got that way; how he lives and what he believes and how he thinks he has come to believe it" (225). While in Europe, Mills realized that his own faltering sense of self was part of a much larger cultural crisis, implied in his reference to "my bourgeois soul, my philistine self, my unsolid identity of which I know so little" (242).

In this sense, Mills's letters to Tovarich functioned as a sort of confessional soliloquy, prompted in part by Mills's reading of Dostoevsky, who had made the investigation into man's divided consciousness a key part of his fiction. As he explained to Tovarich, Mills had once spent an entire summer reading the Russian writer, an experience that "nearly killed me" (224) but one that taught him much about self-scrutiny. Dostoevsky's fiction was populated with characters in dialogue with others or with readers, ambivalent about themselves, desperate for some acknowledgment, and compulsively confessing their desires, all of which were found to be grounded in a particular historical moment. From Dostoevsky, Mills realized that autonomy did not mean a complete elimination of the past or of any restraining context. Like the confessant in *Notes from Underground*, Mills understood that autonomy was gained only through the continual recounting of an individual's own history, a process of writing the self that linked together the multiple roles played by the individual and the multiple vocabularies he mouthed into a coherent narrative that located the individual in time and in space. For Mills, writing the self was "another name for the creating and the maintaining of a more or less orderly mind of your own, and so a sense of your own identity" (255). But such an identity was not the function of some radical originality or the result of an excavation of some substantial self with ontological priority. Given the social character of man's identity, any autobiographical project was less a mode of self-discovery than a "little drama" produced between the individual and the others around him. Writing the self in this sense only took place in an interlocutory situation. Mills recognized that the response of the other served both to dislodge any autonomous self-representation constructed solely from within and to reinforce the fundamentally relational quality of the self. "This experience of self is a crucially interpersonal one," argued Mills; "its basic organization is reflected from surrounding persons to whose approbation and criticism one pays attention."[97] For Mills, Tovarich served that purpose.

Using Tovarich as his interlocutor allowed Mills to view own life through the gaze of the ultimate Cold War other. Mills's limited travel experience in Europe brought him to this conclusion. "Traveling in foreign countries," Mills explained to Tovarich, "of course, turns you in upon yourself; you get away from your routines; and you begin to sort yourself out. At the same time, it makes you feel the need to tell the strangers around you what you are all about. You want to look at self and world together before the strangers."[98] In this way, Mills hoped such a dialogue would place his own experience within a larger framework. "Feelings, however vague," observed Mills, "are the infant beginnings of a political traffic when you start to interchange them" (224). Consequently, in order to find "some kind of theme" running through his autobiography, Mills tried to gather the moments of his life together by unearthing the often contradictory motivations he had inherited. Mills recognized that his father's job as a traveling salesman meant that he had been raised with no experience of an intimate family, an upbringing that left him feeling quite alone and that explained in part his isolation as an academic. He recognized that his intellectual ambitions were a product of his mother's own frustrations living in the stifling environment of Texas. Mills recognized that his mother had given him many "feminine qualities" that helped him to escape the maddening military environment he encountered as a cadet at Texas A&M. Mills also recognized that his father's confused relationship with the family's Catholic heritage had made Mills, despite his own experience as an Irish Catholic altar boy, equally lonely in a spiritual sense. Finally, Mills recognized that his slow political awakening during World War II meant that he had few political traditions to which to cling, having been born too late for Progressivism or New Deal liberalism. As he explained to Tovarich, "the great energies" that his search for an identity "demanded and created, the burdens of loneliness that often accompanied it, and the difficulties of achieving any durable and really deep 'human relations' have thus arisen out of quite specific social and cultural contexts" (30). Mills in this sense was just as adrift as the people about whom he wrote. All of his writings centered on the problems associated with how individuals drew connections between their own isolated activities and the larger cultural milieu.

In several of his letters, Mills referenced Walt Whitman as the American exemplar of his own autobiographical approach. Whitman was an excellent model for Mills—a writer who, in his attempt to provide "'some authentic glints, specimen-days of my life'" (292), had discovered that claims to authenticity often covered over a fundamentally divided consciousness. Writing an autobiography for both Mills and Whitman was a way of noting the singularity of each individual life while simultaneously undermining the ontological grounds upon which such singularity stood. Mills knew that no individual voice could ever be effectively cleansed of the vocabularies that helped to constitute it. The seemingly solitary voice was in reality always inhabited by the voices of others, voices that were part of various social, religious, and political traditions in various states of consolidation. According to Mills, "the motivations of men, and even the varying extents to which various types of men are typically aware of them, are to be understood in terms of the vocabularies of motive that prevail in a society and of social changes and confusions among such vocabularies."[99] In this sense, memory never recovered an unadulterated past; a considerable degree of interpretation, projection, and fantasy accompanied any personal recollection. Memory remained distorted by an already constituted vocabulary of interpersonal values, a vocabulary that determined in part what "may be better remembered than what we cannot thus locate."[100] For instance, he knew that most of the stories he told about himself were hyperbolic—from the anecdotes about driving trucks across Texas oil fields to the pithy quotes supposedly mouthed by his grandfather. "But that's merely posing again—perhaps even seeking a 'background,' or trying to invent one or imagine one," explained Mills; "in truth, I don't know a single thing my grandfather ever said."[101] Conversing with Tovarich served to shatter Mills's own sense of self-sufficiency and to demonstrate the futility of any attempt at self-enclosure. "As for the past," admitted Mills, "like almost everyone, I've got several different pasts that I find variously useful, and comforting; and all of them are equally convincing" (247). Writing about his past was for Mills a never-ending process of trying to stake out the boundaries of his own self that was in actuality never completely formed and that was always unable to escape the voices that inhabited it.

But writing the self was also an unavoidable project with both personal and political implications, a means of confronting the pressures of social life and a means of articulating desires oftentimes unrecognized in the modern world. It was also a way to merge past selves with present and future identities, to draw together the range of subject positions, past and present, in which the self was embedded. Indeed, the biography of a person was a record of the transformations in character produced by the abandonment of certain roles and the appropriation of others. "To understand the biography of an individual," argued Mills, "we must understand the significance and meaning of the roles he has played and does play; to understand these roles we must understand the institutions of which they are a part."[102] The narrative of the life of the subject was written just as much by participating respondents, institutional authorities, and cultural traditions. Character structure was inescapable but negotiable. For Mills, the romantic modernist self was so trapped in its own uniqueness, so proud of its purging of any identification with anything outside itself, that any sense of the social was lost. As he argued, "the answer to the 'façade self' and the 'real self' dichotomy is found not by trying to jump past the socialized portions of the personality and finding something more 'genuine' in the psychic or organic 'foundations,' but by viewing the social process of the self in a longitudinal way, and 'finding' a 'genuine self' that is buried by later socializations."[103] Mills refused to eliminate agency by reducing the self to a passive spectator within the symbolic order, yet he also refused to grant the subject the power of limitless self-fashioning. Even the most intimate features of a person's biographical makeup were in fact scattered throughout the institutional scenes in which those features took shape and received or were denied satisfaction. In this way, the individual fashioned a self through the languages he learned, developing his own inner speech and own voice through the appropriation of the discourse of others, particular and generalized, with whom he conversed. Autobiography therefore was not decoration but an ideologically charged and politically essential process. Writing the self was a means of achieving uncertain unity amid chaos, permanence amid change. For both Mills and Goffman, then, the self was not merely an actor assigned to play a series of roles but a speaking self capable of integrating those roles in a unique and meaningful way—a stable character in its own right.

CHAPTER FIVE

Beyond Primitivism and the Fellahin: Receiving James Baldwin's Gift of Love

During the first testing of the atomic bomb on July 16, 1945, in the New Mexico desert, the scientific personnel who witnessed the explosion related how they were unable to translate their experience into adequate words. Those who did offer words realized that even their hyperbolic statements failed to express what was ultimately inexpressible. "Most experiences in life can be comprehended by prior experiences," said Navy commander Norris Bradbury, "but the atom bomb did not fit into any preconceptions possessed by anybody."[1] This sense of awe in the face of an inconceivable event, that is, a situation comparable to "that state of the soul, in which all its motions are suspended, with some degree of horror," was what philosopher Edmund Burke famously referred to as the sublime.[2] Originally invoked in the eighteenth century to mark man's experience with the often terrifying grandeur of the natural order, notions of the sublime reemerged during the Cold War to signify the awe felt over the ghastly images of mushroom clouds hovering over Japan. Although stemming not from the immensity of the starry heavens or the stormy sea that Romantic poets once experienced, this "nuclear sublime" similarly provoked the drives for shelter and self-preservation that Burke associated with the sublime experience: "Terror is in all cases whatsoever, either more openly or latently the ruling principle of the sublime."[3] Cowering before the explosion, the scientists in New Mexico were the first ones to recognize the inadequacy of language to describe both the seemingly limitless force of the atomic blast and the feeling of insignificance in the face of such destruction.

In many ways, this experience of the "nuclear sublime" did more than any other single event to shape the contours of mid-century modernism. As Norman Mailer argued in his infamous 1957 essay "The White Negro: Superficial Reflections on the Hipster," "probably, we will never be able to determine the psychic havoc of the concentration camps and the atom bomb upon the unconscious mind of almost everyone alive in these years."[4] The bomb seemed to be both the culmination of a process of industrialization and rationalization begun during the Enlightenment and a fundamental rupture in history itself. All of the utopian visions and progressive dreams that marked nineteenth-century thought were now defunct, leaving romantic modernists, if not everyone, scrambling not merely for security but also for salvation. Some, like William Burroughs, saw this international trauma in very personal terms. Having suffered from continuous sinus trouble as an adolescent while living in St. Louis, Burroughs had been sent by his parents to the Los Alamos Ranch School in New Mexico, a sprawling 400-acre campus that was eventually purchased by the United States government and converted into the official site for the Manhattan Project. This ironic connection between America's most belligerent modernist and the most famous site of military research was not lost on Burroughs, who once claimed that "it seemed so right, somehow" that he had personal experience of Los Alamos.[5] Indelibly embedded within the aesthetic practices of both Mailer and Burroughs was this scarring experience of a world on the brink of catastrophe.

In this, Burroughs and Mailer were joined in the 1940s and 1950s by other romantic modernists such as the New York school of painters who reformulated their artistic practices in relation to this upturned landscape. Loosely grouped as abstract expressionists, painters such as Jackson Pollock, Mark Rothko, Barnett Newman, Clyfford Still, Willem de Kooning, and others revolutionized Western art by transforming painting from being a reflection of external reality to being a reflection of the interior landscape of the artist, a move inherent to the project of romantic modernism. In so doing, these painters, like Burroughs and Mailer, were trying to salvage their own selves from a chaotic American society seemingly on the verge of collapse. Years later, Barnett Newman sketched the circumstances that gave expression to his early work: "You must realize that twenty years ago we felt the moral crisis of a world in shambles, a world devastated by a great depression and a fierce world war."[6] Unable to continue painting "flowers, reclining nudes, and people playing the cello," Newman and his colleagues, like those who followed the lead of Wilhelm Reich, "actually began, so to speak, from scratch."

In order to gain an analytic lens with which to confront this global catastrophe, Newman began studying the natural sciences, taking classes in the early 1940s at the Brooklyn Botanic Garden and graduate courses in botany, ornithology, and geology at Cornell University.[7] Soon he incorporated biological themes addressing the origins of life into his aesthetic practice, a move not uncommon within the tradition of romantic modernism. For instance, his 1945 painting *Gea*, which is a reference to the Greek goddess who was the child of Chaos and who gave birth to the earth itself, features a white, fertilized circle that Newman once referred to as "a kind of void from which and around which life emanated—as in the original Creation."[8] He repeated this theme about the cosmic regeneration of life through images of cellular forms in subsequent paintings such as *Pagan Void*, *Genetic Moment*, *Genesis—The Break*, and *The Beginning*.

Other New York school painters followed his lead. Mark Rothko, for instance, studied biology as an undergraduate at Yale University in the 1940s, and he connected his artistic creations to what he referred to as the search for "biological immortality."[9] Borrowing themes from the natural sciences, Rothko traced the rise of man's consciousness back to a primordial essence. His 1944 painting *Slow Swirl at the Edge of the Sea*, with its two schematic figures standing at the water's edge, mixed the evolutionary and the spermatozoal to suggest the generation of life from a primeval couple. Anatomical forms were also reduced to cellular entities, protozoic organisms, and microscope structures in *Genetic Instant*, *Primeval Landscape*, and *Beginnings*. Like Wilhelm Reich and others, these romantic modernists searched for some sort of biological grounding that they often translated into a search for the protozoic. They also searched for a form of politics that reflected this new artistic stance, aligning themselves, like other romantic modernists, with anarchism. When once asked what one of his paintings actually meant, Barnett Newman responded: "My answer was that if he and others could read it properly it would mean the end of all state capitalism and totalitarianism."[10] Defending heroic individualism in the face of what Clyfford Still called "the omnivorousness of the totalitarian mind," Newman, Still, and Rothko protested any curtailment of personal freedom, whether in the form of bureaucratic demands or authoritarian political programs.[11] But with the world seemingly on the brink of annihilation, simplistic references to the biological or to anarchism did not seen comfort enough.

Indeed, even before the United States had reeked "psychic havoc" upon the world with the bombing of Hiroshima, many romantic modernists argued that the sheer devastation of World War II was so incomprehensible that artists needed an entirely different language with which to address this type of total warfare. For instance, Mark Rothko, like many abstract artists, began to portray the tragic consequences of a world at war through references to archaic myths. Rothko's eclectic blending of iconographic elements was vividly demonstrated in his 1942 painting *The Omen of the Eagle*, a reference to Aeschylus's Agamemnon trilogy. The painting, with its horizontal tiers of images, is an oblique nod to the choral omen at the beginning of Aeschylus's drama in which two eagles, representing the forthcoming ruthlessness of Agamemnon's assault during the Trojan War, devour an innocent hare. Since the mythic portent of barbarism needed no translation in 1942, Rothko decided not to subordinate his work to deliberate pictorial images, explaining that "the picture deals not with the particular anecdote, but rather with the Spirit of the Myth, which is generic to all myths at all times."[12] In one hybrid image composed of Greek masks, surrealist-inspired bird heads, and twisted human forms, Rothko represented the violence of modern war through reference to ancient mythology. As he explained in "Art in New York," a 1943 WNYC radio broadcast, "those who think that the world of today is more gentle and graceful than the primeval and predatory passions from which these myths spring, are either not aware of reality or do not wish to see it in art."[13]

Even more than Rothko, Barnett Newman extrapolated the castrating experience of the nuclear sublime into a universal condition. Noting the apocalyptic terror under which modern man lived, Newman drew a parallel between the atomic age and the primitive age. In a 1946 article written in conjunction with the "Art of the South Seas" exhibition at the Museum of Modern Art, he argued that "the reason primitive art is so close to the modern mind is that we, living in times of the greatest terror the world has known, are in a position to appreciate the acute sensibility primitive man had for it."[14] Newman went on to compare the terror felt by the South Sea islanders in confrontation with "the mysterious forces of nature, the unpredictable sea and the whirlwind" to the catastrophic events of World War II. Indeed, much of Newman's early work referenced the cataclysmic power of the atomic bomb, including his 1946 painting *Pagan Void*, which represents not just the cellular regeneration of life but also the destructive effects of the bomb that had produced such a void. Frightened on the one hand by the rise of collectivist politics that had decimated the rights of the individual and on the other hand by the development of mechanized means of destruction, Newman saw a spiritual kinship between modern artists who felt overwhelmed by the experience of World War II and primitive men who similarly struggled to make sense of the forces of the natural world. In fact, his references to Oceanic art in paintings such as *The Command* and *The Beginning* were just a few of the many invocations of primitivism throughout romantic modernist discourse. As Newman noted in a 1948 *Tiger's Eye* article, "the sublime is now."

Of course not all modernists in the postwar period dealt with the recent global catastrophe in such a defiant manner. Those late modernists who were determined to unravel the metaphysical certainties of their compatriots worried over this effort by romantic modernists to shore up their own individual sense of identity through an appropriation of primitive cultures. The most vocal critic of this turn in the trajectory of romantic modernism was the novelist James Baldwin, whose early fiction, including *Giovanni's Room* (1956) and *Another Country* (1962), unearthed the racial and sexual assumptions embedded within bohemian discourse. An expatriate like many other modernists, Baldwin recognized the pressures that had compelled numerous artists to seek refuge from a declining American culture through either a metaphoric escape into the deep recesses of the psyche or a literal flight into the underground avant-garde of a recently rebuilt Western Europe. In a 1961 *Esquire* article, "The New Lost Generation," Baldwin reflected upon the circumstances that had shaped the artistic spirit of his generation, telling the tragic story of his close friend—a black man and a committed socialist—who had, in a moment of despair, taken his own life. Recounting his last conversation with his friend, in which the two had debated whether or not the world was possible to redeem, Baldwin finally recognized that his friend's pain was in fact also his own. The only difference between them was that Baldwin, unlike his friend, did not believe at that moment in any redemptive power, including love, to fix their pain. "Love! You better forget about that, my friend," Baldwin explained to his troubled compatriot, "that train has *gone*."[15] With such staunch language, Baldwin had not only disappointed his friend but had revealed the utter emptiness within such hopes. Soon after their conversation, Baldwin's friend jumped off the George Washington Bridge, a tragic end that Baldwin claimed was much too common in the postwar world.

Reflecting upon this experience and regretting the language he had used, Baldwin recognized that his initial response to his friend was far too commonplace among men of his generation, a response that revealed a lack of faith in any form of communion. Unable to believe in any collective project, many had turned to visions of individual redemption, beginning "to believe in formulas" such as "the idea of the world being made better through psychic and sexual health" (308). Baldwin recognized at that moment that he and his generation were stuck between two unfortunate poles—between lapsing into the despair that had consumed his friend and forfeiting any claim to the world or turning to "formulas for the improvement of the private . . . life" such as those offered by Wilhelm Reich. Both choices were for Baldwin ultimately the same—both were motivated by a desperate drive for separation and individual redemption, what he referred to as "a certain euphoric aura of well-being." Unable to lose himself in either option and unwilling to reconcile with an American culture seemingly devoid of possibilities, Baldwin fled to Paris in 1948, a decision that he readily admitted saved his life. But the experience also revealed to him the futile desperation of his fellow modernists who believed that redemption was possible through any form of escape—whether through a metaphorical alignment with primitive cultures, a scholastic interrogation of ancient mythologies, a road trip into the Mexican desert, or any of the endless paths of evasion taken by American artists. In the end, Baldwin recognized, as his departed friend had once tried to explain, that redemption was possible only through the experience of love, that is, through a political and aesthetic project centered on the recognition of the inextricable bond between the self and others, a love that built bonds of community, established practices of recognition, and ended artificially imposed forms of isolation. In so doing, Baldwin, like David Riesman and Norman Brown, offered an image of the self built around "the experience of others" (313). In *Another Country*, Baldwin exposed the existential limitations of romantic modernism and posited a different vision of redemption, one that aligned him with the late modernist visions of Riesman, Brown, and others.

Modernism and Primitivism

In his 1947 essay "The First Man Was an Artist," Barnett Newman coyly noted that "in the last sixty years, we have seen mushroom a vast cloud of 'sciences' in the fields of culture, history, philosophy, psychology, economics, politics, aesthetics, in an ambitious attempt to claim the nonmaterial world."[16] Noting that the scientific method had become a new theology, Newman argued that the modern scientist searched for a "descriptive knowledge" of reality, asking only "the specific question, *what?*" instead of deeper metaphysical ones. In response, Newman encouraged artists to look instead to primitive art, in particular, Oceanic and Native American traditions, to counter this naïve faith in technology to better the current situation. More important, Newman turned to primitive art to rethink the nature of the self in a landscape seemingly overrun by group psychology. Indeed, many romantic modernists like Newman turned to primitive art in the 1940s in a desperate search for man's origins, believing that the reductive element within these cultural forms expressed a more fundamental unity between man and his surroundings. As literary critic Thomas Weiskel has noted, for many artists the paralysis produced by the experience of the sublime was often only temporary. The modern artist's contemplation of such grandeur often led to an identification with the "superiority" of the sublime object, offering the privileged witness a "sense of inward greatness."[17] Thus, the original sense of infinitesimal smallness in the face of impending annihilation was quickly replaced in romantic modernism, through a comparison with primitive man, with a renewed feeling of importance. Once again, Newman signaled this transformation in the experience of the sublime, most notably in his 1950 painting *Vir Heroicus Sublime*, which borrowed from a Latin title, "man, heroic, and sublime," to acknowledge the buried potential of man. Newman referenced the sublime experience of primitive man not merely to describe his own incapacitated state but to find a way, like his primitive ancestors, to overcome it. Primitive man, whose imaginary wholeness and self-sufficiency reflected a prior stage of innocence, served as a point of critique for the supposedly shattered nature of civilized society. The sublime, in this sense, offered redemption.

Romantic modernists who searched for a biological instinct with which to ground the self also referenced images of their primitive ancestors as a source of spiritual regeneration. Wilhelm Reich, for instance, borrowed heavily from Bronislaw Malinowski's studies of the Trobriand Islanders of Melanesia, a society Reich romantically depicted as a sexual paradise free of social restraints. According to Reich, "the sexual life of Trobriander children develops naturally, freely, and without interference through all stages of life with full sexual gratification."[18] Primitive man was corporeality itself, an example of man freed from all character armor and psychological baggage. Echoing Reich's turn to ethnographic studies, many romantic modernists began their own investigations into the world of primitive man.[19] Barnett Newman, for instance, was instrumental in his role as curator, critic, and artist in promoting the association between avant-garde painting and primitive art. His interest in Native American art stemmed in part from his friendship with the surrealist artist Wolfgang Paalen, who had visited Pacific Northwest Coast settlements to study their sculptural achievements.[20] Following Paalen's example, Newman organized the "Pre-Columbian Stone Sculpture" exhibition in 1944 at the Wakefield Gallery in New York with aid from the American Museum of Natural History, and in 1946, he organized the "Northwest Coast Indian Painting" exhibition at the Betty Parsons Gallery. In his prefatory comments to the catalogues accompanying his shows, Newman argued that "it is becoming more and more apparent that to understand modern art, one must have an appreciation of the primitive arts."[21] With this in mind, he also helped organize an influential 1947 modern art exhibit, "The Ideographic Picture," which connected the work of Mark Rothko, Clyfford Still, and others to the abstract designs of the Kwakiutl artists of the Northwest Coast Indians. In his introduction, Newman praised Kwakiutl artists for their rejection of any faulty obsession with artistic representations of "inconsequential" tribal concerns (107).[22] Instead, the true tribal artist, like the romantic modernist, left "the everyday realities" to the "toymakers" and created instead "ideographic" representations of deeply held ideas, ideographs that made "contact with the mystery—of life, of men, of nature, of the hard, black chaos that is death, or the grayer, softer chaos that is tragedy." The primitive artist, according to Newman, understood that aesthetic production was a "metaphysical exercise" and therefore practiced a "non-voluptuous art" concerned with "the hidden meanings of life."[23]

Most romantic modernists, including Jackson Pollock, Mark Rothko, Clyfford Still, and Adolph Gottlieb, immersed themselves in local traditions, appropriating forms from Northwest Coast Indian, Eskimo, Mexican, and Oceanic traditions. A series of exhibitions at the Museum of Modern Art including "African Negro Art" (1935), "Prehistoric Rock Pictures in Europe and Africa" (1937), "Twenty Centuries of Mexican Art" (1940), "Indian Art of the United States" (1941), and "Ancestral Sources of Modern Painting" (1941) introduced many abstract artists to non-European styles. Ethnographic inspiration was also culled from the permanent collections at the American Museum of Natural History, the Brooklyn Museum, the Museum of the American Indian, and the Heye Foundation. The frail, primordial figures of Mark Rothko's *Slow Swirl at the Edge of the Sea* (1944), for instance, were borrowed not just from the protozoan figures found in the works of Joan Miró or André Masson but also from Navajo sand paintings such as *Sky Mother and Earth Mother*, which was shown at the 1941 Museum of Modern Art exhibition "Indian Art of the United States."[24] Similarly, Jackson Pollock's study of the ceremonial objects at the same exhibition inspired his 1943 painting *Mural*, in particular, the Hohokam pottery bowls of southwest Arizona tribes that depicted a humpbacked Pueblo spirit, which Pollock translated into the rhythmic, colorful patterns of his painting.[25] To continue such studies, Pollock purchased twelve volumes of the *Annual Report of the Bureau of American Ethnology*, a series of works that illustrated the traditions of Native American tribes and offered him hundreds of ritual images to appropriate and transform, images that Pollock reproduced in *Guardians of the Secret* and *She-Wolf*.[26]

Although romantic modernists in America turned to Oceanic and Native American traditions instead of the African artifacts appropriated by their European counterparts, they too reflected modernism's long-standing fascination with primitive cultures. This recovery of the primitive by romantic modernists was done in the midst of the apparent failure of Western society to prevent its own oblivion and done as the means to recover some lost vitality or to return to an organic unity. As such, the primitive served as the ultimate fetish, functioning simultaneously as recognition of modern man's irredeemable lack in the face of castrating institutional control and as a disavowal of such powerlessness through fantasized images of an untainted wholeness.[27] The primitive marked a self that was topographically unlocatable, a self residing beyond its biographical, historical, and institutional embodiment, and a self no longer overwhelmed by the ubiquitous presence of psychological and physical mechanisms of authoritarian control. Unlike modern man, the primitive was liberated from all forms of character armor and freed from the dysfunctions of the ego. In this sense, the primitive was unmarked by the passage of historical traditions and political regimes and therefore was the closest link in an evolutionary chain connecting mankind through the ages to a primary unity. The primitive, according to romantic modernists, was the new man, the original man, and the last man.

Of course, many romantic modernists recognized that there was something disingenuous about making a metaphorical connection between primitive and modern man. For example, Mark Rothko argued that artists needed to demonstrate the actual embeddedness of the archaic past in the present moment by showing how mankind's mythic heritage was ever present within the mind of contemporary man. Most of Rothko's early works, particularly those composed between 1938 and 1946, referenced a mythic story or character, and he borrowed heavily from the works of Aeschylus, Sophocles, Plato, Shakespeare, and Nietzsche as well as from the Bible.[28] His use of mythology allowed Rothko to break with what he saw as the staid traditions of European art and the obvious provincialism of American regionalism. In fact, Rothko claimed he had stopped painting in 1940 for almost a year in order to study ancient mythology, mostly through his reading of Sigmund Freud's *Interpretation of Dreams*, James Frazer's *The Golden Bough*, and Friedrich Nietzsche's *The Birth of Tragedy*, books that intensified his frantic search for some collective myth to redeem a world in decay. Upset at critic Edward Jewell's befuddlement over the annual exhibition of the Federation of Modern Painters and Sculptors, Rothko uncharacteristically responded in a 1943 letter to the *New York Times* in which he professed a "spiritual kinship with primitive and archaic art."[29] Thus, Rothko in his paintings throughout the 1940s made frequent use of themes concerning buried memories (*Ancestral Imprint*, *Prehistoric Memory*, *Tentacles of Memory*), trial and sacrifice (*Gethsememe*, *The Sacrifice of Iphigenia*), primitive magic (*Vessels of Magic*, *Implements of Magic*), rebirth (*Baptismal Scene*, *Entombment*), and dreams (*Archaic Phantasy*, *Geological Reverie*).[30]

This interest in ancient mythology as a window onto the turbulent modern world was reflected in the profound interest among many romantic modernists in the work of Swiss psychologist Carl Jung, whose theories came into vogue in American intellectual circles in the 1930s and 1940s. One of the most important popularizers of Jungian psychology and one of the most influential theorists of romantic modernism was Philip Wylie, a journalist for the *New Yorker*, *Vanity Fair*, and *Redbook* and a staunch libertarian who denounced Communism, labor unions, big business, and large-scale government. Wylie gained nationwide fame for his 1942 nonfiction book *Generation of Vipers*, which was reprinted in abbreviated form in countless magazines and which stayed on the *New York Times* bestseller list for months. Echoing the language of many romantic modernists, Wylie attacked America's failure of nerve in confronting international and national ills and criticized intellectuals, religious leaders, scientists, and congressmen for allowing the country to fall into barbarism. Claiming that America had "cancer of the soul," Wylie called for a scientific investigation into man's basic instincts: "To the extent that we have denied the power of our instincts—to the extent that we have really believed the extravagant piffle that we are Christian, rational, and legal—they have kicked us to pieces."[31] Believing that such "instinctuality" was an inseparable part of man's heritage, Wylie turned to Carl Jung, who, "by studying collections of ancient legends and by studying primitive people," had demonstrated how man had "*personified* his instincts" in mythology. Wylie was introduced to Jungian psychology in 1936 when he entered therapy after divorcing his wife and after his brother's untimely death. As Wylie explained, he had made an incredibly long journey from his childhood Presbyterianism to his prewar atheism to his philosophical appropriation of Jungian psychology.

Like Rothko and Newman, Wylie argued that the incapacitating experience of the nuclear sublime had irreversibly changed man. In *An Essay on Morals*, Wylie claimed that "the latest large event—the engineering of a large-scale atomic chain-reaction, because it involves not just the opinions but the bodies of our species, too—has waked up every archetype, every instinct, in the billion-year-old breast of humanity."[32] The atomic explosion had demonstrated man's recent separation from himself—a "compelled Judas" (70) forced to betray, as Carl Jung had maintained, his cosmic self. Indeed, as Wylie explained, "the day the old ape decided he was more than a beast—the day he found the temporal pleasure of his ego, the day of the original sin—marked the beginning of the blunder" (65). In response, Wylie turned to Jung to re-engage with man's deeper self. Challenging the rudiments of psychoanalysis, Jung offered a three-tiered image of man's unconscious: the personal unconscious, the collective unconscious, and the forever buried and untranslatable part of the collective unconscious. The personal unconscious was constituted from repressed material from the individual's life, material that was continuously replenished and transformed on a daily basis. The collective unconscious contained archetypes that, as universal forms in the Platonic sense, gave meaning to daily experiences. These archetypes represented inherited forms that guided behavior, arising within the individual psyche in dreams and intuitions when the individual faced unresolved problems. "The archetype," explained Jung, "is essentially an unconscious content that is altered by becoming conscious, and by being perceived, and it takes its colour from the individual consciousness in which it happens to appear."[33] From these archetypes emerged an endless series of characters and symbols that offered the individual a pathway into his unconscious. Through his cross-cultural study of mythology, Jung catalogued an almost endless list of archetypal images—the trickster, the hero, the old wise man, the virgin, the great mother, and the many others—that gave man guidance in confronting a series of universal events such as birth, parental separation, marriage, and death. The collective unconscious was the repository of these myths, fairy tales, and religious stories. "Thanks to the labours of the human spirit over the centuries," explained Jung, "these images have become embedded in a comprehensive system of thought that ascribes an order to the world, and are at the same time represented by a mighty, far-spread, and venerable institution called the Church" (304). According to Jung, man's nature was to produce myths from the flux of human experience, myths of significant emotional intensity that helped to guide behavior.

The goal of Jungian therapy was to tap into the images offered by the collective unconscious to help understand those buried individual elements. Such archetypal images, usually taken from dreams, helped to compensate for the unknowing one-sidedness or misguidedness of the individual ego. Dreams for Jung were purposive, existing not merely as signs of repressed wishes but as symbols of man's unconscious heritage. As Jung explained, "the dreamer descends into his own depths, and the way leads him to the mysterious water" (313). Jungian theory helped romantic modernists translate their ambiguous notion of man's primordial instinct into the recognizable form of the archetype. Romantic modernists, in an attempt not merely to shatter the fragile shell of man's personality but to escape the horrid landscape of a post-Hiroshima world, began a vertical descent into this mythopoetic part of man's being. As Mark Rothko observed, "the myth holds us, therefore, not through its romantic flavor . . . but because it expresses to us something real and existing in ourselves, as it was to those who first stumbled upon the symbols to give them life."[34] For artists like Rothko, Jung offered an image of man grounded not in the detritus of the contemporary world but within a much larger universal context and an image of man capable of transcending his individual ego.

Of course, as Rothko explained, romantic modernists were not simply illustrating the collected works of Carl Jung; instead, they were searching through their backgrounds to find sources of personal significance. Jackson Pollock, for instance, was introduced to the theories of Jung from a number of sources, including two of his therapists, Joseph Henderson and Violet de Staub de Laszlo, both of whom were associated with the Analytical Psychology Club in New York and both of whom spoke with Pollock frequently about psychoanalytic concepts.[35] Both therapists admitted in particular to discussing Jungian formulations of man's basic birth-death-rebirth cycle, a process that Jung had connected to man's individual development. As the artist himself explained, "I'm very representational some of the time, and a little all of the time. But when you're painting out of your unconscious, figures are bound to emerge. We're all of us influenced by Freud, I guess. I've been a Jungian for a long time."[36] Pollock was also influenced by Polish painter and art theorist John Graham, whom Pollock once proclaimed was the "one man who really [knew] what [his art was] about."[37] Graham's oft-cited book on modern art *System and Dialectics of Art* depicted artistic creation as a heroic journey into man's unconscious: "The purpose of art in *particular* is to re-establish a lost contact with the unconscious . . . and develop this contact in order to bring to the conscious mind the throbbing events of the unconscious mind."[38] Of course, neither Pollock nor Graham was interested in directly translating Jungian myths. The obscure images that formed Pollock's more representational phase in the early 1940s were derived from myriad sources—Native American cultural traditions, modernist works by Pablo Picasso and Joan Miró, and the murals of Mexican artists such as David Alfano Siqueiros and José Clemente Orozco. Pollock mingled the mystical and the transcendental with Jungian invocations and modernist references in a series of works, including his 1941 painting *Birth*, which reflected his therapist's claim that "a psychic birth-death-rebirth cycle was essential to the maintenance of Pollock's sanity."[39] The serpent motif in *Birth* was borrowed from an Eskimo mask illustrated in Graham's well-known article "Primitive Art and Picasso," which Pollock combined with explicit references to Picasso's *Demoiselles d'Avignon*, a juxtaposition that signaled Pollock's attempt to move modernism forward by turning to primitive influences in the same way that his father figure, Picasso, had done. In so doing, Pollock was one of many romantic modernists trying to redefine the role of the artist.

The Modern Artist as Shaman

In his 1947 essay "The First Man Was an Artist," Barnett Newman noted the anthropological priority of the aesthetic act over any strictly utilitarian one. Referencing both the first chapter of Genesis in which Adam's first act was to eat from the Tree of Knowledge in an attempt to replicate "the life of a creator" and the recent findings of archaeologists who noted that "the God image, not pottery, was the first manual act," Newman connected man's struggle with the forces of nature to the creative act.[40] According to Newman, "man's hand traced the stick through the mud to make a line before he learned to throw the stick as a javelin." Art, as Newman maintained throughout his life, was a metaphysical exercise. The artist created an "entirely different reality" out of the "chaos of pure fantasy and feeling," a reality devoid of "any known physical, visual, or mathematical counterpart" or any quotidian references (163–64). In this sense, the importance of the primitive object was not merely its facticity but its anthropomorphic quality; as Newman stressed, the human was not essentially separate from the natural or the magical. Romantic modernists, as Newman explained, partook in the same mystical processes that primitive artists did. In claiming that the aesthetic process was closer to a magical act than a technical one, he was intentionally invoking the image of the shaman, that priestly figure of Eskimo, Subarctic, Northwest Coast, Southwest, and Plains Indian cultures whose role as a healer and magician and whose use of mythological lore elevated him to a revered position in many non-Western societies. Through ritual acts, the shaman practiced a form of magic that allowed him to travel to the supernatural world and coerce the spirits to do his bidding. Indeed, the spirits spoke to and through the shaman, who operated as an ecstatic vessel for their messages and as a seer existing in communion with the unknown spiritual realm. The shaman was simultaneously a prophet of the future who could predict coming calamities and an archivist of his tribe's past who could pass judgment on prior events. More important, the shaman could also directly influence the world's mana—that supernatural force that pervaded and bound the natural world together. He could heal the sick, avert plagues, interpret dreams, handle fires, raise the dead, and recover lost souls. Although at times tinged with madness, the shaman played a multitude of roles—sorcerer, soothsayer, physician, priest, and prophet—that made him the tribe's spiritual authority.

The artist who most fully articulated the creative process as a form of shamanism was Clyfford Still, who followed Newman in equating art and metaphysics. Still's interest in Native American traditions began sometime in the late 1930s after he had painted his "way out" of prior European traditions—"whether Realist, Surrealist, Expressionist, Bauhaus, Impressionists, or what you choose"—until he found artistic freedom elsewhere: "I worked through the idiomatic means to which my culture had subjected me, until the way became clear. And freedom from the structuring mechanics of the contemporary social ethic representing a totalitarian trap could be identified with its primitive origins."[41] He had encountered Native American traditions when, as an art instructor at Washington State College, he taught summer school in the late 1930s on several local Native American reservations, and he soon began inserting references to shamanistic powers and symbols into his works.[42] For instance, Still's painting *1938-N No. 1*, originally titled "Totem Fantasy," features a dark, imposing shaman figure rising into the night sky; his painting *1943-J* features a stele-like presence that art historian Stephen Polcari has traced to images of the thunderbird spirit presented in the "Shaman Mnemonic System of the Grand Medicine Society," published by the Bureau of Indian Affairs in 1853; and his painting *1945-K* depicts a shaman drumstick used to commune with the dead.[43] In most of his paintings from this period, images of bones, birds, snakes, and feathers often bleed into each other, producing abstract forms that depict the regeneration of man through the shaman-artist's supernatural powers. As Mark Rothko explained in his introduction to a 1946 exhibition at Peggy Guggenheim's Art of This Century gallery, Still's paintings were at their essence images of "the Earth, the Damned, and the Recreated" (102). While Rothko tended to project his own interest in mythic archetypes onto Still's work, he did capture the sense of transformation—death from cultural asphyxiation and rebirth through spiritual regeneration—that marked Still's interest in shamanism. Similarly, Still's former instructor Clay Spohn, in an epigraph written in 1947, made a similar connection: "After seeing many of Clyfford Still's works I have come to the conclusion that he is a sorcerer with powerful magic . . . Nay! An Earth Shaker" (95).[44] Still's mythic Earth Shaker was also an allusion to the Native American shaman whose incantatory powers allowed the shaman to commune with the supernatural world and thereby heal the sick.

Even without specific references to Native American traditions, other romantic modernists turned to shamanism as an antidote to an irredeemable cultural decay. *An American Dream*, Norman Mailer's eerily spiritual fourth novel, is a vision of a world in which the magical and the quotidian meet and a world in which demons and angels whisper in the ears of those characters courageous enough to listen. The story's protagonist, Stephen Rojack, whose painful submission to his domineering wife symbolizes his Reichian character armor, has lost contact with the theological. His alternatives rest somewhere between suicide, which he contemplates on an apartment balcony in the book's opening scene, and acquiescence to the multitude of powers (his wife, his father-in-law, his television producer) parasitically occupying his being. Rojack traces his psychic collapse to his wartime confrontation with four German soldiers when he hesitates at the sight of the final one after having disposed of the first three. Unable to commit the final act and receive the ultimate form of "grace," Rojack sacrifices spiritual knowledge because of his timidity. However, he is saved from his self-imposed fate by several spiritual voices that speak to him throughout the novel. Through their guidance, Rojack becomes "separated from myself forever" by the insurmountable "distance" between his television personality and his "secret frightened romance with the phases of the moon."[45] In a world of lecherous materialism, Rojack comes "to believe in spirits and demons, in devils, warlocks, omens, wizards and fiends, in incubi and succubi" (37). Having proven himself willing to move beyond good and evil by sacrificing his lecherous wife, Rojack becomes prehistoric man confronting the brutality of existence itself, feeling "just as some creature locked by fear to the border between earth and water . . . might feel on that second when its claw took hold" (80), an image of primordial emergence not unlike Mark Rothko's *Slow Swirl at the Edge of the Sea*. By the end of the novel, Rojack has become a modern-day shaman, a "new breed of man" (81) who courts madness to purge himself of those in possession of his being and who has the spiritual power to commune with his dead girlfriend. Rojack has, as Mailer explained, moved "not forward to the collectivity which was totalitarianism in the proof but backward to the nihilism of creative adventurers."[46] In the end, disgusted with the spiritually deserted landscape of Las Vegas, Rojack leaves the decadence of America for the "primitive" energies of Guatemala. Other romantic modernists had already led the way for him.

Racial Surrogacy and the Return of the Fellahin

In the foreword to the "Pre-Columbian Stone Sculpture" exhibition at the Wakefield Gallery in 1944, Barnett Newman hoped that this "growing aesthetic appreciation" of native art would lead to the development of what he referred to as an "inter-American consciousness."[47] Newman believed that the fundamental "spiritual aspirations of human beings" detailed within Jungian psychology helped to reveal a "common hemispheric heritage" between the once flourishing native populations and contemporary man. To that end, Newman encouraged inter-American relations, working briefly for the diplomatic journal *La Revista Belga* of the Belgian office for Latin America, for which he wrote several essays linking pre-Columbian art in Latin America to the forms found in traditional Native American sculptures. Equally important, he linked the abstract compositions of artists such as Adolph Gottlieb and himself to these indigenous forms. By turning to primitive cultures in the Western hemisphere not associated with the African forms appropriated by their European counterparts, the New York school tried to create a strictly American version of modernism comprising indigenous elements. But as Newman continuously made clear, the romantic modernist appropriation of these cultures was not merely an ethnographic project; instead, this inter-American consciousness he helped to forge supposedly had a redemptive purpose.

Of course Newman was not the only modernist to propose a larger inter-American consciousness as an antidote to Western decay. Most Beat writers turned to primitive cultures as well to transform their own artistic practices, looking to indigenous traditions for inspiration and ultimately for redemption. But instead of turning to Jungian psychology, Burroughs, Kerouac, and

Ginsberg appropriated the historical writings of the German theorist Oswald Spengler, whose *The Decline of the West*, with its mixture of romantic nationalism and philosophical idealism, offered an image of Western society on the verge of collapse, a theme that echoed their own pessimism about modern society. History for Spengler was not a linear project but a cyclical one, a process that did not conform to any evolutionary movement, as Hegelian philosophers had maintained, but that conformed to a more organic process of birth, growth, and decay. Adopting a physiogmatic approach to historical study, which dispensed with the strictly rational methods of trained historians, Spengler claimed he was able to grasp intuitively the hidden meaning behind history. Tracing the development of the eight "high cultures" of recorded history—Indian, Babylonian, Egyptian, Chinese, Mexican, Arabian, Greco-Roman, and Western European—Spengler challenged Enlightenment claims that Western civilization was the culmination of a progressive development and argued instead that modern society was in a state of decline that paralleled the fall of Roman civilization. According to Spengler, who borrowed his language from Goethe, Western society had become a Faustian one, dominated not only by decadence but also by the naïve belief that the tools of scientific inquiry were forging a more advanced civilization. For romantic modernists railing against crass materialism, nuclear proliferation, and authoritarian politics, Spengler's narrative of decline offered a philosophical framework for their own pessimism. Sometime in the late 1940s William Burroughs, for instance, introduced Jack Kerouac to the writings of Spengler, handing him a copy of *Decline of the West* and instructing him to "edify yer mind, me boy."[48] But even more compelling was Spengler's prophetic vision in which he argued that the inevitable disintegration of Western civilization would lead to the rise of those groups displaced by modernization—those preindustrial, artisanal, and agricultural populations on the margins of society, what Spengler referred to as the *fellahin*. The residue of this collapse was "the Fellah type," descendants of the ancient, primitive, pre-Christian peoples such as "the Jews and Persians of the Seleucid age, the 'Sea-peoples,' [and] the Egyptian Nomes of Menes's time" who had been displaced by the "world-historical cultures" of "imperial" nation-states.[49] As such, they were the inheritors of a postimperial, postnational, and postcivilized world supposedly in the making.

The historical and metaphysical claims offered by Spengler provided evidence for many romantic modernists that their enthusiasm for primitive cultures was justified. The classic example of this Spenglerian paradigm within romantic modernism was Jack Kerouac's *On the Road*, which not only portrays America as a society in decline but also points to the rise of the fellahin as a source of redemption. Kerouac's tale of two discontents, Sal Paradise and Dean Moriarty, traveling the country looking for women and kicks, reaches a climax when the two friends sojourn to Mexico for new adventures and begin to recognize the artificiality of national boundaries: "'It's the world,' said Dean, 'My God!' he cried, slapping the wheel. 'It's the world! We can go right on to South America if the road goes. Think of it!'"[50] Traveling through Mexico opens their eyes to the displaced populations left behind by modernity. The "Fellahin Indians" of North America, as Sal Paradise explains, are that "essential strain of the basic, primitive, wailing humanity" that has been forgotten by "silly civilized American lore" (280). Following Spengler, however, Sal argues that their redemption will soon come, emerging from the wreckage of a postapocalyptic world to reclaim their rightful place. As Sal argues, "for when destruction comes to the world of 'history' and the Apocalypse of the Fellahin returns once more as so many times before, people will still stare with the same eyes from the caves of Mexico as well as from the caves of Bali, where it all began and where Adam was suckled and taught to know" (281). But more important than clinging to a pastoral vision of an inter-American landscape is Sal and Dean's hope that their contact with the fellahin will somehow serve as a regenerative force for their own selves. Mexico City is envisioned as the original source of man and as the site for their own reincarnation: "This was the great and final wild uninhibited Fellahin-childlike city that we knew we would find at the end of the road" (302). Like abstract expressionists who borrowed from classical mythologies and Native American traditions to rethink their own identitites, Sal and Dean travel to Mexico less to befriend these marginalized groups and more to recognize that the spiritual capacities exhibited by the fellahin were in fact inherent to the Beat poets themselves.

Indeed, Kerouac and his fellow Beat writers did not actually imagine that Mexico was the site of a forthcoming revolution or that the fellahin were revolutionary subjects. Instead, they hoped that they could find a way to inherit the redemptive qualities of these marginalized people. In this sense, the romantic modernist served as a surrogate for the vanquished fellaheen, emerging from the decay of modern civilization as the only remaining heir of the plentitude and vastness of the North American landscape.[51] Kerouac in fact was always invested in his family's genealogy, determined to pinpoint some connection between himself and the fellahin to justify his aesthetic project. His uncles helped Jack to mythologize his family's ancestors, telling him repeatedly that their distant relative, Baron François Louis Alexander Lebris de Kerouac, had valiantly fought in the Seven Years War and for his heroics had acquired an Iroquois princess as his bride. Lebris de Kerouac's six or seven sons, as the tale went, transplanted their families either to the new Iroquois tribes up north or to the textile mills of New England, making the Beat writer an heir to the redemptive legacy of Native Americans.[52] Similarly, in *Satori in Paris*, Kerouac traced his father's heritage to Brittany, only to discover that this once noble birthplace was "considered a hickplace by the popular wits of Paris, because of its distance from the capital," thus making his family situation comparable to "a New York Negro" whose roots traced "back to Arkansas."[53] As Kerouac himself admitted in his more honest moments, his fascination with primitive cultures and the fellahin in particular was part of his personal search for a scene of origins not connected to a seemingly totalitarian American society. The problem for Kerouac and others was how to move forward.

James Baldwin's Gift of Love

In his 1961 essay "The New Lost Generation," in which he described the fate of his longtime friend who was driven to suicide after falling into an insurmountable despair, James Baldwin recounted the vast social and economic changes brought about by World War II that had irrevocably altered life in the United States, changes that Baldwin had personally experienced. Unfit physically for military service and unfit financially for college, Baldwin had moved with another close friend, Emile Capouya, to Belle Mead, New Jersey, in 1943, both of them getting employment in a defense-related industry.[54] But with lingering dreams of becoming a writer and with little patience for the high level of racial prejudice in the Garden State, Baldwin had trouble holding onto his job and was forced to move back in with his family in Harlem, a neighborhood that, as Baldwin explained, had fallen into financial and spiritual ruin as its young men were shipped overseas and a neighborhood that would eventually explode in a bloody riot later that year, coincidentally on the same day that Baldwin buried his deceased father. But the confusions in Harlem to which Baldwin returned were for him part and parcel of numerous national upheavals in the mid-1940s—marriages that did not survive the course of the war, soldiers who, in the absence of their wives or girlfriends, "had homosexual encounters in CO camps or in the service," chastity promises that ended with hasty abortions "before husbands returned from overseas," decency and decorum replaced by experimentation with drugs, sex, and "minor infringements of the law," and Saturday evening parties that ended with "someone, possibly oneself, [who] would have a crying jag or have to be restrained from murder or suicide."[55] Everything that was solid, as Baldwin's suicidal friend had discovered, had begun to melt away. Baldwin recalled that "life was beginning to tell us who we are, and what life was—news no one has ever wanted to hear." In this, he was merely repeating the sentiments of modernist writers of all persuasions who recognized that the experience of total war, which climaxed with the horrifying encounter with the nuclear sublime, had forced Western society to come face to face with a landscape now devoid of solidity.

Like Jackson Pollock, Jack Kerouac, and Allen Ginsberg, Baldwin's emergence as an artist coincided with the catastrophe of World War II. When he returned to Harlem in 1943, Baldwin held an endless series of part-time jobs, including meatpacking, garment making, and dish washing, that did little to improve his personal situation, a veritable dead end that probably would have led to his own collapse if he had not stumbled upon the postwar bohemian artistic circles in Greenwich Village. Inspired by the eccentric crowd he met, Baldwin began working on his first novel, tentatively titled *Crying Holy*, which detailed in stark prose his troubled upbringing. Like Pollock, Kerouac, and Ginsberg, Baldwin too struggled with how to redeem a world in crisis, a problem that was not merely an academic one but for Baldwin a deep existential one. In this sense, his early career paralleled that of most romantic modernists. In words that echoed those of Barnett Newman and Norman Mailer, Baldwin openly admitted that he felt a sense of "failure, elimination, and rejection" (309) in a sterile, disenchanted American landscape. In response, he fled to Paris in 1948, joining Richard Wright, Asa Benveniste, and others in building a new American artistic community abroad. Baldwin, like his compatriots, recognized the scars on the bodies of his fellow Americans—on his fellow Harlem residents suffering under the legacy of racial oppression, on returning World War II veterans unable to escape the memories of the atrocities abroad, and on the wives left behind who struggled to hold their families and themselves together. In large measure, argued Baldwin, the palpable sense of despair after 1945 was connected to a lack of any political certainties. "All political hopes and systems," said Baldwin, "seemed morally bankrupt: for, if Buchenwald was wrong, what, then, *really* made Hiroshima right?" (308) Those individuals like himself who had fled to Paris after the war (what the newspapers referred to as "the 'new' expatriates") sought different answers, dispensing with "all formulas and all safety in favor of the chilling unpredictability of experience" (309). He had hoped, naïvely enough, that such rootlessness would lead to growth.

But of course, Paris was, as William Burroughs, Allen Ginsberg, and other denizens of the Beat Hotel were to discover, a disappointment—a "large, inconvenient, indifferent city" littered with aggressive police officers, sexually reserved French citizens, and poor indoor plumbing. Determined to escape the puritanical culture of their homeland and angry at the direction of American politics, this "lost generation" tried to evade the creeping tide of political and social repression by rediscovering themselves abroad, a project that, according to Baldwin, was doomed to fail. "We had been perfectly willing," explained Baldwin, "to refer to all the other Americans as children—in the beginning; we had not know what it meant; we had not known that we were included" (311). As he said in another context, his fellow writers were searching for a purity that did not exist, and in so doing, much like the members of the Eisenhower administration who refused to recognize that the world had changed, were in fact running from themselves. "It seems to me," argued Baldwin, "that the confusion is revealed, for example, in those dreadful speeches by Eisenhower, those incredible speeches by Nixon, they sound very much, after all, like the jargon of the Beat Generation . . . Jack Kerouac says 'Holy, Holy' and we say Red China does not exist. But it really does."[56] This search for purity was a symptom of a certain kind of madness. As Baldwin explained, "the converts [to Reich], indeed, moved in a certain euphoric aura of well-being, which could not last. They had become more generous, but less, not more open, but more closed."[57] In clinging to characterological release as the medium for authentic expression and by shuffling to Europe in search of a new frontier, this lost generation had in actuality forfeited themselves. When he returned home in 1956, Baldwin had come to reject the limitations of romantic modernism and had begun, like many others, to rethink his artistic practices.

Baldwin served as the perfect commentator on this trend within the American avant-garde community. A devotee of Henry James, a friend of the abstract painter Beauford Delaney, and a regular contributor to literary journals such as *Partisan Review*, Baldwin was one of many postwar writers who turned away from the realist fiction and protest novels that characterized the literature of the Popular Front era and who looked to the complexity, ambiguity, and dissonance of modernist forms to offer a more nuanced account of man's psychic life. In many ways, Baldwin straddled the line between high modernism and romantic modernism, having close friends and associates in both circles and writing literary and cultural criticism that echoed their themes. Baldwin recognized that the traumatic experience of World War II and the threat of impending nuclear catastrophe had shaken the core of man, revealing, in this recently castrated state, the fundamental lack at the center of his being. Recent economic and social dislocations had precipitated this widespread psychological trauma, and the experience of the nuclear sublime confirmed it. "The world [has] prepared no place for you," observed Baldwin, "and if the world had its way, no place would ever exist."[58] But like David Riesman, C. Wright Mills, and Ralph Ellison, Baldwin refused to engage in the metaphysical speculations that drove the artistic projects of Kerouac, Newman, Rothko, and others. He refused, in other words, to view the self in a strictly vertical way, unwilling to believe that the present historical crisis could be overcome by viewing the self only through reference to archaic mythologies, Jungian archetypes, or primitive cultures. This search for a form of purity uncontaminated by the flux of time was not only immature but nonsensical. Baldwin directly challenged those artists who were "in the grip of a weird nostalgia, dreaming of a vanished state of security and order, against which dream, unfailingly and unconsciously, they tested and very often lost their lives" (290).

All of Baldwin's writings confronted in one way or another what he saw as the desperate attempt by many to flee from the historical conditions that gave birth to them and to posit themselves in a realm of unconditioned and untainted freedom. This perpetual escape was for Baldwin part of the larger cultural madness at the center of the American scene, exemplified best by the appearance of the hipster and the beatnik in American literature and in urban coffeehouses. In a 1954 *Partisan Review* article, "A Question of Identity," Baldwin argued that this new bohemian culture, in its desperate panic to shore up the borders of the self from characterological entrapment or from the cancer of totalitarianism, was ironically engaging in the most American of projects. As Baldwin explained, "this little band of bohemians, are grimly single-minded as any evangelical sect, illustrate, by the very ferocity with which they disavow American attitudes, one of the most American of attributes, the inability to believe that time is real."[59] Historical time was evaded for mythological or primitive time, all as part of an escape from contaminating influences. According to such a perspective, "society, it would seem, is a flimsy structure, beneath contempt, designed by and for all the other people, and experience is nothing more than sensation—so many sensations, added up like arithmetic, give one the rich, full life." But to view experience in such a way was to ignore the historical forces that provided the grounds for being. "The American confusion," argued Baldwin, seems "to be based on the very nearly unconscious assumption that it is possible to consider the person apart from all the forces, which have produced them" (94). This search for purity, whether as a drive for illicit pleasures or for a moment of grace, was destined to collapse upon itself. Jack Kerouac himself acknowledged as much in the melancholic ending of *On the Road*.

But even more troubling, according to Baldwin, was the fact that this moment of purity so sought after was aided by the appropriation or usurpation of marginalized groups to whom these bohemians looked to shore up their own sense of identity. In a 1961 *Esquire* article, "The Black Boy Looks at the White Boy," Baldwin famously confronted the most blatant use of racial surrogacy—Norman Mailer's promotion of the philosophy of hip in "The White Negro." In this piece, Mailer announced the emergence of the hipster as the new cultural vanguard—a philosophical and existential psychopath who had dispensed with the trappings of character armoring, had delved into the deepest recesses of the human mind, had confronted the madness at the core of man's being, and had thereby escaped the trappings of an overcivilized, totalitarian world. Emerging from the wreckage of World War II, Mailer's hipster had learned to dispense with the baggage of the past and to live in the ever-evolving present, rejecting all of the staid visions, political programs, and remedies that had come before and appearing instead as a mystical shaman with the ability to commune with the spiritual world. But the hipster was neither born from a virgin birth nor created ex nihilo. Instead, the hipster originated in the unlikely marriage between the white bohemian world and the downtrodden, primitive world of black Americans. As Mailer explained, "in such places as Greenwich Village, a ménage à trois was completed—the bohemian and the juvenile delinquent came face-to-face with the Negro, and the hipster was a fact in American life."[60] The hipster in this sense had not joined in revolutionary solidarity with his marginalized companion; he had instead appropriated his libidinal energy and had emerged as a new man himself. "The hipster had absorbed the existentialist synapses of the Negro," said Mailer, "and for practical purposes could be considered a white Negro" (341). The hipster, as this "white Negro," had emerged out of the American urban landscape like "the wise primitive in a giant jungle" (343) and had freed himself from the trappings of civilization.

In his *Esquire* response, Baldwin described his troubled yet passionate relationship with Mailer, challenging not only the critical language Mailer had used against him in *Advertisements for Myself* but also the cultural politics of Mailer's brand of modernism. Baldwin had met Mailer while in Paris, and he described his admiration and envy of the writer, who had already achieved literary success. But Baldwin admitted that during their few weeks together he remained distant from Mailer, increasingly concerned about this white writer who was desperate to befriend the black jazz musicians with whom they fraternized and with whom Mailer assumed he shared a great deal. Baldwin recognized that Mailer was dangerously close to appropriating the primitivist caricatures found within romantic modernism, a move that was for Baldwin an abandonment of Mailer's more ambitious project in both *The Naked and the Dead* and *Barbary Shore*. As Baldwin explained, "Norman appeared to be imitating so many people inferior to himself, i.e., Kerouac, and all the other Suzuki rhythm boys."[61] Believing that the redemption of American society could only occur through the spiritual resources of its marginalized racial groups, Mailer, like Kerouac and others, stepped into the heralded, revolutionary place reserved for these groups and tried to internalize their imagined traits and powers. In displacing the fellahin, whose own redemption was never discussed, Mailer and Kerouac were desperately trying to rescue themselves from the national catastrophe in which they found themselves, yet doing so, according to Baldwin, in the most naïve way possible—by projecting their own sense of loss and pain onto others who were actually disenfranchised and then using them as a supposed model for a life lived in either pastoral simplicity or in reckless abandon. For Baldwin, this was merely another example of the endemic problem of naïve Americans "who believe the world is theirs and who, albeit unconsciously, expect the world to help them in the achievement of their identity" (298). Consequently, the unacknowledged void at the center of the self was filled by assuming the fantasized place of the primitive, whether in the general form of an imagined fellahin or in the specific form of African Americans or Native Americans.

In a 1951 *Partisan Review* essay, "Many Thousands Gone," Baldwin sketched out the origins of this problem, rooted in the pathological denial of any fundamental relationship between whites and blacks. For Baldwin, the images of African Americans bandied about in the novels of Kerouac and Mailer were derived from the long-standing drive on the part of white Americans to keep their fellow citizens at a distance, that is, to treat them as a social problem instead of a personal one. For centuries, African Americans were seen through a distorting sociological lens—"statistics, slums, rapes, injustices, remote violence"—all in an attempt to keep them in the shadows of American society and in the shadows of the American psyche.[62] Accordingly, "one may say that the Negro in America does not really exist except in the darkness of our minds." As a sociological category, a stereotype, and a phantom, African Americans were an imagined, not real, presence in American life, seemingly devoid of any traditions, customs, historical legacies, or intellectual sophistication, and therefore devoid of complexity. In so doing, African Americans had been deprived of any past—treated as beings existing in an eternal present and living in an eternal vacuum. For romantic modernists intent upon abstaining from the flux of history and time, this image of African American served a recuperative function, allowing them to imagine a place fundamentally separate from their restrictive American culture. As Baldwin explained in another context, "what they do see when they look at you is what they have invested you with. What they have invested you with is all the agony, and pain, and the danger, and the passion, and the torment—you know, sin, death, and hell—of which everyone in this country is terrified."[63] This recuperative function that Kerouac and Mailer invested in African Americans was built, according to Baldwin, paradoxically upon the belief in a fundamental divide between whites and blacks (in terms of culture, history, and identity), a divide crossed only by those courageous few willing to risk their own outdated selves by traveling uptown to clubs in Harlem or by sojourning to impoverished towns throughout North America. Romantic modernists engaged in both a fantasy of mastery in which the individual purged himself of all polluting attachments and character armoring and a fantasy of transcendence in which the individual removed himself from historical circumstance and from historical time by aligning with the imagined world of the primitive.

Like C. Wright Mills and David Riesman, Baldwin argued that it was impossible both to purify the self in such an elementary way and to escape from historical time in general. "People are trapped in history," argued Baldwin, "and history is trapped in them."[64] In a 1960 address, "In Search of a Majority," Baldwin laid bare the seemingly indissoluble problem of identity in America, a problem built upon the elaborate constructions used to ward off inevitable feelings of anxiety, pain, loss, and uncertainty. Any sense of identity, according to Baldwin, was a very fragile construct, built upon an endless series of unstable identifications and attachments that the self made or was forced to make. The mixture of admiration, envy, guilt, and hatred with which many Americans viewed persons of color stemmed in large measure from the projection of their own fears onto others, fears concerning love, sexuality, status, power, and the nature of identity itself. Baldwin observed that "in a way, if the Negro were not here, we might be forced to deal with ourselves and our own personalities, with all those vices, all those conundrums, and all those mysteries with which we have invested the Negro race."[65] Frightened over their unstable economic and social status and worried about their ability to resuscitate their own selves in a disenchanted world, many projected their fears and ironically their salvation onto blacks as a timeless, pastless, and primitive group. In so doing, they denied blacks of any claim to a concrete past and therefore denied themselves of any such past too. The choice then remained to fortify social and psychological segregation in the ultimate form of denial or to engage in the racial crossing and racial cross-dressing of many romantic modernists. Both solutions for Baldwin were pathological. As he argued, "the necessity of Americans to achieve an identity is a historical and a present personal fact and this is the connection between you and me" (234). By establishing and then appropriating this imaginary other—this primitive being whose powers of enjoyment, mobility, and timelessness seemed antithetical to the actual structures of society—romantic modernists negated the real presence of blacks and in so doing negated their own presence as well. In an attempt to concretize their identities through reference to some ontological grounding outside of history, they ironically furthered their original problem.

The only solution, according to Baldwin, was to remain rooted within the American landscape, a lesson he himself learned after he had sequestered himself in the mountains of Switzerland to escape his past. Although he believed this isolation from his homeland was essential to find himself, Baldwin admitted that he succeeded only by listening to Bessie Smith records and reinvesting himself in his past childhood experiences and therefore in his country. The self, explained Baldwin, was indissolubly connected to the march of history, a common, shared history that kept blacks and whites tied together through a joint yet unrecognized experience: "The one thing that all Americans have in common is that they have no other identity apart from the identity which is being achieved on this continent" (234). Bloated with a sense of grandeur stemming from the unacknowledged internalization of the imagined traits of marginalized groups, romantic modernists had forfeited any point of commonality for a sense of individual solidity. But for Baldwin, the only possible solution was to accept the fluidity of selfhood, of a lack of any total sense of coherence, and to acknowledge that the self was forever implicated and fused with those surrounding groups. "Whether I like it or not, or whether you like it or not, we are bound together forever," argued Baldwin, "we are part of each other. What is happening to every Negro in this country at any time is also happening to you" (234). For Baldwin, this marked the unlikely but unavoidable "marriage" between whites and blacks, a marriage based upon that principle "that we have not as yet been able to define" called love. Indeed, Baldwin's major contribution to the cultural politics of modernism was his reinvention of love as a guiding social principle.

This notion, which linked his modernism to the early work of Norman Brown, was elaborated most clearly in his 1962 novel, *Another Country*, which unearths the racial politics found in the bars, clubs, and apartments of Harlem and Greenwich Village in the 1950s. *Another Country* tells the story of a group of Manhattan companions who are, individually and collectively, forced to come to terms with the suicide of their friend Rufus Scott, a black jazz musician who fell into a pit of despair after the dissolution of his relationship with Leona, a southern white woman who was trying to make a new life for herself in New York. Overcome by the legacy of racial oppression in America and therefore unable to maintain any coherent sense of himself, Rufus jumps off the George Washington Bridge, leaving his friends and his sister Ida Scott to confront their complicity in his death. At the center of this struggle is Vivaldo Moore, an "Irish wop" who is at the time the closest to Rufus and the person in the best position to help him.[66] But Vivaldo's failure, particularly during their last night together when Vivaldo recognizes Rufus's pain but is unable to provide comfort, is for Baldwin endemic of the failure of white society in the 1950s to confront the legacy of racism. Vivaldo is, as Rufus repeatedly points out, a "liberal white bastard" (24) who is sympathetic to Rufus's plight but unable to understand the complexity of racial identity. More important, Vivaldo is emblematic of the new bohemian occupying Greenwich Village park benches reading Kierkegaard but refusing to recognize in any real way the void at the center of his own self. Vivaldo is a "parody of a hipster" (303), a bohemian writer who cannot finish his novel because his characters have become too distant from him, who is ever fearful of selling out to commercial interests like his friend Richard, and who abets his own loneliness by making frequent visits to Harlem prostitutes. Vivaldo's journey to jazz clubs and Harlem bars is for Baldwin symptomatic of the entire bohemian culture of New York—those who, like Jack Kerouac and Norman Mailer, believed redemption could come through associations with marginalized groups. In this, Vivaldo "had felt more alive in Harlem, for he had moved in a blaze of rage and self-congratulation and sexual excitement, with danger, like a promise waiting for him everywhere" (132). Of course Vivaldo is in reality in flight from himself; as he soon learns, "he had merely been taking refuge in the outward adventure in order to avoid the clash and tension of the adventure proceeding inexorably within" (133). In large measure, Vivaldo is trying to escape his past, in particular, his troubled childhood in the streets of Brooklyn that left him with lingering hostility toward his parents, a lingering fear of his own personal weaknesses, and an inexpressible sorrow over the person he has become. Equally troubling, Vivaldo is consumed, in subtle and unacknowledged ways, with the feeling that he failed Rufus in his moment of need.

After Rufus's death, Vivaldo falls in love with Rufus's sister Ida, a relationship that Vivaldo naïvely assumes can help both of them overcome their shared loss. Throughout the novel, Vivaldo struggles with his love for Ida, unable to get beyond the seemingly impenetrable divide between them. Most pointedly, the difficulty stems from Vivaldo continuing to view Ida, in many ways unconsciously, through fantasized images of her, unable, in a manner similar to his relationship with Rufus, to understand how scarred her position in society has made her. Vivaldo cannot understand why Ida is angry and why she in part blames him for Rufus's death: "I know, I failed him, but I loved him, too, and nobody there wanted to know that. I kept thinking, They're colored and I'm white but the same things have happened, really the *same* things, and how can I make them know that?" (113). Similarly, Vivaldo cannot see or hear Ida; he cannot see beyond her "mysterious and impenetrable" (171) face with which he has invested so much of himself, and he cannot hear what she hears in the blues songs she endlessly sings. As a result, he sees her only through a cultural screen that has demarked her in particular ways, viewing her simultaneously as a whore with an endless list of lovers and as a delicate virgin whose sexual secrets can redeem mankind. As Baldwin explained in a different context, "the white American regards his darker brother through the distorting screen created by a lifetime of conditioning."[67] Despite his bohemian façade, Vivaldo epitomizes what Baldwin saw as a form of liberalism invested in color-blind sameness but a form of liberalism unconsciously invested in race. Ida endlessly challenges Vivaldo's assumptions about her, her brother, and their background, especially at those moments in which he declares, "I'd give up my color for you" (308). As the months pass by, both of them struggling with their careers (his failed novel and her stalled singing career), their frustration eventually turns into silence, as "great areas of the unspoken, vast minefields which neither dared to cross" (320) begin to separate them.

In this sense, Baldwin was just as invested as Theodor Adorno and other high modernists in discovering the psychological sources of prejudice as well as the socioeconomic sources of this cultural screen through which individuals made sense of the world. Indeed, many of the concerns that marked high modernist discourse—mass culture, mass society, and mass politics—were part of Baldwin's early focus. His first published essay, appearing in 1948 in *Commentary* (the journal sponsored by the American Jewish Committee), investigated the problem of anti-Semitism within the African American community. "The Harlem Ghetto" explored the link between white racism and black anti-Semitism, both as examples of the common problem of religious and racial discrimination in America at large. In language that paralleled a larger discussion about the sources of prejudice, Baldwin argued that the anti-Semitism found in Harlem was the result of the internalization of self-hatred by the black community, caused by centuries of discrimination projected onto the Jewish community. Similarly, Baldwin joined the chorus of modernist critics lambasting mass culture. His contribution, for instance, to a 1959 seminar sponsored by the Tamiment Institute and attended by figures such as Hannah Arendt, Leo Lowenthal, and William Phillips echoed other modernist claims questioning the common assumption "that the cultural level of the people is subject to a steady rise."[68] Although he disliked the elitism and bourgeois mentality of defenders of high culture, he worried, like Dwight Macdonald, that the fantasies offered by mass culture did little to help Americans "to re-establish their connection with themselves, and with one another" (123). In fact, he spent most of his career lambasting the moral and political failings of his fellow Americans. In particular, despite his criticisms of what he saw as the simplistic, overly sociological depiction of damaged African Americans in the protest fiction of Richard Wright, Baldwin was deeply invested, as is evident in his anguished depiction of Rufus Scott, not just in unearthing the sources of prejudice but also in explaining to Americans the troubled legacy of racism.

But Baldwin avoided the most obvious and readily available solutions. He refused to defend the tenets of psychoanalysis or to advance a staid image of ego autonomy as high modernists had done. As he explained in *Another Country*, he "did not believe in the vast, gray sleep which was called security, did not believe in the cures, panaceas, and slogans which afflicted the world he knew."[69] Baldwin spent considerable effort denouncing some of the simplicities in conventional psychoanalytic theory. But he also did not believe in the racial surrogacy so prominent within the literary circles of the American avant-garde. The solution to these naïve proposals was not to lapse into notions of an intractable racial difference or into a form of identity politics, both of which, according to Baldwin, mirrored this search for purity. In many ways, Ida Scott in *Another Country* represents this opposing, if not reactionary, impulse—so desperate to protect herself from the forces that led to her brother's tragic end, she isolates herself from those around her, including Vivaldo, using them for her own gain. Her forced distance from Vivaldo is a product of her need for protection. But as Baldwin continuously explained throughout his writings, "the unprecedented price demanded—and at this embattled hour of the world's history—is the transcendence of the realities of color, of nations, and of altars."[70] The theme in all Baldwin's writings was this need to present not just a new image of man but a new image of communion.

In *Another Country*, Baldwin pointed to a revived notion of love as a redemptive tool—as a psychic, social, and political force that offered a new image of selfhood and of community. In this, he was not echoing the liberal notion of love offered in works such as Erich Fromm's *The Art of Loving*, in which the German theorist offered an image of love as a form of intimacy between autonomous, self-actualized individuals freed from the trappings of self-love and dependency. Fromm argued that "only the person who has faith in himself is able to be faithful to others, because only he can be sure that he will be the same at a future time as he is today, and therefore, that he will feel and act as he now expects to."[71] The art of loving for Fromm was predicated upon ego autonomy. Baldwin instead argued that love was a disruptive force, one that did not provide comfort, stability, or solidity but one that challenged, if not dismantled, the boundaries of the self. As Baldwin explained, "I use the word 'love' here not merely in the personal sense but as a state of being, or a state of grace—not in the infantile American sense of being made happy but in the tough and universal sense of quest and daring and growth."[72] Aesthetic self-affirmation or self-discovery did little to heal social ruptures or individual traumas and did little to heal the distance between antagonists or between lovers. This distance was overcome only by accepting an active relation to another. For Baldwin, love was dependent upon the radical unsettling of the borders of the self, upon a moment in which the self accepted the intrusion of alterity and thereby risked its own coherence. In so doing, love created a provisional moment of communion and discovered a new way of speaking that acknowledged the vulnerability and pain of others. Love was marked, according to Baldwin, by the "halting attempt to relate the terms of my experience to yours; and to find out what specific principle, if any, unites us in spite of all the obvious disparities, some of which are profound, and most of which are entirely misunderstood."[73] In this sense, love was for Baldwin the most difficult and the most imperative of projects.

The personal and political nature of love is revealed most fully in *Another Country* in the strained relationship between Vivaldo and Ida, one unable to confront his personal pain and his personal assumptions about race and the other unable to offer anything to her lover (or to the world at large) because of her abounding and legitimate fears of self-destruction. As Vivaldo openly admits, "love was a country he knew nothing about," and his affection for Ida is motivated unconsciously by the color of her skin and therefore her difference from him: "Perhaps it was only because she was not white that he dared to bring her the offering of himself."[74] The turning point for Vivaldo comes when he begins to recognize that he failed his friend Rufus, or more directly, when he admits that he loved Rufus but failed him. In a conversation late in the novel with Eric, his actor friend who has recently returned from France, Vivaldo admits with much grief that his desperate desire to save Ida is connected to his unremitting sorrow that he failed Rufus in his most dire moment. Unable to acknowledge the social roots of Rufus's pain, Vivaldo was unable to overcome the divide between them. Rufus's accusations against Vivaldo were a product of Vivaldo's failure to tell his friend that he loved him: "But, oh Lord, when he died, I thought that maybe I could have saved him if I'd just reached out that quarter of an inch between us on that bed, and held him" (343). After their conversation, Vivaldo falls asleep, with Eric's head on his chest, and dreams of his deceased friend, a dream about himself being chased in a strange country by an unseen enemy only to be saved by Rufus, who sacrifices himself to let Vivaldo live. As he slowly awakens from this dream, admitting to Rufus at that moment that he loved him, Vivaldo finally recognizes Eric's embrace, making Vivaldo see that Eric loves him too. Their brief sexual encounter transforms Vivaldo, allowing him for the first time to become passive and to give himself over to the love of another. In so doing, Vivaldo's entire identity is briefly destabilized, no longer bound by the definitions or restrictions he had once willfully imposed: "He felt that he had stepped off a precipice into an air which held him inexorably up . . . and seemed to see, vastly and horribly down, into the bottom of his heart, that heart which contained all the possibilities that he could name and yet others that he could not name" (386). In this way, Vivaldo's own self becomes paradoxically both more mysterious and more opaque.

Of course Eric and Vivaldo recognize that this moment of tenderness cannot last; both have other lovers to whom they must attend. But this transformative experience finally allows Vivaldo to love Ida in the way that she needs. Soon after, he returns home and is able, for the first time, to accept her confession—her anguished admittance that not only had she slept with Steve Ellis, a lecherous record producer, but that she had originally gotten together with him to save herself from Rufus's fate. In large measure, as Ida explains to him, she had spiraled out of control because Vivaldo "didn't want to know what was happening to [her]" (422). Unwilling to acknowledge the particularities of her situation as a disenfranchised, marginalized African American woman, Vivaldo had originally believed that the distance between them could easily be overcome. But in the end, Vivaldo recognizes his responsibility in this breakdown of communication—of a failed love hampered by a seemingly incommensurable difference. In the beginning, Vivaldo could accept the presence only of Ida in his life; he could not accept the intrusion of her story—an individual past driven and restrained by the boundaries of race, gender, and class—in his life and could not accept his complicity in the trajectory of her story. Love, as a form of generosity and responsiveness, entailed accepting responsibility for the past on both an individual and collective level. His long history of racial surrogacy—his frequent trips to Harlem for joy, for kicks, and for sex—was indelibly tied to the pain of Ida's own life, for which Vivaldo finally begins to accept responsibility. Ida does not want, as she explains to him, "understanding" (430); she wants acknowledgment. In this provisional moment of togetherness, Vivaldo is stripped of his purity and is forced to recognize that his own identity is inextricably mixed with Ida's own story as well as the stories of all those around him. In the end, "her long fingers stroked his back, and he began, slowly, with a horrible, strangling sound, to weep, for she was stroking his innocence out of him" (431). As the two embattled lovers recuperate, having finally broken through to each other, the rainy sky begins to clear up and the darkened clouds start to disappear.

But love, defined by Baldwin as both the open disclosure of the self to another and the acceptance of the self's implication in the story of another, was not just a personal force. Love had social and political parameters as well. In part, love was about subjects who came together in a form of communion, willing to risk their own individual purity. The goal for Baldwin was to produce a demonstrable form of solidity between lovers without lapsing into a gross homogeneity. As he explained, "if you can examine and face your life you can discover the terms with which you are connected to other lives, and they can discover, too, the terms with which they are connected to other people."[75] The only way to do so was to acknowledge that the self was not a metaphysical entity but a lived, historical being, that is, to accept that the self could discover itself only in and through the historical traditions, customs, and forces in which it was situated. "The great force of history," argued Baldwin, "comes from the fact that we carry it within us, are unconsciously controlled by it in many ways, and history is literally *present* in all that we do."[76] The grounds of communication that love required could be established only by accepting an abiding tradition holding individuals together, a tradition constructed from a multiplicity of voices, stories, and experiences. The lens of history provided not only a framework for self-understanding and self-articulation but also a common point of identification in which the alterity of the other was neither neglected nor obliterated but recognized. "We become social creatures," argued Baldwin, "because we cannot live any other way."[77] Love, as Baldwin explained in his novel, was not merely a communal force but, in a certain sense, the grounds for another country entirely, a country in which the tragedies, traumas, and disruptions were individually and collectively acknowledged and in which the implication of the self in the lives of others was accepted. Rufus himself recognizes this connection while standing on the subway platform at Fifty-ninth Street: "Many white people and many black people, chained together in time and in space, and by history, and all of them in a hurry."[78] This connection is symbolized throughout the novel by the cufflinks that Eric had given to Rufus years ago, which are then taken by Ida, who converts them into earrings; they were, as Rufus realized, a "confession of [Eric's] love" (24), a love that in many ways held them all together. Such a love required a loosening of the boundaries of the self. To do otherwise was to risk catastrophe. As Baldwin repeatedly emphasized, "the climate and the events of the last decade, and the steady pressure of the 'cold' war, have given Americans yet another means of avoiding self-examination."[79]

CHAPTER SIX

Masculinity, Spontaneity, and the Act: The Bodily Ego of Jasper Johns

At a 1960 solo exhibition in New York, the abstract artist Jasper Johns presented his bluntest statement about the hostile atmosphere of the New York art scene. Having recently achieved notoriety for his 1958 one-man show at the Leo Castelli Gallery, where he exhibited his infamous painting *Flag*, Johns spent the next several years deconstructing the assumptions about art within the abstract expressionist movement. His *Flag* painting, for instance, challenged the widespread ban on direct representation by offering a literal translation of the iconic American image, a rigid design that was clearly out of place in art galleries filled with the explosive canvases of Jackson Pollock and his followers. But with his 1960 work *Painting with Two Balls*, Johns was criticizing more than just the aesthetic norms of abstract expressionism; he was also criticizing the posturing and arrogance of artists like Pollock and Barnett Newman. His painting was a chaotic landscape of colorful, gestural brushstrokes composed on three separate panels with two painted balls forced into a darkened slit between the top two panels. The energy of his brushwork echoed the work of other abstract expressionists but the title of the painting and the obvious anatomical reference within the work itself reflected Johns's personal concerns. A gay man and a reserved man, Johns had little respect for the overtly masculine displays of his fellow artists who believed that the potency of their brushwork, either dripped, splashed, or poured across the canvas, testified in some way to their heroic natures. Such artists, according to Johns, who created "ballsy painting" or art that was painted "with two balls," naïvely believed that their paintings were a reflection of their masculinity and therefore a representation of some pristine, autonomous self that created artwork uncontaminated by any social or cultural baggage.[1]

Marginalized in such an art world, Johns struck back, revealing in *Painting with Two Balls* the absurd pretensions within abstract expressionism. His use of encaustic instead of enamel to build up his exuberant brushstrokes gave his painting an almost frozen quality that mimicked the techniques of action painters like Pollock but that drained such techniques of their presumed dynamism. He was concerned that abstract expressionists had naïvely reduced modern art to being merely a representation of themselves or had simplistically reduced the artistic process to being merely a "cathartic process" or "release of energy."[2] Johns was clearly not painting in the same potent manner and not in the same anatomically derived way. Johns recognized that the widespread defense of abstract painting as a masculine enterprise was in fact part of a larger cultural panic about shifting gender identities in the new economic landscape of the early Cold War. In *Painting with Two Balls*, Johns exposed the not-so-subtle connection between aesthetic debates within modernist circles over the nature of art and a corresponding debate about the nature of male subjectivity. For romantic modernists, their project to dismantle the artificial boundaries of the ego was dependent upon the release of libidinal energy, a project that was intimately connected to their aesthetic practices. But this project was also intimately connected to a larger cultural panic over the perceived loss of autonomy in modern society, which many believed was caused by the loss of any sense of masculinity in a world of castrated, dependent men. For many romantic modernists, the autonomous individual toward which Reichian therapeutic practices were directed seemed almost extinct. In response, many took it upon themselves to reclaim their own masculine identities within this damaged landscape, whether through aggressive sexual displays, alcoholic drinking binges, or spontaneous styles of artistic production.

In response, Johns openly mocked this modernist panic. "It's a phrase I used to hear all the time," Johns explained in reference to the critical discourse about his fellow painters, "that 'he was really painting with two balls'—I thought perhaps that was intended" (156–57). Obviously, Johns had little patience for those artists whose works were imbued with this kind of anxiety. Two things in particular bothered Johns about the aggressive masculine displays rampant within the New York school. First, he was not only personally intimidated by the often rough treatment he received as a gay man in a social network consumed by an existential panic disguised by an artificial machismo but also professionally frustrated by the limitations placed upon modernist art. Unlike Jackson Pollock and Willem de Kooning, who believed that their work was in some foundational way an undistorted expression of their true selves and a definitive example of their artistic potency, Johns believed that modernist art needed to forgo such lingering romantic notions. "There was this idea associated with Abstract Expressionist painting that the work was a primal expression of feeling," argued Johns, "and I knew that that was not what I wanted my work to be like" (256). Like Kenneth Burke and others, Johns argued that art need not be a simple reflection of the artist himself, that the actions of an artist made on the canvas were not primarily designed to refer to some private inner realm but to the complicated interaction between the individual and his surrounding milieu. As Johns explained, "my work is largely concerned with relations between seeing and knowing, seeing and saying, seeing and believing" (122). Indeed, Johns was interested in complicating the ways in which the individual encountered and navigated his way through a cultural landscape imbued with a surplus of meaning and with endless possibilities. The problem was to make the individual aware of such possibilities. Second, Johns argued that such an aesthetic practice required a radical reconception of the individual subject. Unlike his fellow artists, Johns refused to believe in simplistic notions of autonomy, of a human subject whose desires and intentions were somehow fundamentally separate from the context in which they were given meaning. In contrast, Johns offered an image of the human subject as inescapably embodied—a being who came into existence through the complicated balancing of the litany of social and psychic pressures impinging upon it. In so doing, Johns helped to rethink the nature of artistic expression and to overturn modernist practices in the 1950s. Wrapped in the symbolism of the American flag, Johns returned modern art to the landscape in which it was created—to its national and cultural origins.

The Crisis in American Masculinity

In a 1958 *Esquire* magazine article, Arthur Schlesinger, Jr., reiterating his concerns about the widespread flight from "the unendurable burden of freedom into the womblike security of the group," connected the loss of any coherent sense of identity in modern life to a perceived decline in "American masculinity."[3] Schlesinger's invocation of a crisis of masculinity to discuss the problem of the weakening of individual ego autonomy was in fact a common trope during the early Cold War. Schlesinger pointed to a number of cultural venues—the theater, the movie house, and the psychoanalyst's couch—in which this "age of sexual ambiguity" was most visible. According to Schlesinger, a number of postwar changes, including the centralization of economic life and the standardization of culture, were depriving the "American male" of any "rugged clarity of outline" (237). Castrated by the "subliminal invasion" of mass culture, men of all social classes had lost any sense of identity, and Schlesinger was uncertain whether or not they had the strength to lead a militarized nation. Schlesinger, as historian K. A. Cuordileone has astutely noted, was one of many Cold War intellectuals who, in the formulation of a new liberal politics antithetical to the extremes of left- and right-wing ideologies, linked the vulnerability of the nation's body politic to a weakening of its "vital center."[4] On the left, according to Schlesinger, were the "Doughface," the progressive, and the fellow traveler—those naïve optimists with "a weakness for impotence" caused by their misguided faith in historical progress and by their pathological projection of "private grievances" onto the public order.[5] On the right were the "plutocrat," the capitalist, and the conservative—those "impotent" organization men who had "emasculated the political energies of the ruling class" (15) and who had allowed "mass production and mass organization" to take "the guts out of" (26) the bourgeois individual. Both the Doughface and the plutocrat had led the masses into "a profound and trance-like political apathy" and had helped to convert "the 'anxious man'" into "the 'totalitarian man'" (159). Looking for a masculine "doer" to revitalize American politics, Schlesinger, like many other Cold War intellectuals, saw only a country filled with "utopians" and "wailers."

The worries Schlesinger expressed in his central work *The Vital Center* were emblematic of a national panic that American men had lost the tough-minded, virile character of the heroic, rugged individual of decades past and that therefore the body politic was too soft to resist penetration by threatening forces. Discussions of the problem of masculine weakness were ubiquitous. Mass-circulation magazines presented articles such as "Masculinity: What Is It?" "The U.S. Male . . . . . . Is He First-Class?" and "What Is a Man?" Even more directly, *Look* magazine published a three-part installment in 1958 on "The American Male," asking "why do women dominate him," "why is he afraid to be different," and "why does he work so hard?"[6] Four factors in particular had supposedly caused the American male to lose the "meaning of 'I,'" that originally unalterable sense of identity and individual worth.[7]

Most notably, the transition from a goods-producing to a service-oriented society had redefined man's economic identity in relationship to meaningless paper shuffling. Best-selling publications such as William Whyte's *The Organization Man* and William Kornhauser's *The Politics of Mass Society* detailed the "softness" of America's office clerks, salespersons, and college-trained professionals whose only acknowledged skills were verbal and interpersonal and whose only career goals were adherence to managerial decisions and the "gray flannel mind." Second, as the brawny industrial laborer from the turn of the century supposedly disappeared, doctors noted an alarming decline in man's physical condition. Mounting work pressures were increasing cases of heart disease and hypertension, in what was popularly termed "the executive crack-up."[8] Magazines such as *Newsweek*, *American Mercury*, and *Time* offered an "anatomy of executive health" and gave housewives instructions on "how to keep your husband alive."[9] Psychologists such as Edmund Bergler and James Slotkin also described a form of "male menopause" afflicting middle-aged men, defined as the inability to confront family responsibilities, work pressures, and the inevitable certainty of death.[10] Third, modern advertising had made men just as susceptible as women to consumerism. As appearance and attire became key markers of occupational status in a service-centered economy, men had seemingly fallen victim to the exhibitionism traditionally associated with feminine display. Indeed, the *New York Times* reported an alarming escalation in the volume of men's cosmetic business, making the American man "as much a slave to the American credo of staying and looking young as any woman."[11]

The most unsettling trend, however, was the realignment of masculinity with fatherhood and family commitment. As massive federal funds made homeownership more accessible and as increasing employment prospects offered larger financial rewards, more and more Americans found security from threatening international and national conflicts in the comforts offered by a new suburban lifestyle. The domestic revival of the postwar years—suburban sprawl, rising birth rates, declining divorce numbers, and so on—marked the ideological importance of the nuclear family as a bulwark against Communist subversion and atomic holocaust.[12] This ideology of domestic containment, in which family roles were carefully delineated, rewrote traditional masculinity in relation to paternal responsibilities. As a litany of popular magazines, child-rearing experts, and Hollywood films pleaded with American men to take seriously their responsibility to be a guiding influence on their children, fatherhood was refashioned as a secure identity for the alienated, corporate-minded professional. But although the middle-class family had become "the center of attention," many remained unconvinced.[13] The "bondage" of the institution of marriage, as psychologist Edith Stern argued in the pages of *American Mercury*, was "a cultural superimposition."[14] Softened by the strictures of family togetherness, the "domesticated male" was often unable to reconcile his new identity with "the image of masculinity that history has bequeathed to him—the image of man the warrior, man the conqueror of animate and inanimate nature, man the explorer, man the amorous predator."[15]

Solutions to this perceived crisis of masculinity were just as prevalent as apparent causes. In typical high modernist fashion, Arthur Schlesinger promoted the aesthetic experience. As he explained, "thoughtful exposure to music, to painting, to poetry, to the beauties of nature, can do much to restore the inwardness, and thereby the identity, of man."[16] The highbrow nature of this solution, however, was not widely translatable, and popular culture, as historian Michael Kimmel has noted, offered more accessible ideas.[17] Fitness gurus such as Jack LaLanne urged the domesticated male to reclaim his physical strength through strenuous exercise. The widespread popularity of woodworking and the arts-and-crafts movement convinced suburban homeowners to convert their basements into mock artisanal workshops. A number of magazines targeted specifically at men such as *Real: The Exciting Magazine for Men* and *Impact: Bold True Action for Men* offered some refuge as did detective novels and Mickey Spillane stories. Hollywood films also sought to help navigate this ideological confusion by presenting a number of roles for the American male—Humphrey Bogart and Gary Cooper portrayed loners, neurotics, and drunken characters left behind by the postwar era, and John Wayne and Marlon Brando, albeit in different ways, rewrote the face of rugged individualism.[18] More pointedly, the libertarian sermons appearing in *Playboy* magazine and in the fiction of Henry Miller and Norman Mailer promoted bohemianism and masculine flight from domestic responsibilities.

Such solutions, however, only touched upon the most alarming threat to fantasized images of normative masculinity—growing anxiety about male virility. In his widely discussed findings concerning American sexual behavior, scientist Alfred Kinsey and his colleagues noted that personal frustrations had led to an alarming decline in proper male sexual functioning.[19] Inadequacies ranging from premature ejaculation to erectile dysfunction to general inhibition were detailed in numerous other studies. As one researcher argued, "Most male sexual inadequacy in our society is caused not so much by deep-seated, particularized psychological disturbances as by a more generalized fear of failure, on the one hand, and sexual Puritanism, on the other hand."[20] Family responsibilities, work pressures, and moral restrictions had unwittingly placed male potency in question. Following Kinsey's study, an explosion of psychological literature challenged the rampant fear and morality surrounding sexual behavior, literature that prefigured the sexual revolution of the ensuing decades. Academic and popular titles such as Edwin Hirsch's *Sexual Fear* (1950), Oliver Butterfield's *Sexual Harmony in Marriage* (1953), Albert Ellis's *Sex Without Guilt* (1958), Ira Reiss's *Premarital Sexual Standards in America* (1960), and James Collier's *The Hypocritical American* (1964) hoped to end the "era of Hush-and-Pretend" regarding sexual practices and to restore proper sexual functioning.[21]

Consequently, the most prominent reaction to concerns over waning masculinity was an overly aggressive phallic display—visible evidence that American men were merely frustrated and not, as many had claimed, impotent. Like the portrait of the weak-willed male breadwinner in Billy Wilder's *The Seven Year Itch*, whose hands were all over Marilyn Monroe like "the creature from the Black Lagoon," images of man's primal sexual nature were ubiquitous. Dime-store novels, pulp-fiction comic books, James Bond films, and *Playboy* centerfolds reaffirmed heterosexual masculinity. As sociologist Pitirim Sorokin noted in his 1956 book *The American Sexual Revolution*, the recent "sexualization of American culture" had resulted in the replacement of "homo sapiens" by "homo sexualis" who was "packed with genital, anal, oral, and cutaneous libidos."[22] Male sexuality, many argued, ran counter to the ideology of domestic containment. Writing in the *American Mercury*, psychologist Edith Stern argued, for instance, that "a raging, albeit often unconscious conflict arises when man's natural proclivity to be footloose and free, promiscuous and irresponsible, is checked by society's demand that he come home in time for dinner."[23] Arguments about man's inability to repress his erotic urges were made by a number of other psychologists including Theodor Reik, who argued that the sexual drive "is entirely incapable of being sublimated . . . [and] the satisfaction of this particular urge cannot be fulfilled by the substitution of another goal," comments supposedly proven true by Alfred Kinsey's findings regarding the high rate of premarital sex in the postwar era.[24]

Romantic modernists who searched for a biological instinct to liberate man from the trappings of character were quite enthusiastic about these discussions of man's rebellious sexuality. In *Generation of Vipers*, Philip Wylie, for instance, argued that American society was too virginal and too repressed. Pointing to "the laws, rules, superstitions, taboos, dirty names, repugnances, and secrets" that impinged upon "our sexual instinct," Wylie called for a more "naturalistic attitude" toward intercourse to help liberate man's character.[25] His claims were soon echoed by other romantic modernists. Noting that "the drive that underwrites almost the whole of behavior" was "the object of every conceivable repressive force," psychiatrist Robert Lindner declared any prohibition on sexuality a "travesty on human nature" and linked most neurotic problems to sexual repression.[26] More important, for Lindner and others, sexuality seemed to counter the most pernicious forms of social control. In his 1957 review of George Orwell's *1984*, critic Irving Howe noted that the author had presented a compelling model of "the totalitarian state in its 'pure' or 'essential' form," but that he had exaggerated the ability of the state to eliminate the drive for "erotic pleasures."[27] Believing such pleasures could not be "violated as thoroughly as Orwell suggests," Howe argued that "these drives may prove to be one of the most enduring forces of resistance to the totalitarian state" (247). Such remarks were championed by the editors of *Playboy* magazine who argued that sex was "so intimately" connected "with the rest of human experience that it is impossible to conceive of a society" without the existence of "the primal sex urge," except perhaps within a "very cold, totalitarian one."[28] As fears about mass society increased, romantic modernists became obsessed with images of sexual potency. References to Jungian archetypes as the key to man's being were quickly replaced by more libidinal notions. Indeed, sex was, as Dean Moriarty explained in Jack Kerouac's *On the Road*, "the one and only holy and important thing in life."[29]

Romantic Modernism and the Cult of the Orgasm

The intellectual justification for the reassertion of sexuality as the foundation of man's inner nature was again provided by Wilhelm Reich, whose early work *The Function of the Orgasm* helped many to rethink male subjectivity. Linking character armor to the compulsive morality of religious and cultural institutions, romantic modernists followed Reich in arguing that most disturbances in man's personality were the result of impediments to proper sexual functioning. Writing to his friends Carolyn and Neal Cassady in 1953, Jack Kerouac, for instance, exclaimed, "for God's sake read and dig Wilhelm Reich's *Function of the Orgasm* before its too late, he has discovered that all neurotic and somatic physical problems arise from lack of straight genital potency, man cock, woman cunt (vagina not clitoris orgasm)."[30] Indeed, many romantic modernists used Reichian theory as a defense for their own bohemian activities. For instance, Saul Bellow used Reich's criticisms of monogamy to engage in extramarital affairs, retreating often, like his friend Isaac Rosenfeld, to the Casbah, a bohemian refuge on Hudson Street in Manhattan for writers and intellectuals seeking sexual fulfillment outside their marriages.[31] Norman Mailer's personal exploits were of course the stuff of legend, and his belligerent defense of what he referred to as "*serious* promiscuity" in the face of the "liquidational" use of marriage was tinged with Reichian language.[32]

Having returned psychoanalysis to a study of the physiological, Reich criticized the social restraints that alienated man from his instinctual energies, and he redirected his therapeutic practices toward the sensory experience of libidinal pleasures. As such, the orgasm became the center of his psychoanalytic theory. Psychic health, according to Reich, was dependent upon "orgastic potency, i.e., upon the degree to which one can surrender to and experience the climax of excitation in the natural sexual act."[33] The "biopsychic motility" toward which Reich's therapy was directed depended upon the dissolution of the muscular rigidity that plagued the "sexually neurotic" individual. The inability to achieve a satisfactory orgasm led to the build up of nondischarged orgone energy, which served in turn to fuel "anxiety neuroses" such as excessive masturbation and "psychoneuroses" such as Oedipal fixations. Committed to the notion of a "sex-economy" within the human body, Reich argued that "the energy source of the neurosis is created by the difference between the accumulation and discharge of sexual energy" (121). Consequently, there were two preconditions for the establishment of orgastic potency. The first was the dissolution of any infantile fixations caused by compulsive parental emphasis on oral and anal functions during childhood. The second was the liberation of sexual energy from its entrapment in psychic neuroses and chronic muscular tension. Only under such conditions could man achieve proper orgasm, which Reich defined as "the capacity to discharge completely the dammed-up sexual excitation through involuntary, pleasurable convulsions of the body" (102). Orgastic potency, however, was inhibited by modern society in several ways: through social barriers such as the ban on premarital intercourse and through psychic barriers such as the moralistic voice of the superego.

Reich's theory of the orgasm soon became the basis for the work of many romantic modernists. The early career of Paul Goodman, for instance, was marked by his enthusiastic promotion of this ejaculatory foundation of the self. Goodman discovered Reich in 1944 when reviewing the work of A. S. Neill for the *New Republic* and plunged deeply into the writings of "perhaps the most brilliant of [this] generation of psychoanalysts."[34] Goodman even underwent analysis in 1946 with a Reichian therapist, Alexander Lowen, finding "great benefit from it both physically and emotionally," and he also incorporated such therapeutic techniques into his own counseling practices.[35] In a sympathetic article, "The Political Meanings Behind Some Recent Revisions of Freud," Goodman praised Reich's work as "a Freudian deviation to the left" and linked his own libertarian position to Reich's sexual politics.[36] Of course, other romantic modernists explored the question of orgastic potency in a much more personal way. For instance, Norman Mailer acknowledged that his overemphasis on orgasmic pleasure as the key component of psychic life was due to his reading of *The Function of the Orgasm*. Later in life Mailer claimed that Reich "was no literary influence, but he gave me one idea—a man's character is in his orgasm, a man's neuroses are in his orgasm, everything is in his orgasm."[37] In a series of short stories, Mailer elaborated on the hipster's understanding that "the good orgasm opens his possibilities and bad orgasm imprisons him."[38] In his 1952 story "The Man Who Studied Yoga," originally intended as a prologue to a series of books never written, Mailer mockingly narrates the spiritual malaise of a former radical, now lowbrow magazine writer, penned in by his unsympathetic wife, by his Freudian analyst, and by "the womb of middle-class life."[39] His desperate search for spiritual answers missing in contemporary religion, mainstream politics, and orthodox psychoanalysis leads to the voyeuristic pleasures found in a pornographic movie, a sad and artificial substitute for the deeper pleasures of the Reichian orgasm.

Spontaneity and the Ejaculating Artist

Besides offering an intellectual defense of unimpeded sexuality as a solution to this perceived crisis in masculinity, Reich's theoretical work was also attractive to romantic modernists because the Austrian analyst promoted the figure of the artist as the true embodiment of genital sexuality and therefore as the true revolutionary vanguard. The modern artist, Reich asserted in the 1946 preface to *The Mass Psychology of Fascism*, had overcome "the superficial layer of character, of self-control, and tolerance" by creating "genuine art" that was "genuinely revolutionary."[40] Recognizing the ever-present threat instrumentality posed to the creative moment inherent within *poiesis*, romantic modernists followed Reich in rejecting Marxism and promoting the artist over the proletariat as the true revolutionary subject. In a 1965 essay, "Art and Work," Harold Rosenberg, for instance, distinguished between art and craft production, the former focusing on the "psychic experience of creation" and the latter focusing on "the object and its qualities, to the exclusion of the personality of the artist."[41] Consequently, the modern artist was the true proletarian, the only figure who was "able *not to be alienated*, because he works directly with the materials of his own experience."[42] Such work was done, according to Rosenberg, "not in obedience to external need but as a necessity of the worker's personality," and it was "spontaneous" in nature.[43] In this sense, Rosenberg was one of many romantic modernists who, in the attempt to reintegrate art and life, forged the postwar "culture of spontaneity," which challenged the rationalizing tendencies of modern technology and the militarism of an uncertain Cold War world.[44] From the poetry of William Carlos Williams and Allen Ginsberg to the gestural paintings of Jackson Pollock and Willem de Kooning to the kinetic dance routines of Merce Cunningham, romantic modernists challenged the formalism of high modernism through recourse to improvisational techniques, chance happenings, and spontaneous compositions. Prioritizing the unconscious over the conscious, the imaginary over the symbolic, and the id over the ego, romantic modernists argued that their spontaneous outpourings were undistorted expressions of their authentic selves. As art critic Meyer Schapiro argued, the romantic modernist artwork was "the occasion of spontaneity or intense feeling," representing "freedom and deep engagement of the self" outside the trappings of "industry, economy, and the state."[45]

Two legendary artistic outpourings marked the importance of spontaneity to romantic modernism. The first instance occurred in 1943 when Jackson Pollock, commissioned by Peggy Guggenheim to create a mural-sized painting for her collection, completed the enormous work in a brief creative outburst, resulting in the gestural rhythms of the aptly named *Mural*. The second moment occurred in 1951 when Jack Kerouac, frustrated over the lack of critical attention for his first book, produced what was to become his most famous novel, *On the Road*, in a three-week creative explosion—an apparently free-flowing composition energized by the writer's overstimulation on caffeine and Benzedrine. In viewing artistic creation as the outpouring of man's libidinal energy, such romantic modernists linked spontaneity, creation, and procreation. Indeed, most descriptions of artistic spontaneity were marked by sexual imagery. Allen Ginsberg's ejaculatory visions in his college dorm room were the most personal, if not most benign, example. More directly, in a famous piece written to William Burroughs, Jack Kerouac related his "spontaneous writing" to the thrust of achieving orgasm. Kerouac encouraged his friend to "write without consciousness in semi-trance . . . write excitedly, swiftly, with writing-or-typing cramps, in accordance (as from center to periphery) with laws of orgasm, Reich's 'beclouding of consciousness.' *Come from within*, out—to be relaxed and said."[46] Even those who never read Reich made similar claims. The works of many abstract expressionists, for instance, contained phallic imagery and themes of fertilization, including Barnett Newman's *Gea* (1945) and *Pagan Void* (1946). In the early 1940s, Clyfford Still even composed a number of works with autoerotic images. When he turned to more abstract compositions in the late 1940s, Still continued to equate exhibitions of his work to his own bodily exposure—"Here I am; this is my presence, my feeling, myself. Here I stand implacable, proud, alive, naked, unafraid."[47] His artistic potency was always linked to masculine display.

Masculine tropes were also ubiquitous in discussions of Jackson Pollock's work, particularly after the painter turned away from the representational works of the early 1940s to his classic "drip" paintings a few years later. Pollock was, according to one critic, the "bush-bearded heavyweight champion" of modern art who "flexed his muscles for the crowd" and whose paintings resulted from his "outpouring of Herculean energy."[48] Similarly, *Life* magazine described his painting process as a "focused fury of creation," and *Time* magazine praised his "great pounding rhythms which batter their way across the 18-ft. canvases."[49] Pollock himself never refrained from linking his work to a form of masculine display. When asked how he knew when a painting was finished, Pollock responded, "How do you know when you're finished making love?"[50] Most of his own descriptions of his method were tinged with sexual innuendoes: his instruments were phallic tools ("sticks rather than brushes"); he physically penetrated the picture plane ("I do step into the canvas occasionally"); and his works possessed libidinal force ("energy and motion made visible").[51] The "key," as Pollock noted in his 1947 painting *Full Fathom Five*, was located both figuratively and literally in the genital region of the veiled figure underneath the painting's layering webs.[52] Thus, despite his adept manipulation of his materials and his insistence upon the crafted production of his works, Pollock often "finished" his paintings with one final, uncontrolled splash of paint to ensure the apparent spontaneity of his technique, a climactic moment found in *Lucifer* (1947), *Yellow Islands* (1952), and a number of other paintings: "I have no fears about making changes, destroying the image, etc., because the painting has a life of its own. I try to let it come through."[53] Pollock, like many of his fellow romantic modernists, always believed his artistic virility was proven by the painterly flows he disseminated across the surface of his canvases.

Late Modernism and the Gonad Theory of Revolution

Many late modernists were quite amused by the sincerity with which romantic modernists promoted ejaculation as the self's authentic grounding; others were more worried about the implications. David Riesman, for instance, fell into the latter group. One of the case studies he included in *Faces in the Crowd* was a profile of Henry Friend, a fifteen-year-old student at a progressive high school in Los Angeles. Friend, according to Riesman, was an example of an anomic, other-directed character who had distanced himself from his family but was unable to adjust to the evaluative pressure from his contemporaries. Unlike his peers, whose political leanings made most of them admirers of Henry Wallace, Friend was infatuated with Wilhelm Reich. According to Friend, his parents had given him a copy of the Kinsey Report, which had perked his interest in sexual matters and eventually led him to read Reich's *The Sexual Revolution*. In his analysis of the interview, Riesman noted that Friend's enthusiasm for Reich stemmed in part from his need to gain a critical perspective on the Stalinist ideology that had captured the imagination of his fellow students. Consequently, Friend uttered grandiose statements concerning the need for spontaneity and libidinal release. According to Riesman, Friend was an example of how the contemporary "concern for autonomy and spontaneity" had become "compulsive," at once a "form of boasting" and a "form of egotism."[54] Clamors for spontaneity might have the ironic effect of hardening the individual against personal growth and social interaction. As Riesman explained, "the only alternative many people see to the organization man is the nostalgic image of the cowboy or the rebellious artist; hard-shelled individualism and a rejection of human solidarity are mistaken as signs of strength and independence."[55] Riesman's worries were echoed by Ralph Ellison and James Baldwin, who criticized romantic modernists such as Norman Mailer for tying this "culture of spontaneity" to retrograde and reactionary stereotypes of African American men whom Mailer used as symbols of genital potency. In a letter to his friend Albert Murray, Ellison expressed obvious frustration—"these characters are all trying to reduce the world to sex, man, they have strange problems in bed; they keep score a la Reich on the orgasm," all of them trying to become "cocksmen possessed of great euphoric orgasms and are out to fuck the world into peace, prosperity and creativity."[56]

Other late modernists issued similar rebukes. In a response to Paul Goodman's "The Political Meanings Behind Some Recent Revisions of Freud," C. Wright Mills mockingly referenced Reich's "gonad theory of revolution."[57] Continuing his criticism of political programs that lapsed into biological essentialism without analyzing the actual motives driving human conduct, Mills argued that the current problem was "not how to release the 'orgastic potencies' of men" but instead "how to make men rationally and critically aware of where their interests lie and how they may realize them collectively" (65). Refusing to reduce freedom merely to the "gratification of protoplasm," Mills challenged romantic modernists to jettison their simplistic references to biology and spontaneity. According to Mills, romantic modernists had trapped themselves in an indissoluble dilemma: "The 'I' of Mead, the 'Superman' of Nietzsche, the 'Liberty' of Marx, the 'creative man' of liberalism, the 'spontaneity' of the newer psychoanalysis (Fromm and Horney), all stand for the problem of how to be free tho determined. They involve a quest for a transcendental sanction in terms of which the occidental man can transform himself. It is in the occident with its ever-changing system of psychic power that such a problem arose."[58] In this, Mills was again following the example of Kenneth Burke, who likewise challenged this modernist search for genital potency. In an epistolary exchange with the modernist poet William Carlos Williams, who encouraged him to read *The Function of the Orgasm* because the book scientifically demonstrated that the orgasm was "the source" of man's "biological energy," Burke challenged the naïvete of Reich's work. For Burke, "the important thing is, of course, to eat when one is hungry—but the Reich sort of thing seems to make one *think* he is hungry for a lot of things that he isn't really very hungry for at all."[59] Burke was troubled by the physiological reductionism involved in Reich's theory of the orgasm. By translating love and desire into a biological function, Reich lost any sense of the tension or the dialectical relationship between "physical gratification" and "social relations" (111). For both Mills and Burke, Reich and his followers had left the most essential parts of Marx behind.

Burke of course had a much deeper criticism of the "culture of spontaneity," whether derived from theories of genital potency or from some other form of reductionism. Well before the vogue of avant-garde poetics in the late 1940s, Burke was aware of the ironic consequences of linking the aesthetic act to biological or neurological processes. The problem rested in the complicated difference between action and motion, the former referring to those demonstrative modes of being peculiar to humans that connote "a 'doing' rather than a being 'done' to" and the latter referring to those forms of "sheer locomotion" produced by a concomitant of forces such as "'instincts,' 'drives,' or other sheerly compulsive properties" acting upon someone.[60] Motion, as Burke explained, described stumbling over something whereas action described the rebuke directed at the person responsible for leaving the object in the way. The problem, as Burke noted, was the tendency to reduce human action to sheer motion, to reduce everything, as behavioral scientists had done, to physiological processes, thereby negating the presence or at least the motivational locus of the responsible agent. In trying to foreground the active powers of the human agent by equating artistic creation with insemination, romantic modernists unwittingly shifted the stress from the agent to the agency or means used for procreation/creation and to the scenic or naturalistic background driving the agent. Action painting, when the logic of its production was followed, became passive painting. Burke argued that "strictly speaking, the act of an agent would be the movement not of one *moved* but of a *mover* (a mover of the self or of something else by the self). For an act is by definition active, whereas to be moved (or motivated) is by definition passive" (40). Despite claims to the contrary, artists such as Pollock and Kerouac often slipped into the passive voice when describing their creative processes—a body that was acted upon instead of a body that acted and a voice that was evoked instead of a voice that spoke. "To consider an *act* in terms of its *grounds*," according to Burke, "is to consider it in terms of what it is not, namely, in terms of motives that, in acting upon the active, would make it passive." The hypermasculine artist, originally depicted as a heroic figure, seemed, under Burke's logic, to be a passive object.

Romantic Modernism and the Act of Creation

Burke, of course, was not the only one who recognized that the problem inherent to action painting was its fundamental passivity. Even without reference to Burke, romantic modernists soon realized that organ display ironically placed the artist in a vulnerable position, leaving him subject to the castrating gaze of the other that such exhibitionism inevitably entailed. For example, Clyfford Still vehemently denounced any curtailments of artistic freedom, believing that art dealers were "the enemy," the art world was an "arrogant farce," and the art museum was a "glorified comfort station."[61] Using language borrowed from high modernism, Still warned against the spectator's projective intrusion, expressing contempt for those unable to see beyond "what his fears and hopes and learning" had taught him to see. For Still, there was "no explanation, logically" of his work since the "tools" of "the psychologists and psychoanalyst" and other interpretive frameworks were much "too clumsy" to offer any adequate understanding, tools that were "death itself."[62] Jackson Pollock, who was the most visible artist of the New York school, bristled against such vulnerable exposure, particularly during the infamous 1950 filming of his artistic practices at his Long Island studio by the filmmaker Hans Namuth. Although he embraced the opportunity to demonstrate the merit of his technique, Pollock had reservations about the intrusion of Namuth's camera. After a series of film shoots, occurring just prior to an important exhibition at the Betty Parsons Gallery and during Pollock's frustration at an ambivalent *Time* magazine review of his work at the Venice Biennale, the artist reached a "breaking point" over the apparent "phoniness" that such celluloid representation entailed.[63] Pollock argued in relation to the "transparent" image of himself in both Namuth's film and the *Time* review that "what they want is to stop modern art; it isn't just me they're after, but taking me as a symbol sure works."[64] Exposure, in this regard, was nothing but deadly: "maybe those natives who figure they're being robbed of their souls by having their images taken have something" (129). Self-representation in art, especially given Pollock's strong association between his painterly style and his own body, appeared to be nothing less than the painter's own death—the lethal moment in which the orgasmic subject, whose spontaneity signified an unimpeded masculinity, became an ejaculated subject whose seminal fluid seemed to be of questionable productive power.[65] For instance, Clement Greenberg noted Pollock's difficulty in naming his paintings or in attaching his signature to them. As Pollock explained to his friend, "signing is more than goodbye, it means the picture is *fixed* in time—it's done, and there's death in that."[66] For Pollock, the materiality of his inscriptions on the canvas signified his ultimate vulnerability, as critics too often wiped away the significance of those inscriptions.

By focusing on the male body as the site of artistic production, romantic modernists had unwittingly focused considerable attention upon the reproductive capacities of the artist. Castration anxiety translated as production anxiety was the inevitable result. For example, Pollock stared at the enormous white canvas that was to become *Mural* for weeks, "getting more and more depressed," because he recognized the difficulty in trying to yield to the "layers and layers of imagery" that constituted his deeper self without turning himself into a residual object.[67] Pollock tried to overcome such anxiety by using fiberboard as a support for many paintings or similar brown-colored fabrics as a way of "relieving the [painter's] eye from the monotony of the white ground" or by immediately tracing the outline of a figure upon the canvas as an "underpainting" which, after moments or days of contemplation, he would obliterate.[68] But despite his bravado, Pollock always expressed deep anxiety about whether or not his paintings were actually art. Clement Greenberg had warned painters early on "how easy it is for the abstract painter to degenerate into a decorator," creating art that lacked "dramatic interest."[69] Decorative art was inconsequential, feminine, and menstrual, art that was drooled instead of art that exploded, the unfortunate moment when Jack the Painter, as *Time* magazine had mocked, became Jack the Dripper. More than his fellow artists, Pollock struggled with the "expressive fallacy" inherent within abstract expressionism.[70] Believing that his explosive lines were representations of a hidden yet authentic subjectivity, Pollock was disturbed when he realized that such representations were merely another form of alienation. The supposed residual force of his seminal fluid morphed into mere thread-like scribblings on the canvas, leaning more toward the feminine than anything else. In response, Pollock tried to reinscribe his artwork at the moment prior to its visibility. Lee Krasner noted that Pollock defined his work as an "aerial form which then landed."[71] His friend, Nicholas Carone, noted a similar hesitancy: "Jackson told me that he wasn't just throwing the paint, he was delineating some object, some real thing, from a distance above the canvas."[72] In this sense, Pollock believed that his art existed just prior to the moment of insemination—ephemeral loops in the air that were undistorted. In this moment of release, Pollock and his artwork were indivisible.

Pollock's desperate attempt to remove his art from its reduction to the stains that appeared on the canvas signaled the profound anxiety felt by many romantic modernists over their original project to integrate art and life. The only solution to such a problem, as Kenneth Burke predicted, was to disentangle the act of artistic creation from any supporting reference, not by becoming finitely engorged but by becoming infinitesimally small. Like the angst-ridden, male breadwinner of the quirky 1957 science-fiction film *The Incredible Shrinking Man*, whose exposure to nuclear radiation results in his eventual disembodiment and his conversion to pure voice, romantic modernists avoided the threat of castration associated with feminine visibility by becoming disembodied enunciators of meaning.[73] Masculinity, originally associated with sexual prowess, was redefined as disengagement from the body. Indeed, the hyperbolization of the penis, which had temporarily solved the postwar anxiety over emasculation, was a much too vulnerable construction, and romantic modernists soon felt the need to veil the organ that supposedly produced the seminal work of art. This subtle move was most apparent in Harold Rosenberg's 1952 landmark essay "The American Action Painters," in which he redefined the artwork as an "arena" in which the movements of the artist were captured. But despite his apparent focus on the "angst-ridden, expressive body of the artist," Rosenberg invoked the physicality of action painting in only a "rhetorical" sense.[74] Since Rosenberg's "pastless" artist was indistinguishable from the canvas upon which he worked, self-alienation continuously occurred when the object of the artist's own reflection was severed from him, converting the artist into a saleable "commodity with a trademark."[75] In response, art needed to become self-referential—unconsumed and unmutilated by public reception. For Rosenberg, the artist escaped "art criticism" through "his act of painting," which served as "an extension of the artist's total effort to make over his experience" (38). The artist, however, was one step ahead of any such representation, forever escaping any momentary embodiment: "To maintain the force to refrain from settling anything, he must exercise in himself a constant NO" (32). In other words, the act of painting had little to do with "self-expression," which merely accepted "the ego as it is," and more to do with "self-creation or self-definition or self-transcendence" (28), which stressed the immaculate origins of the artist. The self-discovery associated with the spontaneity of the act was in reality a form of self-hyperbole in which the artist not only created himself but his painted canvas as a "world" liberated from "the 'nature,' society and art already there" (30).

The abstract expressionist who best exemplified Rosenberg's rewriting of the artistic process as a primal act of creation was Barnett Newman. As Rosenberg explained in his survey of the artist's work, "the ultimate subject of Newman's paintings is himself—not the biographical self of neighborhoods lived in, schools attended, people met, jobs held, not the self of 'expressionism' magnifying the accidental 'I,' but the self . . . of artistic creation he took to be subjectively parallel to God's creation of the universe, the sanctification of space (places), the deeds of heroes and prophets, the descent of light (grace)."[76] As the engorged, spontaneous artist gave way to the disembodied enunciator, the images of cellular generation and floral insemination, which appeared in Newman's early works such as *Gea* (1945) and *Genetic Moment* (1947), were replaced by invocations of creation from the elemental void of human existence. His most famous work, *Onement* (1948), a small, unassuming painting with a reddish-brown background divided by a central orange stripe or "zip," marked Newman's effort to create an artwork that was neither "a matter of personal indulgence" nor "a display of emotional experience" but a metaphysical statement concerning the "hidden meanings of life."[77] His line, completely devoid of figuration, was an act of renewal—a reference to God's separation of light and darkness in the book of Genesis and to the creation of Adam as a Giacometti-like figure from the primordial clay of the earth.[78] The "zip" was of pure origin, the mark of the artist wresting "truth from the void" like "the Creator" who assembled the world from nothingness.[79]

Of course abstract expressionists were not the only romantic modernists to flee from any discernible embodiment. For instance, Norman Mailer was very literal in his worries over male potency, whether artistic or sexual. He repeatedly warned his readers that too much sexual intercourse actually posed a threat. According to Mailer, "you can get killed, you literally *can* fuck your head off, you can lose your brains, you can wreck your body, you can use yourself up badly, eternally."[80] Virility, as Mailer eventually clarified, implied more than "the stamina of a stud"; instead, it offered "power, strength, the ability to command, the desire to alter life" (297). As a result, Mailer ironically developed a Catholic attitude toward birth control. To engage in sex, Mailer explained, was to confront the possibility of creating life—to do otherwise was to reduce ejaculation to simple waste. According to Mailer, "if you're not ready to make a baby with that marvelous sex, then you may also be putting something down the drain forever. . . . One might be losing one's future" (142). Simple orgasm then was not the solution. Instead, the orgasm needed to move beyond the present and into the future; it needed to become mystical. The "apocalyptic orgasm" for which Mailer searched marked the path to God, not as a transcendent being but as a God who was "located in the senses of [the hipster's] body."[81] After a checkered political past in which he bounced from Trotskyism to anarchism, Mailer, too, turned to religion: "To be a real existentialist (Sartre admittedly to the contrary) one must be religious, one must have a sense of the 'purpose'" (341). That purpose was not passive submission to a benevolent being but a commitment to working with God in his never-ending battle with the Devil. If God was in reality found in the life-blood or orgones of man, then God was ironically "in bondage to the result of man's efforts."[82] Thus, immanent within man was God himself, that "navigator at the seat of [man's] being," expressed through creative and procreative sexuality.[83]

William Burroughs, however, was the most graphic in his depiction of the human body as a "soft machine" that was subject to assault, possession, and disease. As Will Lee discovers in *Naked Lunch*, state regulation inevitably took the form of castration: "'All right, Lee!! Come out from behind that strap-on! We know you' and pull the man's prick off straightaway."[84] For Burroughs, even sexual freedom was another form of control. Images of the repressive desublimation of modern culture filled his books: the commodification of degenerate behavior for the amusement of urban sophisticates ("Hassan's Rumpus Room" in *Naked Lunch*), the Boschian sexual fantasies offered to hapless victims in the Garden of Delights (the "man-eating trap" in *Nova Express*), and the violent fluctuations of pain and pleasure of the Orgasm-Death-Gimmick (the Puerto Joselito fantasy in *The Soft Machine*). Consequently, the only way to transcend either biological control or death itself was to evacuate the violated body: "The hope lies in the development of non-body experience and eventually getting away from the body itself, away from three-dimensional coordinates and concomitant animal reactions of fear and flight."[85] Salvation as such was only possible through "biologic alterations," and Burroughs developed his famous literary technique, the cut-up, to aid the process. Borrowing from the literary experiments of Tristan Tzara, Gertrude Stein, and, more directly, his friend Brion Gysin, Burroughs randomly reassembled passages of prose that he had cut from his own writings. The resulting jumbled, distorted sentences were designed to disassemble conditioned patterns of perception. Thus, the cut-up moved beyond syntax, logical thought, and time-bound perceptions, allowing the reader to enjoy the totality of experience in the absence of plot or continuity. The cut-up technique also allowed Burroughs to elude representation altogether by taking no responsibility for his works ("I am a recording instrument"), thereby rescuing himself from any violence done by readers to his texts, readers who were, as proof of Burroughs's own disengagement, invited to "cut into *Naked Lunch* at any intersection point."[86] Separated from traditional meanings, from conventional emotional reactions, and from staid conceptions of time, both reader and writer were thrust into a nontemporal and completely spontaneous mode of living. The cut-ups, in this way, prepared reader and writer for life without a body—Burroughs's ultimate vision of the liberated self.

Bodily evacuation was of course merely speculation. Burroughs's fascination with the experience of astronauts as a pathway to space-time travel seemed too fantastic. Instead, many romantic modernists decided that the only way to free themselves from "the impediments of memory, association, nostalgia, legend, myth, or what have you" was, in the words of Barnett Newman, to make "cathedrals" out of themselves.[87] In a number of paintings, including *Cathedra*, *Vir Heroicus Sublimis*, *Uriel*, and *Adam*, Newman referenced biblical themes, not in the form of any specific exegesis, but in reference to man's desire to approach divinity. Mark Rothko expanded upon Newman's notion of divine escape and received a commission to paint a mural cycle for an ecumenical chapel in Houston. Similarly, Jackson Pollock, along with artist Alfonso Ossorio and Tony Smith, designed plans to construct a Catholic church composed of stained-glass windows and murals from his work. Although never constructed due to lack of interest, if not hostility, from solicited Catholic contributors, the planned church was "to be like a honeycomb, interlocking and cantilevered" with an "undulating ceiling with a band of stained glass," all designed by Pollock.[88] More pointedly, when he died in 1980 at the age of seventy-five, Clyfford Still bequeathed his entire collection of works to any "American city that will agree to build or assign and maintain permanent quarters exclusively for these works of art," with the requirement that no other works from other artists were exhibited and that none of his own works were sold or lent to other galleries.[89] The artist had become the grand enunciator. Unlike the "cold scientist," the modern artist, as Philip Wylie explained in *An Essay on Morals*, found "his transcendence by losing himself," becoming the "art of living," his "own masterpiece," through the "solar chemistry come alive, knowledgeable, expressive and creative."[90] Phallic authority, in romantic modernist language, was reinscribed as divine creation.

The Bodily Ego of Jasper Johns

In *A Grammar of Motives*, Kenneth Burke predicted that the logic of romantic modernism would eventually lead to the comparison, if not elision, between the artistic act and divine creation. Burke himself had of course made the act central to his aesthetic theory. Unwilling to reduce action to merely the reiteration of things in the present tense, Burke turned to the constitutive or symbolic act as the means by which something new entered the world. For Burke, as noted earlier, artists who had reduced the act to a motivating instinctual force had drained the act of its novelty by ironically revealing it to be fundamentally passive. They had unfortunately located the source of the act in something else and thereby had deprived the act of its own motivational locus. "An act has an element of 'arbitrariness' or 'magic,'" explained Burke in

A Grammar of Motives, "insofar as it contains a motivational element requiring location under the heading of the term *act* itself."[91] Given the inherent tension between the act and other pentadic terms (scene, agency, purpose, and agent), Burke understood the desire by romantic modernists to link the artistic act to the most demonstrative act of all: "Indeed, the Creation as an act of God was a total novelty; and it was magic because, just as the magician would make it seem that he pulls a live rabbit out of an empty hat, so God made *everything* out of *nothing*" (65). The act of creation easily became the paradigm for artistic creation because it avoided the difficulties inherent in self-expression—how to avoid reducing the act to being merely the residue of an expressive agent. Pure art, according to the logic of romantic modernism, was art not situated within any discernible scene, not originating from any embodied agent within that scene, and not done for any purposes extrinsic to the act itself.

Burke had two criticisms of this seemingly unfortunate turn in the aesthetic theory of romantic modernism. First, if art, according to Burke's definition, was in part a quest for selfhood, then nothing was more absurd than fleeing from any discernible embodiment in the name of an ever-elusive purity. For Burke, art was an attitude toward the human condition, not an evasion of it. More specifically, art was inextricably connected with those psychological, sociological, political, and familial elements in which the self was grounded. Like Erving Goffman, Burke refused to remove the self from the scene in which its life unfolded. As he explained in his criticism of the "art of escape" offered by Harold Rosenberg, "in freeing oneself *perpetually*, one would in a sense remain perpetually a prisoner, since one would never have definitively escaped" (36). Romantic modernists, argued Burke, attempted to escape from social entrapments first by freeing themselves from the identifications of the ego they had dismissed as character armoring and then by fleeing from the body itself in an act of complete divestiture. But this search for absolute purity ironically produced the exact opposite result. "Note that, dialectically," argued Burke, "the concept of 'pure' personality itself contained its dissolution as its ultimate destiny. For, by the paradox of the absolute, a 'pure' person would be an 'im-person'" (80). Burke sympathetically recognized that with "the increasing depersonalization brought about by industrialism" there would emerge as "over-compensation" a cult of "pure personality" (86). But such a stance avoided the much deeper problem concerning the relationship between artist and audience and between expression and exchange. Thus, Burke argued that "written under an esthetic of pure 'expression,'" despite protests to the contrary, was the "*anguish* of communication," that is, the anguish of courtship, love, and commitment.[92] Such an "art of escape," in this sense, served neither the artist who wished to exalt the self nor the other to whom such art was addressed.

Burke's second problem with the "culture of spontaneity" was the lingering romantic impulse attached to its understanding of the creative act. "The strategy of romantic philosophy," noted Burke, "was to identify the individual Self metaphysically with an Absolute Self, thereby making the reflexive act the very essence of the universe, a state of affairs that is open to lewd caricature."[93] Although he found some of the more outlandish claims of romantic modernists laughable, Burke did recognize the need to define the creative act without reducing it to some form of motivational response arising from another pentadic element. In the first, the act was reduced to some physical reaction to outward stimuli. In the second, the act was reduced to a strict scenic product, whether sociological, economic, or otherwise. As Burke explained, "there could be *novelty* only if there were likewise a locus of motivation within the act itself, a newness not already present in elements classifiable under any of the other four headings."[94] But unlike romantic modernists who posited a disembodied act of creation as the foundation of aesthetics, Burke turned to the work of the pragmatist philosopher George Herbert Mead to present a much more complicated vision of the creative act. Mead had demonstrated to Burke that human action was neither simply an unreflexive response nor an entirely imaginative enterprise but a complex development emerging from a long process of self-reflection. To describe the fruition of the act, Mead distinguished between the self as process and the self as object, that is, between the "I" as the initiator of action and outward thrust of movement and the "me" as a private world of self-communication among the various identifications that made up the ego. Burke noted that "once a complex world has been built up, no one is just talking to himself. Each individual contains several roles of personalities which have been built out of his situation. And he learns how to develop a thought by a process that could be reduced to alternating statements and rejoinders."[95] In other words, the "me" outlined, defined, and structured the situation while the "I" reacted, often unpredictably, to such guidance. The act, then, was something more than mere reaction but something less than a sovereign invocation. "It is this ability (implemented by the character of language) to put oneself in the role of the other," explained Burke, "that human consciousness is made identical with self-consciousness, that the subject can see itself as object (an 'I' beholding its 'me'), and that the subject can mature by encompassing the maximum complexity of roles."[96] This "internalization of objective relationships" that marked man's coming into being provided the means for self-conversation.

In this sense, the act was composed of a variety of elements—motives, plans, desires, perceptions, feelings, demands, and so on—woven together, none serving as the solitary locus for the act itself but merely helping to further its formation. Consequently, the creative act, according to Burke, was something constructed rather than something released. At least this was how Burke explained the process to those participants at the "Western Round Table on Modern Art" in San Francisco in 1949. Despite claims by interlocutors such as Marcel Duchamp, who insisted that artistic work was based on "emotion" and that critical work was based on "intellectual translation," Burke argued that the two processes—the function of the artist and the critic—were inseparable, that "a critical function is an integral part of the creative act."[97] Extending Mead's idea of "taking the attitude of the other" to the artistic process, Burke described the artist as a participant in a conversation about his work with a set of internalized others: "if we apply such a dialectical explanation to account for the producing of a work of art, we find that an artist is not merely expressing himself; he is considering the 'attitude of the other,' he is anticipating objections. There is thus a critical function interwoven with the creative function." Unwilling to grant the modern artist the power of unlimited creation, Burke argued that the expressive act came from a range of motivational loci that gave each act the sense of novelty so desperately sought.

Burke's effort to unpack, through logical examination and deliberate punning, the metaphysical, if not theological, assumptions of romantic modernism was matched by arguably the most visible late modernist in the 1950s, the abstract artist Jasper Johns. Unlike Burke, who remained marginalized within a literary academy dominated by the New Criticism and who was ignored by young bohemians searching for salvation, Johns succeeded in challenging, if not displacing, the entire generation of action painters who had dominated the New York art scene in the early 1950s. But like Burke, Johns was an unlikely candidate to foment a paradigm shift within American modernism. A southerner and a dropout of the University of South Carolina and Hunter College as well as a commercial art school, Johns moved to New York in 1952 after serving in the U.S. military for two years, working endless odd jobs while trying to establish himself in the tight-knit Manhattan art world. Having befriended Robert Rauschenberg, Merce Cunningham, and John Cage, all of whom offered their own critiques of romantic modernism, Johns struggled in the early 1950s to find his own aesthetic voice, even destroying his earliest work because of its obvious derivative quality. Like his friends, Johns was clearly searching for an alternative to abstract expressionism which was dominating the New York scene. Johns himself acknowledged his predicament: "The 1940s did something valuable with the work of Pollock and others. In the 1950s there was a hangover where they were not producing private pictures but painting public pictures and refining statements. I am not interested in refinement. I try to avoid resemblances."[98] More than anything else, Johns believed that modern art had grown stale. In a loft on Pearl Street, Johns struggled with his craft and with his own sense of self until the art world finally "discovered" him and pronounced him "a beacon for young artists all over the world" because of his deliberate challenge to the "jaded sensibilities" of most modernist connoisseurs.[99]

Beginning with his first one-man show at the Leo Castelli Gallery in 1958, where he exhibited several landmark paintings including *Target with Four Faces*, *Green Target*, and *Flag*, Johns pointed beyond the limitations of romantic modernism, a move readily acknowledged by several prominent figures such as Alfred Barr, who immediately purchased three of Johns's paintings for the Museum of Modern Art. Johns's early works—replications of flags, targets, numerals, maps, flashlights, and lightbulbs—marked a heralded reintroduction of realism into the modernist vernacular, signaling his almost obsessive concern with art as object. Like Burke, Johns directly challenged the romantic modernist promotion of art as a vehicle for the recovery of some lost depth or as a literal translation of the transcendental. Although Johns had considerable respect for the artistic revolution Jackson Pollock had helped to initiate, he had little patience for Pollock's anti-intellectual bravado. As Johns repeatedly argued throughout his career, "the artificial construction people make is that painting is not intellectual and does not involve much thinking, but involves psychic or subconscious pressures which are released through the act of painting."[100] All of the artists who followed him or borrowed from his example—Robert Rauschenberg, Andy Warhol, Roy Lichtenstein, to name a few—were indebted to his intellectual assault on the "culture of spontaneity" and in particular to his decision to prioritize the art object over and above strictly subjective concerns.

In large measure, then, Johns deflated the excesses of romantic modernism, not merely through ironic detachment as many have claimed, but through an intense reconsideration of the expressive act itself. The classic example of Johns puncturing the inflated language of abstract expressionism was of course his 1960 work *Painting with Two Balls*, which challenged the explicit connection romantic modernists had made between artistic expression and sexual potency and which unveiled abstract expressionism as a strictly masculine enterprise. Like others who criticized the absurd notion of a "gonad revolution," Johns bristled against the gendered politics of modernism. In *Thermometer* (1959), for instance, Johns deconstructed the heroic gestures of Barnett Newman, replacing the God-like "zip" running down the center of *Onement I* with a simple thermometer that not only measured the temperature of abstract expressionism but exposed that temperature as lukewarm at best. "The whole business here in America," explained Johns, "of my training and even more the people before me, was rooted in the mythology that the artist was separated and isolated from society and working alone, unappreciated, then dying and after that his work becoming very valuable, and that this was sad" (94). Painting, according to Johns, need not involve the "kind of martyr situation" in which the artist approached divinity through the act of self-divestiture. In *Fool's House* (1962), for example, Johns laid bare the instruments of the modern artist, attaching household items to the canvas that function ostensibly as art tools. A large broom has become a paint brush, a drinking cup has become a paint mixer, and a kitchen towel has become a paint rag. In this world of common objects, Johns cleared the artist's studio of all of the mystifications and sacredness invested there by abstract expressionists. Like Burke, Johns revealed the pentad of elements that brought the work of art into existence—the scene in which it was created (the studio), the agencies used (brushes, rags, paint), the act committed (the deliberate application of the paint), the agent of the work (the painter within the studio), and the purpose of the work (the exposure of such elements). In *Fool's House*, Johns demonstrated how little respect he had for those who saw art as a reflection of their own pristine natures.

Along with his friend, lover, and fellow artist Robert Rauschenberg, Johns turned American modernism away from its metaphysical themes and back to the real cultural debris littering the American landscape—back to the iconic images, the beer cans, the forks and spoons, and the light bulbs ever present within modern consumer society. In part, Johns considered the modernist flight into abstraction a failure. Arguing that the expressive strokes and dripped paint of abstract expressionism had declined, through endless imitators, into stereotypical mannerisms, Johns questioned the efficacy of such techniques to translate highly subjective content. More important, he argued that such artists, in their compulsive quest to reclaim their own masculinities, had forsaken any contact with their own culture, trying to remain aloof from a world on the brink of catastrophe. As Johns said, "I'm interested in things which suggest the world rather than suggest the personality" (113). Beginning with his infamous 1954–55 painting *Flag*, which was a flat, rigid, two-dimensional translation of the iconic image, Johns returned American painting to its national origins and in so doing deliberately invoked the tone of the Cold War. Although traditionally interpreted as a comical swipe at the intellectual pretensions of modernism and as a demonstrative return to the image in an art world that had long ago dispensed with representation of any kind, Johns's *Flag* was "flown" at the same time that President Eisenhower signed into legislation on Flag Day in 1954 a bill that added the phrase "under God" to the Pledge of Allegiance, an obvious nod to the militarization of the American landscape in the recent Cold War climate and to Eisenhower's attempt to add a religious dimension to this conflict. As critic Moira Roth has astutely noted, Johns's early work was a "warehouse of Cold War metaphors," dealing with "spying, conspiracy, secrecy and concealment, misleading information, coded messages, and clues."[101] In this sense, like all modernists, Johns fretted over the fate of the self in the early Cold War; he was petrified, like William Burroughs and Wilhelm Reich, of social, political, and psychological control. In one of his favorite metaphors, the artist in the modern world needed to become a "spy," that is, one who operated within the national security state but who escaped subordination through the manipulation and extraction of vital information and secrets. According to Johns, "the spy must be ready to 'move,' must be aware of his entrances & exits. . . . The spy designs himself to be overlooked."[102] He recognized, like Burroughs, that the enemy was poised to infiltrate the "entrances & exits" of the individual at any moment of weakness. Even art, Johns argued, was not immune. By hiding behind the American flag, Johns as a Cold War spy was able to think through the nature of artistic expression in a cultural landscape determined to repress such practices.

The complicated origins of Johns's flag signaled the artist's intermingling of personal and political concerns within a highly charged national image. Johns in fact acknowledged the inspiration for his painting. As he explained, "one night I dreamed that I'd painted a flag of the United States of America, and I got up the next morning, and went out, and bought materials and began to paint this flag" (123). Johns began his painting on a sheet, explicitly referencing the original source for his idea and thereby making the work a representation of his dream, not an unusual modernist move. Using pieces of newspaper collage and enamel to construct the stars and stripes, Johns painstakingly built up his image.[103] The sheet was then fixed to a plywood backing to retain its flat shape. But Johns was soon dissatisfied with the use of enamel, which dried very slowly and was unable to retain in any real fashion the traces of his brushstrokes. Dispensing with enamel, Johns turned to encaustic, blending heated wax with paint and newspaper to create a thick, almost sensual, mixture that hardened soon after its application and thereby preserved the character of each individual brushstroke. As Johns explained, "the encaustic technique emphasizes the object character of the pictures," in this way "freezing" the wild, expressive gestures of recent American painting into the stiff character of his flag.[104] Early critics, particularly those associated with high modernism, obsessed over Johns's return to representation, arguing that the painter had solved the riddle of how to return to the image without reinvoking illusionism or three-dimensionality. Most, like Clement Greenberg, argued that Johns was ironically using the painterly methods of abstract expressionism to construct an image of a flag that was also a literal object in its own right. Greenberg asserted that "everything that usually serves representation and illusion is left to serve nothing but itself, that is, abstraction; while everything that usually serves the abstract or decorative—flatness, bare outlines, all-over or symmetrical design—is put to the service of representation."[105] Accordingly, Greenberg argued that such a work demonstrated not an expansion of modernist practices but a "certain narrowness." But whether critics appreciated Johns's reformulation of modernism or rejected it, all assumed that Johns was invoking the playful spirit of Dadaism or Surrealism by presenting highly familiar objects—flags, targets, or numerals—but depriving them of any context or meaning. For many, Johns seemed to be playing a game.

But Johns's deliberate use of encaustic, which gave his early works not just a painterly quality but a tactile one as well, signaled that he was not trying to create an art of detachment or an art of ironic dismissal. The uncertain nature of Johns's flag demonstrated that something more was going on. Indeed, despite the fact that Johns was determined to both deflate the sense of grandeur associated with abstract expressionism and circumvent its obsessive concern with exposing the artist's feelings, Johns was neither lapsing into mere representation nor handing his art over to some formalist interrogation of the properties of his medium. Just as much as action painters, Johns connected his flags and targets to his own sense of self; as he explained later in life, "I think my early work exposed me just as much as any other bit of my work."[106]

But his images of flags, targets, maps, and numerals were obviously not about the excavation of a self with ontological priority. Instead of presenting the self as a disembodied enunciator as Barnett Newman and others had done, Johns returned the self to the scene of its emergence—to its national, cultural, and psychic formation. Like other late modernists, Johns argued that individual identity was derived from specific forms of cultural intervention. In this sense, Johns exchanged a focus on psychic interiority for a focus on corporeal exteriority, returning in his artwork to the materiality of the body itself. Whereas the body within the language of romantic modernism was merely a vehicle for the expression of a private interior, Johns argued that any sense of self was derived from the body and its complicated interaction with social and psychic forces. Accordingly, Johns recognized that although much was made of the expressive gestures of artists like Jackson Pollock, for instance, very little was made of his actual body. Like Burke, Johns wanted to return art and the artist to the complex scene in which both were situated.

Johns argued that the body existed on the delicate threshold between the inner and the outer, and he explored in his work the complicated ways in which the self was physically bound to the cultural iconography of modern America. In so doing, Johns followed other late modernists in arguing that the self was as much a horizontal construction as a vertical one. As he explained, "the boundary of the body is neither a part of the enclosed body nor a part of the surrounding atmosphere."[107] In this, Johns was invoking, in a fashion similar to Norman Brown, the concept of a bodily ego first elaborated by Freud in *The Ego and the Id*; as Johns once declared, "I love Freud's writings" (187). Complicating his original formation of ego autonomy, Freud argued in his later work that the ego was in fact formed through the complicated interaction between libidinal impulses, erotogenic zones, and external reality in what was a difficult process of balancing exogenous and endogenous stimuli. For Freud, the subject had to confront two difficult tasks. The first was to unify the myriad sensations that composed experience into the properties of a single subject that received, reacted to, and remembered what were ultimately disconnected sensations, that is, to forge a seemingly stable identity that was separate from but confirmable by those experiences. Only in this way did the subject come into being. The ego was of course the site of this unity but was not a preexisting or ontologically prior entity. Instead, the ego was the result of a complicated process of psychosocial interaction, constructed over time by the myriad sensations that impinged upon the subject's body and that helped to provide a general outline of its boundaries. Freud asserted that "the ego is ultimately derived from bodily sensations, chiefly from those springing from the surface of the body. It may thus be regarded as a mental projection of the surface of the body, besides, as we have seen above, representing the superficies of the mental apparatus."[108] In this, Freud was presenting a postural model of the body—one built up from the endless forms of contact and endless sensations that impinged upon it. The second task for the ego was to mediate the libidinal drives from within that were over time connected to particular erogenous zones and that established an investment in the body overall. Resulting from the intensity of the drives, certain organs and orifices were given a particular erotic significance as the individual progressed through the pre-Oedipal and Oedipal stages of development. The ego developed in response to the need to negotiate this discharge of excitations in relationship to the demands of the outside world, thereby separating the interior from the exterior. Consequently, as Freud explained, "the ego is first and foremost a bodily ego; it is not merely a surface entity, but is itself the projection of a surface."[109] For Freud, the ego emerged as the constructed projection of the boundaries of the self in relationship to both interior and exterior pressures. The ego was metaphorically and literally a psychic map—a cartographic surface generated from particular psychical, libidinal, and social investments in the surface of the body. In offering this image of the bodily ego, Freud challenged simplistic notions of individual autonomy that ignored the complicated process of differentiation that brought the subject into being.

In following Freud, Johns returned modernism to a study of the body, not as merely a carrier for some psychic interior, but to a study of the body as flesh or skin. Indeed, Johns was preoccupied throughout the 1950s and 1960s with the status of the body, stressing the tremendous difficulty in maintaining the divide between the interior and the exterior. In this, Johns followed others in trying to reformulate an image of the ego not bound by notions of autonomy but an image of the ego formed in relationship to a complex of psychic and social forces. As Johns himself warned, "beware of the body & the mind. Avoid a polar situation."[110] The most direct example of Johns's formulation of this bodily ego was a series of works titled *Studies for Skin, I–IV* (1962). Covering his face and hands with baby oil, Johns pressed them against engineering standard form paper and then rubbed charcoal onto the moistened image. He then filled in the standard box in the bottom corner with the title and supplies used for the composition. The effect was a series of odd, distorted portraits of the artist, with the detailed outlines of his face and hands seemingly pressing up against the paper itself. The blurring caused by the charcoal and by the movement of Johns's face when he pressed against the paper created an image of the artist struggling simultaneously with his imprisonment, with his expression, and with his own self. In this, the *Studies for Skin* series represented the ambiguous nature of the bodily ego. On the one hand, the rigidness of the engineer's paper, serving as a metaphor for the hardness of social reality itself, is flattening Johns's self, thereby inscribing its own demands onto the artist; on the other hand, Johns's own self is pressing for recognition from within, desperately tracing the outlines of its own boundaries onto the paper. Johns's ego then rested on this precarious point between the exterior and the interior, both of which were instrumental in his own self coming into being.

For Johns, then, the ego was less a protective shield against external stimuli and more a surface upon which the demands of social reality were imprinted, a theme evident even in his earliest works. In fact, Johns described his translation of commonplace images as "a play between the subjective and the objective" (287), highlighting his frustration with the rigid dichotomy traditionally made between subject and object, thought and desire, and self and society. For instance, his series of *Target* paintings in the late 1950s explicitly addressed the ambiguous position of the human body. In *Target with Plaster Casts* (1955), Johns introduced another flat, two-dimensional object that, like the American flag, served a specific function but was also imbued with a surplus of meaning. The blue-and-yellow target on a red background was set on a stretcher with attached boards on each side. On top, Johns placed a row of boxes containing casts of various body parts painted in different colors—a foot, a face, a hand, a breast, an ear, a penis, and a heel. In merging these casts of a body in fragments with an enormous target, Johns followed other modernists in depicting the violence done to the body by social forces. In this work, the human body was dissected—cut into separate elements, drained of any sense of wholeness, and placed into confined, closeted compartments. The corporeal fragmentation represented in the painting was the product of unnamed social forces directly aiming for the subject. "Any broken representation of the human physique is touching in some way," explained Johns, "maybe because one's image of one's own body is disturbed by it" (201). In all of his *Target* paintings, Johns meditated on the way in which the functions (and possibilities) of the body were limited by the meanings imposed upon it—by a social reality that channeled desire and bodily functions in regimented ways. The target was the point of entry for such forces, rendering the body immobile and fixing it in place.

Indeed, Johns warned that the painter as a "spy" needed to remain "aware of his entrances and exits," and he exposed the ways in which patterns of cultural and political identification were implanted into the subject. Exemplified by his original dream of the American flag, such identifications, according to Johns, served as material for the emergence of the unconscious itself. Following Freud, Johns exposed the role that bodily orifices played in receiving and taking in the outside world and in transmitting and channeling desire. In all of his early work, Johns commented upon the means through which the human body was disciplined, trained, and coerced, that is, the way in which "preformed, conventional, depersonalized, factual, exterior elements" (113) became a part of the subject. In his numerals paintings such as *Gray Numbers* (1957) and *White Numbers* (1959), which monotonously repeat the sequence of single-digit numbers on a grid-like structure, Johns stressed the use of repetition to train the subject to count. In his *Map* paintings from the early 1960s, which recreate the image of the United States, Johns noted the rudimentary use of such drawings to locate the subject both geographically and nationally. In his alphabet paintings such as *Gray Alphabets* (1956) and *Alphabet* (1959), which repeat the linear sequence of letters over and over again, Johns pointed out the role of memorization in forcing the subject to accede to language. In his *Flag* paintings, which recreate the iconic image in numerous formats, Johns stressed the role of nationalism in training the body to salute. In numerous other works, Johns similarly incorporated rulers, thermometers, and tools to demonstrate the importance of human measurement in mapping out the subject's relationship to the surrounding world.

But Johns did more than symbolize the ways in which the human body was shaped by a barrage of social pressures; he also argued that such forces were literally mapped upon the human body. In using encaustic to build up his images, Johns, as he directly demonstrated in his *Skin* drawings, transformed his tactile, sensuous canvases into a fleshy repository for these inscriptions. For Johns, the flat surface of the canvas was a representation of the surface of the body. In his sketchbooks, Johns made the connection explicit, referring to "encaustic (flesh?)" (56) as his chosen medium. According to Johns, the body as canvas was the site of a series of inscriptions—numerals, alphabets, flags, and others—imposed upon the subject's flesh. As critic Joan Carpenter has diligently discovered, most of the collage elements Johns used to create his encaustic paintings were items with personal and social significance.[111] In *Target with Four Faces*, his collage elements included a laundry ticket, newspaper horoscopes, a photograph of Billy Graham, an address label from a hotel, and most pointedly, a newsprint with the title "History and Biography," an obvious reference to the intermingling of the personal and the political endemic to his work. Similarly, the collage elements of *Flag* were, not surprisingly, taken from the business pages of newspapers (job postings, stock prices, insurance quotes, and real estate listings) and from political advertisements for the Eisenhower administration. *Flag*, as recent investigators into the artist's background have revealed, was not merely a commonplace, two-dimensional object chosen randomly by Johns to reintroduce, in a playful way, representation into an art world that had dispensed with such concerns; instead, Johns's *Flag* possessed considerable political and personal baggage.

Pointedly, both Johns and his father, William Jasper Johns, were named after Sergeant William Jasper, the famed Revolutionary War hero who had died while valiantly defending the city of Savannah, Georgia, against British troops in 1779. In two separate battles, Sergeant Jasper had heroically rescued the American flag from capture by the British, receiving in his last effort a gunshot wound that would ultimately be fatal. As Johns himself explained in describing the background of his *Flag* painting, "the only thing that I can think is that in Savannah, Georgia, in a park, there is a statue of Sergeant William Jasper. Once I was walking through this park with my father, and he said that we were both named for him. . . . Sergeant Jasper lost his life raising the American flag over a fort."[112] Prompted to paint the image after a dream he had had, Johns was obviously making a statement about his own sense of identity. Comparing his past struggle for artistic independence to the bloody quest for national independence two centuries prior, Johns linked his personal family history to this national image. He continued his explanation: "But according to this story, the flag could just as well be a stand-in for my father as for me." As critic Jill Johnston has noted, Johns's unveiling of *Flag* at the Leo Castelli Gallery in 1958 occurred soon after his father's death, indelibly linking Johns's emergence as the new voice of the art world to the end of his troubled relationship with his father.[113] By most accounts, William Jasper Johns, who died in 1957 at the age of fifty-six, had failed as a father, leaving his own father to raise his son, Jasper, as he struggled with alcoholism and a failing business. The obvious melancholy of *Flag* reflects in part Johns's difficult family history and his feelings about his father. But of course Johns's *Flag* was not merely a representation of Johns's troubled self; such an image in the early Cold War conjured up an obvious national signification. Johns's flag was also a metaphorical representation of the individual body overcome by the ideological content imprinted upon it by the national security state, a body in which any traces of the real, corporeal entity underneath had been erased.

Uncertain of his role not just in an art world that clung to normative images of masculinity but in a national culture that did as well, Johns demonstrated, within the frozen stars and stripes of his painting, how the claustrophobic climate of the Eisenhower years had reduced individual identity to a reflection of stale national pride.

Over time, however, Johns came to believe that his early work was too passive and that he had leaned more toward the objective at the expense of the subjective. Despite the subtle autobiographical connection, Johns's flag said little about Johns the person. In many ways, Johns had rendered the self too immobile by unfortunately dissolving the agent into the scene that had generated it. This was of course an obvious overreaction to the grandiose claims about the expressive power of the subject emerging from romantic modernist circles in the 1950s. His numeral and alphabet paintings, in which he used encaustic to build up an endless series of either numbers or letters to emphasize, as noted earlier, the way in which counting and memorization became the primary patterns of thought, left little room for spontaneity or improvisation. For example, Johns produced a series of paintings titled *0 Through 9*, all of which, with obvious variations in color and style, generated this numerical sequence in an overtly mechanized way. The self, in Johns's early work, often seemed merely an automaton. But beginning with his 1959 painting, *False Start*, whose title emphasized Johns's self-declared break from his previous work, he began to explore the ways in which the subject broke free from such physical and psychological entrapments, not by some flight into purity or nonbodily existence but by figuring ways to make individual expressive gestures that mattered on an everyday basis. In part, Johns was aided by his reading of the Austrian philosopher Ludwig Wittgenstein, who helped him to avoid the solipsism of abstract expressionism and whose infamous studies of language paralleled a similar exploration of linguistic behavior among many late modernists in America. As Johns admitted, he was "terrified of Wittgenstein," a philosopher who starkly revealed the limitations of traditional Western thought.[114]

Johns saw within Wittgenstein's deconstruction of the metaphysical assumptions embedded within traditional philosophy the same criticisms he was making about abstract expressionism. Like Wittgenstein, Johns was uninterested in trying to penetrate phenomena to reveal some underlying essence that would provide the true grounding of being. Like Johns did in his early work, Wittgenstein also meditated on the ways in which individual behavior was guided, in subtle and not so subtle ways, by the tools, practices, and signs inherent to the historically specific forms of life from which such behavior arose. These rules and signs created regulated patterns of action—rules and signs that compelled the particular use of an object or that demanded a particular relationship to an object. "The rule, once stamped with a particular meaning," argued Wittgenstein, "traces the lines along which it is to be followed through the whole of space."[115] Such ingrained practices made it seem as if all steps, all conclusions, and all effects had already been accounted for even before any action commenced, appearing, as Wittgenstein described, as "a visible section of rails invisibly laid to infinity." Following a rule in any sense—taking directions, obeying commands, learning the proper response, repeating what had been taught, and so on—often led to automatism. A life lived according to such rules was a life lived along a section of rails that allowed for no deviation. As Johns noted, "what happens is you form habits, ways of doing things, and you're so used to moving your body in certain ways, and your mind as well, that you never think to do another kind of action which would give you a different result."[116] Whether through a flag that demanded to be saluted or through a sequence of numbers that demanded to be memorized, the individual was trained in a series of practices that over time became mere habit.

Of course Wittgenstein was attempting to do more than merely demonstrate the power of concepts, language, and tools to entrap individuals into repeatable and predictable behaviors. Modernists of all persuasions—from Theodor Adorno to William Burroughs to Kenneth Burke—had demonstrated how the current landscape had rendered individual expression almost meaningless. Wittgenstein, however, refused to resort to discussions about some inner psychic realm shielded from outside influences that might provide autonomy. He saw within all of Western philosophy a futile attempt to explain inner processes deemed private or autonomous. Such attempts produced an inexorable set of problems that often led, according to Wittgenstein, to solipsism. "One thinks that one is tracing the outline of the thing's nature over and over again," argued Wittgenstein, "and one is merely tracing round the frame through which we look at it."[117] In response, he dropped this search for psychological propositions with which to translate some privileged inner world and instead explored the linguistic forms through which the individual expressed himself. In this, Wittgenstein argued that philosophers should stop searching for some essence behind appearances and examine the concrete use of language to express psychological states. For Wittgenstein, it was only through the grammar of psychological concepts—a language of pain, pleasure, contentment, frustration, and other feelings—that any particular psychological state gained meaning. The sheer complexity of language gave individual experience this perceived depth. The use of words to describe particular states was connected to what Wittgenstein referred to as language games—those endlessly diverse patterns of linguistic protocols that established the use and purpose of words and that thereby gave meaning to particular activities. "The term 'language-game,'" said Wittgenstein, "is meant to bring into prominence the fact that the speaking of language is part of an activity, or of a form of life" (11). A limitless number of language games—games involving orders, measurements, movement, counting, exercise, devotion, love, and so on—provided, according to Wittgenstein, the grounds for the coherence of human expressions, games that gave meaning to individual sensations, gestures, and thoughts. Unlike other modernists who searched for some ultimate essence, Wittgenstein, in invoking the everyday use of language, argued that "everything lies open to view" (50).

Eventually, Johns began to translate Wittgenstein's lessons into his art, effectively revolutionizing modernist practices in America. Most obviously, Johns referenced Wittgenstein's critique of traditional understandings of how language was acquired and used. Classical Augustinian philosophy had argued that language acquisition stemmed from simply attaching names to particular objects, what Wittgenstein referred to as ostensive definition. For Wittgenstein, this was an overly simplistic understanding of how language worked; in response, he argued that words were neither abstract entities nor a system of signs but were an embedded part of ordinary life and therefore used in a variety of ways and given a variety of meanings. Accordingly, language had a flexibility to it that allowed for the endless manipulation of words and expressions. This was Johns's essential point in paintings such as *False Start*, a landscape of colorful brushstrokes with incorrectly stenciled names of each color painted on top. In a deliberate jab at abstract expressionists who attributed some metaphysical attribute to their colors, Johns demonstrated that even the colors used by painters were connected to a language game that determined the boundaries of each particular color. According to Johns, "'red' only exists once there's been widespread agreement that there is such a thing."[118] Like Wittgenstein, who argued that there was no such thing as an expression or feeling untranslatable into common terminology, Johns argued that there was no such thing as a private language in art as Still, Pollock, and others claimed. *False Start* was in many ways a Pollock painting filtered through the lens of a common language of color. Johns wanted modernists of all persuasions to acknowledge certain human limitations, to bring art back from the metaphysical realm in which they had placed it and to its everyday, if not commonplace, use. Too many romantic modernists, according to Johns, were trying to escape those forms of life that gave coherence to their actions.

Of course, like Wittgenstein, Johns argued that innovation could occur through the manipulation of the boundaries of this common language. Johns wanted simultaneously to demonstrate how viewers had been trained to respond in particular ways to particular images and to demonstrate how to subvert those responses. This was done by changing the context in which something was situated, by shifting the rules with which something was used, or by manipulating the available modes of response to something. "I am concerned with a thing's not being what it was," explained Johns, "with its becoming something other than what it is, with any moment in which one identifies a thing precisely and with the slipping away of that moment" (93). In all of his works—from *Flag* to *Book* to *Coat Hanger*—Johns tried to defamiliarize everyday images, signs, and objects; as Johns described, he was "concerned with the invisibility those images had acquired" (128). Whether by making something fluid into something solid or by grossly exaggerating the properties of an object or by subverting the use of an object, Johns hoped to break down customary ways of thinking about or doing things and to reveal the contingency behind everything taken as foundational. He asserted that "there seems to be a sort of 'pressure area' 'underneath' . . . language which operates in such a way as to force the language to change. (I'm believing painting to be a language, or wishing language to be any sort of recognition)" (53). In *Fool's House* (1962), for instance, a common broom used to sweep floors is affixed to a canvas and treated as a brush, even though ostensively the written word "broom" has already signified its use, an obvious Wittgensteinian reference that Johns repeated in *M* (1962) and *Zone* (1962).

In this sense, Johns followed Wittgenstein in arguing that the self was not a preexisting entity with ontological priority but an entity that came into being through an engagement with lived reality. Johns's sense of self was intimately connected to his use of artistic materials that limited, directed, and controlled his gestures. In so doing, Johns erased the metaphysical attributes given artistic tools (brushes, paint, canvases, etc.) by romantic modernists and returned them to their everyday uses. Any action (painting or otherwise) was made within a complex world of known rules, procedures, and coordinates, those "unavoidably formed unconscious habits" (153) that formed the basis for action. In contrast to the wildly expressive gestures of Pollock, which supposedly signified his inner flows, Johns began with guided movements, created mostly through his famous "device circles." Beginning with *Device Circle* (1959), in which a stick attached to the painting is used to trace a circle on a multi-colored canvas, Johns argued that the expressive act was just as much a guided response as a self-generated movement. In an endless number of paintings such as *Good Time Charley* (1961), *Liar* (1961), *Device* (1961–62), and *Voice* (1964–67), Johns laid bare the devices—rulers, sticks, wires, printing blocks, and others—that controlled his gestures, thereby making impossible any grand statements divorced from concrete reality. But acknowledging limits was not the same as abandoning self-expression; for Johns, innovation occurred when new techniques were introduced, when new means of utilizing tools were created, and when new connections between disparate elements were made. As Johns explained, "in focusing your eye or your mind, if you focus in one way, your actions will tend to be of one nature; if you focus another way, they will be different" (92). Despite the fact that the practice of using tools in particular ways was indelibly connected to an extended history of training, such established patterns of acting and responding, through focused attention to nuances, differences, and shades of meaning, were open to manipulation. Like Burke, Johns argued that something new entered the world not through some magical act but through a critical rethinking of given practices and rules.

For Johns, the subject gained autonomy not by fleeing into some sort of nonbodily existence but by learning to master and manipulate those acquired forms of life given within a particular historical context. According to Johns, there were endless types of action—saluting, counting, memorizing, speaking, dancing, loving, eating, drawing, tracing, pressing, reflecting, and so on—that were open to subversion, what he referred to as those "questionable areas of identification and usage and procedure" (145). This was how Johns's Cold War "spy" operated. The task was to take an action and see which way it led, what new meanings might be found, and what new applications might be discovered. "To trick one's thinking," argued Johns, "which seems to me to be a valuable thing to do, one might make something happen which would not have happened had one simply relied on what one was assured of" (90). But to approach art in such fashion meant acknowledging the materiality of the human body itself—how the body's movements and boundaries were already implicated in a cultural landscape with ontological priority. Thus, the way in which the individual artist responded to a given situation was determined by his particular mastery of certain linguistic and nonlinguistic techniques. Unlike romantic modernists who fled the body, Johns returned a corporeal dimension to any sense of self. Johns clearly felt the same pain, anguish, and longing that his fellow artists like Pollock and Newman felt; he was willing, however, to live in a world of contingencies and uncertainties. This entailed, as it did for Burke and other late modernists, a radical reconception of the human subject. Accordingly, for Johns, the human self was simultaneously active and passive, simultaneously a speaking subject and a controlled object, and a self that existed on the delicate line between autonomy and conformity.

CHAPTER SEVEN

Rethinking the Feminine Within: The Cultural Politics of James Baldwin

In 1954 Jack Kerouac completed his only science fiction story, "cityCityCITY," a portentous, dystopian vision of America. Written during the Army-McCarthy hearings and reflecting his concerns about the excessive use of power by the Wisconsin senator, Kerouac's story, as he described to Allen Ginsberg, had a "wildly hip political flavor."[1] Prefiguring William Burroughs's own science fiction adventures, Kerouac offered a disturbing portrait of an overpopulated civilization in which every inch of the Earth's surface is inhabited and in which the entire population is systematically controlled by an authoritarian regime. Aided by the Computer of Infinite Merit ("one of the most, if not THE most complicated mechanical brains ever put together"), the rulers of cityCityCITY maintain control through the installment of "Deactivator disks" to monitor the activities of every citizen, through hypnotic television programming that brainwashes viewers, and through the electrocution of dissident individuals.[2] Because he was accidentally delivered to his father at birth with no deactivator disk, thirteen-year-old M-80 is saved from electrocution when his father secretly sends him into space on a homemade ship. Having finally escaped the "Overpopulated Totalitarian trap" and entirely alone in space with only a cargo of food, M-80 is given comfort at the end of the story from a prayer contained in a letter from his father, a prayer in which he promises his son that his "reward is without end" (213).

Modeled in part on the comic book *Superman*, which similarly tells the story of an orphaned son sent into space, Kerouac's story was a reiteration of romantic modernist fears concerning governmental control of hapless populations, a theme echoed in novels such as George Orwell's *1984*, Raymond Bradbury's *Fahrenheit 451*, and William Burroughs's *Nova Express*. Despite the sentimental tone of his more popular works, Kerouac was just as vitriolic about the rise of mass politics as his fellow Beat writers were. Kerouac's story contained numerous personal references to this insidious system. Challenging the authorities in cityCityCITY are the Activationists, who distribute illicit drugs that counteract psychological control, and the Loveless Brothers, who reject social norms through their shiftless, nonproductive activities, two groups obviously reminiscent of Kerouac and his friends. But what distinguished Kerouac's dystopia from the litany of other visions offered in the 1950s was the gendered description of the authoritarian government he used. Controlling the entire cityCityCITY system is "the inner core of the High Women," a group that uses "Multivision Love Broadcasts" to seduce the male population into compliance. As M-80's father explains: "Son, the day women took over all the central organization of world government, wow, lookout, that was it. . . . The day my grandfather envisioned, he told me too, when women get a hold of the whole works and you have to kowtow every morning to a dike martinet, that's your red wagon" (193). In this sense, Kerouac's "very hip, very tea-head writ, sinister" tale was a portrait of the modern totalitarian state as a matriarchy, run by domineering women who maintain authority through psychological and military means.[3]

Indeed, connected to postwar discussions over a perceived crisis in American masculinity was a corresponding fear that paternal authority as such had dissolved and had been replaced by an even more sinister maternal order. As Kerouac's story demonstrated, the figure lurking behind modern totalitarianism—behind the police, the government, the media, the CIA, the corporation, the suburban family, and the advertising agency—was, according to romantic modernists, the Devil, that figure of temptation and seduction who had weakened man's will and sterilized his environment. The Devil, as a symbol of waste, cancer, and institutional life, was metaphorically and literally envisioned within the art of romantic modernism as a feminine presence. Whether through the image of the queen of the chessboard controlling the action in Burroughs's *Queer* or the queen of diamonds lurking behind American politics in Richard Condon's *The Manchurian Candidate*, critics in the early Cold War presented an image of a ubiquitous feminine presence within American culture as a description of totalitarian power. In this sense, the fantasies of violence against women that filled the art of romantic modernism were symptoms of this overwhelming fear. In an endless series of paintings and novels, romantic modernists constructed an elaborate mythology of feminine control, a world in which the rugged, pioneering male of the frontier era and the independent, self-mastering entrepreneur of industrial capitalism were removed from all centers of power—from the family, the boardroom, and the government. As William Burroughs wrote in *Nova Express*, the "Present Controller," who is "coming in loud and clear," is "the American Woman."[4]

The reactionary politics of many romantic modernists was not lost on other modernists who routinely criticized the hypermasculine, if not belligerent, attitude of their fellow artists. In the same way that Norman Brown challenged the obvious homophobia of Theodor Adorno and others, late modernists such as James Baldwin and Jasper Johns mocked the obvious insecurities and sexual panic of William Burroughs, Jack Kerouac, and others. Always the gadfly within American modernist circles, Baldwin in particular continuously undercut the assumptions embedded within romantic modernism. In a 1949 essay, "The Preservation of Innocence," originally published in *Zero*, Baldwin challenged, in sweeping language, what he saw as the desperate attempt by American male writers in the postwar period to cling to outdated images of masculinity. Although he singled out the crime novelist James Cain, Baldwin clearly believed that Cain's confusion was only one example of the confusion over "the nature of man and woman and their relationship to one another."[5] As Baldwin noted in relation to Cain's novels, "men and women seem to function as imperfect and sometimes unwilling mirrors for one another; a falsification or distortion of the nature of the one is immediately reflected in the nature of the other." Baldwin traced such distortions to two factors in particular. First, postwar social and economic changes, which had destabilized traditional gender roles, had led to a widespread panic among American men that the opposite sex had begun to usurp traditional male prerogatives. Such panic was reflected in the "remarkable preoccupation with the virile male" (598) in postwar literature, a preoccupation that stemmed not merely from the sexual revolution ushered in by Reich and others but from hyperbolic fears about female empowerment. As Baldwin argued, "the woman, in these energetic works, is the unknown quantity, the incarnation of sexual evil, the smiler with the knife," someone determined to gain the ultimate revenge. Ever fearful of castration, such writers clung to outmoded images of male virility to preserve their own innocence. Second, this sexual panic over the emancipation of women signified a larger insecurity that fluctuating gender roles had begun to undo masculinity itself. This fear was exemplified not merely by the endless images of vitriolic women throughout postwar fiction but by the overwhelming preoccupation with homosexuality among Cain and others. For Baldwin, these two fears—the emancipation of women and the widespread appearance of homosexuality—were indelibly connected in the minds of most male writers, a belief not only that men were losing ground to women but becoming feminine themselves. Cain's *Serenade*, like so many other postwar novels, "contains a curious admission on the part of the hero to the effect that there is always somewhere a homosexual who can wear down the resistance of the normal man by knowing which buttons to press" (599). Such simplistic reasoning represented not just the limitations of many male writers but a wider inability to confront the actual complexity of human beings. Like Norman Brown, Jasper Johns, and others, Baldwin made a determined effort to rethink gender and sexual identities in this changed landscape. "Without the passion," argued Baldwin, "we may all smother to death, locked in those airless labeled cells, which isolate us from each other and separate us from ourselves" (600).

The "Womanization" of America

Writing in a 1958 issue of *Playboy* magazine with his usual sardonic tone, Philip Wylie lambasted what he saw as "the womanization of America," detailing the guiding presence of a feminine touch in every corner of the nation—from the color of office buildings and homes (no longer "factory yellow" but "chartreuse and beige") to the alcoholic beverages consumed at parties (no longer martinis but "apricot ambrosia" and "orange blossom").[6] Doomed to an early grave because of outlandish economic demands, American men, according to Wylie, had abdicated control of the home and the workplace to their wives who, as doctors repeatedly noted, had a much higher life expectancy. Befuddled and angry, Wylie had difficulty understanding why the men of his generation had passively abdicated their authority. Wylie's rant, reiterated by countless other critics, reflected a growing anxiety that the waning of masculinity in American men was caused not merely by economic changes but by the pervasive presence of women in public and private life. As many historians have recently noted, the lives of many middle-class and working-class women often ran counter to traditional assumptions about domestic retrenchment in this period.[7] Even as the conservative bent of the Eisenhower administration repaired the dislocations of World War II and female employment declined from the great heights reached during the war, many middle-class, married women, because of the escalating costs of living, entered the workforce. By 1960 one-third of American workers were women, representing an increase of approximately 7.6 million female workers since 1947.[8] Equally troubling was the sense that women were searching for employment not just for financial reasons but also for a sense of self-fulfillment. No longer wanting to be "just a housewife," many middle-class women were publicly unable to "find [their] apron strings."[9] Furthermore, many such women had begun to carve out a larger public role for themselves. Many women increased their involvement in the labor movement, flooding into service-sector unions in the hotel, telephone, and confectionary industries and challenging wage inequities and gender discrimination.[10] Similarly, many joined political movements including civil rights organizations, nuclear disarmament campaigns, peace organizations, and community service groups.[11] But even more visible was the apparent infiltration of women into traditional male arenas such as sporting events, bars, clubs, and fitness centers. In fact, the *New York Times* issued a "lament for the male sanctuary," noting how men's organizations were imperiled by a large number of wives demanding entrance, or even worse, membership.[12]

These changes in public roles were paralleled by changes in private ones as well. Encouraged by advertising campaigns offering limitless consumer wonders, wives had, according to critics, supposedly usurped decision-making power in the household and had foisted obscene expectations upon "the poor coated necktie-throttled male."[13] Corporate managers had also enlisted the aid of the "executive wife" to ensure that the family as a whole remained committed to the company through proper consumer choices and familial satisfaction, in what William Whyte termed the corporate "wife problem."[14] According to doctors and psychologists, their husbands, as the primary breadwinners, were the ones who suffered from such pressure. In a 1958 article "The American Male: Why Do Women Dominate Him?" *Look* magazine staff writer J. Robert Moskin pointed to the tremendous stress under which middle-class men lived: "Wives may say they want their husbands to ease up, but they still hold out the carrot to lead their husbands up the hill to success—and toward two cars in the garage."[15] Even worse, wives now demanded male participation in household chores and had transferred traditional child-raising duties to their husbands. "The American man," Arthur Schlesinger lamented in his discussion about the waning of masculinity, "is found as never before as a substitute for wife and mother—changing diapers, washing dishes, [and] cooking meals."[16] In the ultimate confusion, critics noted that American husbands had lost authority in the bedroom too, as wives now controlled decisions over sexual contact and birth control and placed priority upon their own sexual satisfaction.

As this apparent flight of women from normative gender roles escalated, critics such as Philip Wylie were joined by numerous psychologists who provided evidence to confirm growing fears about the "masculinization" of American women. For instance, psychiatrists Ferdinand Lundberg and Marynia Farnham, in their popular 1947 book *Modern Woman: The Lost Sex,* argued that career-minded women had become a "bundle of anxieties" caused by "the price of feminine relinquishment."[17] According to Lundberg and Farnham, "the more importance outside work assumes, the more are the masculine components of the woman's nature enhanced and encouraged." Calling for federal subsidies to encourage women to forfeit employment outside the home, their book was one of many volumes to criticize the apparent psychological imbalances caused by the movement of women from the home. In her two-volume opus *The Psychology of Women*, psychoanalyst Helene Deutsch similarly detailed this widespread identity crisis in American women. According to Deutsch, the social and economic demands of World War II had aroused "active and aggressive" tendencies within many women, placing them in psychic conflict "with the woman's environment and above all with the remaining feminine inner world."[18] Similar arguments about this escalating "masculinity complex" were found in Erik Erikson's *Childhood and Society* (1950), Talcott Parsons's *Family, Socialization, and Interaction Process* (1955), and Edward Strecker's *Their Mothers' Daughters* (1956), all of which meditated on the disastrous effects of women's employment outside the home.

Male anxieties over these changes were summarized in a 1962 *Playboy* panel on "The Womanization of America," attended by Norman Mailer, psychologists Ernest Dichter and Theodor Reik, anthropologist Ashley Montagu, and *Life* editor Alexander King. Pointing to the "growing national awareness of the degree to which women have come to power," the editors at *Playboy* hoped to "illuminate [the] cause and effect of this process" in the hopes of stemming its tide.[19] The panel, not surprisingly, reiterated the conventional wisdom that relations between the sexes had changed for the worse. Economically independent and politically empowered, modern women had not only usurped control of most public spaces but had also done irreparable damage to their husbands and sons. Alexander King placed this transition into a larger historical perspective: "Now, with the liberation of the woman from housework and chores, and with her getting the vote and feeling her new freedom, an uneasy period has set in. . . . And the man, sheepishly and very foolishly, I think, has in some ways resigned his prerogatives, and by default woman has taken over" (47). With considerable resentment, the panel wondered if men possessed the fortitude to reassert their authority. The party jokes and nude photographs throughout the pages of *Playboy* were only one element of this struggle. As part of their cultural project, the editors at *Playboy* also highlighted the importance of modern artists—from Pablo Picasso to Jackson Pollock to Jack Kerouac—in this struggle to reclaim American culture for men and frequently promoted these artists through lengthy portraits of their lives and critical discussions of their works.

Norman Mailer's presence on the *Playboy* panel testified to the anxiety many romantic modernists felt at the growing presence of women in public and private life. As the editors at *Playboy* recognized, modernists such as Mailer, Kerouac, and Pollock were not only part of a new avant-garde but also part of a larger male revolt against this female incursion. Romantic modernist discussions over male potency were indelibly connected to hostile, often openly misogynistic, attitudes toward the apparent emancipation of women. The violence committed by both Norman Mailer and William Burroughs against their respective partners (Mailer's stabbing of his wife, Adele Morales, during a Manhattan party and Burroughs's fatal shooting of his wife, Joan Vollmer, during a drunken evening in Mexico City) were the least subtle examples. Mailer in particular always seemed unapologetic; as he explained repeatedly in his 1962 book of poems *Death for the Ladies*, "so long as you use a knife, there's some love left."[20] Such retribution was derived from fantasies of women as implacable enemies to a collapsing male order. Jack Kerouac, for instance, exhibited a certain hostility toward women throughout his life, desperate for their affection but ambivalent about their love. Most of his sexual relationships were clouded by his anxiety about the destructive power of women, imagining them as hustlers and thieves and imagining their genitals as a *vagina dentate*. In his encounter with Mardou Fox in *The Subterraneans*, for instance, narrator Leo Percepied fantasizes about her actual intentions: "I now wonder and suspect if our little chick didn't really intend to bust us in half" with the "contraction and great strength" of her "vice-like" womb.[21] Kerouac's fear even led him to abstain from sex for an extended period of time, particularly after his heralded conversion to Buddhism. Such images of castrating women were constructed by most romantic modernists, even by many members of the New York school whose paintings frequently referenced mythological stories of witches and demons. For example, Barnett Newman's 1945 painting *Song of Orpheus* refers to the great musician of Greek antiquity who, after he swore off the love of women following the death of his wife, was torn apart in an ecstatic frenzy by Maenads, the female worshippers of Dionysus and exemplars of unchecked feminine aggression. Similar stories of aggressive women were also referenced in Newman's *Slaying Osiris*, Adolph Gottlieb's *Sorceress*, and Mark Rothko's *Rites of Lilith* and his *Sacrifice of Iphigenia*.[22]

More directly, Jackson Pollock and William Burroughs, both of whom had part of a finger severed when younger (Pollock in a childhood accident, Burroughs in a despondent moment in college), expressed a lifelong anxiety about castration. This sense of loss was readily visible in a number of Pollock's paintings including *Circumcision*, *She-Wolf*, and *Moon-Woman Cuts the Circle*, all of which testified to his concerns about male performance. Burroughs was just as explicit. Writing to Allen Ginsberg in 1954 to explain his self-imposed exile from his homeland, Burroughs argued that "the U.S. simply does not provide the sustenance for a man," evidenced by the fact that "women outlive men by a wide margin."[23] Modern America was, as Burroughs repeatedly explained throughout his life, matriarchal, and his fiction contained countless scenes of women castrating men. In *Naked Lunch*, A.J. and his associates are assaulted by "a horde of lust-made American women," whose vengeance places the men's "very cocks at stake" and who are stopped only through their violent decapitation by Burroughs's alter ego.[24] Even when Johnny removes Mary's "vaginal teeth," he is still "drawn in by a suction of hungry flesh." For Burroughs, relations between the sexes were nothing but violent; in the fantasized landscape of *The Soft Machine*, the "war between the sexes" has "split the planet into armed camps right down the middle" (153). In many ways, Burroughs's lifelong treks through the impoverished towns of Mexico and the male brothels of Tangier were not simply part of his self-imposed exile from the censoring authorities in the United States but part of his larger search for a male-dominated frontier world not yet eclipsed by rising female power.

Momism, Modernism, and Male Sexuality

In his 1941 study of criminal behavior *Dark Legend*, psychologist Frederic Wertham argued that the appropriate mythological framework through which to view contemporary culture was not the story of Oedipus but the story of Orestes, the son of Agamemnon and Clytemnestra, who, according to Greek legend, avenged the murder of his father at the hands of Clytemnestra's lover, Aegisthus, by killing his mother. Designating the subsequent condition the Orestes complex, Wertham contended that the defining impulse within modern man was not patricide but matricide, that is, the compulsive need to redeem the paternal legacy by punishing the mother for apparent transgressions against the father or by fleeing from her aggressive sexuality.[25] According to Wertham, as the influence of American women increased, more and more men would adopt affectionate attitudes toward their emasculated fathers and adopt violently hostile feelings toward their mothers. The most influential translation of the Orestes complex was Philip Wylie's *Generation of Vipers*, in which he coined the term "momism" to warn against the psychologically destructive influence overprotective mothers had on their children. Wylie connected the alarming rise in emotionally dependent and sexually confused men to the reign of tyrannical mothers who had "taken possession of the spirit" of their sons.[26] Once again, Wylie appropriated the psychological theory of Carl Jung to criticize the excessive identification with femininity on the part of American men. Jung had taught Wylie that the most influential archetypes within man's unconscious were the animus and the anima, the often latent and contrasexual tendencies that gave men and women access to the qualities of the opposite sex. The anima, as Jung explained, was "what is not-I, not masculine," those characteristics of compassion and togetherness that helped to balance man's obsession with individuality.[27] Noting that "Jung's studies of the female principle in the male personality" were "unknown" by most lay readers, Wylie argued that "when the conscious mind is seized by one definite instinct the 'liability' of its opposite instinct is set up with exactly equal force in the unconscious mind."[28] However, the problem, according to Wylie, was not that man had tapped into his masculine side at the expense of his feminine one, but that his anima, often deceptive and bewitching, was imposing emotional states not conducive to any practical response to the modern world: "A man who is good and mad will be frightened out of his masculinity and suddenly start behaving in a womanish manner."[29]

As an explanation for the apparent instability of traditional gender roles, Wylie's vitriolic attack on the "destroying mother" became a common trope to explain the nation's vulnerability to a number of infestations, including political deviance, juvenile delinquency, alcoholism, and crime.[30] In part, Wylie's turn to the mother as the source of dysfunction in the child was prompted by the rise of ego psychology in psychoanalytic circles in the 1940s. Originating in Freud's own revisions in *The Ego and the Id* (1923), where he argued that the development of the ego in the pre-Oedipal phase was just as essential as the development of the superego in the Oedipal moment, ego psychology, as outlined in the work of Karen Horney and Donald Winnicott, declared the mother-child relationship the cornerstone of individual development. As the original source of care, the mother was the parent who navigated the child through the pre-Oedipal stages of infantile helplessness and object loss. Thus, ego psychologists were less concerned with the father as the symbol of authority and warned instead that the mother's nurturance of her child impacted the development of an integrated ego even more—either by aiding the child's separation from her through a controlled process of development or by disturbing such growth by damaging the child's sense of boundaries. Maternal factors—feelings of affection, recognition, and security—were essential components of psychic development; maternal failures in that regard—overaffection and smothering—were the primary sources of neurotic behavior. Such arguments were soon incorporated into American social sciences, elaborated in a number of books including Edward Strecker's *Their Mothers' Sons* (1946), Geoffrey Gorer's *The American People: A Study in National Character* (1948), and Betty Friedan's *The Feminine Mystique* (1963).

As popular characterizations of Wylie's tyrannical mother abounded in the national media, vehemently referred to as "the overprotective mother" and "the encapsulating mother," one psychologist went so far as to translate the Orestes complex into a universal condition.[31] In a number of influential books, including *The Basic Neurosis* (1949) and *Neurotic Counterfeit-Sex* (1951), psychiatrist Edmund Bergler argued that the key stage in a child's development was not identification with the father under the auspices of the Oedipus complex but the prehistory of that phase in which the newborn had to negotiate threats to his "infantile megalomania" from the mother as caregiver. According to Bergler, the infant maintained fantasies of omnipotence until subjected to the painful discovery that feeding times and sleeping schedules were regulated by the "Giantess of the nursery." Forced into an insufferably passive role, the infant either reacted sadistically to this "witch" who now seemed "capable of starving, devouring, poisoning, choking, and castrating him" or, under the vicissitudes of the drives, reacted masochistically by accepting, if not enjoying, such punishment.[32] The only antidote to such a situation was the child's identification with the father who, because of his strength, was able to demote "the threatening and fear-inspiring 'witch' of boyhood from her position of power." But the eclipse of paternal authority under the recent accession of maternal power had negated this transition to "asexual filial affection" (51). The result, according to Bergler, was a lingering libidinal attachment to the passive position in the nursery, in what he termed "psychic masochism." Finding satisfaction in failure and erotically attached to punishment, the psychic masochist courted dependent relationships. For Bergler, "those children who carry too large a remnant of early pre-Oedipal passivity with them into the rescue station of the Oedipal phase express this passivity in *feminine identification.*"[33]

Even more disturbing than the apparent emancipation of women was the belief that such changes were usurping men of their masculine identities. Psychoanalyst Theodor Reik argued in the *Playboy* panel that "there is a law—a law as binding as the laws of chemistry, or of physics—namely, that a masculinization of women goes with the womanization of man, hand in hand."[34] Reik's worries were echoed by the editors of *Life* magazine, who, noting that there was "some deep-lying disturbance of a psychological nature" affecting society, convened a panel of psychiatrists in 1956 to comment on the "changing roles in modern marriage." Pointing to an increasing divorce rate, the panel argued that "spottily and sporadically, but increasingly, the sexes in this country are losing their identities."[35] But while psychologists such as Reik were merely interested in addressing some of the limitations of orthodox Freudianism, romantic modernists inflated these worries into a dread of maternal power, presenting the mother of the pre-Oedipal moment as the literal example of an omnipresent threat of incorporation. Once again, William Burroughs was the most explicit, linking the rise of state power in the early Cold War to the rise of matriarchal rule. In the ninth routine of *The Soft Machine*, Burroughs portrayed the bodily control of the local population in the jungles of South America by a cult of priests as a form of institutionalized gender inversion: "The Comandante spread jelly over Carl's naked paralyzed body. The Comandante was molding a woman. Carl could feel his body draining into the woman mold."[36] Such state-sponsored regulation occurred through the usurpation of the male body by an imposed feminine presence. The goal of democracy, as Will Lee learns in *Naked Lunch*, is the elimination of difference—sexual, physical, and personal—until there is only one sex in the world. In *Naked Lunch*, the forces of democracy, led by the Divisionist Party, want to populate the world with "exact replicas of themselves," and they instill control by tying each replica to a controlling maternal presence.[37] Freedom of movement is eliminated as the replicas "must periodically recharge with the Mother Cell," a situation Burroughs believed was readily apparent in postwar America.

A similar, although less abrasive, attempt to address the masculine and feminine imbalances within the male psyche was found in the early work of Jackson Pollock, who, like Philip Wylie, appropriated Jungian ideas to describe this disturbance. The artist, as his biographers have noted, was always ambivalent about the influence of women in his life, in particular, his mother, with whom Pollock seemed to have an anxious relationship. Supposedly burdened by a caregiver who "could walk through a stone wall," Pollock was ever conscious of a lingering maternal presence within his psyche. One of Pollock's former Long Island neighbors detailed Pollock's psychological vocabulary: "Of my excavating, be it by dozer, crane, or tractor shovel, he pointed out that I was really digging into 'Mom—back to that old womb with a built-in tomb.'"[38] In part, Pollock's hostility, exemplified by the inappropriate drunken behavior detailed by friends over the years, was characteristic of the predominantly male avant-garde milieu in which he operated and reflected, in particular, the attitudes of his two artistic heroes, Pablo Picasso and John Graham. For example, Clement Greenberg noted Pollock's often blatant anger: Pollock "was hostile to women. He said it himself: 'I'm angry against women and so is David Smith'" (212). Frightened of intimate relationships with women and full of bravado but sexually insecure, Pollock struggled with a lifelong ambivalence about his own masculinity. The most specific representation of Pollock's worries, knowing that "in society's eyes to be an artist was queer in the homosexual sense" (213), was his 1942 painting *Male and Female*.[39] With its two totemic figures (a curvaceous, flirty-eyed woman and a rigid, masked man), the painting represents the difficult sexual differentiation of men and women from an unconscious imbued with masculine and feminine traits. Neither a representation of a union between the two sexes nor a rendition of some psychological wholeness, the painting, much like Wylie's own work, summarized Pollock's frustration over the power of the anima in his own psyche. If anything, the painting is a celebration of this differentiation, as the male figure affirms his identity through the yellow and red fluid spouting from his erect penis. In fact, what assures the separation of these two figures is the presence of a series of diamond shapes in the center, the lingering presence of his father figure, Pablo Picasso, from whose 1932 painting *Girl Before a Mirror* Pollock appropriated these shapes.

Pollock's fears were also exhibited in his interest in the "dark side" of the moon as a lingering maternal presence, an idea referenced in a series of paintings—*The Mad Moon-Woman* (1941), *The Moon-Woman* (1942), and *The Moon-Woman Cuts the Circle* (1943). His wife, Lee Krasner, and his friend Tony Smith have noted Pollock's obsession with the moon, simultaneously cursing and praising it, and one of his therapists, Violet de Laszlo, attributed this obsession to Pollock's anxiety about his masculinity: "He had an affinity for the moon, which I associated with the feminine element in his nature, and in these disparate drawings—little improvisations, or whatever you wish to call them—quite often a half moon would appear."[40] The symbol of the moon, as art historian Michael Leja has pointed out, was an abiding interest for Jungian psychologists in the 1930s, particularly the Analytical Psychology Club in New York, which helped disseminate Jungian ideas to practitioners such as Violet de Laszlo and Joseph Henderson, as noted earlier, two of Pollock's therapists.[41] The different phases of the moon, as key symbols not just for Jungian analysts but also for many of the Native American traditions that inspired Pollock, represented the different forms of feminine power—the terrible mother, the life-giving lunar goddess, the mysterious temptress, and the castrating witch. As such, the moon was the symbol of that mysterious, uncontrollable force that determined man's fate. As Leja has explained in relation to Pollock's work, "women often symbolized the powerful force fields that had to be negotiated by the conscious, rational part of the subject—gendered as masculine—in his quest for balance, harmony, and resolution of conflict."[42] Painting, then, became the site for self-exploration and self-confrontation—a continual escape from the castrating influence of a softer and more maternal society.

Many other romantic modernists introduced into their works similar Jungian invocations of a gender imbalance within the male psyche. For instance, the existential journey of Stephen Rojack in Norman Mailer's *An American Dream* is described as a mythical encounter with the "Great Bitch" herself—the devouring mother, the castrating wife, and the female archetype. Like Jackson Pollock, Rojack carries on a "secret frightened romance with the phases of the moon," and, as a symbol of rebirth but also a symbol of terror, the moon serves as the central image of Mailer's novel.[43] The moon, "giving a fine stain" to the night sky on the German battlefield, witnesses Rojack's spiritual failure; the moon, "baleful in her radiance," also stands in judgment of Rojack on the night of his wife's murder; and finally, the moon presides over the desert world of Las Vegas to which Rojack retreats at the end of the novel. Indeed, the moon is a "platinum lady with her silver light," a seductive blonde whom Rojack needs to court and ultimately surpass to gain redemption and who is personified most dramatically by his wife Deborah, the "lioness of the species" gnawing at Rojack's flesh (13, 147, 9). Deborah is the moon in the night sky demanding punishment for the crimes Rojack has committed; she is Artemis, Selene, Diana, and Luna, the goddesses of the moon; and she is the huntress, the witch, and the beautiful maiden whose secrets remain impenetrable until Rojack finally appropriates her quiver of psychic arrows that have tormented him most of his life.

Historically, modernists such as Mailer, anxious about their shared social position with women in a marginalized realm outside the masculine sphere of economic production, have always expressed great concern over contamination by or accusations about their supposed femininity.[44] As both members of a supposedly effeminate artistic class and presumably defenders of a rugged individualism, modernists have struggled with their ambiguous social position. Long after Jackson Pollock's death, Willem de Kooning, for instance, defended his friend against public accusations: "The suggestion that he was gay is crazy! We used to kiss each other drunk, roughhouse, but he never was not knowing the difference between a friend and a gay. . . . If he was, he couldn't *paint* the way he did."[45] Even those who engaged in same-sex romances such as William Burroughs, Jack Kerouac, and Allen Ginsberg repeatedly insisted that they were not "fags." Such men, as Burroughs argued in *Queer*, were the ultimate representation of a possessed, infected psyche—men who had succumbed to effeminacy and therefore to the lure of state power. For example, the battlefield scene in Norman Mailer's *An American Dream*, in which Stephen Rojack begins his spiritual quest to recapture the grace he lost at the sight of the fallen German soldier he was unable to kill, is depicted as an extended homosexual encounter. The German soldiers whom Rojack battles are all victims of maternal overprotection: "a great bloody sweet German face, a healthy overspoiled young beauty of a face, mother-love all over its making, possessor of that overcurved mouth which only great fat sweet young faggots can have when their rectum is tuned."[46] Homosexuality, defined by Mailer as the possession of the male psyche by maternal attachment, was the pathway to authoritarianism. In fact, the figures holding state power in many of Mailer's novels (General Cummings in *The Naked and the Dead* and Leroy Hollingsworth in *Barbary Shore*) are latent homosexuals.

This fantasy of maternal omnipotence was buttressed by the notion that the paternal order as a whole had collapsed. As literary critic Alice Jardine has argued, one of the essential features of American fiction after 1945, particularly for romantic modernists, was the absence of the father as a component of the symbolic; instead, the father was portrayed as a defeated, disenfranchised, or even dead figure.[47] Oedipus had been replaced by Orestes, as the mother, not the father, became the figure to overcome. Thus, the goal of liberation was not only the end of fusion with the mother but the end of any form of representation that left the male artist vulnerable. The romantic modernist whose personal life most dramatically emphasized this was Jack Kerouac, whose fiction, beginning with his first novel, *The Town and the City*, was haunted by the absence of his father.[48] For Kerouac, the history of his family was in part the history of the financial and physical decline of his father, Leo. Working variously as a typesetter for several local newspapers in the 1920s, Leo eventually achieved some financial success and was able to open his own print shop, *The Spotlight Print*. But his shop soon felt the tremors of the Depression, and when a flood damaged his equipment in 1936, Leo was bankrupt. Kerouac's father was also physically bankrupt, suffering from rheumatism, developing asthma as he grew older, and eventually dying in 1946 of cancer of the spleen. In *On the Road*, Kerouac told the tale, as he explained later in life, of "an ex-cowhand and an ex-footballer driving across the continent north, northwest, Midwest and southland looking for lost fathers, odd jobs, good times, and girls and winding up on the railroad."[49] His story of Sal Paradise joining the "holy lightning" that is Dean Moriarty for a series of cross-country adventures portrays a culture bereft of manliness and paternal authority.[50] Their actual motivation for these trips, as Dean openly admits, is to find his "father wherever he is and save him" (184). Dean's father, like Kerouac's own, had been displaced by the Depression and never recovered, "once a respectable and hardworking tinsmith" who had become "a wine alcoholic" (39). While the two men search for Dean's "raggedy father" in slums and train yards across the American continent, Sal is haunted by the spirit of his own father, entering into "a temporary trance" at a racetrack in New Orleans when a horse named "Big Pop" conjures up memories of his long-departed father.

In this sense, the Beat Generation was for Kerouac a raggedy collection of young men, full of lunacy and desperate to redeem the legacy of their fathers. Beat was also part of Kerouac's own patrilineal background, traced to his Breton ancestors, who "were the most independent group of nobles in all old Europe and kept fighting Latin France to the last wall," to his grandfather Jean-Baptiste Kerouac, who challenged from his front porch the "big thunderstorms" that threatened the Canadian landscape, and to his father, who hosted "wild parties" in the 1920s and 1930s.[51] But the failure of the two heroes to find Dean's father testified to the difficulties Kerouac had in imagining any restoration of the paternal order. Recognizing that the world of his father is eroding, Sal empathizes with his friend's forlorn condition: "Every new girl, every new wife, every new child was an addition to his bleak impoverishment. Where was his father? –old bum Dean Moriarty the Tinsmith, riding freights."[52] Of course, romantic modernists like Kerouac, through their reading of Wilhelm Reich, were not interested in simply reconstituting Oedipal identity as the proper foundation for subjectivity. But continuously impeding Sal and Dean's journal of reckless abandon is the Shrouded Traveler, a demonic force intent upon catching them before they reach the Protective City that Carlo Marx (Allen Ginsberg) identifies as "the mere simple longing for pure death" (124). Indeed, supposedly buried at the core of their respective egos is this death drive pushing them toward suicidal dissolution, a drive they have to overcome to reach the pure core or "IT" of their beings. Unbinding the ego in the name of Reichian therapy meant, in this regard, confronting this latent death drive that Kerouac metaphorically associates at the end of *The Subterraneans* with the image of his mother's face in the moon in the night sky.

Purging the Feminine

In this sense, the romantic modernist self, as literary critic David Savran has pointed out, was split into an aggressive masculine part and a passive feminine part, the former psychically dominating the latter on the way to self-mastery.[53] The traditional categories demarking gender differences—mind and body, culture and nature, activity and passivity, sun and moon, day and night, father and mother, intelligence and sentiment—became part of a divided masculine psyche. In the *Playboy* panel on the "womanization" of American society, Norman Mailer openly acknowledged such confusion: "The artists always have a great sensitivity to the poles of their nature. They're aware of what's feminine in them. By this I don't mean any crude equation to homosexuality or bisexuality. One can be aware of the feminine side of one's nature without being overcome by it."[54] By acknowledging and even embracing their passive position (dependent upon a fickle art market, threatened by castrating critics, and forced to submit to a perceived feminine order), romantic modernists took almost sadistic pleasure in the violent purging of their own femininity in the name of virility. Artistic creation was seen as a confrontation with the Other—nature, madness, unconscious, death—all those abject forces threatening the masculine self. Paradoxically, then, romantic modernists expressed paranoia over painfully constrictive psychic boundaries but also over the loss of any such boundaries. Indeed, the dismantling of ego constructions in the name of Reichian therapy entailed not simply the release associated with orgasm but, more important, a regression to the infantile stage of psychological development to confront the libidinal tie with the mother that had apparently taken possession of the male psyche. The dream of self-mastery connected to theories of artistic creation inflated into the dream of self-paternity, as romantic modernists imagined a libidinal drive with no permanent connection and no terminus.

The most dramatic example of this attempt by romantic modernists to purge themselves of any feminine attachment was Willem de Kooning's third solo exhibition, "Paintings on the Theme of Woman," at the Sidney Janis Gallery in 1953. After having become the crowned king of abstract art with the unveiling at the Venice Biennale in 1950 of his painting *Excavation*, de Kooning returned to figurative painting despite the taboo on representational art.[55] The history of these portraits, in particular *Woman I*, reveals de Kooning's uncertainty over the project as a whole.[56] Beginning in June 1950, he sketched an endless number of female figures, the starting point for an eighteen-month project that was abandoned in January 1952 but revisited later that year after encouragement from art historian Meyer Schapiro. De Kooning then spent months frantically reworking these images until his anxiety produced heart palpitations serious enough for his doctor to warn him: "You've got to calm yourself. You're overanxious. This whole idea of painting a figure and destroying it . . . this is doing something to you."[57] Originally echoing the seated figures painted by Picasso in the 1930s, *Woman I* soon lost this Cubist influence, as de Kooning started to overlay different body parts and facial features, including most famously a cutout of a young woman's mouth from a cigarette advertisement. Believing that any form used by an artist "ought to have the emotion of a concrete experience," de Kooning noted that the image changed each working day according to his own emotional state: "Then I could sustain this thing all the time because it could change all the time; she could almost get upside down, or not be there, or come back again, she could be any size."[58] In the end, de Kooning presented a visually fragmented figure composed of broken, stark brushstrokes that at times spatially bled into the background—an imposing womanly figure with sagging breasts, a toothy grin, and an engulfing, demonic stare. In returning to figurative painting, de Kooning claimed that his figure originally represented "the female painted through all the ages," akin to "the idol, the Venus, the nude" (77–79). But the woman in the final version, with her high-heel shoes and makeup, was much too contemporary to refer to a classical figure. Explaining his painting to his friend Al Copley, de Kooning noted that his figure was closer to the modern scavenging consumers found at Klein's department store, the "elegant" women who, when they came "to the bargain table," acted like "animals."[59] In part, then, *Woman I* was an image of the classical nude transformed into the modern icon, the moment when highbrow culture bled into mass culture, an image of woman as Venus who had entered mid-twentieth-century culture as the typical American woman.

But underlying these general connotations was a much more personal reference. Although he intended at one point for the images to reference the banality of young American women, he realized that when the paintings were finished those girls were "not there, only their mothers." In fact, de Kooning associated the context for *Woman I* not with an urban American landscape but with the waters of Holland where he had been born: "*Woman I*, for instance, reminded me very much of my childhood, being in Holland near all that water." [60] What began as an apparent mockery of cigarette advertisements transformed into a monstrous representation of a middle-aged bourgeois woman, most likely a reflection of de Kooning's own mother. Elaine de Kooning associated her husband's work with his childhood experiences, in particular his hysterical mother who had a penchant for verbal abuse: "The turbulence came from his image of women, of his consciousness of their role—and it was not sweet."[61] De Kooning himself admitted in a 1968 interview that the women from the 1950s may have had "something to do with my mother."[62] Early reviews made similar associations. Writing in *Art Digest*, critic Hubert Crehan pointed to the Sidney Janis exhibition as a sign of de Kooning's own "woman trouble," and *Time* magazine's art editor, Alexander Eliot, who reviewed de Kooning's work at the Venice Biennale in 1954, argued that the painter's portrait of "a creature he calls 'woman'" bore a striking "resemblance to the Mom made infamous by Author Philip Wylie."[63]

However, *Woman I* was not a traditional portrait of a seated bourgeois woman. With its battleground of slashing brushstrokes, the painting was the record of the artist's struggle with the female image—a tale of frustration and sexual violence that was less about the monstrous mother figure and more about the artist himself. For instance, Harold Rosenberg, a close friend and prominent defender, argued that de Kooning's painting was more an exploration into the artist's personality than an exposition of a real object. According to Rosenberg, it contained "forms emerging spontaneously from the action of the brush bringing to light areas of the psyche in which feelings had not yet crystallized into an identified image."[64] Action painting, in this sense, was a therapeutic reworking of the self, an immersion into the murky realm of the unconscious to confront the shadowy figures residing there. De Kooning argued that his artistic process was an immersion into and out of the "yoghurt" that was his canvas: "I am always in the picture somewhere. The amount of space I use I am always in, I seem to move around in it, and there seems to be a time when I lose sight of what I wanted to do, and then I am out of it."[65] As such, the environment in which de Kooning worked was a fluid mixture "already there," a "stew" or a "soup" into which the artist stuck his hand, if not his entire body, to "find something."[66] Using an odd mixture of turpentine, oil, and dammar varnish, de Kooning intentionally kept his canvas greasy and wet. In this sense, immersion into the canvas was an immersion into himself. As de Kooning explained years later, his *Woman* series was in fact about him: "Maybe in that earlier phase I was painting the woman in *me*. Art isn't a wholly masculine occupation, you know."[67] Purged of maternal identification once he was separated from his canvas, de Kooning had projected his own femininity onto his canvas, producing a fetishized object that functioned as a mirror for his own narcissism, exhibitionism, and castration and therefore paradoxically as a sign of his own self-mastery.

De Kooning's formulation of the artistic process as a purging of the artist's own femininity was a common trope for romantic modernists. In 1947, the Stanley Kootz Gallery in New York held an exhibition titled "Women," which staged a number of paintings of the female figure by modern artists including Adolph Gottlieb, Hans Hofmann, and Robert Motherwell. In the accompanying catalogue, modernist poet William Carlos Williams summarized this interest in "woman": "I don't know how you could make a painting presenting man without including woman. But woman, somehow, lends herself to painting in her own right as man does not. Somehow the painting IS woman."[68] She was irresistible but insurmountable, and the male artist had no choice but to challenge her—"What is he to do? Impregnate her? Kill her? Avoid her? You see, it all amounts to the same thing: do what he will she remains in spite of his greatest doing or not doing the same thing, woman." Romantic modernists, especially those who borrowed their language from Wilhelm Reich, made a similar association. In *Cannibals and Christians*, Norman Mailer defined the novel as the "Great Bitch," a cruel temptress who must be dethroned: "The novel is like the Great Bitch in one's life. We think we're rid of her, we go on to the other women . . . and then we turn a corner on a street, and there's the Bitch smiling at us, and we're trapped."[69] Borrowing mythological imagery and military references, Mailer defined this confrontation with "the Great

Bitch" as a desperate attempt to ransack the "palace" of the unconscious and bring forth "the real secrets" that she so jealously protected. Thus, writing was, for Mailer, a form of mastery over the castrating influence of such weakness, the moment when the hipster overcame "the buried weaker more feminine part of [his] nature."[70]

In this way, romantic modernists detailed a desperate struggle to purge the feminine attachments lingering from the pre-Oedipal moment that haunted the male psyche. Their assault upon man's armored character structure in the name of Reichian therapy was an implicit acknowledgment that the ego was founded in part upon an identification with the lost maternal object. In so doing, romantic modernists returned to the mother, declared her guilty of a host of transgressions, subsequently handed out punishment, and, through such perceived heroism, reclaimed their identities. Masculinity was not something given; instead, it was something gained, as Mailer explained, from "an existential series of victories and defeats."[71] Whether through Allen Ginsberg's invocation of "feminine chatter" to which he succumbed when writing or through the "infantile pileup of scatological buildup words till satisfaction is gained" that marked Jack Kerouac's regressive form of spontaneous prose or through the vaginal landscape of Jackson Pollock's *The Deep* into which the artist submerged himself, romantic modernists tried to eradicate the ego in the name of libidinal release by purging the psyche of those identifications upon which the ego itself was founded.[72] Forever vulnerable and subject to viral infection, masculinity was for romantic modernists in need of rigid defense.

The Cultural Politics of Jasper Johns and James Baldwin

In a 1959 *Arts* magazine review of the "Beyond Painting" exhibition at the Alan Gallery in New York, which brought together the work of George Cohen, Joseph Cornell, Robert Motherwell, and others, art critic Hilton Kramer singled out Jasper Johns and Robert Rauschenberg for his harshest criticism. Confused by the popularity of these two young artists, Kramer argued that they were merely "visual publicists" whose heralded return to imagery simply reflected the uncritical tastes of an uninformed art world and the uninspired visions of two mediocre painters. Accordingly, Kramer saw "no difference between [Rauschenberg's] work and the decorative displays which often grace the windows of Bonwit Teller and Bloomingdale's."[73] Continuing his critical assault, Kramer linked Johns derogatorily to the Dada movement but also argued that the radical bent of this tradition was missing in Johns's work: "Dada sought to repudiate and criticize bourgeois values, whereas Johns, like Rauschenberg, aims to please and confirm the decadent periphery of bourgeois taste." For Kramer, the art world had succumbed to the decorative displays of two banal artists. In a highly unusual move, Johns wrote a response to the editor of *Arts* magazine, one of the few times Johns directly answered his critics. In large measure, Johns was responding to what he saw as the deliberate attempt to disparage him and Rauschenberg on the basis of their personal relationship. The two had become intimate several years prior, a rather scandalous situation in a New York art scene centered on the overtly masculine displays of Jackson Pollock and his compatriots at the Cedar Bar. Kramer's innuendos about the sexuality of both painters, embedded in comments about the "sheer decorative sweetness" (50) of Johns's work, angered the young artist. In response, he knocked Kramer for his "rottenness" and for the "abundance of false labels" in his piece, a review that seemed less like art criticism and more like the personal ramblings of a man determined to "evaluate, defame, [and] categorize" any and everyone.[74] Such an insinuation about Johns's sexuality was nothing new for the artist; as soon as he was publicly recognized as one of the fomenters of the shift away from abstract expressionism, critics began to make coded references to his homosexuality. For instance, Johns was described in 1959 by *Time* magazine as a "fair-haired boy" and a determined "bachelor" who "works in a neat, spacious loft" in New York.[75] Both Johns and Rauschenberg recognized that such personal descriptions, reiterated in countless reviews of their art, were in stark contrast to the masculine depictions of Pollock and others over the years, and both admitted that the rumors about their relationship had a negative effect on their lives. As Rauschenberg explained, "what had been tender and sensitive became gossip. It was sort of new to the art world that the two most well-known, up and coming studs were affectionately involved."[76] This was the constraint under which these two lovers lived and worked and because of which their relationship ultimately ended.

Throughout his career, Johns struggled with his identity in an artistic landscape that shunned such a relationship. Responding to his critics and to the litany of rumors about him, Johns began to incorporate specific references to gay American poets such as Walt Whitman, Hart Crane, and Frank O'Hara in paintings such as *In Memory of My Feelings—Frank O'Hara* (1961), *Periscope (Hart Crane)* (1963), and *Land's End* (1963), all of which reflected Johns's melancholic state after the end of his relationship with Rauschenberg in 1961. But even in his early works, Johns expressed his difficulty in coming to terms with his sexuality in a social world that disavowed same-sex desire and that portrayed homosexuality as a pathology. For instance, in *Target with Plaster Casts* (1955), which he painted at the beginning of his relationship with Rauschenberg, Johns portrayed the homosexual body under siege by social forces in the postwar period. The target, as described in Chapter 6, represents the violence done to the body—hacked to pieces, dissected into separate components, and trapped inside closeted boxes for surveillance. The painting was in this sense a metaphor for the social prioritization of heterosexuality at the expense of same-sex attraction; as Johns obliquely described in his sketchbook, "An object that tells of the loss, destruction, disappearance of objects. Does not speak of itself. Tells of others."[77] All of his *Target* paintings, in this sense, spoke to the destructive assault upon the gay male body by the outside world.

In his monumental 1962 painting *Diver*, Johns presented his most complex image of the self, offered in response to what he saw as the obvious limitations of romantic modernism. Begun as a large charcoal drawing of a diving board with the hand and footprints of a man doing a swan dive, *Diver* was eventually translated into a mural-sized painting reminiscent of the size and scope of Jackson Pollock's early murals. The title of the painting is a reference to Friedrich Schiller's poem "The Diver," which Johns probably discovered through his reading of Sigmund Freud's *Civilization and Its Discontents*, where the famed psychoanalyst used the poem to describe the origins of religious feelings. Schiller's poem tells the tale of a young man who undertakes the heroic task set forth by his king to retrieve a golden goblet from the depths of the boundless sea into which the king had thrown it. With the promise of the king's daughter's hand in marriage and a knighthood in the king's court, the page willingly dives into the stormy depths as "it boils and it roars and it hisses and seethes." When tempted a second time to complete the task after the first retrieval is successful, the page is swallowed up by the "ocean-womb" and never seen again. In this sense, the sea in Schiller's poem represents not just the torrid force of the natural world but also the deep recesses of the unconscious that continually pulls at man and threatens to overwhelm him. More pointedly, in Schiller's poem the whirlpool into which the man drowns is also, as Karen Horney has suggested, a metaphor for the lure of women—as a symbol of man's longstanding dread of castration in the face of female enchantment.[78] This was of course why Freud referenced Schiller's poem. Meditating on the sources of the oceanic feeling that generated religion, Freud, who openly admitted that he was unable to discover such a feeling in himself, turned to Schiller's poem as an example: "I am moved to exclaim in the words of Schiller's diver: 'He may rejoice, who breathes in the roseate light.'"[79] Freud argued that the origins of monotheistic religion were found in man's need to save himself, through the intervention of the all-powerful father, from the powerlessness of this oceanic oneness that he equated with the pre-Oedipal position. Thus, within religion, Freud saw the classical Oedipal narrative, which was also detailed in Schiller's tale of a young man desperate to break from the maternal realm of the pre-Oedipal moment by gaining the paternal throne for himself and marrying the king's daughter.

Johns's reference to Schiller's poem thus served two purposes for the painter. First, he equated the drowning of the young page to the real-life suicide of the American poet Hart Crane, who struggled for years with his own sexuality and eventually perished because of his inability to gain recognition. In so doing, Johns was criticizing the widespread cultural defense of proper Oedipal development as the only foundation for individual autonomy. Johns had made a well-known distinction between man as a spy and as a watchman, his most explicit statement concerning the nature of man's being. As Johns explained, "the spy must be ready to 'move,' must be aware of his entrances and exits. The watchman leaves his job & takes away no information."[80] Johns's notion of the watchman was presumably also taken from his reading of Freud, who had metaphorically described the psychic agency of man's superego as a watchman: "For what prompted the subject to form an ego ideal, on whose behalf his conscience acts as watchman, arose from the critical influence of his parents . . . to whom were added, as time went on, those who trained and taught him."[81] In displacing the watchman for the figure of the spy, whose mobility reflected a concerted effort to evade the demands of social and political authorities, Johns took an obvious swipe at the psychoanalytic pretensions of high modernists who had prioritized Oedipal identity as the proper trajectory for autonomous and therefore heterosexual development. Johns refused to believe that the internalization of paternal authority was the only source of a stable, coherent identity. Second, he was criticizing the notion proffered by romantic modernists that artistic creation was at its essence a desperate struggle to liberate the self from maternal immersion and from the pre-Oedipal moment in general. Schiller's diver, like the American action painter, represented this widespread cultural panic over the power and influence of women; as Karen Horney has explained in relationship to Schiller's poem, "always, everywhere, the man strives to rid himself of his dread of women by objectifying it."[82] In the countless images offered by De Kooning, Rothko, Pollock, and others, Johns saw a futile attempt to shore up male subjectivity from feminine contamination. In this sense, Johns's spy was not the disembodied self of romantic modernism that had dispensed with all visible representation and all psychic attachments. Accordingly, Johns offered an image of selfhood not bound by the parochialism of romantic modernism, which simply reflected, according to Johns, a larger cultural panic over the supposedly feminine nature of the American male. In so doing, Johns, like Norman Brown and many other modernists, saw the self as a complex formation held together by the endless series of identifications made by the ego.

Measuring fourteen feet long and over seven feet high, *Diver* is a composite of the styles—from expressionistic to controlled—that Johns had incorporated into his works over the years. Divided into five panels, the work is also a tapestry of a range of available subject positions linked together in subtle and diffuse ways. In the first panel, Johns included a multicolored device circle—a stretcher bar scraping thick, bright colors onto a gray-stained canvas, once again representing his understanding of individual expression as a manipulation of the tools and measurements of everyday life. In the second panel, Johns painted a vertical row of rectangles, beginning with a black one at the top of the canvas and progressing downward through a series of increasingly lighter gray ones. The strict ordering of these geometrical units reflects the controlled ordering of the environment inherent to any form of life—those endless rails that Wittgenstein described that reduced behavior to patterned, ordered expressions. If the first two panels, then, represent the mediation of social demands by an internalized superego that limits individual expression, the third and fourth panels, which retrace Johns's original drawing of a diver, represent man's complex psychic interior and his psychic history. Unlike romantic modernists who fought, through their artistic mediums, to free themselves from the pre-Oedipal moment that Schiller's poem violently describes, Johns's diver acknowledges the possibilities inherent in such a position, accepting that identification with the pre-Oedipal mother is just as legitimate as identification with the Oedipal father. Johns's diver sees the compulsive drive for autonomy by romantic modernists, that is, their search for a form of identity that excluded outside attachments, as pathological. The fifth panel is an expressionistic landscape of colorful brushstrokes with the stenciled names of primary colors (echoing his breakthrough in *False Start*) combined with a bundle of silverware held together by several wires. The expressionistic landscape reiterates Johns's original deconstruction of action painting, and his inclusion of cutlery reflects his concern with consumption, orality, and nourishment, that is, with the pre-Oedipal moment in which the subject first confronts the complicated and ambiguous divide between the inner and the outer. The entire composition is loosely held together by Johns's numbering of the panels, by a tape measure running part of the length of the canvas, and by a block of paint crossing the break between the fourth and fifth panels. The self depicted in *Diver* is one in continual oscillation between subject positions, at times active, at times passive, a self with an openness to the vicissitudes of the instinctual life, to all of the available objects of attachment, and to the restrictions of the outside world. Johns's diver, in this sense, represents a less defensive, less restricted, and more flexible form of identity, one that recognizes the complementary relationship between the pre-Oedipal and Oedipal positions and between intrapsychic and intersubjective forms of being.

Of course Johns was not the only postwar artist to challenge the mainstream notions of the American avant-garde. Like the young painter, who struggled with the language and cultural assumptions of abstract expressionism, James Baldwin fought a similar battle against the posturing within the New York literary scene, trying to defend himself from the criticisms issued against him by high modernists like Irving Howe and by romantic modernists like Norman Mailer. In particular, Baldwin had a hard time digesting the theoretical claims of high modernism, in particular, the ubiquitous use of Freudian psychology to dissect the American character. Baldwin was of course doubly scarred by the "imprecise science of psychiatry."[83] As a homosexual, Baldwin had to defend his sexual identity from claims that his attraction to men marked a narcissistic, weakened condition. Moreover, as an African American, Baldwin had to defend his racial identity from claims made by postwar social scientists, liberal and conservative alike, that the legacy of racial oppression and the supposed dysfunctional nature of the African American family had left those in his community psychologically immature. As historian Daryl Michael Scott has demonstrated, African Americans in the early Cold War, much like homosexuals, were depicted by social scientists as psychologically damaged and therefore as pathological personalities. In works such as Abram Kardiner's *Mark of Oppression* and Kenneth Clark's *Dark Ghetto*, social scientists, in language borrowed from *The Authoritarian Personality*, argued that the lack of paternal figures as models of discipline and emulation had led to a generation of African American children raised within a matriarchal culture and therefore lacking any internalized paternal image to ensure proper psychological growth. In most of his works—from *Go Tell It on the Mountain* to *Another Country*—Baldwin challenged those "encyclopedias of physiological and scientific knowledge" that depicted his maturation as a black man and a gay man as an arrested form of development.[84]

Of course Baldwin was not naïve enough to present merely celebratory accounts of both the black and gay communities. He found it impossible to argue that the historical legacy of racism and homophobia had not had long-standing effects. He was as determined as Theodor Adorno and Lionel Trilling, for example, to offer an image of an autonomous personality strong enough to confront the psychic assaults on the ego launched by a dysfunctional world. But like David Riesman and other modernists, Baldwin refused to believe that a strong ego formed by the internalization of paternal authority was the only healthy personality structure. In response to most modernists who depicted such problems in broad historical strokes, Baldwin turned to his personal struggles. Throughout his career, as literary critic William Spurlin has noted, Baldwin had to deal with accusations and assumptions about his sexuality, evidenced most famously by a *Time* magazine cover story in 1963 that downplayed Baldwin's role as a black leader in the civil rights movement and emphasized instead his "effeminate" mannerisms and his "nervous, slight, almost fragile figure."[85] In fact, over the years Baldwin had to rebuke continuous criticisms from a series of writers—from his mentor Richard Wright to Alfred Kazin to Eldridge Cleaver—that his works were no more than "quivering novels of sensibility by an over-conscious stylist."[86]

But like Jasper Johns, Baldwin saved his most pointed criticisms for Jack Kerouac, William Burroughs, and Norman Mailer, all of those romantic modernists whose lifelong struggles with their own masculinities seemed to the gay, black writer symptomatic of a larger cultural madness. Forever confronting the stereotypes of black male sexuality scattered throughout such works as Norman Mailer's "The White Negro," Baldwin tried to rethink the nature of sexual and gender identities. "I think I know," explained Baldwin, "something about the American masculinity which most men of my generation do not know because they have not been menaced by it in the way that I have been."[87] Baldwin's first attempt to address the limitations of the psychoanalytic theories to which most modernists clung was his 1954 *New Leader* article "The Male Prison," in which he criticized the sexual confessions made by André Gide in his memoirs. Although partly concerned about Gide's Protestant moralizing, Baldwin was more exacerbated by the French writer's frank but immature admission of his homosexual encounters. Unlike Lionel Trilling, Philip Wylie, or Gide himself, Baldwin was uninterested in debating the etiology of homosexuality: "That argument, for example, as to whether or not homosexuality is natural seems to me completely pointless—pointless because I really do not see what difference the answer makes."[88] Refusing to reduce questions about human affairs to discussions about a supposed natural state, Baldwin saw Gide's personal dilemma, in which the writer confessed to his homosexual activities with numerous men while clinging desperately to the hand of his beleaguered wife, as representative of this larger modernist panic over the contours of American masculinity. "It is important to remember," argued Baldwin, "that the prison in which Gide struggled is not really so unique as it would certainly comfort us to believe, is not very different from the prison inhabited by, say, the heroes of Mickey Spillane" (105).

Burdened by accusations of effeminacy, Gide had locked himself in a "male prison," desperately trying to cling to his own purity by distancing himself both from his wife and from the men with whom he had sex. In the former case, he constructed a hypertrophic, idealized image of his wife to avoid acknowledging her as a concrete individual: "And this is because then he could no longer have loved Madeleine as an ideal, as Emanuele, God-with-us, but would have been compelled to love her as a woman, which he could not have done except physically" (103). But just as much as he had entrusted his wife with his purity, Gide had also distanced himself from his male lovers, continuously despising them for what they represented in himself. Unable to relate to either the men or the women in his life, Gide searched, like other modernists, for a place of isolation or purity. "It is worth observing," argued Baldwin, "that when men can no longer love women they also cease to love or respect or trust each other, which makes their isolation complete" (105). Of course, this was not just an academic question for Baldwin; he had had to deal with this cultural panic for most of his life. In a different context, Baldwin described his extreme sensitivity as a young boy about his slender physical appearance and his slightly feminine voice, painfully aware that he was continuously mocked as he walked down the streets of Harlem. More important, however, after he had fled the restrictive confines of his neighborhood for the bohemian world of Greenwich Village, Baldwin was shocked that restaurant patrons at the Calypso where he worked were determined to decipher the etiology of the young black man's sexuality.[89] As Baldwin explained, the question "'Do you really *like* your mother?'" which he was asked by countless inquiring companions who had latched onto psychoanalytic clichés, "did not cause me to wonder about my mother or myself but about the person asking the question."[90] Never an avid admirer of "Freud, Horney, Jung, [or] Reich,"

Baldwin worried that his fellow modernists had trapped themselves into "psychiatric formulas" that did not help to deal with the actual vicissitudes of human desire. Moreover, he worried that this widespread panic over the nature of masculinity had irreparably damaged relations between the sexes, forever locking men and women into prisons of their own making.

Baldwin's most detailed discussion of this male prison was his second novel, *Giovanni's Room*, which continued the argument found in his essay on Gide. *Giovanni's Room* was in many ways a corrective to his first novel, *Go Tell It on the Mountain*, from which he had been forced at the urging of his publishers to excise most of the homosexual subtext. But the frank content of his second novel could not be eliminated and was therefore turned down by his editors at Knopf, who told Baldwin that he should "burn the manuscript" or risk ruining "his reputation as a leading young black writer."[91] Eventually published by Dial Press in 1956, *Giovanni's Room* continued the discussion of sexual identity Baldwin had begun in several short stories such as "The Outing." The novel also explored this "new lost generation" that had fled to Europe supposedly to rediscover themselves. *Giovanni's Room* tells the tale of a young American man, David, who has fled to Europe to escape his troubled relationship with his father, his uncertain future and self-destructive behavior, and, more important, the memory of an adolescent homosexual encounter with a young black boy. Like his fellow expatriates, David wants, as he explains, "to find myself," an ambiguous task that leads him into a relationship and eventual engagement with an American woman, Hella, whom he meets in a Parisian bar.[92] But her trip to Spain, which she makes to contemplate David's marriage proposal, leads him to explore the gay subculture of Paris and to his eventual tortured relationship with an Italian bartender, Giovanni, whom David both loves and pushes away. A meditation on the relationship between two men in a homophobic culture, *Giovanni's Room* is also Baldwin's most frank discussion about the nature of masculinity.

In fleeing to Europe in the hopes of discovering himself, David imagines he can overcome the corrupting influences of his American home life that has generated his forlorn condition; more important, David also hopes to find in the streets of Paris a pristine but rugged environment in which to redeem himself. In turning to France, David admittedly invokes his European forebears who had escaped the feudal structures of their homeland for the uncorrupted lands of North America. As David says, "my ancestors conquered a continent, pushing across death-laden plains, until they came to an ocean which faced away from Europe into a darker past" (3). Invoking images of the rugged, inner-directed frontiersman of the American past, David hopes to regain the "innocence and confidence" that he has lost. Indeed, David's assertion of his independence is echoed by his denial of any form of dependence, familial or otherwise; as David himself admits, he is one of those people "who believe they are strong-willed and the masters of their destiny" and "who pride themselves on their willpower" (50). Embedded in his fantasies of Paris are David's dreams of omnipotence and purity. But Paris of course is not the untainted paradise that David had hoped. As Baldwin subtly notes, France, just like most of Western Europe after the rise of NATO, had become a site of American military and economic expansion in the early Cold War, a land littered with Coca-Cola bottles, Gary Cooper movies, and drunken American sailors. "It's cold out here in the Old World" (134), observes David's girlfriend Hella. As a result, his flight to Europe to escape the confines of America and thereby redeem himself is inevitably doomed to fail.

Of course David's flight did not begin when he boarded the plane to Europe. As he himself notes, his flight began years ago as a teenager when he had his first homosexual encounter with his friend Joey. After a spirited summer day whistling at girls sunbathing at Coney Island, David returned with Joey to his family's apartment in Brooklyn where an innocent moment in the shower horsing around with wet towels led to a night of intense passion. While their encounter was full of tenderness, joy, and mutual love, David awoke the next morning to terrible confusion, simultaneously recognizing that his friend's body was "the most beautiful creation" he had ever seen but also recognizing that his own body was "gross and crushing" and that the desire within it was quite "monstrous" (8–9). Finally realizing the implications of that night, David recoiled from Joey's body, which "suddenly seemed the black opening of a cavern in which I would be tortured till madness came, in which I would lose my manhood." David's fears of castration and therefore obliteration also produced within him tremendous shame as he recounted to himself all of the stories of perversion he had heard and internalized over the years. Soiled and impure, David fled from Joey's bedroom in the morning and ultimately from Joey himself. Embarrassed, David spent years fleeing from the memories of his encounter with Joey, a flight that ultimately leads him to Paris. Unable to accept the reality of his desires, David is only able to associate his latent homosexuality with the loss of his own masculinity, that is, as a form of castration that he associates with the aggressive, domineering spirit of his long-departed mother.

Indeed, *Giovanni's Room* is in many ways a meditation on the dread of maternal power embedded within the culture of romantic modernism and on the paranoia and self-destruction emanating from that dread. Baldwin saw this paranoia at the heart of American psychoanalytic literature. As Freud had explained, the child's separation from the pre-Oedipal mother was predicated not simply upon a declaration of his independence but upon establishing barriers to guard against any regression to this previous stage of development. Although the common method for dealing with object loss according to Freud was the process of identification, whereby the lost object was psychically integrated into the ego, male development was predicated upon the denial of any such feminine identification.[93] The result was that the maternal figure, repudiated and denied, reemerged as an even more frightening, omnipotent, archaic figure buried deep within the male psyche. Like many romantic modernists, David exhibits an intense panic over his relationship with his mother. Her death, much like Orestes' murder of Clytemnestra, converts David's mother from a concrete family member to an omnipotent, archaic figure, emphasized by her photograph that "stood all by itself on the mantelpiece" and "proved how her spirit dominated that air and controlled us all" (11). David's psyche is in fact littered with fantasies of his mother as a devouring presence bringing neither comfort nor warmth but death: "I scarcely remember her at all, yet she figured in my nightmares . . . straining to press me against her body; that body so putrescent, so sickening soft, that it opened, as I clawed and cried, into a breach so enormous as to swallow me alive." Like the images in Willem de Kooning's paintings, David's mother emerges not as a substantive being and self-possessed individual but as a creature to overcome and subdue. Less interested in offering an etiology of homosexuality than in exploring the causes of this male panic over maternal identification, Baldwin wondered why his fellow artists and writers were so fearful of any psychological or physical dependence and unwilling to recognize the possibility that the sources of their identities were outside themselves. "It need scarcely be said," explained Baldwin, "that I have no interest in hurling gratuitous insults at American mothers."[94] David can only imagine paternal rescue as a solution to his situation, a rescue that, much like Jack Kerouac's personal story, seems impossible given the seemingly castrated position of his father. David's father, described as an incorrigible drunk and as a delinquent paternal figure, had supposedly, when David was a young boy, "left something, somewhere, undone" between them, a failure caused in part by his father's refusal to avoid "utter nakedness" in his relationship with his son.[95]

This drive toward paternal authority, in any form, represented for Baldwin an intense cultural sickness. In fact, Baldwin suggests that David's troubles stem not simply from the haunting memories of his mother but from his confused relationship with his father. In detailing David's troubles with both his parents, Baldwin was making problematic not just traditional psychoanalytic theories of male sexual development but also the nature of identification and psychological growth overall. David's panic over the supposedly castrated condition in which he had been placed during his encounter with Joey aroused a culturally induced panic that he was losing his masculinity by aligning himself with the passive position of women. David is desperate to redeem his failures as a man by purging himself of those seemingly feminine attachments within his psyche that had led to his perverse behavior, in particular, by forgoing desire for his mother in traditional Oedipal fashion by identifying, not with her (which, according to Baldwin, the logic of psychoanalytic theory seems to maintain) but with his father. But to identify with the father, under the vicissitudes of the drives, would seem according to Baldwin to reveal an underlying homoerotic attachment to the father that has been repressed. David becomes in many ways the melancholic subject of heterosexual culture that theorist Judith Butler has unearthed as a fundamental part of traditional gender formation. As Butler explains, if a boy becomes a man by renouncing love for his mother and identifying with his father, that identification must have been the result of the prohibition that barred the father as an object of desire and installed him as part of the ego, that is, as an incorporated object that haunts the subject as the melancholic residue of an object lost and subsequently disavowed.[96] David's desire for men therefore becomes a love that he cannot describe or acknowledge. "I did not *want* [my father] to know me," exclaims David in highly guarded language, and "I did not want anyone to know me."[97] But David lingers over his father's sexual relations, forever frightened that his path and his father's own might cross one day. "I could scarcely ever face a woman," says David, "without wondering whether or not my father had, in Ellen's phase, been 'interfering' with her" (15). In fact, during his passionate encounter with Joey, David, both repelled and liberated by the experience, can only imagine that he has in some fashion betrayed his father: "Then I thought of my father, who had no one in the world but me, my mother having died when I was little" (9). With his masculinity unraveled by this encounter, David is desperate for the intervening blow from the law of the Father to foreclose this flood of desire. As David pleads, his father "wanted no distance between us; he wanted me to look on him as a man like myself. But I wanted the merciful distance of father and son, which would have permitted me to love him" (17). Traditional masculinity, in this sense, represented for Baldwin a reaction formation. Under prescribed heterosexual norms, the fundamental oscillation between identification and desire at the root of Freudian theory was denied, and they were treated instead as mutually exclusive operations. The result, according to Baldwin, was the American male's endless flight from femininity and his drive toward an incorruptible masculinity that was in fact anything but untainted.

While he is in Paris, the prison that David has so artfully constructed begins to collapse after he is introduced to the young Italian man named Giovanni who bartends at a restaurant owned by their mutual acquaintance Guillaume. Their subsequent affair is for David "strange beyond belief," mixed with feelings of shame, regret, satisfaction, and frustration, as he is unable to accept his feelings for Giovanni or to let Giovanni care for him in any meaningful way. In many ways, the metaphor of Giovanni's room (the bartender's small studio apartment in a less than idyllic part of the city) operates on several levels as a description of David's predicament. Most prominently, the room functions as a metaphor for David's personal retreat. After his experience with Joey, David decides "to allow *no room* in the universe for something which shamed and frightened me" (20), a statement that serves as an odd foreshadowing of things to come. On a basic level, Giovanni's room represents the forbidden relationship between these two men, something private that exists "beneath the sea" and outside the flux of "time" (114) and something secluded from his previous life where "neither my father nor Hella was real." As such, the room is a retreat from traditional masculine norms. David of course continues to view the room as Giovanni's property, hence his continual use of the possessive. David posits the room as the objective embodiment of Giovanni's sexuality and as a possession that Giovanni owns and to which David has no relationship. Consequently, as David explains, "the room was not large enough for two," allowing him to abstain from any responsibility for it. Indeed, Giovanni is the one who "had had great plans for remodeling the room" (86). Unable to accept their relationship, David repeatedly stares "at the room with the same, nervous calculating extension of the intelligence and of all one's forces which occurs when gauging a moral and unavoidable danger" (87). Thus David sees the room as a site of continuous "disorder," a representation of his own confused masculinity. David claims that the "key to this disorder" is "not to be found in any of the usual places," not a "matter of habit or circumstance or temperament" but a "matter of punishment and grief." Therefore, as a site of transgression, the room also represents a metaphorical and literal prison. The social enforcement of heterosexuality locks David and Giovanni into the closeted confines of the room. For Giovanni, "they measure the gram, the centimeter, these people, and they keep piling all the little scraps they save, one on top of the other, year in and year out, all in the stocking or under the bed" (36). The effort by postwar intellectuals to categorize desire into psychiatric norms places an extreme burden upon both characters. The "anguish and fear" of their private relationship becomes the "surface" on which they "slipped and slid, losing balance, dignity, and pride," an anguish that drives David away from his lover and that leads Giovanni to murder the restaurant owner Guillaume in a desperate fit of rage and to his eventual arrest and execution.

In this way, David's flight from both Hella and Giovanni is for Baldwin emblematic of the flight of American men in the middle of the twentieth century from themselves. Unable to mourn Giovanni's death or admit his love for him, David is forced into what Baldwin describes as a state of "melancholy," akin to "the shadow of some predatory, waiting bird" (146). Having denied the loss of his mother and Giovanni, David is unable to integrate the various identifications he has made into a complex whole. Like those who turned to spontaneous release, orgasmic convulsions, and other therapeutic measures to avoid any form of self-representation, David searches for his own purity: "I succeeded very well—by not looking at the universe, by not looking at myself, by remaining, in effect, in constant motion" (20). David is, as he himself notes, "a wanderer, an adventurer, rocking through the world, unanchored" (62). Desperate to maintain a sense of wholeness, David is left staring at his naked body at the end of the novel: "I look at my sex, my troubling sex, and wonder how it can be redeemed, how I can save it from the knife" (168). The only possibility to avoid this passivity and therefore castration is for David, like romantic modernists such as William Burroughs and Jackson Pollock, to flee from his own body by denying any and every form of attachment: "I move at last from the mirror and begin to cover that nakedness. . . . I must believe, I must believe, that the heavy grace of God, which has brought me to this place, is all that can carry me out of it" (169). In his last act of flight, David takes the blue envelope announcing the date of Giovanni's execution and tears it "slowly into many pieces, watching them dance in the wind, watching the wind carry them away." But of course David's refusal to recognize his culpability does not succeed as "the wind blows some of them back" toward him.

Like Norman Brown and Jasper Johns, Baldwin offered an image of man's sexual and psychological development in much more complicated terms than his modernist compatriots did, continuously overturning the oppositional categories of femininity and masculinity guiding traditional assumptions about gender. Instead of a rigid polarity between masculinity as a form of activity and mastery and femininity as a form of passivity and domination, Baldwin argued instead that gender was neither a fixed nor coherent position. David mistakenly believes that autonomy is based upon the disavowal of any form of dependence. "I wanted to be inside again," explains David, "with the light and safety, with my manhood unquestioned, watching my woman put my children to bed" (104). As a form of self-denial and self-deception, David's nostalgia for the purity of the heterosexual family romance, untainted by the perverse nature of homosexual desire, is for Baldwin an endemic part of a failed American culture. He saw the American ideal of masculinity, to which many romantic modernists clung, as "an ideal so paralytically infantile that it is virtually forbidden—as an unpatriotic act—that the American boy evolve into the complexity of manhood."[98] Unlike those who turned "to Wilhelm Reich and perished in orgone boxes" (688) or those like David who desperately tried to escape from their own bodies and desires, Baldwin challenged his fellow artists to risk the coherence of their identities by recognizing not just that the boundaries of the self were quite permeable but that the ego itself was in fact constructed by the identifications that it made. "If you can examine and face your life," argued Baldwin, "you can discover the terms with which you are connected to other lives, and they can discover too, the terms with which they are connected to other people."[99] To obliterate the ego by purging the psyche of all attachments as William Burroughs and others proposed was to risk losing any sense of connection, coherence, or grounding. It was also to lose any possibility of conversation or collaboration with others; as Baldwin explained, "in order to learn your name, you are going to have to learn mine" (16).

The key in overcoming these limitations was to acknowledge a more inclusive image of the self, one that incorporated the possibility of multiple identifications within the psyche. Baldwin challenged his fellow modernists to cease making the feminine a threat to the boundaries of their own selves and to cease positing those repudiated identifications onto outsiders or onto the canvases of their paintings and instead to work through them. This sense of self that Baldwin imagined cut across traditional paternal and maternal subject positions, composed of multiple identifications that formed the basis for the complicated assumption of gender. "But we are all androgynous," argued Baldwin, "not only because we are all born of a woman impregnated by the seed of a man but because each of us, helplessly and forever, contains the other—male in female, female in male, white in black, and black in white."[100] Any refusal to recognize this had two tragic consequences for Baldwin. The first was to continue to treat homosexuality as a perversion of traditional Oedipal development or at least to cling to a particular notion of masculinity, an effect of the assumption that identification with the father foreclosed not just desire for the mother under the threat of castration but also desire for the father. But for Baldwin, identification and desire were not necessarily opposed—masculinity did not necessarily preclude desire for a man. The second consequence was this continuing male panic, projected in endless ways onto the public and private spheres, over a lingering feminine presence controlling their livelihoods and their lives. The result was, as Jack Kerouac's personal story revealed, simultaneously an idealization of women as goddesses or angels and an intense fright over women as threats to male sexuality. As Baldwin explained, "communion between the sexes has become so sorely threatened that we depend more and more on the strident exploitation of externals, as, for example, the breasts of Hollywood glamour girls and the mindless grunting and swaggering of Hollywood he-men."[101] Sometimes, as de Kooning's *Woman* series revealed, these contrasting images existed together. In so arguing, Baldwin made the politics of identification, that is, the social and personal significance of the psychic attachments that brought the self into being, the key to a refashioned cultural politics, a move quite evident throughout not just his own work but the work of Norman Brown, Kenneth Burke, and others.

PART III

The Challenge of Late Modernism

CHAPTER EIGHT

Rhetoric and the Politics of Identification Writ Large: The Late Modernism of Kenneth Burke, C. Wright Mills, and Ralph Ellison

One late summer evening William Burroughs appeared in front of the Moka Bar, a London establishment that had recently offended him through poor table service and unappetizing cheesecake, and blasted a tape recording of street noise and other assorted sounds.[1] Burroughs continued his auditory assault for over two months until the bar officially closed, a spectacle he repeated at other places he deemed lacking. His victory signaled to the Beat writer the efficacy of his cut-up technique as a form of cultural resistance. Over the years, Burroughs had extended his technique beyond written material to include auditory material such as street sounds, snatches of conversation, radio and television static, and crowd noises that he recorded and then spliced together in random fashion. Burroughs's goal, as with his literary cut-up technique, was to introduce irrational, nonlinear, and illogical modes of thought. More important, Burroughs was trying to disrupt the operation of language itself. Arguing that the human body was a "soft machine" under constant siege from a host of parasites, Burroughs considered language the ultimate form of junk because of the demonic way words built up patterns of associations, concepts, and images within the individual. The current system of communication, which was dominated by the loudspeaker of the culture industry, was monolithic, acting as a form of hypnotic and subliminal control. As he explained, "there are certain formulas, word-locks, which will lock up a whole civilization for a thousand years."[2] In the midst of such endless chatter, any attempt at communication using the available language was to participate in the mindless exchange of tainted concepts.

Burroughs's understanding of the stultifying effects of language derived from the semantic theory of Polish-born scientist Alfred Korzybski, whose lectures Burroughs attended at the University of Chicago in 1939 and whose 1933 book *Science and Sanity* challenged Aristotelian logic, and from Burroughs's introduction in the late 1950s to the theory of Dianetics formulated by L. Ron Hubbard, the founder of the Church of Scientology. Both theories, albeit in different ways, proved to Burroughs that language itself was a viral element—that the conditioned system of language not only gave rise to patterned associations of thought that limited the range of possibilities contained in the natural world but also served as a tool of entrapment by conditioning the body through the inscription of language directly onto the flesh. In *The Nova Express*, he said, "those colorless sheets are what flesh is made from—Becomes flesh when it has color and writing—that is Word And Image write the message that is you on colorless sheets determine all flesh."[3] If the tradition of romantic modernism that Burroughs helped to fashion was driven by the quest to purge the self of feminine identification as a pathway to bodily liberation, then such liberation also demanded release from all forms of communication that perpetuated psychological control. This bodily liberation meant, in other words, liberation from language itself. Burroughs's cut-up technique was designed to unlink the connection between words and objects produced by conditioned chains of association. By blasting street and crowd noise at establishments such as the Moka Bar, Burroughs believed he could disorient the psyches of patrons and servers and thereby end their attachment to that particular establishment. As he explained in *The Soft Machine*, "Cut word lines—Cut music lines—Smash the control images—Smash the control machines—Burn the books—Kill the priests—Kill! Kill! Kill!"[4] His goal was not a form of liberated discourse but the end of discourse itself—"communication must become total and conscious before we can stop it."[5] The goal was liberation from the body and from language by moving into a state of silence. The tape recorder became for Burroughs the essential tool in this struggle.

Worried about the mystifying techniques utilized by the purveyors of mass culture, many high modernists shared Burroughs's concern with the self-imprisoning nature of communication and language in general. For instance, Theodor Adorno, in "On Lyric Poetry and Society," argued that the mimetic element essential to high modernist art needed to evade the distortions inherent in common language. Given the ubiquitous nature of the culture industry, modernist art could not speak in any meaningful way; it could only negate. This meant that art "spoke" to its audience in a nontraditional manner, that is, through the negation of any possible communicative function. It had to move beyond any rhetorical, persuasive, or dialogic motive and testify to the failures of intersubjective communication overall. The question for Adorno was whether or not an artwork could achieve the "status of something universal" while remaining impervious to conceptual modes of thought thereby "making manifest something not distorted, not grasped, not yet subsumed."[6] Consequently, Adorno distinguished between language as a form of communication and language as a form of poetic expression, the former limited to the exchange of tainted concepts and the latter affirming the possibility of a nonreified discourse. Of course Adorno recognized that for an artwork to be something more than merely an individual expression of resistance to an administered world it had to move beyond the level of monologue, that is, it had to turn from the subjective to the objective to possess any cognitive function. Therefore, the poetic work had to play upon this "double" nature of language. Reluctantly, Adorno scooted closer to Symbolism and to the aesthetic vision of his friend Walter Benjamin in arguing that the subject "has to make itself a vessel, so to speak, for the idea of a pure language" (52). The only way to negate the distance between the subject and society was to hint at a nonreified language, the historical traces or "the linguistic and psychic residues" of a "prebourgeois condition" (46). Thus, according to Adorno, the artwork "reveals itself to be most deeply grounded in society when it does not chime in with society, when it communicates nothing, when, instead, the subject whose expression is successful, reaches an accord with language itself, with the inherent tendency of language" (43). As such, language, according to Adorno, could only approach the universal by drifting away from its communicative function and by seeking refuge from the banal liberal notion of the communicability of each and every thought. While not promoting Burroughs's state of silence, Adorno did agree that communication was the fundamental stumbling block to any project of liberation, aesthetic or otherwise.

This frustration with language was symptomatic of all modernist practitioners and led to Kenneth Burke's ambitious project in *A Grammar of Motives* and *A Rhetoric of Motives* to rethink the connection between communication and aesthetics, a project that set the framework for his late modernist perspective. Although he recognized the philosophical concerns of his fellow modernists, Burke challenged their disapproval of ordinary social communication and argued instead that modernists needed to work in and through the complications of language and not avoid them. He began with the startling claim that word using was temporally prior to tool using in the development of mankind, making *homo dialecticus* prior to and more fundamental than *homo faber*; for Burke, man was at essence a "symbol-using animal."[7] Beginning with the distinction he drew between motion and action, that is, between those forms of movement driven by instinctual urges and those forms of expression driven by individual intent, Burke argued that any framework for action required language—those symbols that allowed not only for abstraction and therefore transcendence of man's immediate environment but also for the externalization and expression of man's intentions. More important, Burke argued that language served as a framework for action by ending man's essential estrangement by helping him to translate his intentions to others. Language in this sense served to bridge the gap between individuals and to establish bonds of community. Language of course, as Burroughs and Adorno argued, was not a neutral medium of communication; the words, the concepts, and the expressions that composed language directed action in particular ways. That was why Burke argued that language was inseparable from rhetoric—the art of persuasion made famous by Greek orators that used the dynamics of language to gain advantage and to convert listeners to a cause or purpose. Rhetoric, Burke asserted, was ubiquitous in modern society, ranging "from the bluntest quest of advantage, as in sales promotion or propaganda, through courtship, social etiquette, education, and the sermon, to a 'pure' form that delights in the process of appeal for itself alone, without ulterior purpose."[8] In this sense, aesthetics, like all forms of knowledge and discourse, was fundamentally connected to rhetoric. Burke's theory of rhetoric was both his rejoinder to a range of modernist practices such as Burroughs's cut-up technique that hoped to produce a private, isolated, speechless, and bodiless form of existence and his major contribution to the artistic vision of late modernism.

The End of Philosophy and the Return of Rhetoric

Burke's turn to a long-forgotten disciple marked the distinctiveness of his philosophical approach. As literary critics John Bender and David Wellbery have noted, the art of rhetoric has had a complicated history beginning with its demonstrative role in the Greek polis beginning in the fifth century B.C. and concluding with its marginalization in academic departments in the twentieth century.[9] During the classical period of rhetoric running roughly from the promotion of the art by Sophist scholars in ancient Greece to Saint Augustine's abrupt departure as an instructor of rhetoric preceding his conversion to Christianity in the fifth century A.D., the art of rhetoric played a prominent role in public oratory, civic disputes, legal proceedings, and pedagogy, serving as the means for building community consensus, deciding political action, and maintaining social commitments. But ever since Socrates in Plato's *Gorgias* demoted rhetoric from an art of persuasion to mere flattery and chastised Sophist practitioners for their willingness to defend both sides of an argument in the name of personal advantage, rhetoric has struggled to retain a place within the philosophical tradition. While diverse figures such as Aristotle, Cicero, Quintilian, and Machiavelli defended the legitimacy of the art over the centuries, charges persisted that rhetoric appealed to the worst and most vulgar aspects of the human personality due to its moral and epistemological obfuscations. Bender and Wellbery list five historical transformations that helped displace the discipline of rhetoric: the emergence of the neutral and nonpositional discourse of science associated with Bacon's *Novum Organum* and Galileo's *Sidereus Nuncius*; the introduction of a subject-centered philosophical discourse ushered in by the discovery of the Cartesian cogito; the creation of an impartial liberal public sphere operating outside personal interests and institutional authority; the replacement of an oral, polis-centered public discourse by a private culture of print as the dominant mode of intellectual exchange; and the birth of the artistic movement known as modernism, which combated the modernizing practices of capitalism with the purity of aesthetic language. In this sense, rhetoric had little place in the philosophical landscape of a post-Renaissance world demarked as modernity in which knowledge claims derived not from persuasion or even forensics but from the neutral scope of science. In his *Critique of Judgment*, Kant summarized the obsolescence of rhetoric in the age of reason, arguing that rhetoric "is a dialectic which borrows from poetry only so much as is needful to win minds to the side of the orator before they have formed a judgment and to deprive them of their freedom."[10] Rhetoric, argued its detractors, remained within the realm of conventional beliefs, worldly encumbrances, and provisional knowledge because of its refusal to join the search for more substantial truths. Consequently, rhetoric historically remained limited by the provisions set forth in manuals such as Aristotle's *Ars Rhetorica* and Cicero's *De Oratore* and was marked as an ethically neutral art of communication that used logic and probabilistic reasoning solely for the purpose of instructing young rhetoricians to speak persuasively in their careers. As elocution became an established part of pedagogy, most followed Plato's lead and contrasted rhetoric as the art of persuasion with philosophy as the site of reason and logos.

But as the challenge to the metaphysical and epistemological claims of modern philosophy commenced in the twentieth century with the works of William James, Ludwig Wittgenstein, John Dewey, and Martin Heidegger, the apparent "end of philosophy" marked for Kenneth Burke the rebirth of rhetoric out of the discipline that had displaced it.[11] As philosophers of all persuasions critiqued the epistemological and ontological claims within traditional theories concerning the mind, the nature of reality, and the protocols of science, the long-standing distrust of rhetoric for its focus on *kairos* or truth's contingent circumstances disappeared. In particular, Burke's turn to rhetoric was prompted by "the verbal tactics now called 'cold war,'" which had forced questions of polemics and persuasion into the open.[12] His purpose in *A Rhetoric of Motives* was twofold: first, to recover the art of rhetoric as a mode of persuasion, and second, to demonstrate the rhetorical nature not just of current political language but of everyday speech as well. Burke wanted to illuminate "rhetorical elements that had become obscured when rhetoric as a term fell into disuse" and to demonstrate that "a rhetorical motive is often present where it is not usually recognized" (xiii). To do so, Burke had to rescue rhetoric from charges of sophistry. He also had to rescue rhetoric from any reduction to a formalized set of procedures for public oratory. Of course enemies of rhetoric in the 1940s had different targets than Sophists. Concerns about the susceptibility of anguished American citizens to the propaganda of Marxist organizations drove anti-Communist liberals and conservatives alike to denounce rhetoric as used in Marxist art; politics as such was deemed inappropriate to aesthetics or any other "pure" activity. Of course Burke noted that such reactionaries disingenuously used rhetoric themselves to unearth Communist politics within American culture and had during World War II infused their own art with anti-Fascist politics. "The fact that an activity is capable of reduction to intrinsic, autonomous principles," said Burke, "does not argue that it is free from identification with other orders of motivation extrinsic to it" (27). For Burke, rhetoric was an inescapable part of any discourse. Despite the differentiation of the domains of science, morality, and art within the philosophical discourse of modernity, the continual presence of rhetoric within technical, political, and artistic languages demonstrated the folly in trying to deny the intermingling of descriptive, normative, poetic, and imperative voices within any regime of action.

In *A Rhetoric of Motives*, Burke addressed the complicated way in which language formed, maintained, and dissolved communities of discourse and uncovered the rhetorical appeal inherent to any form of communication, aesthetic or otherwise. In so doing, he revised his original definition of rhetoric offered in *Counter-Statement* where he had linked the art of appeal to certain universal psychological forms. He also criticized high modernist critics who reduced any aesthetic form to merely the configuration of poetic elements outside the interested intentions of artists and appreciators. Rhetoric, explained Burke, "is rooted in an essential function of language itself, a function that is wholly realistic, and is continually born anew; the use of language is a symbolic means of inducing cooperation in beings that by nature respond to symbols" (43). Rhetoric was a means of inducing action—a call to arms, an appeal to join forces, a gesture of courtship, and a desire to harmonize voices. It was also a means to interrupt the complacency of everyday life by engaging others (whether through flattery, dialogue, or violence) in the hopes of eliciting a response or, more ambitiously, a commitment. In this sense, the art of appeal served an integrating function by inviting auditors to become participants in the traditions and narratives in which their lives were indelibly connected. "Rhetoric," argued Burke, "remains the mode of appeal essential for bridging the conditions of estrangement 'natural' to society as we know it" (211). In helping to form some provisional agreement or some form of communal "we," rhetoric served to bind participating interlocutors to each other through affective ties.

In reclaiming the art of persuasion both for its efficacy in establishing communities of discourse and for its subtle but ubiquitous presence in everyday language, Burke was not merely resuscitating the technical lessons concerning oratory contained in works such as Aristotle's *Ars Rhetorica*. Burke was careful to contrast the "old rhetoric," which focused merely on careful reasoning as the most important mode of persuasion, from his "new rhetoric," which dealt with the more subtle and often unnoticed ways in which language served to bridge the difference between antagonists. For instance, Aristotle had argued that proper rhetoric did not operate by arousing emotions but by persuading through argumentative procedures, that is, by avoiding the use of clichés, exaggerations, distortions, or emotions and employing enthymemes or inductions to prove a point. He had also limited rhetoric to polis-oriented deliberation, in particular, decisions involving judicial matters, epideictic matters, and deliberative or future-oriented matters. Consequently, classical rhetoric privileged the active voice of the rhetor over the receptive ears of the audience. Insofar as its language was directed *at* the members of the polis and not *with* or *for* them, Aristotelian rhetoric was didactic and monological. Burke argued instead that rhetoric was predicated upon an element of responsiveness between subjects, and he rejected the stress on fixed ends, universal judgment, and logical appeal that Aristotle had proffered. Rhetoric was effective, according to Burke, only insofar as it was based not solely on reasoned appeal but on sympathy, care, trust, and acknowledgment; as such, the "new rhetoric" favored a mutually active relationship between addressor and addressee. The rhetor did not act *upon* the audience but *with* them and no longer maintained a privileged locutionary position. "A rhetorician," explained Burke, "is like one voice in a dialogue. Put several such voices together, with each voicing its own special assertion, let them act upon one another in co-operative competition, and you get a dialectic that, properly developed, can lead to views transcending the limitations of each."[13] Successful forms of appeal were those that arose from historically specific contexts and that addressed the exigencies of a particular situation. Such forms were also directly attuned to the needs, desires, and demands of those within earshot. A persuasive rhetorician acknowledged the specific languages, specific forms of life, and special modes of reasoning practiced by his audience: "You persuade a man only insofar as you can talk his language by speech, gesture, tonality, order, image, attitude, idea, *identifying* your ways with his."[14] A rhetorician was successful, in other words, only insofar as he disclosed himself in an open fashion in the name of mutual understanding. The estrangement endemic to rhetoric was overcome only by "the principle of courtship" that linked the interests of interlocutors together. In this way, the "new rhetoric" covered all forms of discourse, not just those forms contained within the polis. Burke noted that "rhetoric includes resources of appeal ranging from sacrificial, evangelical love, through the kinds of persuasion figuring in sexual love, to sheer 'neutral' *communication*" (19). Consequently, rhetoric involved elements of persuasion and, ultimately, identification and love.

Of course Burke was unwilling to overdetermine the efficacy or even the legitimacy of rhetoric to promote a benign and communal form of dialogue, and like many postmodernists who emerged after him, Burke recognized the ever-present tendency of social differences and cultural antagonisms to disrupt conversation. As he explained, "in the War of Words, there is nothing to prevent contestants from hitting one another with anything they can lay hands on" (104). Rhetoric, by definition, was an agonistic instrument. Burke also saw little difference between orators in the ancient Greek polis persuading fellow citizens to adopt a course of action and modern advertisers selling their wares in newspapers and on billboards. But in a social landscape marked by a precipitous decline in sustained traditions and bonds of community, Burke argued that the art of rhetoric was the only means to produce some form of consensus, no matter how provisional. As the growing divisions within modernity forced artists, scientists, and intellectuals back into their own separate spheres of development and reduced many to the status of mere technicians, Burke hoped that the force of rhetoric might overcome such divisions. "The human agent, *qua* human agent," according to Burke, "is not motivated solely by the principles of a specialized activity, however strongly this specialized power, in its suggestive role as imagery, may affect his character" (27). Consequently, he challenged the "liberal apologist" who defended applied science as "a *good* and *absolute*" and endowed its methods "with the philosophic function of *God* as the grounding of values" (30). But he also challenged high modernists whose focus on the "exclusively aesthetic" had lapsed into the same form of abstention and whose "vandalism" had unfairly denigrated the "structures" of rhetoric.[15] All activities, regardless how autonomous they might appear, were indelibly situated within a wider context of interests. Therefore, Burke hoped a study of rhetoric would "lead us through the Scramble, the Wrangle of the Market Place, the flurries and flare-ups of the Human Barnyard, the Give and Take, the wavering line of pressure and counterpressure, the Logomachy, the onus of ownership, the Wars of Nerves, the War," that is, through postmodernity.[16]

Rhetoric, Identification, and Selfhood

Burke's recourse to rhetoric as the means by which both art and communication operated exposed the difficulty not only in safeguarding art from contamination by utilitarian purposes but in safeguarding the individual from persuasive voices from without. The rhetorical nature of all forms of symbolic action—art, advertising, propaganda, parliamentary procedure, conversation, flirtation, and love—demonstrated the indissoluble connection between communication and desire, politics and psychology, and society and self. As Burke explained, there was "no chance" of separating the "meanings of persuasion, identification ('consubstantiality') and communication" (46). In other words, the force of rhetoric was based not simply on appeals to logic, reason, and utility but also upon deeper personal and often unconscious influences. Consequently, any communicative attempt needed to address preforensic and prepolitical levels of experience. As rhetoric emerged from the seeming end of philosophy so did an inevitable concern with the physical and psychical relationship between the self and the other, that is, a concern with how the other served simultaneously as a threat, as an object of desire, and as a potential audience for a subject seeking rhetorical advantage. Burke had little use for the attempts by Clyfford Still and Theodor Adorno to safeguard the subject from the suasive use of language, if not from communication in general, and the attempts by William Burroughs and Norman Mailer to make the subject's bodily and psychic parameters safe from foreign contagion. For Burke, the polemics of politics in the early Cold War demonstrated the folly in holding onto the obfuscations of "bourgeois naturalism" that treated individual identity as a private, peculiar substance. To counter this tendency, Burke returned to Freud's notion of identification to complicate the seemingly simple problem of the self's relation to itself and to others and the delicate relation between interior and exterior. He also turned to Freud to understand the true workings of rhetoric. "The key term for the old rhetoric," observed Burke, "was 'persuasion' and its stress was upon deliberate design. The key term for the 'new' rhetoric would be 'identification,' which included a partially 'unconscious' factor in appeal."[17] In this way, Burke opened up rhetoric to its conscious and unconscious, deliberate and dreamlike, modes of operation.

Freud's notion of identification went through numerous revisions throughout the course of his career.[18] Originally, Freud had defined identification merely as a form of mimicry or imitation, that is, as the process by which a subject modified his behavior by copying by rote the actions, patterns, or skills of another, not in the name of some libidinal attachment but merely as the means to ward off mental collapse. In *The Interpretation of Dreams*, for instance, Freud related this form of mimicry to the actions of hysterical patients who "expressed in their symptoms not only their own experiences but those of a large number of other people."[19] But after his discovery of the Oedipus complex and his theoretical appropriation of the mythological totem meal in *Totem and Taboo* (1913), Freud described the process of identification as a sadistic form of incorporation in which the subject, in his simultaneous wish to be united with the desired other and to overcome his dependency on the outside world, devoured the object cannibalistically, both as a form of revenge and as a form of love. As such, identification was linked to orality—as a holdover from the pregenital stage where ingestion and sexuality were not yet differentiated. Identification was therefore a violent form of incorporation in which the desired other was ingested in the name of mastery, control, and insatiable hunger, precisely why Freud compared it to the mythological moment that the band of brothers murdered the despotic father of the primal horde and devoured him in the hope of acquiring his strength. Of course Freud soon realized he had oversimplified the process of identification by limiting it merely to the internalization of the properties of a libidinal object through its sadistic destruction. The lesson learned from the totem meal did not concern merely the psychical notion of oral ingestion but also the ambivalent nature of identification overall. As the nature of the Oedipus complex had proven, the loss of a libidinal tie with an object often led to a reversal of relations, as the abandoned object was not so much swept away as set up within the ego as a substitution for the actual loss. The original love for the object was transformed into an identification, and the object was established as an autonomous but integral part of the psychic structure, what Freud referred to as an *introject*. The model for the operation of introjection was of course the Oedipus complex, in which the abandoned desire for both parents was transformed into an identification with them and led to the establishment of the parental imago or the superego within the individual's psychic structure. Under this model, the subject was not so much the aggressor but the passive victim of an infiltrating object, a vulnerable and unaware recipient of an introjection from without, in what Diana Fuss refers to as the "disease model of alterity."[20]

These separate understandings of identification set the framework for how modernists of all persuasions understood subject formation. William Burroughs, for instance, saw identification only as incorporation, that is, as the cannibalistic destruction of a rivalrous other. Theodor Adorno, on the other hand, saw identification as the means by which the subject fell into the collectivity of the group through a libidinal attachment with the Fascist leader and the rivalrous embrace of the band of brothers. Burroughs hoped to purge the subject of any polluting attachments; Adorno accepted, in his poetic moments, identification with only the aesthetic object, or, in his troubled moments, identification with the Oedipal father. But buried within Freud's writings was the sense that identification, despite its complications, was in fact the only means by which identity or ego formation took place. Indeed, Freud's theory of identification brushed aside simplistic notions of self-sameness, revealing that the very constitution of the ego was dependent upon other bodies, other people, and other objects outside the self to which it remained inexorably connected. Identification was not merely the means by which introjects were instantiated but also the means by which they were challenged and surpassed. Identification was the way in which the subject moved beyond its own narcissistic reflection. It led to the continual modification of the subject's psychic structure by loosening parental introjects and opening the self to outside attachments and emotional ties. "Identification," Burke noted, "is hardly other than a name for the *function of sociality.*"[21] Identification, in this sense, was simply the relation of the self to the other, of the subject to the objects it consumed and desired, and of its psychic inside to the tangible outside.

Psychoanalysis, for Burke, had revealed the complicated psychic history from which the self emerged. Identity, as Freud had revealed, was never ontologically given, never secure, and never easily discernible. Burke used psychoanalysis to extend his critique of the metaphysics of substance to a critique of notions of the self as a substantive, secure thing. Psychoanalysis had "discovered accurately enough that identity is *not* individual, that a man 'identifies himself' with all sorts of manifestations beyond himself" (263). But instead of envisioning identification as merely a weakening or shrinking of the ego and thereby setting "about trying to 'cure' him of this tendency" as modern psychoanalysts did, Burke saw this process as the grounds of being itself. Identification, as the process by which the self drew in the other or related itself to another, was, according to Burke, the psychical mechanism that instantiated and organized identity. Any sense of self was grounded in the way "we spontaneously identify ourselves with family, nation, political or cultural cause, church, and so on."[22] The history of the subject's identifications was therefore the subject's personal history. How the self related to others was, in this sense, part and parcel of how the self related to its own being. As Burke explained, "the so-called 'I' is merely a unique combination of partially conflicting 'corporate we's.'"[23] Psychoanalysis had revealed the ego to be merely the precipitate or history of current and abandoned object-cathexes.

Identification, however, was not merely a private psychical act but also a social and historical one. Burke noted the "disparate moods and attitudes," "sub-identities," "subpersonalities," and "voices" inhabiting the self and pointed to the role that fantasy, desire, cultural iconography, familial ties, religion, work, and politics played in forming multiple identifications within the same self according to the social landscape in which the subject was located (184). Identifications were neither private nor evasive nor wholly personal;

they were also never freely chosen. Burke argued that "identity is *not* individual . . . a man 'identifies himself' with all sorts of manifestations beyond himself" (263). To exist, that is, to maintain some form of identification, was therefore to be rhetorically aligned. The subject was drawn into an identification or an attachment by the persuasive voice of the other or by a conscious or unconscious motivation from within, making rhetoric an inescapable element in the formation of individual identity. "A way of life is an *acting-together*," said Burke, "and in acting together, men have common sensations, concepts, images, ideas, attitudes that make them *consubstantial*."[24] Freud's theory of the development of the superego was only the most obvious example. Burke contended that "the *ego* with its *id* confronts the *superego* much as an orator would confront a somewhat alien audience, whose susceptibilities he must flatter as a necessary step towards persuasion" (38). In this sense, the subject sustained itself through a never-ending process of assumption and negation of its relationship to others, and rhetoric was the means by which such personal and psychic shifts occurred. Rhetoric demonstrated, according to Burke, that the self, due to its difficulty in maintaining any psychic division between what was inner and what was outer, was perpetually other to itself. Of course Burke was unwilling to dispense with any notion of the individual. "In being identified with B," explained Burke, "A is 'substantially one' with a person other than himself. Yet at the same time he remains unique, an individual locus of motives. Thus he is both joined and separate, at once a distinct substance and consubstantial with another" (21). Each subject was a unique combination of identifications, most of which were never permanent, never fully revealed, and never fully constituted.

This was why Burke defined all art as a form of rhetoric. Aesthetics, as Burke maintained throughout his career, dealt primarily with this connection between communication, persuasion, and identity. Aesthetics, in a certain sense, was inseparable from psychology and sociology—all three fields desperately trying to define a personal or social situation, to demark apparent problems and obstacles, to offer an appropriate attitude or orientation, and to point the way to an eventual transcendence, if not redemption. The aesthetic realm, like the psychoanalyst's couch, helped to reveal the complicated processes of identity formation—how the self was implicated in a variety of attachments ranging from the familial to the corporate to the political, attachments that were at times debilitating, reactionary, and possibly destructive. Consequently, the artist, as Burke maintained, was always an evangelist and a psychologist, hoping to lead the attentive reader through the complicated process of conversion and rebirth. Art, at its essence, was about the symbolic sacrifice and rebirth of the individual. The aesthetic object was designed to undo the self by purging it of its polluted and reactionary parts (in the way that high modernists hoped) but also to put the self back together in the name of redemption. Every "symbolic slaying of an old self," explained Burke, "is complemented by the emergence of a new self."[25] But such a transformation was not reducible to individual psychology. For Burke, "symbolic regressions, involved in rebirth, are kept *public, collective* inasmuch as the artist is required for purposes of communication, to retain his contact with the forensic texture."[26] Symbolic regression was therefore not neurotic regression. Such regression merely helped to produce those boundary-disturbing moments that loosened life-denying attachments. Aesthetics was concerned primarily with confronting those "reigning symbols of authority" that constituted the psychic and corporeal dimensions of the subject. Under the guise of rhetoric, appeals to autonomous agents or autonomous activities made no sense given the wider context in which such agents and actions were situated.

Burke's theory of rhetoric demonstrated that there was no formally empty or universal reader and that there was no easy way to discourage or encourage identifications except through persuasion, conscious or unconscious. High modernists, in their focus on craftsmanship, had assumed that the aesthetic object in and of itself could dismantle atavistic identifications and soften the boundaries of the ego by fully releasing the subject into contours of the contemplated object. Burke argued instead that the rhetorician needed to acknowledge, respect, and challenge the idiopathic identifications of the audience: "only those voices from without are effective which can speak in the language of a voice within."[27] Rhetoric operated in "an intermediate area of expression," one that was "not wholly deliberate, yet not wholly unconscious" (xiii). In other words, rhetoric was "midway between aimless utterance and speech directly purposive." Aesthetics was burdened by matters of strategy and presentation—how to reinterpret a particular situation, particular social arrangement, or particular understanding of human nature and how to persuade auditors that such a reconfiguration was more useful than previous understandings. Such rhetorical forms were designed to help the "victims" who were "educated in wrong meanings and values by the 'priesthood' of pulpit, schools, press, radio and popular arts."[28] Aesthetics was inseparable from psychology; politics was inseparable from rhetoric; and power was inseparable from language. Aesthetics was also inseparable from romance. The mystery and secretiveness attached to the notions of love and courtship, according to

Burke, hid the "communion of estranged entities" that was predicated on an original "persuasive communication between kinds."[29] In this sense, Burke's late modernism marked his attempt to reconnect the aesthetic, the psychological, and the political, an ambitious project that borrowed freely from Freud, Marx, Aristotle, and Veblen.

The Sociological Poetry of C. Wright Mills

Burke's reclamation of rhetoric from the dustbin of intellectual history marked the theoretical distinctiveness of his modernist vision. The suasive use of language to create attachments between strangers, to appeal to common motives, and to instigate collective action was for Burke the key to any aesthetic project. Rhetoric was also a way of loosening the multiple identifications within the self and reopening the psyche to the vicissitudes of fantasy, desire, and expectation. A writer, explained Burke, did not persuade someone merely by raising a problem or even by offering a reasoned argument but only by "ringing the bells" of that person's trained responses. Burke, of course, did not have the disciplinary tools to translate his theory of rhetoric into a coherent program of action, but his work did provide inspiration for the sociology of C. Wright Mills, who agreed that any persuasive form needed to feature both the symbolic and the forensic. In two early essays, "Language, Logic, and Culture" and "Situated Actions and Vocabularies of Motive," and in his 1953 textbook *Character and Social Structure*, Mills invoked Burke's "new rhetoric," in particular, the problems of strategy and presentation, to formulate his own sociological project. Indeed, Mills's understanding of the social nature of human conduct was "indebted" to his reading of Kenneth Burke's *Permanence and Change*, which offered "several leads" in the study of motivation.[30] Following Burke, Mills argued that the psychic structure of the individual was a product of a particular network of identifications within the individual, identifications fostered by libidinal attachments to particular persons, political orders, economic structures, and social roles.

In appropriating Burke's theory of rhetoric, Mills began by arguing that the formation of the self occurred in large measure through discursive practices. Indeed, forgotten in most of the literature on Mills's sociological legacy is his work on language. If the individual was a composite of internalized social roles, argued Mills, then language was the mechanism through which such internalizations occurred, language that served not as a neutral medium of communication but as a system of signs specific to an institutional role that guided conduct and demarked permissible actions. Language, as "a social acquisition and a personal performance," was not derived from dictionaries but from concrete engagement with others and their own particular use of words and therefore was the "prime carrier" of purport and the primary way in which action gained meaning.[31] The internalization of any particular role went hand-in-hand with the internalization of a discursive system with its attendant prescriptive, normative, and, most important, motivational demands. As Burke argued, any statement about how the world functioned was attributable to an internalized orientation or vocabulary of terms, a "bundle of judgments as to how things were, how they are, and how they may be."[32] Such an orientation provided a sense of causation, of relationships, of expectations, and of the good life, what Mills referred to as a vocabulary of motive. "Our motives," he argued, "are imparted to us by others before they are avowed by ourselves."[33] Vocabularies of motive imputed beliefs, values, prejudices, and categories for perception. Such vocabularies also demarked the boundaries of permissible discourse by delineating acceptable modes of life and normative prescriptions concerning actions. In this sense, individual psychic needs were a product of the symbolic universe as a whole. As Mills explained in *The Sociological Imagination*, "it may well be that the most radical discovery within recent psychology and social science is the discovery of how so many of the most intimate features of the person are socially patterned and even implanted."[34] Different roles entailed different motives. More important, any vocabulary of motive served an inherently social purpose, helping to integrate spectators into a circle of action, to win allies for an intended goal, and to provide a commonly accepted rationale for conduct. "As a word," explained Mills, "a motive tends to be one which is to the actor and to other members of a situation an unquestioned answer to questions concerning social and lingual conduct."[35] Since any sense of identity was filtered through a number of interpretive devices, references to a solely private or autistic self were nonsensical.

Of course such vocabularies of motive had a political and social history, and Mills attached the development of such vocabularies in the current age to the rise of what he termed the "cultural apparatus." Mills's ideas concerning the social production of knowledge coalesced in an unpublished manuscript, "The Cultural Apparatus," he was writing just before his death, a book that was an extension of an earlier 1944 *Politics* magazine article, "The Powerless People: The Role of the Intellectuals." In a letter to historian William Miller, Mills claimed that the book was to be "a good, heavy-duty, full-of-awe, but what's-it-all-about book," one that served as a culmination of his social and political criticism.[36] The function of the cultural apparatus, according to Mills, was the development of legitimating symbols that sanctioned particular political and economic institutions and legitimating narratives that explained the origins and evolution of those institutions. These symbols perpetuated certain attitudes toward work, certain assumptions about economic distribution, certain beliefs about political participation, certain prejudices about racial and sexual differences, and certain notions about national and international events. "Such master symbols," explained Mills, "relevant when they are taken over privately, become the reasons and often the motives that lead persons into roles and sanction their enactments of them."[37] This apparatus was operated by private individuals (parents, relatives, and neighbors), social organizations (churches, schools, and universities), public figures (politicians, advertisers, radio broadcasters, and journalists), and entertainment outlets (publishing companies, film studios, theaters, museums, and music distributors). For Mills, the cultural apparatus comprised the "observation posts, the interpretation centers, the presentation depots" of society that establish the boundaries of epistemological certainty.[38] It was "the lens of mankind through which men see; the medium by which they interpret and report what they see." Man's sense of self originated from this uncomfortable mixture of beliefs, vocabularies of motive, and stories inherited from family members, historical traditions, mass culture, literature and poetry, and religious institutions. "Were the cultural apparatus suddenly to stop its production and distribution of ideas, techniques, and images," explained Mills, "there would result a crisis in the affairs of mankind of a scale and depth never before known in world history."[39] Every utterance had a history loaded with ideological assumptions. In this sense, for Mills, there was no strict divide between the normative, the prescriptive, and the descriptive as functions of discourse. All elements of language were fundamentally connected to the cultural apparatus.

However, unlike high modernists such as Theodor Adorno, Clement Greenberg, and Dwight Macdonald, Mills refused to believe that the cultural apparatus operated through one hegemonic voice or that the possibility of symbolic action had been eliminated. In fact, Mills argued that the formation of public opinion was a highly complicated procedure: "in the enormous flow of words, signs, images, sounds, and entertainments there is much that is openly controversial, much that is critical—it does not add up to one, standardized, official image of the world. . . . It contains various images and, to a considerable extent, they compete with one another."[40] For Mills, the individual operated under several vocabularies of motives, leading to conflicting and oftentimes contradictory beliefs and actions. Mills's analysis of the formation of public opinion began with a project he conducted in coordination with Columbia University's Bureau of Applied Social Research under the direction of sociologist Paul Lazarsfeld, a study that was originally intended for publication in *Amerika*, the Russian-language journal of the State Department. Written in 1950, "The Sociology of Mass Media and Public Opinion" represented Mills's subtle understanding of opinion formation that borrowed heavily from Lazarsfeld's notion of the "two-step flow of communication." In his analysis, Mills charted a three-stage development in the formation of public opinion: in eighteenth-century democratic society, political institutions were subordinate to the demands issuing from "innumerable discussion circles knit together by mobile people" who formed "autonomous organs of public opinion"; by the late nineteenth century, these primary publics had been ousted by a "mass society of media markets" that had monopolized the "opinion business" (579); and by the twentieth century, these organs of mass advertising and mass communication had been overtaken by the state with the emergence of totalitarian regimes. In that phase, four elements characterized the totalitarian nature of mass society: the displacement of face-to-face, primary publics by a mass communications industry, the centralization of the opinion process itself, the authoritative and manipulative nature of such media, and the use of coercive and physical sanctions in securing consent. What was emerging in American society, however, was "a sort of synthesis" of the opposing regimes of democracy and totalitarianism in which "both mass media and person-to-person discussion are important in changing public opinion" (586). Postmodern America, for Mills, had developed beyond a world of decentralized democratic publics but also beyond a world of manipulated mass publics.

Naturally, Mills recognized the heuristic importance in maintaining a theoretical difference between "primary publics" and "mass society." The nostalgic image of the former served as a normative constraint upon the latter. In recognizing the complicated role of both mass media and person-to-person discussions, Mills maintained that "it is a question of which is the more important in different areas of opinion, at different times, and of just how the two, as forces causing opinion change, sometimes work together, and sometimes clash." Mills was interested in the causes of public opinion—how the ordinary, the everyday, the existential, the imaginary, the unconscious, and the intimate influenced how political and economic developments were translated and given meaning. In this sense, person-to-person discussions were neither a reflection of unmediated, lived experience nor a tool for the spontaneous generation of undistorted community opinion. Experience was always "mediated and organized in stereotypes" (592). As Mills explained, "the kind of experience that might serve as a basis for resistance to mass media is not experience of raw events, but experience of meaning" (593). The interpretive framework with which individuals made sense of the world around them was limited by their class, social, and educational positions, the extent of their daily exposure to mass media, the psychological baggage that channeled their desire, the strength of their identification with their institutional roles, and their psychic investiture in the symbolic order as a whole. Rhetoric became an indispensable element in social change—whether through political criticism, aesthetic practice, or sociological investigation. According to Mills, "so far as power is concerned then, there are two steps involved: (1) the repossessing of the apparatus, and (2) the reshaping of it and the using of it for new cultural and political purposes."[41] Such marked the beginning and end of his project.

For Mills, then, sociology became oppositional only when it became aesthetic, that is, when it became less concerned with empirical analysis or technical jargon and focused instead on what Burke termed symbolic action. Too many sociologists, according to Mills, were content with only describing a situation. For Mills, persuasion was just as essential as empirical accuracy. To counter what he saw as current academic limitations Mills offered "the sociological imagination," that is, "the capacity to shift from one perspective to another, and in the process to build up an adequate view of a total society and of its components."[42] The sociological imagination was a strategy for encompassing a situation—for assigning values, attributing motives, establishing causes, and casting blame. The modern sociologist needed to play with the fluidity of boundary lines between the aesthetic and the political, the social and the familial, and the normative and the descriptive. The sociological imagination was "the capacity to shift from one perspective to another—from the political to the psychological; from examination of a single family to comparative assessment of the national budgets of the world; from the theological school to the military establishment; from considerations of an oil industry to studies of contemporary poetry" (7). By demonstrating how the most impersonal and remote transformations impacted the private lives of individuals and by showing how the most intimate features of the self were bound to the most public events, Mills hoped the sociological imagination would serve as a disciplinary tool to loosen reactionary vocabularies of motive and thereby loosen the boundaries of the self. Mills argued that the sociologist debunked a scheme of thought not by offering an entirely new one but by demonstrating that such a scheme, when followed to its logical conclusion, was inadequate or outdated. "We control another man," argued Mills, "by manipulating the premiums which the other accepts; we influence a man by naming his act in terms of some motive which we ascribe to him."[43] The sociological imagination, by revealing the intimate connection between the personal and the political, helped to loosen the hold of the cultural apparatus and to demonstrate how the historical scene affected the lens through which the individual viewed his life and expectations, serving in this sense as "a sort of therapy in the ancient sense of clarifying one's knowledge of self" (186).

The most practical form for the provocateur to utilize was, according to Mills, "sociological poetry," a style of writing and a style of persuasion that was simultaneously instrumental and artistic, realistic and surrealistic. Sociological poetry was a "style of experience and expression that reports social facts and at the same time reveals their human meanings" and a style that stood "somewhere between the thick facts and thin meanings of the ordinary sociological monograph and those art forms which in their attempt at meaningful reach do away with the facts."[44] Sociology could not remain merely descriptive; it had to become aesthetic. Similarly, art could not remain disinterested and autonomous; it needed to become persuasive. Once again, Mills turned to Burke, who had borrowed from the "dart-like" style of modernists such as Friedrich Nietzsche and James Joyce to explain the persuasive effects of aesthetics. Two elements were essential. First, the sociologist or the artist needed to loosen his procedures by interjecting surrealist practices into his work. In his famous section "On Intellectual Craftsmanship" at the end of *The Sociological Imagination*, Mills encouraged his colleagues to keep an enormous file or journal, composed of formal notes, empirical examples, random thoughts, and qualitative descriptions. Such a filing system allowed the sociologist "to capture 'fringe-thoughts': various ideas which may be by-products of everyday life, snatches of conversation overheard on the street, or, for that matter, dreams."[45] Since vocabularies of motive operated as unconscious analytic lenses, they could only be unearthed, in large measure, through psychoanalytic excavation. Once such a file was adequately complete, the sociologist needed to loosen his imagination and his disciplinary bias by allowing chance to help in the organizational process. As Mills explained, "you simply dump out heretofore disconnected folders, mixing up their contents, and then re-sort them. You try to do it in a more or less relaxed way" (212). Echoing the practice of surrealists, who allowed chance to organize the construction of their collages and poems, Mills believed that such a process offered "an attitude of playfulness toward the phrases and words with which various issues are defined." Spontaneity, chance, irrationality, and play—all of those elements associated with modernist practice—became an essential element in sociological work.

Second, the sociologist needed to confront established vocabularies of motive by challenging the expectations and orientations of readers. This was accomplished not by simply offering another vocabulary but by challenging the internal logic of the available ones. To do so, Mills, borrowing from Burke again, claimed that sociological practice needed to offer "perspective by incongruity." Symbolic action was a loaded response to a particular situation and an attack on piety through the intentional subversion of linguistic protocols. The social critic transcended a situation by renaming it or rearranging the elements to reveal a new landscape or by inverting the hierarchy of contained elements: "the release of imagination can sometimes be achieved by deliberately inverting your sense of proportion" (215). Perspective by incongruity undermined the normative and the prescriptive by enlarging or reducing the traditional ratio among objects, by making something grotesque or comical through the enlargement of its features, or by parodying or deflating the language of authority. "Often you get the best insights by considering extremes," argued Mills, "by thinking of the opposite of that with which you are directly concerned" (213). Whether through puns and jokes, through caricature and exaggeration, or through the incongruous juxtaposition of ideas, the sociological critic practiced Burkean rhetoric. In "The Cultural Apparatus," Mills observed that "the adequate defining of realities is a set of continuing tasks, and the way to carry it on in a publicly relevant manner is to set up a sort of intellectual and political drama and to enact it."[46] This form of sociological poetry was Mills's response to the limitations of high modernist practice; it was also his own form of cultural politics. Throughout his career, Mills expressed his frustration over high modernism: "The canon of the three brows may be and often is a serious and intelligent response to realities of culture; but it does not enable the critic to confront the causes of these realities and it is more likely to obscure than to solve the real problem: the task of creating a culture for publics, as against masses on the one hand and snobs on the other, the one out for distraction, the other for the use of culture for ulterior purposes of prestige," he noted in the same essay. His use of Burkean rhetoric to stretch the norms of sociological practice marked his own modernist project and set the agenda found in *The Power Elite* and *The Cuban Revolution*.

Ralph Ellison and the Tradition of Late Modernism

However, the clearest use of rhetoric as a mode of persuasion, identification, and transformation was in the work of Ralph Ellison, whose 1952 novel *Invisible Man* translated, in large measure, Burke's philosophy of language into literary form. Ellison first met Burke in 1937 at the Congress of the League of American Writers where Burke gave his controversial paper "The Rhetoric of Hitler's Battle," and he quickly consumed Burke's early books such as *Counter-Statement* and *The Philosophy of Literary Form*, helping to formulate his own rhetorical practice. As Ellison explained in a letter to his friend late in life: "I always tried to turn your insights back to the necessities of fiction."[47] Throughout the writing of *Invisible Man*, Ellison used Burke's philosophy of literary form—the movement from purpose to passion to perception—to characterize the narrative arch of his protagonist. More important, Burke provided Ellison with an image of aesthetic transformation not burdened by the limitations of high modernism. Less interested in formal aesthetics, Ellison, like Burke, was interested in how art functioned within the context of lived experience and therefore fashioned a form of cultural politics in the same vein as the famed literary critic and as C. Wright Mills. In this sense, Ellison's work was neither a form of existential anguish nor high modernist practice but a form of Burkean rhetoric, which became the axiomatic principle of his aesthetic project. As he explained, "in college and on my own, I had studied a little psychology, a little sociology, you know, dribs and drabs, but Burke provided a *Gestalt* through which I could apply intellectual insights back into my own materials and into my own life."[48] For example, Ellison participated in a three-week American studies seminar in Salzburg, Austria, in 1954, giving a series of lectures entitled "The Role of the Novel in Creating the American Experience" that focused specifically on the "rhetorical problems of the American novel." In his lectures Ellison argued that the importance of the novel was its "rhetorical nature," that is, its ability "to define, to evaluate the abiding patterns of experience."[49] As such, "narrative must be constructed from things known by the prospective audience" and must "seek to break through those defenses which we call civilization, in order to put the reader once more in touch with the irremediable, those forces which threaten to undo him." If not, the narrative simply became a "case history of characters," an inappropriate construction of "description" that made no pointed contact with the intended audiences. For Ellison, narrative was "concerned with [the] psychology of [the] reader" and "has to do with identification between reader and public." To do otherwise was to ignore "what the reader brings to [the novel]."[50] In the detailed announcement for his lectures, Ellison gave a list of suggested readings that included Burke's *Counter-Statement* and *The Philosophy of Literary Form*.

Critics over the years, however, have argued that Ellison remained trapped within an aesthetic framework that prioritized the cultural project of the meritocratic artist over the practical needs of oppressed populations, that he saw "artistic transcendence [as] the one unsuppressable means through which human freedom is imagined."[51] Ellison's career in many ways did conform to the pattern of many postwar intellectuals who appropriated high modernism. Born in Oklahoma and educated at Tuskegee Institute, Ellison began his political and artistic education when he moved to New York in 1935 to escape the confines of southern life. His introduction to artistic circles in New York came when he befriended Langston Hughes.[52] Through Hughes, Ellison eventually met Richard Wright, who asked Ellison to contribute a short story to an edition of the journal *New Challenge*. Ellison, who was both a practicing writer and musician, gladly agreed. His literary career continued when he joined the Federal Writers' Project in 1938, where he worked for the next four years. His involvement in political circles began in this period as well, as he wrote for such radical journals as *Direction, Negro Quarterly, New Masses,* and *New Challenge*. Though he did not "think too much of the so-called proletarian fiction" of the time, Ellison wrote articles in support of the Communist Party and in defense of social realism as an aesthetic form.[53] Early in his literary career, Ellison defended the "protest fiction" of authors like Richard Wright who attempted to link the fate of black Americans with the fate of the international working class. But Ellison was never completely committed to the political imperatives of the Communist Party. His early short stories from the 1940s, the "Buster and Riley" stories, focused more on the distinctiveness of Ellison's Oklahoma background, on southern traditions, and on southern culture. Moreover, Ellison was slowly attracted to modernism as a way out of the confines of social realism. As he detailed, "in 1935 I discovered Eliot's *The Waste Land* which moved and intrigued me but defied my powers of analysis—such as they were—and I wondered why I had never read anything of equal intensity and sensibility by an American Negro writer" (7). The result of such studies was Ellison's appropriation of many modernist techniques into his writing, including surrealism and perspectivism. His admitted attachment to the writings of James Joyce, Fyodor Dostoevsky, T. S. Eliot, and Gertrude Stein coincided with the appropriation of high modernism occurring in literary journals such as *Partisan Review.* But his reading of Burke pushed Ellison beyond high modernism. "The diversity of American life," argued Ellison, "with its extreme fluidity and openness seemed too vital and alive to be caught for more than the briefest instant in the tight, well-made Jamesian novel."[54]

Most of Ellison's literary criticism in fact borrowed heavily from Burke's reformulation of rhetoric, in particular, Ellison's well-known essay "The Little Man at Chehaw Station: The American Artist and His Audience." In this piece Ellison recounted the chiding he received at the Tuskegee Institute at the hands of his accomplished piano instructor Hazel Harrison after Ellison's disappointing trumpet recital in front of several faculty members. Dismayed by their criticism of his supposed sterile musicianship, Ellison turned to his teacher for sympathy or at least for a clarification of the high standards to which his critics had held him. Instead, she criticized Ellison's failure to recognize that whenever and wherever he played, even if in the waiting room of Chehaw Station, there was "a little man hidden behind the stove" who knew the standards and traditions of musicianship fundamentally required for any trumpet player. Miss Harrison's reprimand was designed not only to deflate the air of elitism surrounding the young musician but also to force him to acknowledge the needs, expectations, and knowledge of the audience consuming his music and to acknowledge the initial resistance inherent to any listeners. "While that audience is eager to be transported, astounded, thrilled," acknowledged Ellison, "it counters the artist's manipulation of forms with an attitude of antagonistic cooperation, acting, for better or worse, as both collaborator and judge."[55] In other words, she was reminding Ellison of the importance of persuasion and courtship to any artistic statement—that is, the importance of rhetoric.

Rhetoric for Ellison was a means of aligning an individual with a particular discursive formation. Communities were formed not through any particular structural or material pattern but through the symbols, folklore, and heritage that bound them together, a linguistic framework that delineated which forms of experience were possible and were permissible. Rhetoric therefore was a persuasive attempt to demonstrate to an individual or group that their particular orientation for categorizing the world was inadequate or, even worse, reactionary. Rhetoric, however, was neither a polemical nor a violent attempt to replace one competing orientation with another but instead a deliberate attempt at finding specific symbolic tools that were able to bridge the gap between distinct linguistic paradigms, tools that worked in and through the particularities of opposing orientations and demonstrated the common points of identification. Ellison observed that "in the field of literature it presents a problem of rhetoric, a question of how to fashion strategies of communication that will bridge the many divisions of background and taste which any representative American audience embodies" (494). In this sense, rhetoric acted as a form of conversion in which certain patterns of orientation were incongruously named or grossly inflated to render them nonsensical. Playing with language helped to challenge "familiar symbols of identity" and "overdependence upon them as points of orientation" by helping to bring "previously unknown patterns, details and emotions into view along with those that are generally recognized" (504, 497). Yet given the diversity within the American landscape, the writer needed to engage in an intense sociological investigation into the plurality of experiences endemic to the culture as a whole. Indeed, "rhetoric depends upon not only a knowledge of human passion, but the specific situations in which that passion is expressed: the manners, the formal patterns, and so on, as well as the political issues around which they are clustered."[56] In this sense, there was no one language of persuasion and no one strategy for change that gained priority over the rest.

Ellison's concern with rhetoric was perhaps most clearly demonstrated in his famous debate with literary critic Irving Howe in the pages of *Dissent* and *The New Leader* in 1963. In a pointed and polemical attack on the work of Ellison and James Baldwin, Howe defended the protest fiction of Richard Wright from Baldwin's claim that Wright had conflated literature and sociology and in so doing had denied black Americans any complexity, humanity, or agency. For Howe, it was impossible for a black writer to escape his particular condition, that "the 'sociology' of his existence formed a constant pressure on his literary work, and not merely in the way this might be true for any writer, but with a pain and ferocity that nothing could remove."[57] Howe was unwilling to partake in the "implausible assertion of unconditioned freedom" (363) that he felt characterized the work of both Baldwin and Ellison. The key point in the debate was his discussion about Wright's character Bigger Thomas, the antihero of the 1940 novel *Native Son*, who under the constraints of his social condition is forced to commit a violent crime. Howe took Bigger as an essential metaphor for the condition of black Americans, simultaneously "a blow at the white man" that "forced him to recognize himself as an oppressor" and "a blow at the black man" that "forced him to recognize the cost of his submission" (355). Through the revelation of the pain of social experience, the black writer gave form to the "'sociology' of his existence." The force of Wright's novel then stemmed from the shock given to "the decent and cultivated white men" who presumably were ignorant of their own culpability for the life of Bigger Thomas. Ellison's inability to recognize the actual presence of Bigger Thomas in the world, according to Howe, stemmed from Ellison's lifelong desire to prove that he had transcended his background. Ellison's response to Howe evaded this charge, not because Ellison felt himself guilty, but because he was trying to change the framework of the conversation. As Ellison commented to Howe, his goal "was not to strike the stance of the 'free artist' against the 'ideological critic.'"[58] Howe focused on Bigger Thomas as a metaphor for existing social conditions; Ellison focused on Bigger as a problem of rhetorical strategy. That was precisely why the two combatants appeared to talk past one another and why Ellison declared that he was "sorry Irving Howe got the impression that I was throwing bean-balls when I only meant to pitch him a hyperbole" (168).

In fact, what Ellison was asking was whether or not Bigger Thomas possessed any rhetorical value as a symbolic representation of the condition of black Americans, not whether or not Bigger actually existed. Placed within the field of the social, would Bigger fundamentally challenge the language or the vocabulary in which individual groups discussed the problem of race? At an existential level Bigger served as appropriate recognition of the despair felt in most settings of the black community. Ellison (despite the pronouncements of many of his critics) was always attuned to political and economic oppression in the United States. As he repeatedly made clear in both the novel and his critical essays, "overcrowded and exploited politically and economically, Harlem is the scene and symbol of the Negro's perpetual alienation in the land of his birth."[59] He agreed that Bigger was the product of that alienation. But, according to Ellison, at a symbolic level, Bigger served an unfortunate reactionary role. Inherently alienating to black readers who saw none of their own humanity or agency within Wright's novel and unfortunately reassuring to white liberal readers who were reaffirmed of their own visions of black life, the symbol of Bigger encouraged no real dialogue or exchange. This, for Ellison, was the basic failure of Wright's novel. According to Ellison, "here the basic unity of human experience that assures us of some possibility of empathic and symbolic identification with those of other backgrounds is blasted in the interest of specious political and philosophical conceits."[60] The problem became one of finding symbolic tools that were able to bridge the gap between distinct communities and that worked in and through the particularities of race and class without transcending them.

For Ellison, the symbol of Bigger Thomas served no such rhetorical value. Bigger did not serve to connect the fate of American society to the fate of black Americans on any real symbolic level. Regardless of the difficulty of such a project, Ellison saw no other use for aesthetics. He recognized that there was no one audience reading his work but a plurality of readers, each with separate motivations, cultural biases, and discourses of representation. Rhetoric, for Ellison, did not consist in replacing one ontological scheme with another, one version of reality with another, or one paradigm with another, but in finding a way to shift the points of identification within a discourse through its own logic. Indeed, "a study in comparative humanity, and the role of the writer, from that point of view, is to structure fictions which will allow a universal identification, while at the same time, not violating the specificity of the particular experience and the particular character."[61] This meant engaging with the particularities of black culture, that "'concord of sensibilities' which the group expresses through historical circumstance and through which it has come to constitute a subdivision of the larger American culture."[62] In Ellison's novel *Invisible Man*, his protagonist's indictment of Brother Tobitt for his unwillingness to consider the particularities of black life in Harlem when developing the Brotherhood's political program stood as a rigid defense of Burkean rhetoric—"ask your wife to take you around to the gin mills and the barber shops and the juke joints and the churches, Brother. Yes, and the beauty parlors on Saturdays when they're frying hair. A whole unrecorded history is spoken then, Brother."[63] The success of Bigger as a symbolic tool rested upon the success of that engagement.

According to Ellison, Howe never recognized that Bigger might in fact possess a timid or even reactionary value. To maintain Bigger as a symbolic presence, no matter how unconscious, was to exert a form of rhetoric. That is why Ellison was quick to argue that what Howe took as descriptive statements about the social experience of black Americans were in fact prescriptive ones, symbolic actions that contained implicit representational force. No matter how fictitious, such statements *became* real through their invocation—"prefabricated Negroes are sketched on sheets of paper and superimposed upon the Negro community; then when someone thrusts his head through the page and yells, 'Watch out Jack, there're people living under here,' they are shocked and indignant."[64] The result of such prescriptive statements was what Burke termed the "bureaucratization of the imagination"—the imposition of one interpretive framework at the expense of all others and its embeddedness "in the realities of a social texture, in all the complexity of language and habits."[65] Injected into the field of the social, Bigger served to block out other possible symbolic actions. Thus Ellison asked in disbelief, "are we to believe that [Howe] simply does not recognize rhetoric when he practices it?"[66]

The Politics of Rhetoric in *Invisible Man*

Ellison appropriated one of the central tenets of Burkean theory—that language was not a transparent medium of expression but a charged way of ordering the field of objects—and invested himself in the language and psychology of his readers. Whereas high modernists were concerned with developing their own linguistic systems, Ellison was preoccupied with the effect of entering into a particular community of discourse—a "cultural heritage"—and examining its implications and contradictions. Ellison's novel was the effect of such an examination. It was an implicit attempt to enter into the language of modernism and open it onto the social field. His tale of one black man's journey from a southern town to a northern metropolis, from blind acceptance to personal outrage, and from purpose to perspective is a classic modernist work. But the narrative is buttressed by a prologue and epilogue that are explicit critiques of the project of high modernism. Ellison's hero travels from his days as a student at a southern college to a job as a worker at a northern industry to service as an orator for a radical socialist organization and realizes that in each setting his identity and sense of self are provided for him, part of the scheme of representation found in each organization. Invisible Man's identity is subsumed under the paternal arrogance of Mr. Norton and under the scientific language of the Brotherhood. The conclusion of Invisible Man's story ends precisely where high modernism does, with the individual hero finding an isolated, ontologically secure point outside the flux and chaos of social reality in the self-imposed hibernation of his "residence underground" (571).

The epilogue, then, is an interrogation of that position, of what high modernism neglected and what purposes it served. The pragmatic approach of Burke always stressed the social embeddedness of the individual, that despite the "unique combination of experiences" that formed the individual, there were always "symbolic bridges" that connected the individual combination to the "social pattern."[67] This is precisely why Ellison's Invisible Man becomes so disturbed by his self-imposed hibernation or what Burke termed the high modernist retreat to "the realm of the uncrowned king."[68] While Invisible Man is able to negate his bodily presence in the world, he is unable to escape the social "frame of acceptance" that he uses to order his experience and thus is unable to remove himself from social reality. Ellison privately described the modernist problem in the following manner: "The most interesting thing about a character living on an isolated island would be his ignorance of the essentials of his time, his negative relation to the background. We see him in the specific novel perspective: that is, we know more about him than he knows about himself. We leave included in our vision the background of the mountains and rivers unknown to him, and only by seeing him in proportion to these rivers and mountains did we give him novel-life. In other words: his novel-character is conditioned not by his narrow island consciousness which conditions his real life, but by distant surroundings with which he has no point of contact whatever."[69] Consequently, Invisible Man's continuing refrain in the epilogue is that "in going underground, I whipped it all except the mind, the *mind*."[70] The reason, as Burke maintained, is that "the mind, being formed by language, is formed by a *public grammar*."[71]

That was why Ellison's work was comprised of vocabularies from separate discourses. For instance, his appropriation of black folklore—from the veterans at the Golden Day to Trueblood's poetic description of his moral transgression to the invocation of blues references throughout the text—was an attempt to recognize the language in which certain segments of the black community discussed racial oppression. Readers who identified with this language found it posited among competing paradigms representing the situation of black Americans. By entering into these separate languages Ellison gained a new vantage point from which to critique them. As such, the novel served as a form of what Burke called "casuistic stretching," that is, the attempt "to 'coach' the transference of words from one category of associations to another" (230), or, in the case of Ellison, from the language of the reader to the language of Invisible Man. By undermining the conceptual categories available to his readers (the prominent ones in the novel include the bourgeois liberalism of Mr. Bledsoe, the scientific Marxism of Brother Tarp, and the black nationalism of Ras the Destroyer) and therefore unveiling the chaos existing outside "the narrow borders of what men call reality," Ellison inserted a new scheme of orientation. Thus, as Invisible Man informs his readers, he is trying "to give pattern to the chaos which lives within the pattern of your certainties."[72] This was Burkean rhetoric at its strongest, a way of shifting back and forth between competing languages or representational fields and finding points of common contact and points of definite disagreement. By delegitimating the conceptual apparatus of his readers, Invisible Man is able to insert his own orientation. The impact of the last sentence stems from the revelation of his rhetorical strategy—"Who knows but that, on the lower frequencies, I speak for you?" (581). The effect is the conjoining of the fate of the readers (from the outcasts, the uncommitted, and the convinced) with the fate of the narrator.

In this sense, the only way to understand Ellison's invocation of the blues is by recognizing the relationship with the rhetorical project he constructed. Ellison's characterization of the blues as a "near-tragic, near-comic lyricism" was an implicit critique of existentialism and a direct attempt at aligning Burkean rhetoric with the cultural tradition of the blues. The main impetus for Ellison's idiom came from his reading of Burke's *Attitudes Toward History*, in which Burke argued that all frames of orientation that divided up the social field fell into two separate categories, tragedy and comedy. The tragic "frame of acceptance" was based upon a sense of personal futility, a sense that the terror of social circumstance was too overwhelming and inevitably fatal. Such an attitude was a method of acknowledging moments of deep social change while simultaneously rejecting the shift in social values that change produced. The social shift was then imbued "with the connotations of crime."[73] Tragedy became a polemical attack on this point of transition through reference to that prior historical moment and the crime that was perpetrated. The individual, according to Burke, fell into the role of spectator, a passive recipient of historical flux who resigned himself to "a sense of his limitations" (38). The result was the inevitable withdrawal from the new social order or, even worse, to an assumed ontological point outside the vicissitudes of time, whether in the realm of art or in an image of a reality prior to the tragic crime. A comedic frame of acceptance, on the other hand, was unwilling to accept the loss of human agency implicit within tragedy. The comic perspective became an explicit attempt to treat the individual as both a spectator and active agent within the flux of historical change. The characteristic attitude was not resignation but embarrassment—a willingness to acknowledge that a crime had occurred but an unwillingness to attribute responsibility to a villainous figure or to material circumstance. The comic figure emerged from the darkness of tragedy and accepted responsibility for his agency. As Burke argued, "when you add that people are *necessarily* mistaken, that *all* people are exposed to situations in which they must act as fools, that *every* insight contains its own special kind of blindness, you complete the comic circle, returning again to the lesson of humility that underlies great tragedy" (41). In that completion, the magnitude of the situation was leveled and the comic figure was no longer bound by a sense of limitations.

Ellison's theory of the blues was derived from his reading of Burke, and the figure of the comic frame of acceptance emerged in Ellison's novel as the "blues-toned laugher-at-wounds who included himself in his indictment of the human condition."[74] As he declared in words reminiscent of Burke, "the blues speak to us simultaneously of the tragic and the comic aspects of the human condition and they express a profound sense of life shared by many Negro Americans precisely because their lives have combined these modes."[75] Thus, the blues served as "a comic antidote to the ailments of politics," that is, as an implicit recognition that the American political system had failed in its promise to the black community and as an affirmation of the perseverance needed to challenge and alter social fate. The downtrodden figures in Ellison's novel—the unexpected heroes and comic masters like Trueblood and Invisible Man's grandfather—are purveyors of the blues. The veteran that the protagonist encounters at the Golden Day and aboard the bus to Washington, D.C., directly imparts the spirit of the blues. Instead of the demoralization connected with tragedy, the veteran offers comic wisdom: "Come out of the fog, young man. And remember you don't have to be a complete fool in order to succeed. Play the game, but don't believe in it - that much you owe yourself. Even if it lands you in a strait jacket or a padded cell. Play the game, but play it your own way—part of the time at least. Play the game, but raise the ante, my boy. Learn how it operates, learn how *you* operate—I wish I had time to tell you only a fragment."[76] In other words, the veteran is offering rhetoric as a way out. By mastering the dominant mode of orientation (its field of objects, the arrangements of those objects, and the meaning assigned to that arrangement), the comic operator is in the position to riff upon that arrangement. As Ellison's friend Albert Murray notes, the blues "is a statement about confronting the complexities inherent in the human situation and about improvising or experimenting or riffing or otherwise playing with (or even gambling with) such possibilities as are also inherent in the obstacles, the disjunctures, and the jeopardy."[77] Willing to risk both embarrassment and implication in the structure of social reality, the comic blues master gains a framework for subversion.

Perhaps the best example of Ellison's prioritization of comedy over tragedy as a frame of acceptance is the bar scene in the novel set at the Golden Day, an implicit reference to Lewis Mumford's 1926 work of the same name. Mumford's book was a deliberate attempt at reconstructing recent American history as a form of tragedy. Mumford promoted the literature of the early nineteenth century, including Melville, Emerson, Thoreau, and Whitman, above what he saw as the instrumental vision of later literary traditions. For Mumford, the philosophical idealism posited in the works of these authors was a proper remedy for the failings of American development. They were the first writers to deal explicitly with the contradictions inherent within the project of modernity. America's protracted break with the Old World and the attempt to ground its institutions and social structures on something other than the inherited customs of European traditions were part of the difficult task of the Enlightenment's replacement of transcendental groundings of truth with self-grounding. For Mumford, "the groups that had most completely shaken off the old symbolisms were those that were most ready for the American adventure: they turned themselves easily to the mastery of the external environment."[78] The pioneer—the emblematic figure in Mumford's usable past—was the figure who, in breaking with the cultural patterns of the Old World and turning to Protestantism and science instead, introduced instrumentalism to American thought. The eradication of transcendental foundations for truth and their replacement by the use of reason resulted in the demystification and the objectification of the natural world. The collapse of "the symbols of the older culture" and the unleashing of the pioneer onto the American wilderness—"innocent of anything to occupy his mind except the notion of controlling matter and mastering the external world"[79]—marked the unleashing of instrumentalism, the dominant theme of American thought. The culmination of this story was the emergence of an American philosophy that preached acquiescence and produced paralysis, the philosophy of pragmatism. Thus, American history became the site of tragedy—the eventual decay of a culture that had no determinant symbols to hold onto or inspired visions to add value to the emptiness of modernity. The transcendentalism of Emerson became the touchstone for the respiritualization of American culture that Mumford sought. Unwilling to yield to the impulses of pure experience, Emerson sought refuge in the recuperation of a universal spirit that served as a foundation for individual behavior and salvation. Having recognized that America had disposed of the cultural symbolism of the prior age, Emerson sought a new symbolism, one that would imbue value and meaning in the new social institutions. Nature became that symbolism—it was not simply a tool for instrumental uses but the site for reclamation and the site of satisfaction for the inner demands of human existence. According to Mumford, "with most of the resources of the past at his command, Emerson achieved nakedness: his central doctrine is the virtue of this intellectual, or cultural, nakedness: the virtue of getting beyond the institution, the habit, the ritual, and finding out what it means afresh in one's own consciousness" (96). The self was detached from its ties with externality and placed within the realm of the transcendent, which became the source of inspiration and salvation.

Ellison's invocation of Mumford's reading of Emerson was an attempt to show the failings of transcendentalism as a source for subjectivity. The two representations of Emerson in the novel (Mr. Norton's invocation of Emerson's work and Mr. Emerson, the potential employer whose son reveals to Invisible Man his fate) are both directly related to Mumford's own representation of Emerson and become an implicit critique of Mumford's romanticism. The character of Mr. Norton—the college donor and the "symbol of the Great Traditions"—represents Mumford's Emerson within the novel. As Ellison publicly explained, Norton is "representative of the New England type of man celebrated in Lewis Mumford's 'Great Tradition.'"[80] His sense of self is connected with his duties as a philanthropist. As he declares to Invisible Man, "I had a feeling that your people were somehow connected with my destiny."[81] His subjectivity is therefore able to overcome the limitations of his circumstances through the fate of the groups he has helped—"through you and your fellow students I become, let us say, three hundred teachers, seven hundred trained mechanics, eight hundred skilled farmers, and so on" (45). Like the power of the college founder before him who "had the power of a king, or in a sense, of a god" (45), Norton believes he has transcended his own particular experience. He is *in* the world of objects but is not *of* it. His identity is part and parcel of objects he can control, but he is not forced to recognize their particularities. As the protagonist notes, Mr. Norton did not "even know my name" (45).

Ellison understood that the transcendental self of Emersonian romanticism required the presence of an other to provide its stability. The transcendental self grounded itself not upon the objects of its experience but the way in which those objects served as vehicles to a truth grounded outside of experience. The particularity of those everyday objects dropped out. Thus, the self's dominance of the other was the precondition of its own appearance and realization. Its presence was dependent upon a negation, that is, the ability to control and dominate the other. The veteran in the Golden Day chastised Mr. Norton for precisely this reason: "to you he is a mark on the scorecard of your achievement, a thing and not a man; a child, or even less—a black amorphous thing" (95). Mumford's image of the Golden Day therefore ignored the way in which the subjugation of black Americans provided the foundation for the transcendental self. That is what provides the shock to Mr. Norton when he enters the Golden Day as portrayed from the point of view of the black community. To fall into the Golden Day is for Mr. Norton to fall into the world of externality, to fall into a world where desire triumphed over reason and where the id triumphed over the superego. It is to fall into time. Ellison's representation of Emerson serves as an implicit critique of the transcendental self of Mumford and, as a result, an implicit sanctioning of the social self elaborated by Burke. This is why Ellison was able to conjoin the situation of oppressed black Americans and the intellectual tradition of American pragmatism. Both were attempting to escape the confines of transcendentalism, "that great false wisdom taught slaves and pragmatists alike, that white is right" (95). Trapped beneath the romantic radicalism offered by Mumford is the forgotten world of the Golden Day and the chaos of social experience.

Of course Ellison recognized the dangers in detaching subjectivity from its transcendental foundations. To place the self within the flux of experience was to risk the collapse of all positive significations of identity. The character of Rinehart represents this precise problem. Prefiguring both the hipster of Beat literature and the centerless self of postmodern writings, Rinehart is Ellison's version of one of the continuing themes of postwar literature—the collapse of stable foundations for subjectivity. As Mr. Norton's secretary and son proclaims to Invisible Man, "who has any identity anyway?" (187). The extension of socialization in the Cold War period destabilized not only the autonomy of the modernist text but also selfhood as well. Like Mailer's hipster, Rinehart represents the radical possibilities inherent in that dissolution. To constantly shuffle between categories of identification is to accept a world without boundaries, a world where social death occurred through the reification of one particular identity, and a world that has jettisoned any remnants of the past. It is a world that exists in the continual present, "a vast seething, hot world of fluidity, and Rine the rascal was at home" (498). Ellison privately explained that Rinehart is one of those "quick-silver personalities that have no social forms to contain them, allowing for constant shifting and change."[82] In this mode of defense, Rinehart remains at the surface of appearances, manipulating particular features of consumer society, identities constructed "not by features, but by clothes, by uniform, by gait."[83] Rinehart is the centerless self, a conglomeration of separate categories—"Rine the runner and Rine the gambler and Rine the briber and Rine the lover and Rine the Reverend" (498). His appearance at the end of the protagonist's search for his own identity marks Ellison's attempt to reconstruct the self at the moment of its dissolution, "that somewhere between Rinehart and invisibility there were great potentialities" (510). Rinehart as the "personification of chaos" provides no reference point, no way of understanding whether or not a particular identity is liberating or not. [84] Unable to posit any positive values of his own, Rinehart partakes of no tradition or cultural heritage.

In this sense, Ellison wanted to reconstruct the self in the face of the chaos that he himself had revealed through his deconstruction of both liberalism and Marxism. His protagonist leaps into that chaos by burning the points of reference from his previous identity, including his high school diploma and Tod Clifton's Sambo doll. But jettisoning his past does not lead to freedom, and liberation is not found in "the freedom of Rinehart or the power of a Jack, nor simply the freedom not to run."[85] The self, for Ellison, was simply the product of the orientation with which it was aligned. Thus, a change in the nature of subjectivity could occur only when the individual recognized the social construction of those frames of reference with which his identity was connected. According to Burke, "the change of identity (whereby he is at once the same man and a new man) gives him a greater complexity of coordinates. He 'sees around the corner.' He is 'prophetic,' endowed with 'perspective.'"[86] In words reminiscent of Burke's, Invisible Man describes his transformation—"and now all the past humiliations became precious parts of my experience, and for the first time. . . . I began to accept my past and, as I accepted it, I felt memories welling up within me. It was as though I'd learned suddenly to look around corners; images of past humiliations flickered through my head and I saw that they were more than separate experiences. They were me; they defined me."[87] Subjectivity was a development that occurred in and through historical time, not above and beyond it in the realm of the absolute or the teleological.

That was why Ellison was so attuned to the cultural images of black experience that were thrown about. While theories of black pathology might shed some light on social and economic oppression in America, they did not help support positive definitions of black life. They did not, according to Ellison, help "to explore the full range of American Negro humanity and to affirm those qualities which are of value beyond any question of segregation, economics or previous condition of servitude."[88] Thus, the affirmation of selfhood was a dialogical operative. It began first when the individual accepted his cultural heritage, when he began "to recognize himself through where he comes from, recognizing his parents and his inherited values. This is a very active, self-creating process. The way to create a false identity is to think that you can ignore what went before."[89] But it also entailed the emergence from the negativity of invisibility to the light of visibility. This entailed positive recognition from social and cultural institutions as a whole. As Ellison claimed in relationship to his novel's narrator, "in the process he found it necessary to come to confront experiences and motives which until closed underground he had avoided."[90] This was why Ellison always claimed that the shared cultural project of America was both a black and white creation. According to Ellison, "to embrace uncritically values which are extended to us by others is to reject the validity, even the sacredness, of our own experience. It is also to forget that the small share of reality which each of our diverse groups is able to snatch from the whirling chaos of history belongs not to the group alone, but to all of us."[91]

This recognition of a common cultural heritage was a recognition of pluralism, "the puzzle of the one-and-the-many," that characterized the American project (207). The struggle for political participation was simply the beginning of a larger cultural project. The respect granted through the legal recognition of full citizenship must eventually translate into the esteem for the unique contribution of an individual or group to the entire community. The problem of race in America, according to Ellison, went "beyond its economic and narrowly political aspects" as defined by the radical Left. [92] What was needed was "not an exchange of pathologies, but a change of the basis of society. This is a job which both Negroes and whites must perform together. In Negro culture there is much of value for America as a whole. What is needed are Negroes to take it and create of it 'the uncreated consciousness of their race.' In doing so they will do far more, they'll help create a more human American" (340). The affirmation of difference in Ellison's project was also an affirmation of the intersubjective character of the self that might lead to more emancipatory and more cooperative forms of identity. To make this affirmation was to enter the field of rhetoric and to recognize that social transformation occurred not solely within the realities of politics but also within the field of the social—that ambiguous point between the political world and the private life where cultural patterns, meanings, and symbols were exchanged and debated. Thus, for Ellison, the novel "is *always* a public gesture, though not necessarily a political one."[93]

CONCLUSION

The Legacy of Late Modernism

On April 21, 1964, Andy Warhol held a public party at the Factory, his fifth-floor art studio on Lexington Avenue in Manhattan. For the first time, Warhol allowed art critics and New York socialites to view his new studio, which he and his assistant Billy Linich had spent several months converting from an old hat factory into a glistening, silver-draped spectacle. The party marked the opening of Warhol's Boxes show at the Stable Gallery in New York, where the young artist first presented his famous collection of Factory-produced Brillo box reproductions.[1] The gallery show was of course a huge success—Warhol continued to perplex critics who were still trying to digest his Campbell soup can paintings from two years before. But Warhol's party was in many ways more important than his gallery show. First, given his rising popularity in the art world because of his deliberate reconsideration of what constituted art, Warhol had seemingly succeeded in brushing aside all of the debates about modernism from the 1950s. All modernists—whether Theodor Adorno, Jackson Pollock, or Ralph Ellison—seemed irrelevant in the mirror-lined, raucous space of Warhol's Factory, where, in dispensing with stale debates over formalism versus expressionism, he had redefined art as an assembly-line, automated production. Second, his party, which was attended by wealthy patrons, homeless actors, New York politicians, movie stars, and junkies, signaled that modern art had officially become a public spectacle. No longer an academic question or a highbrow style, modern art had poured out onto the streets and had become an official part of the larger culture of the 1960s. While the escalating costs of a Jackson

Pollock painting soon after his tragic death in 1956 had already demonstrated that high art was not exempt from commodification, Warhol's party, with rock music blaring and neighbors complaining, had ushered in a new cultural landscape. Modernism had taken another radical turn.

Debating the Fate of Modernism

But the academic debates over modernism for which Warhol had little use had not officially ended. Most pointedly, in a 1959 essay, "Mass Society and Post-Modern Fiction," Irving Howe continued the debate between high and romantic modernism, almost beating to death what had been a decade-long argument. Predictably, Howe argued that certain modern writers—the "angry young men" in England and the "beat generation" writers in San Francisco—were the most prominent examples of contemporary artists unable to come to terms with mass society. For Howe, the difficulty for modern writers rested in the character of this new landscape—"a relatively comfortable, half welfare and half garrison society in which the population grows passive, indifferent and atomized"—that had made traditional issues of class conflict irrelevant.[2] The problem with romantic modernists, according to Howe, was that they were unable to thematize the historical shift prompted by the socioeconomic prosperity of the previous decade and therefore had retreated into facile discussions about "personal identity and freedom," in what were vague discussions of man's consciousness. "In their contempt for mind," argued Howe, "they are at one with the middle-class suburbia they think they scorn" (205). Howe's diatribe felt dated even in 1959; he himself would acknowledge as much ten years later in a reprint of his article in which he argued that the kind of literature he had ridiculed in 1959 had already been replaced by a new kind of "postmodern fiction," one that signaled the "breakdown of the modernist impulse" (207). Having prematurely identified the Beats as postmodern, Howe was forced to retract that label and reserve it for a new generation. Indeed, he decried throughout the 1960s what he saw as the end of modernism: "A lonely gifted survivor, Beckett, remains, to remind us of the glories modernism once brought. . . . For what seems to await [modernism] is a more painful and certainly less dignified conclusion than that of earlier cultural movements: what awaits it is publicity and sensation, the kind of savage parody which may indeed be the only fate worse than death."[3] Howe's funeral oration for modernism was repeated by a number of other critics such as Cleanth Brooks and Harry Levin who similarly wondered about the status of modernism in the early 1960s. As Levin claimed, "we may choose whether or not we wish to be modern, and the present drift seems to be toward the negative choice and away from the hazards of controversial involvement."[4] In this sense, it was no coincidence that at the same time Warhol was letting visitors into the Factory many high modernists were announcing that the project of modernism was over.

Howe was right that high modernism had become the most obvious casualty of this tumultuous decade. All of the major premises of high modernism—formalism, the autonomy of art, the democratic personality, orthodox psychoanalysis, and the others—came to seem highly questionable, if not reactionary, to the generation that came of age in the 1960s. To the growing student movement, high modernism seemed the worst form of elitism and the worst example of undemocratic sentiment. Even more, high modernists, with their almost compulsive anti-Soviet politics, seemed complicit with the national security state and complicit with a corrupt university system that had forfeited its long-standing goal of influencing societal development. High modernists had supposedly abdicated direct engagement for ivory tower speculations. Of course many high modernists, including Theodor Adorno, Lionel Trilling, and Allen Tate, would make themselves easy targets for this new generation by making disparaging remarks about the student movement. As poet Frank O'Hara would explain in "Personal Poem," he and his friends would often "go eat some fish and some ale it's / cool but crowded we don't like Lionel Trilling / we decide, we like Don Allen we don't like / Henry James so much."[5] In fact, many high modernists, in particular, many New York intellectuals, eventually came to reject the cultural project they had long defended, seeing in the tumults of the late 1960s the worst excesses of modernism. Lionel Trilling and Daniel Bell, for instance, would criticize the supposed denigration of standards in America caused by the avant-garde, arguing, as Bell would do in *The Cultural Contradictions of Capitalism*, that "the singular fact is that as a creative cultural force—creative in aesthetic form or content—modernism is finished. . . . The sensibility of the 1960s is relevant simply as evidence that the aesthetics of shock and sensation had only become trivial and tedious."[6] As their universities were soon forcefully taken over by members from Students for a Democratic Society and some were even ushered from their offices, many high modernists became cultural and political conservatives.

But more important, the overall project of high modernism appeared antiquated in the cultural revolution of the 1960s. First, high modernists' attempt to carve out a realm for individual autonomy came to seem merely a form of nostalgia to the new counterculture interested in community building. Lionel Trilling, for instance, seemed to have little relevance to the visions found in Marshall McLuhan's *The Medium Is the Massage*, Timothy Leary's *The Psychedelic Experience*, and Theodore Roszak's *Making of a Counter Culture*. Similarly, the high modernist defense of Oedipal identity as the only proper framework for psychological development and as a correction to group psychology seemed completely reactionary, an outdated image of man left over from a paranoid, postwar generation. A range of criticisms appeared in the 1960s that debunked the theoretical claims of high modernists: in works such as Carl Wittman's *Refugees from Amerika: A Gay Manifesto* and Dennis Altman's *Homosexual: Oppression and Liberation*, the gay liberation movement challenged the obvious homophobia of high modernists and others; in works such as Shulamith Firestone's *The Dialectic of Sex* and Nancy Chodorow's *The Reproduction of Mothering*, the feminist movement challenged their defense of the patriarchal culture of early capitalism; and in works such as Thomas Szasz's *The Manufacture of Madness*, Ken Kesey's *One Flew Over the Cuckoo's Nest*, and Michel Foucault's *The Birth of the Clinic*, the antipsychiatry movement criticized their simplistic psychoanalytic formulations. Similarly, as the violence of the Vietnam War caused a crisis of confidence over the role of the United States in the Cold War, their notion of a "democratic personality" became circumspect. Of course high modernism survived, albeit in a much more restrained form, having failed in its original project of promoting autonomous art as a corrective to the failures of modernity. High modernism remained a living presence in university classrooms, in art museums, in publishing companies, in auction houses, and in classroom textbooks. But in a world of absurdist theater, happenings, drug experimentation, psychedelic music, communalism, and sexual liberation, high modernism struggled to remain relevant.

In many ways, then, romantic modernists were much more successful in translating their artistic sensibilities into a larger cultural movement throughout the 1960s. Many of those who survived the 1950s—from Allen Ginsberg to Norman Mailer to William Burroughs—were instrumental in shaping the counterculture of the following decades. The politics of romantic modernism—antiauthoritarian, libertarian, sexual, expressive, and participatory—were part and parcel of the politics of the 1960s. Investigations by romantic modernists into the liberating potential of human sexuality obviously exploded into the sexual revolution of the ensuing decades.

Although most practitioners of this new counterculture had never heard of Wilhelm Reich, they were obviously indebted to the theoretical arguments he had made years earlier. The notion of "free love" had its roots in Reich's *The Function of the Orgasm*. Equally important, investigations by romantic modernists into the supposed deep recesses of the human mind, via their reading of Carl Jung and various Eastern philosophies, helped give rise to the age of Aquarius. Whether through Mark Rothko's enthusiastic reading of world mythologies or Jack Kerouac's interest in Buddhism or William Burroughs's exploration of Scientology, romantic modernists helped to introduce new strains of thought into American culture. Similarly, the proliferation of New Age philosophies—from crystal healing to Reiki to biorhythmic therapy—as a way to find a spiritual grounding uncontaminated by the current political landscape began with the mythological and transcendental investigations of romantic modernists. For instance, Allen Ginsberg's relationship with many of the key figures of the counterculture including Bob Dylan, Timothy Leary, and John Lennon helped to transform their spiritual practices, in effect keeping romantic modernism relevant in the 1960s and 1970s. Romantic modernism even made a number of recruits from high modernist circles who were energized by this new participatory culture. For instance, Frankfurt school member Herbert Marcuse, who remained in the United States after Theodor Adorno and Max Horkheimer moved back to Germany, wrote encouraging remarks about romantic modernism in his 1969 manifesto *An Essay on Liberation*, where he praised this "new sensibility" in art that marked the "end of the segregation of the aesthetic from the real, but also the end of the commercial unification of business and beauty."[7] Similarly, Dwight Macdonald, unlike other New York intellectuals, was supportive of the student movement, famously visiting Columbia University during the 1968 student occupation of the campus and defending the New Left in the face of many detractors.

But as both an aesthetic and political practice, romantic modernism too faced difficult challenges. As an artistic form, romantic modernism suffered from gross assimilation, repetition, and lewd caricature. Art deemed spontaneous, authentic, and above critique quickly became devoid of innovation. The difficulty, for instance, that Jackson Pollock had in moving beyond his famous drip paintings of the late 1940s demonstrated the bind of romantic modernism, a problem that also plagued Mark Rothko, Barnett Newman, and Jack Kerouac. The image of the chain-smoking, half-drunk, romantic artist slinging paint across canvases or words across paper was quickly absorbed by the culture industry, even before the suicidal gestures of Pollock and Kerouac. As Kerouac himself explained, "what horror I felt in 1957 and later 1958 naturally to suddenly see 'Beat' being taken up by everybody, press and TV and Hollywood borscht circuit to include the 'juvenile delinquency' shot and the horrors of a mad teeming billyclub New York and L.A. and they began to call *that* Beat, *that* beatific."[8] Over time, romantic modernism became a cliché. Pop artist Roy Lichtenstein, for instance, poked fun at the "culture of spontaneity" in his 1965 painting *Brush Stroke*, which revealed the commodification of such artistic practices by converting the expressive gestures of abstract expressionists into stereotyped, benday-dot composed brushstrokes. For many later critics such as Christopher Lasch and Tom Wolfe, the obsessive concern with authenticity and spontaneous release by artists in the 1950s had transformed in the ensuing decades into the self-centered, narcissistic "Me generation" of the 1970s. Moreover, the reactionary tendencies of romantic modernism increasingly became suspect. Many, like Norman Mailer and William Burroughs, continued to espouse an antifeminist politics throughout the years, aided by the efforts of Hugh Hefner and others to promote the *Playboy* lifestyle. But in the wake of the modern feminist movement, a litany of critics, in works such as Kate Millett's *Sexual Politics* and Jo Freeman's *The Politics of Women's Liberation*, took Mailer and Burroughs to task for their retrograde notions. Some, like Joyce Johnson and Carolyn Cassady, who were personally associated with many romantic modernists, told of their frustration with the aggressive posturing of these artists. Equally influential, the gay liberation movement challenged the explicit homophobia of romantic modernism, helped in part by the examples set forth by James Baldwin and Jasper Johns, among others. Andy Warhol, for instance, made a series of "oxidation" paintings reminiscent of Pollock's abstract paintings, yet created not by dripping paint but by urinating on canvases, an obvious rejoinder to the hypermasculine nature of abstract expressionism. By the time poet Robert Bly started the mythopoetic men's movement in the 1970s, which had its origins in the revival of Carl Jung in the work of Rothko, Pollock, and others, the gender politics of romantic modernism had become cartoonish.

In this sense, Irving Howe was correct that the defining cultural trend in the 1960s was the emergence of postmodernism, a loosely defined movement determined to debunk simultaneously the elitist posturing of high modernism and the metaphysical claims of romantic modernism. The movement from utopia to dystopia that characterized American culture in the 1970s signaled the almost total exhaustion of earlier modernist practices. As a number of historians have recently argued, the rise of postmodernism, in all its forms, was connected both to the global economic crisis that began in the 1970s, erasing, at least in America and in parts of Europe, the era of abundance associated with the postwar period, and to the supposed failures of the social movements of the 1960s, whose actual achievements seemed to many to have failed to live up to their original utopian sentiments.[9] But even before the age of stagflation, political scandals, soaring energy prices, and deindustrialization, many artists, exemplified by the opening of Warhol's Factory, had begun to refashion their practices according to a fundamentally new aesthetic. For instance, Warhol's party occurred at the same time as the publication of critic Leslie Fiedler's "The New Mutants" and critic Susan Sontag's "One Culture and the New Sensibility," two seminal essays that defended the excesses of popular culture against the obnoxious elitism of high modernism and that thereby announced the arrival of postmodernism. In "The New Mutants," Fiedler described a fundamental shift in Western culture in which the long-standing tradition of humanism that had guided Christian, liberal, democratic thought for centuries had broken down and had been replaced by a new antihumanist, antibourgeois, and anti-elitist culture created by a generation of "dropouts from history."[10] Similarly, Susan Sontag defended the new art of the 1960s that was pluralistic, anti-elitist, and populist, what she described as art that was "less snobbish, less moralistic."[11] Although this new postmodernist sensibility competed with the other practicing forms of modernism throughout the decade, the movement had gained enough adherents by the 1970s to prompt one critic to offer the first attempt at canonization. Ihab Hassan's 1971 book *The Dismemberment of Orpheus: Toward a Postmodern Literature* offered a list of postmodern writers and served a similar purpose for this new sensibility to that of Edmund Wilson's 1931 book *Axel's Castle: A Study in the Imaginative Literature of 1870–1930* for the first canon of modernists writers. According to Hassan, modernism had been the literature of the urban landscape, of technology and automatism, a literature of experimentalism, primitivism, and alienation; postmodernism, on the other hand, was the literature of the global village, of the computer age, of a new participatory culture, a literature of a postindividual world and of an antielitist culture.[12]

Postmodernism, in all its forms, centered on three related themes: the end of man, the end of history, and the end of metaphysics. Most famously, postmodernists began to argue that the era of the autonomous individual was over. For many, the immensity of technological advancements, which had destroyed traditional notions of time and space, the escalating rise of multinational corporations, which had begun to dismantle national boundaries, and the overwhelming influence of the culture industry, which had erased any division between art and commerce, had left no room for individual development. Hysterical and frayed, the individual self seemed merely a psychic reflex of this new landscape. Of course, some like Andy Warhol saw this as something to celebrate; others like literary critic Fredric Jameson saw this as the ultimate defeat. Either way, by the 1960s, many began to thematize the end of the subject: Warhol's Factory-produced Brillo boxes and silkscreen images were drained of any personal elements; Roy Lichtenstein's reproductions of comic book images mirrored the processes of consumer society; the novels of Thomas Pynchon, John Barth, and John Hawkes contained depthless, empty characters; and the structuralist and poststructuralist theories of Jacques Derrida, Roland Barthes, Paul de Man, and others, which were ubiquitous in literature departments by the 1970s, displaced the individual author or the autonomous text as the grounds for meaning. Art and literary criticism were completely transformed. The postmodern artist was neither a grand enunciator in the tradition of Jackson Pollock nor even a much more subdued, expressive subject in the vein of Jasper Johns but a *bricoleur* who took delight in simply reorganizing the cultural debris around him. By the 1970s, Michel Foucault had replaced Wilhelm Reich; James Rosenquist had replaced Barnett Newman; Don DeLillo had replaced Norman Mailer; and Paul de Man had replaced Lionel Trilling. All of these practitioners declared, albeit in different ways, the disappearance of the individual in the face of an entirely new landscape.

Of course, postmodern artists could deal with this cultural debris in such a haphazard fashion because they had already declared the end of history. Such a grand announcement was the result of two related transformations. First, the collapse of utopian politics in all its forms—the teleological visions of Marxism, the progressive vision of classical liberalism, the transcendentalism of the counterculture, and the rest—made it seem as if traditional radicalism as such had died. Second, the spread of capitalist relations into all aspects of life made it seem as if any deviation from the present moment was impossible, thereby making all past cultural traditions antiquated in the hyperreality of consumer capitalism. In an age of mass media and computer technology, the materiality of everyday life seemed to have been erased by an endless stream of signs and images, creating a world where commodification was inescapable. Theorists and artists as diverse as Marshall McLuhan, Andy Warhol, Guy Debord, Jean Baudrillard, Claes Oldenburg, Nam June Paik, Jeff Halley, and others highlighted the ceaseless flow of media images, consumer fantasies, and artificial signs that had supposedly transformed lived reality into a simulated illusion. In such a world, the postmodern artist abandoned the grand themes of modernism and instead turned to popular culture, making irony and pastiche the key aesthetic elements. Postmodern architects such as Charles Jencks and Robert Venturi revolted from the purity of long-standing modernist forms, choosing instead to play with historical styles, ornamentation, and decoration that better reflected the discontinuous nature of the electronic age. Similarly, postmodern novelists, in particular those who turned to science fiction such as William Gibson and Neal Stephenson, played with the ambiguous line between lived and virtual reality. Other novelists such as Umberto Eco and E. L. Doctorow blended detective fiction, history, science fiction, and war stories to create novels that reflected the fragmented, almost schizophrenic nature of modern society. In such a world, conventional notions of history and historical progress made no sense.

Finally, postmodernism heralded the supposed end of metaphysics, a philosophical revolution that had its origins in the work of a range of figures including Friedrich Nietzsche, Ludwig Wittgenstein, Martin Heidegger, John Dewey, and others, but that exploded in the 1970s and 1980s. A range of philosophers such as Jean-François Lyotard, Jacques Derrida, Richard Rorty, and Gilles Deleuze began to break down the divisions between academic fields, working across the disciplinary boundaries between history, philosophy, psychoanalysis, and literature. In so doing, they rejected traditional notions of epistemological certainty grounding most of Western philosophy, thereby abandoning the search for fixed meaning in favor of contingency, multiplicity, and relativism. This philosophical revolution not only impacted traditional forms of knowledge but transformed conventional notions of human identity, decentering long-standing ways of thinking about sexuality, gender, race, ethnicity, and so on. The result was an explosion of new fields such as gender studies, queer theory, postcolonial theory, cultural studies, and critical race theory. Unlike their modernist predecessors, whether those who clamored for individual autonomy or those who searched for some metaphysical truth, postmodern theorists confronted what they saw as the fragmented, decentered, and constructed nature of identity. By the 1980s, all of the debates over modernism that occupied American intellectual life after World War II had seemingly been negated by this new theoretical landscape. The culture as a whole had turned in a new direction.

Revisiting Late Modernism

Given the force of this intellectual and cultural revolution, the contributions of Kenneth Burke, Ralph Ellison, Erving Goffman, and others in exposing the limitations of earlier forms of modernism have often been overlooked. Postmodern theorists, with coy prose and biting irony, had a lot of fun in the 1970s and 1980s deflating the excesses of their modernist predecessors, a task that was highly needed and rightly pursued. But in the process, late modernism was reduced to being merely a footnote in the rise of postmodernism. For instance, in his 1979 manifesto *The Postmodern Condition: A Report on Knowledge*, French theorist Jean-François Lyotard announced the end of modernity in a world of uncertainty and skepticism. Although his book centered on his reading of Ludwig Wittgenstein, Norbert Weiner, and others, Lyotard buried in his notes references to C. Wright Mills and Erving Goffman, both of whom had already announced the transition to a postmodern age and had dealt in depth with the role of performativity that Lyotard saw as an integral part of this new landscape. Similar obfuscations were also found in the early work of Jean Baudrillard, Ihab Hassan, Alain Touraine, and Amitai Etzioni, all of whom made a litany of guarded references to American sociology. Of course some late modernists did not live long enough to defend their legacies or to even see the changes of the 1960s that made their work seem so prescient. C. Wright Mills died in 1962, having failed to complete his manuscript on the cultural apparatus and having failed to publish his confessional letters to his imaginary Russian friend. In the ensuing years, his more digestible books were absorbed by the New Left, resulting in the flattening of his sociology into the political framework of the student movement. The endless books and essays written on Mills over the years have reduced him to being merely a godfather of the New Left and have thereby not given enough attention to the breadth of his sociological imagination. For instance, Stanley Aronowitz has defended the maverick sociologist as "a model for those who wish to become intellectuals" in contrast to current academics who have followed "the path of least resistance by writing the same articles and books over and over."[13] But in fact, most defenders of Mills's legacy like Aronowitz have themselves been continuously writing the same articles on Mills over the years, praising his more political and more pedantic works over his others that slip into what historian Kevin Mattson mockingly refers to as "passive, almost Germanic language."[14] Missing from the studies written by Aronowitz, Mattson, and others is any attention to Mills's meditations on the nature of language, selfhood, rhetoric, and role-playing, those elements that gave his work an intellectual edge and theoretical rigor and that addressed the key questions of the postmodern age.

Indeed, the flattening out of the intellectual legacy of many late modernists by those unwilling to engage in a close reading has resulted in the abandonment, dismissal, or misinterpretation of their works. Like Mills, David Riesman has suffered from a litany of superficial readings by writers who have simply lumped *The Lonely Crowd* into the plethora of postwar books lamenting the rise of postindustrialism. For example, historian James Gilbert has recently reiterated conventional readings of Riesman's famous book, arguing that the sociologist was obsessed with "how to be a man in an increasingly feminized world of mass culture, consumption, and conformity."[15] Riesman fought against such misreadings for decades, trying to get his fellow sociologists to acknowledge the complexity of his book, in particular, his guarded enthusiasm for those forms of subjectivity later associated with postmodernism. Of course, Riesman never matched the success of *The Lonely Crowd*, although he published numerous sociological studies of leisure practices, consumer trends, work patterns, and housing trends as well as commonsensical pieces on Cold War diplomacy, all of which continued the ambitious task he set forth in *The Lonely Crowd* and *Faces in the Crowd*. But he eventually moved away from the sociology profession and focused on the problems of higher education. As the student movement began to take over the universities in the 1960s, Riesman unfortunately seemed to many to be an antiquated and complicit figure, in what was an unfortunate foreshortening of his work. Some late modernists, of course, did not help their own cause. Norman Brown, for instance, got swept up into the cultural tumult of the 1960s, exchanging his theoretical investigations into Freud for much more mystical and metaphysical speculations that echoed Allen Ginsberg and others. As such, Brown has long been reduced to merely a footnote in the history of the counterculture. Most commentators have focused on "the apocalypse of Norman O. Brown" and not his actual academic contributions.[16] But his work predated the absorption of Lacanian psychoanalysis and other Freudian deviations into American academic departments and represented the first systematic challenge, along with the work of Wilhelm Reich and Herbert Marcuse, to orthodox psychoanalysis and ego psychology. In particular, his return to Freud's earlier speculations about the "bodily ego" echoes the current theoretical interest in the role of desire and the body in political and social subjection.

Others similarly were pushed aside by the movements of the 1960s, appearing far too conservative in an age of sexual and political experimentation. Ralph Ellison and James Baldwin, for instance, were quickly dismissed by the black nationalist movement, which argued that these two writers were promoting a form of pluralism that had little relevance in a world of urban riots, police brutality, and a failed welfare state. Most famously, Eldridge Cleaver ridiculed James Baldwin in his 1968 memoir *Soul on Ice*, not only for what Cleaver saw as Baldwin's unreflective interest in white culture but for his supposedly immature, if not pathological, sexuality. As Cleaver explained, "homosexuality is a sickness, just as are baby-rape or wanting to become the head of General Motors," a critique that many others leveled against Baldwin in the 1960s.[17] Although he continued to write fiction and nonfiction well into the 1980s, Baldwin, who was uninterested in the kind of identity politics prominent within the American Left, seemed to have little to offer. But his work, like that of Norman Brown, was an essential part of the rethinking of sexuality in the 1970s and readily cited by the gay liberation movement. Similarly, Ralph Ellison had trouble surviving critiques similar to the ones leveled at Baldwin. Despite the resounding success of his first book, Ellison, for personal and professional reasons, failed to produce a second one. As a result, he was often dismissed as merely another conservative high modernist. The charges made against Ellison over the years have been he refused to look beyond aesthetics to the world around him or that he believed "social and political engagement may be antithetical to his artistic pursuit."[18] According to such interpretations, Ellison promoted high modernism precisely at the moment that others were in the process of debunking it, an interpretation that unfortunately fails to recognize the breadth of Ellison's cultural criticism. Indeed, the manuscript for his uncompleted work *Juneteenth* and his countless essays over the years drew upon the best of Burkean rhetoric to elaborate upon the American experience.

Other late modernists got trapped within the shifting terrain of their own academic fields. For instance, the work of Erving Goffman had little force in the 1960s in a sociology discipline increasingly split between structuralism and empiricism. Goffman continued to produce subtle investigations into the effect of institutions, role-playing, and language upon everyday life (investigations that echoed the work of many postmodernists). But Goffman's so-called microsociology remained only an underground force in a field dominated by Talcott Parsons and others. Goffman, however, would be revisited in the 1970s and 1980s when many sociologists took a more "cultural turn" that linked questions of power and control to the kinds of institutional and cultural forms that Goffman had analyzed in the early 1960s. In fact, his last three books, *Relations in Public* (1971), *Frame Analysis* (1974), and *Forms of Talk* (1981), not only elaborated upon his dramaturgical perspective but paved the way for the linguistic turn in the humanities years later. Similarly, Kenneth Burke was marginalized within an academy originally dominated by the New Critics and then by poststructuralists, and most of his work was ignored in English departments, except for the occasional reference by critics such as Irving Howe who ridiculed those who spent time reading "reams of Kenneth Burke."[19] His work would persist, however, picked up by an odd range of intellectuals in the ensuing decades, from philosopher Calvin Schrag to literary critic Frank Lentricchia, who have been interested in finding an indigenous alternative to French literary criticism. Even the most successful late modernist, Jasper Johns, whose work was incredibly influential on numerous artistic trends in the late twentieth century and who still has many successful shows, has often been relegated in art history textbooks to being merely a forerunner of Pop art in the 1960s. Art historian David Hopkins has written, "New York Pop stepped up Johns's and Rauschenberg's critique of Abstract Expressionism's bombast through cool impersonality," an oft-repeated statement that ignores the personal and political elements throughout Johns's work.[20] Like many others, Johns simply became a transitional figure.

But the contribution of these artists and intellectuals in refashioning, if not rehabilitating, modernism cannot be ignored, a contribution that has much to say to our present-day concerns. Unlike many postmodernists like Andy Warhol or Charles Jencks, late modernists still believed in the redemptive power of art, refusing to abandon the long-standing modernist claim that the aesthetic was one of the privileged sites for social transformation. But of course they were unwilling to accept the simplicities offered by other modernist critics who spoke either of art's autonomy from social contamination or of art's power to reflect the pristine interior of the individual artist. Instead, the aesthetic practices of late modernism were centered on what Kenneth Burke and Ralph Ellison referred to as symbolic action—the process of unearthing the shared vocabularies of motive driving human conduct, examining the implications within each vocabulary, formulating new and possibly more liberating forms of action from the possibilities inherent to each vocabulary, and convincing readers, through studied attention to their own interests, to side with the artist's reorientation of these shared vocabularies. They conceived of any form of human action, whether political, ethical, or artistic, as a form of symbolic action—a demonstrative attempt to acknowledge, persuade, seduce, and transform those within earshot. As Ralph Ellison explained, "the work of art is, after all, an act of faith in our ability to communicate symbolically."[21] This meant treating the artwork primarily as a form of communication, one that examined the shared historical, cultural, and political traditions that made experience meaningful and that pointed out how such traditions provided possibilities for both unity and division. Such symbolic action played upon trained forms of response and upon embedded cultural assumptions, what Ellison referred to as "the rhetorical levers within American society."[22] In this way, late modernists like Ralph Ellison, Kenneth Burke, and C. Wright Mills reinterpreted the aesthetic form, if not all attempts at communication, as a form of rhetoric. They noted the inescapability of such discourse—whether the monologues of television commentators, the speeches of politicians, the visual cues of mass media, the arguments of next-door neighbors, or the aesthetic visions of contemporary artists—in shaping individual opinion.

This meant for late modernists that any aesthetic project succeeded or failed in large measure in relationship to its communicative appeal. Rhetoric, at its essence, was, as Aristotle originally claimed, an art form, one that exposed the limitations inherent to any form of life, not through any wholesale dismissal, but through a sustained unearthing of the assumptions within that form of life that revealed unseen prejudices, shortcomings, or failures. By bringing to light the unacknowledged ideological frameworks (economic, political, or social) of any common culture, rhetoric served, through its myriad tools such as perspective by incongruity, casuistic stretching, rituals of rebirth, and so on, to make the implications of such a culture appear grotesque, comical, tragic, or utopian. For Ralph Ellison, "experience tends to mold itself into certain repetitive patterns, and one of the reasons we exchange experiences is in order to discover the repetitions and coincidences which amount to a common group experience" (372). Of course, this did not mean that the artist as rhetorician was simply a grand enunciator, a con man, or a bully; if anything, Ellison and others were determined to recast the modern artist as merely one voice in the aesthetic experience, a voice in dialogue with a heterogeneous audience trying to create some form of consensus. "The work of fiction comes alive through collaboration between the reader and the writer," asserted Ellison, "this is where rhetoric comes in" (158). The artwork as such was addressed to an audience not easily persuaded, an audience often times quite skeptical and quite protective of its separateness. The task for the modern artist was to search through the histories and traditions of this diverse audience, recognizing that each member "has his own hierarchical ranking of human values" and "his own range of pieties—filial, sacred, racial" that operated as "the rhetorical 'stops' through which his sensibilities are made responsive to artistic structurings of symbolic form."[23]

Of course, the goal of late modernists like Ellison or Burke was not merely to refashion aesthetics as a form of rhetoric or symbolic action. More important, they were interested in constructing an entirely different image of the self, an image that took into account the myriad forces—political, social, familial, and others—that provided the context for individual identity. They argued, unlike many of their postmodern followers, that it was impossible to get rid of all vocabulary of the self, that despite such overwhelming economic and political changes, an image of the self as *subject* was still essential. But unlike their modernist predecessors who obsessed over notions of individual autonomy, late modernists offered a much more restrained image of the self, one that cried, breathed, answered, performed, cursed, and struggled, a self of action, of response, and of commitment. For instance, C. Wright Mills tried to demonstrate throughout his work that the self was neither a closed system nor an autonomous entity but something forged through a continuous negotiation with the outside world. "Surely we ought occasionally to remember that in truth we do not know much about man," Mills wrote in *The Sociological Imagination*, "and that all the knowledge we do have does not entirely remove the element of mystery that surrounds his variety as it is revealed in history and biography."[24] In so doing, late modernists made the process of identification the key to any understanding of the psychical birth of the self. "In forming ideas of our personal identity," argued Burke, "we spontaneously identify ourselves with family, nation, political or cultural cause, church, and so on."[25] Through the process of identification, all of those external experiences—relationships with significant others, training in particular language games, confrontations with authorities, instruction in certain ideological perspectives, and others—were internalized and made part of the person in a meaningful way. Any form of identity therefore was in reality a composite of a series of identifications, an identity that was neither given nor complete but an ongoing development with an often troubled, conflicted history. But late modernists like Burke and Mills always stressed that the individual was not merely the sum total of all of the identifications made but the result of the ordering and reordering of such identifications into a coherent whole. "The uniqueness of the individual—the particular composition and unity which he achieves," noted Mills, "arises from his differing experiences and from his cumulative ordering of these experiences."[26] As such a combination, the individual was neither alienated by these past identifications nor overcome by them; instead, the individual tried to piece together, however fragile, an account of himself that in turn provided the basis for self-identity.

In this sense, the legacy of late modernists in the 1950s was not only their reformulation of art, if not all types of communication, as a form of symbolic action but their attempt to rethink the role that identification played not just within the aesthetic realm but within the political, economic, social, and familial realms as well. As C. Wright Mills explained in *The Sociological Imagination*, "our basic definitions of society and of self are being overtaken by new realities."[27] In offering a form of cultural politics centered on the process of identification, late modernists opened up a range of concerns missing from other modernist visions in the 1950s, blending together politics, aesthetics, and personal transformation and rethinking the fundamental nature of the self—from sexuality, gender, and race to the body itself. That is why so many late modernists appeared as gadflies in the 1950s—C. Wright Mills and Erving Goffman challenging the theoretical assumptions of conventional sociology, Norman Brown undermining orthodox psychoanalysis, Jasper Johns toying with the practices of abstract expressionism, and Kenneth Burke endlessly poking fun at formalist literary practices. Their reconceptualization of the self—one found in language, love, and significant others—helped produce the postmodern turn of the 1970s. But as Burke always maintained, his goal was not merely to debunk established norms and practices. Instead, his goal was to offer a form of cultural politics that paid particular attention to the forms of life and institutional settings through which the individual struggled to emerge, a cultural politics that was centered not just on the subversion of discursive and nondiscursive practices but on the consolidation of new and possibly more liberating practices. As philosophers, literary critics, and artists begin to move beyond postmodernism, absorbing its warnings, skepticism, and force, one can hope that the contributions of those who composed the tradition of late modernism will help point the way forward, contributions that helped to rethink the connection between selfhood, aesthetics, and social transformation.

NOTES

Sources for quotations are given in a note for the first instance, and subsequent page references appear parenthetically in the text.

Introduction

1. Douglas MacAgy, ed., "The Western Round Table on Modern Art," in *Modern Artists in America* (New York: Wittenborn Schultz, 1949), 26.

2. Quoted in "The Western Round Table on Modern Art," 27.

3. Quoted in "The Western Round Table on Modern Art," 27.

4. Quoted in "The Western Round Table on Modern Art," 33.

5. Quoted in "The Western Round Table on Modern Art," 33.

6. Quoted in "The Western Round Table on Modern Art," 32.

7. Kenneth Burke, *Permanence and Change: An Anatomy of Purpose*, 3rd edition (Berkeley: University of California Press, 1965), xlix.

8. Irving Howe, "The Culture of Modernism," in *Decline of the New* (New York: Harcourt, Brace, and World, 1967), 15.

9. Cleanth Brooks, *Modern Poetry and the Tradition* (New York: Oxford University Press, 1965), viii.

10. Howe, "The Culture of Modernism," 5.

11. Lionel Trilling, "William Dean Howells and the Roots of Modern Taste," in *The Moral Obligation to Be Intelligent*, ed. Leon Wieseltier (New York: Farrar, Straus and Giroux, 2000), 218. See Robert Genter, "'I'm Not His Father': Lionel Trilling, Allen Ginsberg, and the Contours of Literary Modernism," *College Literature* 31, no. 2 (Spring 2004): 22–52.

12. See Peter Burger, *Theory of the Avant-Garde*, trans. Michael Shaw (Minneapolis: University of Minnesota Press, 1984).

13. See Astradur Eysteinsson, *The Concept of Modernism* (Ithaca, N.Y.: Cornell University Press, 1990); and Art Berman, *Preface to Modernism* (Urbana: University of Illinois Press, 1994).

14. On the origins of this debate, see Thomas Hill Schaub, *American Fiction in the Cold War* (Madison: University of Wisconsin Press, 1991).

15. Harold Rosenberg, "The American Action Painters," in *The Tradition of the New* (New York: McGraw-Hill, 1959), 28.

16. Brooks, *Modern Poetry and the Tradition*, viii.

17. Andrew Ross, *The Failure of Modernism: Symptoms of American Poetry* (New York: Columbia University Press, 1986), 211.

18. Howe, "The Culture of Modernism," 33.

19. Brian McHale, *Postmodernist Fiction* (New York: Routledge, 1987).

20. Fredric Jameson, *Postmodernism or, the Cultural Logic of Late Capitalism* (Durham, N.C.: Duke University Press, 1991), 305.

21. Albert Murray and John Callahan, eds., *Trading Twelves: The Selected Letters of Ralph Ellison and Albert Murray* (New York: Vintage, 2000), 157.

22. Ralph Ellison, "The Little Man at Chehaw Station," in *The Collected Essays of Ralph Ellison*, ed. John F. Callahan (New York: Modern Library, 1995), 492.

23. See, for instance, Ihab Hassan, *The Postmodern Turn: Essays in Postmodern Theory and Culture* (Columbus: Ohio State University Press, 1987).

24. William S. Burroughs, *The Letters of William S. Burroughs, 1945–1959*, ed. Oliver Harris (New York: Viking Press, 1993), 293.

25. In this, I am following the lead of other critics who have begun to carve out a genealogy of late modernism. See Charles Jencks, "Postmodern vs. Late-Modern," in *Zeitgeist in Babel: The Postmodernist Controversy* (Bloomington: Indiana University Press, 1991), 4–35; Tyrus Miller, *Late Modernism: Politics, Fiction, and the Arts Between the World Wars* (Berkeley: University of California Press, 1999); and Anthony Mellors, *Late Modernist Poetics: From Pound to Prynne* (Manchester: Manchester University Press, 2005).

26. Kenneth Burke, "The Definition of Man," in *Language as Symbolic Action: Essays on Life, Literature, and Method* (Berkeley: University of California Press, 1966), 5.

27. Eduardo Cadava, Peter Connor, and Jean-Luc Nancy, eds., *Who Comes After the Subject?* (New York: Routledge, 1991). My work on late modernism has been deeply influenced by the work of Calvin Schrag, who has tried to reconstruct the self in the wake of postmodernism. See, for instance, Calvin O. Schrag, *The Self After Postmodernity* (New Haven, Conn.: Yale University Press, 1997).

Chapter One. Science, Postmodernity, and the Rise of High Modernism

1. Vannevar Bush, *Science: The Endless Frontier* (Washington, D.C.: U.S. Government Printing Office, 1945), 5.

2. Alvin Weinberg, "Impact of Large-Scale Science on the United States," *Science* 134, no. 3473 (July 21, 1961): 161–64.

3. "The Great Science Debate," *Fortune* 33, no. 6 (June 1946): 116–20, 236–45.

4. James Conant, "The Role of Science in Our Unique Society," *Science* 107, no. 2769 (January 23, 1948): 77.

5. See Paul Forman, "Behind Quantum Electronics: National Security as Basis for Physical Research in the United States, 1940–1960," *Historical Studies in the Physical and Biological Sciences* 18, no. 1 (September 1987): 149–229; and Stuart Leslie, *The Cold War and American Science: The Military-Industrial-Academic Complex at MIT and Stanford* (New York: Columbia University Press, 1993).

6. Dan Kevles, "Cold War and Hot Physics: Science, Security, and the American

State, 1945–1956," *Historical Studies in the Physical and Biological Sciences* 20, no. 2 (March 1989): 245.

7. See S. S. Schweber, "The Mutual Embrace of Science and the Military: ONR and the Growth of Physics in the United States After World War II," in *Science, Technology, and the Military*, ed. Everett Mendelsohn, Merritt Roe Smith, and Peter Weingart (Boston: Kluwer Academic, 1988), 21.

8. National Manpower Council, *Proceedings of a Conference on the Utilization of Scientific and Professional Manpower* (New York: Columbia University Press, 1954), 18. See David Kaiser, "Cold War Requisitions, Scientific Manpower, and the Production of American Physicists After World War II," *Historical Studies in the Physical and Biological Sciences* 33, no. 1 (September 2002): 131–59.

9. "Summary of Study by Committee on Scientists and Engineers," *New York Times* (December 1, 1957): 58.

10. John Rudolph, *Scientists in the Classroom: The Cold War Reconstruction of American Science Education* (New York: Palgrave, 2002).

11. "Sharp Rise Found in Science Study," *New York Times* (September 7, 1958): 140.

12. "Wizards of the Coming Wonders," *Life* 36 (January 4, 1954): 92–94.

13. "American Scientists: Men of the Year," *Time* 77, no. 1 (January 2, 1961): 40.

14. On the conflicting images of postwar scientists, see Paul Boyer, *By the Bomb's Early Light: American Thought and Culture at the Dawn of the Atomic Age* (Chapel Hill: University of North Carolina Press, 1994).

15. Alvin Weinberg, "Big Science—Marvel or Menace?" *New York Times Magazine* (July 23, 1961): 15.

16. C. P. Snow, *The Two Cultures*, intro. Stefan Collini (New York: Cambridge University Press, 1998), 8.

17. Lionel Trilling, "The Leavis-Snow Controversy," in Wieseltier, *The Moral Obligation to Be Intelligent*, 419.

18. J. Robert Oppenheimer, *Science and the Common Understanding* (New York: Simon and Schuster, 1953).

19. Herbert Marcuse, *One-Dimensional Man: Studies in the Ideology of Advanced Industrial Society* (Boston: Beacon Press, 1964), 1.

20. Theodor Adorno, "Scientific Experiences of a European Scholar in America," in *The Intellectual Migration, Europe and America, 1930–1960*, ed. Donald Fleming and Bernard Bailyn (Cambridge, Mass.: Harvard University Press, 1969), 369.

21. Max Horkheimer and Theodor Adorno, *Dialectic of Enlightenment*, trans. John Cumming (New York: Continuum, 1996), 12.

22. Max Horkheimer, *Eclipse of Reason* (1947; New York: Continuum, 1974), v.

23. Dwight Macdonald, "A Corrupt Brightness," *Encounter* 8, no. 6 (June 1957): 75. On Macdonald's career, see Stephen Whitfield, *A Critical American: The Politics of Dwight Macdonald* (Hamden, Conn.: Archon Books, 1984).

24. Dwight Macdonald, *The Root Is Man* (New York: Autonomedia, 1995), 93.

25. Dwight Macdonald, "The Bomb," *Politics* (September 1945): 260.

26. Gerald Graff, "What Was the New Criticism?" in *Literature Against Itself: Literary Ideas in Modern Society* (Chicago: University of Chicago Press, 1979). On the politics of the New Criticism, see Mark Jancovich, *The Cultural Politics of the New Criticism* (New York: Cambridge University Press, 1993).

27. John Crowe Ransom, *The New Criticism* (Norfolk, Conn.: New Directions, 1941), 44.

28. Jürgen Habermas, *The Philosophical Discourse of Modernity*, trans. Frederick Lawrence (Cambridge, Mass.: MIT Press, 1987).

29. On the complex history of the phrase "post-modern," see Margaret A. Rose, *The Post-Modern and the Post-Industrial: A Critical History* (Cambridge: Cambridge University Press, 1991).

30. C. Wright Mills, *The Sociological Imagination* (New York: Oxford University Press, 1959), 165–66.

31. Peter F. Drucker, *Landmarks of Tomorrow* (New York: Harper and Brothers, 1957), x.

32. Bernard Rosenberg, "Mass Culture in America," in *Mass Culture: The Popular Arts in America*, ed. Bernard Rosenberg and David Manning White (Glencoe, Ill,: Free Press, 1957), 5.

33. Macdonald, *The Root Is Man*, 40.

34. Theodor Adorno, "The Essay as Form," in *Notes to Literature*, volume 1, trans. Shierry Weber Nicholsen (New York: Columbia University Press, 1991), 6.

35. On Adorno's aesthetics, see Peter Osbourne, "Aesthetic Autonomy and the Crisis of Theory: Greenberg, Adorno, and the Problem of Postmodernism in the Visual Arts," *New Formations* 9 (Winter 1989): 31–50; Shierry Weber Nicholsen, *Exact Imagination, Late Work: On Adorno's Aesthetic* (Cambridge, Mass.: MIT Press, 1997); and Albrecht Wellmer, "Truth, Semblance, Reconciliation: Adorno's Aesthetic Redemption of Modernity," *Telos* 62 (Winter 1984–85): 89–113.

36. Theodor Adorno, "Valery's Deviations," in *Notes to Literature*, 1: 143.

37. Clement Greenberg, "Avant-Garde and Kitsch," in *Clement Greenberg: The Collected Essays and Criticism*, volume 1, ed. John O'Brian (Chicago: University of Chicago Press, 1986), 10.

38. Adorno, "Valery's Deviations," 143.

39. Clement Greenberg, "The Decline of Cubism," in *Clement Greenberg: The Collected Essays and Criticism*, volume 2, ed. John O'Brian (Chicago: University of Chicago Press, 1986), 213.

40. Theodor Adorno, *Minima Moralia*, trans. E. F. N. Jephcott (New York: Verso, 1978), 226.

41. Theodor Adorno, "On Lyric Poetry and Society," in *Notes to Literature,* 1: 40.

42. On the New Criticism, see Art Berman, *From the New Criticism to Deconstruction: The Reception of Structuralism and Post-Structuralism* (Urbana: University of Illinois Press, 1988); William Cain, *The Crisis in Criticism: Theory, Literature, and Reform in English Studies* (Baltimore: Johns Hopkins University Press, 1984); and

Murray Krieger, *The Play and Place of Criticism* (Baltimore: Johns Hopkins University Press, 1967).

43. Ransom, *The New Criticism*, 92.

44. Cleanth Brooks, *The Well Wrought Urn: Studies in the Structure of Poetry* (New York: Harcourt, Brace, 1947), 18.

45. As William Phillips explained, Greenberg gave "the new painting a plastic definition, much like the textual definition of poetry by the New Criticism." See William Phillips, *A Partisan View: Five Decades of the Literary Life* (New York: Stein and Day, 1983), 66.

46. Clement Greenberg, "Modernist Painting," in *Clement Greenberg: The Collected Essays and Criticism*, volume 4, ed. John O'Brian (Chicago: University of Chicago Press, 1993), 86. On Greenberg's aesthetics, see David Carrier, "Greenberg, Fried, and Philosophy: American-Type Formalism," in *Aesthetics: A Critical Anthology*, ed. George Dickie and R. J. Sclafani (New York: St. Martin's Press, 1977), 461–70.

47. Michael Fried, "How Modernism Works: A Response to T. J. Clark," in *Pollock and After: The Critical Debate*, 2nd edition, ed. Francis Frascina (New York: Routledge, 2000), 90.

48. Clement Greenberg, "The Crisis of the Easel Picture," in *Collected Essays*, 2: 224.

49. Clement Greenberg, "Abstract and Representational," in *Clement Greenberg: The Collected Essays and Criticism*, volume 3, ed. John O'Brian (Chicago: University of Chicago Press, 1993), 191.

50. T. S. Eliot, *The Use of Poetry and the Use of Criticism* (London: Faber and Faber, 1933), 34.

51. John Crowe Ransom, "Wanted: An Ontological Critic," in *Beating the Bushes, Selected Essays* (New York: New Directions, 1972), 2.

52. John Crowe Ransom, *The World's Body* (New York: Charles Scribner's Sons, 1938), 334.

53. John Crowe Ransom, "Art and Human Economy," in *Beating the Bushes*, 129.

54. John Crowe Ransom, "Poetry: A Note on Ontology," in *The World's Body*, 111.

55. John Crowe Ransom, "An Address to Kenneth Burke," in *Beating the Bushes*, 64. From John Crowe Ransom's *Beating the Bushes* to Allen Tate's *Reason in Madness*, from Theodor Adorno's *Minima Moralia* to Herbert Marcuse's *Eros and Civilization*, and from Clement Greenberg's *Art and Culture* to Cleanth Brooks's *The Well Wrought Urn*, high modernists referenced Kantian theory as the basis for their aesthetics.

56. Greenberg, "Modernist Painting," 85.

57. Immanuel Kant, *Critique of Judgment*, trans. J. H. Bernard (New York: Hafner Press, 1951), 16.

58. Ransom, "An Address to Kenneth Burke," 63.

59. Ransom, "Wanted: An Ontological Critic," 12.

60. Brooks, *Well Wrought Urn*, 189.

61. Adorno, *Minima Moralia*, 224.

62. See Berman, *From the New Criticism to Deconstruction*, 47.

63. Adorno, "Lyric Poetry and Society," 53.

64. Adorno, *Minima Moralia*, 77.

65. Clement Greenberg, "Cezanne and the Unity of Modern Art," in *Collected Essays*, 3: 83.

66. Clement Greenberg, "Cezanne: Gateway to Contemporary Painting," in *Collected Essays*, 3: 116–17.

67. Clement Greenberg, "Master Leger," in *Collected Essays*, 3: 167.

68. Clement Greenberg, "New York Painting Only Yesterday," in *Collected Essays*, 4: 22.

69. Clement Greenberg, "Review of Exhibitions of Mondrian, Kandinsky, and Pollock," in *Collected Essays*, 2: 17.

70. Clement Greenberg, "'American-Type' Painting," in *Collected Essays*, 3: 225.

71. J. M. Bernstein, "'The dead speaking of stones and stars': Adorno's *Aesthetic Theory*," in *Cambridge Companion to Critical Theory* (New York: Cambridge University Press, 2004): 139–64.

72. Clement Greenberg, "The Case for Abstract Art," in *Collected Essays*, 4: 76.

73. Brooks, *The Well Wrought Urn*, 92.

74. "The Cover," *Saturday Evening Post* 235, no. 2 (January 13, 1962): 1. The popular reception of high modernism is detailed in Leonard Diepeveen, *The Difficulties of Modernism* (New York: Routledge, 2003).

75. Clement Greenberg, "The Jackson Pollock Market Soars," in *Collected Essays*, 4: 107.

76. Aline Louchheim, "Who Buys What in the Picture Boom," *Art News* 43, no. 9 (July 1944): 12–14, 23–24.

77. Delmore Schwartz, "The Literary Dictatorship of T. S. Eliot," *Partisan Review* 16, no. 2 (February 1949): 119–37; Karl Schapiro, "The Three Hockey Games of T. S. Eliot," *Antioch Review* 22, no. 3 (Fall 1962): 284–86.

78. David Hollinger, "The Canon and Its Keepers: Modernism and Mid-Twentieth-Century American Intellectuals," in *In the American Province: Studies in the History and Historiography of Ideas* (Bloomington: Indiana University Press, 1985), 74–91.

79. Clement Greenberg, "Review of the Whitney Annual," in *Collected Essays*, 2: 117.

80. Lionel Trilling, "The Situation of the American Intellectual at the Present Time," in *The Moral Obligation to Be Intelligent*, 287, 284.

81. See Mark Krupnick, *Lionel Trilling and the Fate of Cultural Criticism* (Evanston, Ill.: Northwestern University Press, 1986), 105–7.

82. See Bradford Collins, "*Life* Magazine and the Abstract Expressionists, 1948–51: A Historiographic Study of a Late Bohemian Enterprise," *Art Bulletin* 73, no. 2 (June 1991): 283–308; and Erika Doss, *Benton, Pollock, and the Politics of Modernism: From Regionalism to Abstract Expressionism* (Chicago: University of Chicago Press, 1991).

83. Russell Davenport, "A *Life* Round Table on Modern Art," *Life* 25, no. 15 (October 11, 1948): 68.

84. Gerald Graff, *Professing Literature: An Institutional History* (Chicago: University of Chicago Press, 1987).

85. Richard Foster, "Frankly, I Like Criticism," *Antioch Review* 22, no. 3 (Fall 1962): 278. See also Irving Howe, "Modern Criticism: Privileges and Perils," in *Modern Literary Criticism: An Anthology*, ed. Irving Howe (New York: Grove Press, 1958): 1–37.

86. On the relation between the New Critics and the New York intellectuals, see Schaub, *American Fiction in the Cold War.*

87. Irving Howe, *A Margin of Hope: An Intellectual Autobiography* (New York: Harcourt, Brace, and Jovanovich, 1982), 141.

88. Lawrence H. Schwartz, *Creating Faulkner's Reputation: The Politics of Modern Literary Criticism* (Knoxville: University of Tennessee Press, 1988).

89. Philip Rahv, ed., *The Great Short Novels of Henry James* (New York: Dial Press, 1944), vii.

90. Clement Greenberg, "The State of American Writing," in *Collected Essays*, 2: 254.

91. Gail McDonald, *Learning to Be Modern* (New York: Oxford University Press, 1993), 176–210.

92. *America and the Intellectuals: A Symposium* (New York: Partisan Review, 1953), 108.

93. Lionel Trilling, *Of This Time, of That Place, and Other Stories* (New York: Harcourt, Brace, and Jovanovich, 1979); Clement Greenberg expressed a similar hesitation: "But it is a fact that there has been a certain regimentation of the avant-garde, a standardization of its attitudes, which—whether the attitude be Henry Miller's or John Crowe Ransom's—threaten to impose a new academicism on us." Clement Greenberg, "State of American Writing, 1948," in *Collected Essays*, 2: 255.

94. Dwight Macdonald, preface to *Against the American Grain* (New York: Random House, 1962), xi.

95. Dwight Macdonald, "Masscult and Midcult," in *Against the American Grain*, 56.

96. Dwight Macdonald, "Looking Backward," in *Against the American Grain*, 79.

97. Russell Lynes, "Highbrow, Lowbrow, Middlebrow," *Harper's* 198, no. 1185 (February 1949): 28.

98. "High-Brow, Low-Brow, Middle-Brow," *Life* 26, no. 15 (April 11, 1949): 113–15.

99. Willem de Kooning, "What Abstract Art Means to Me," in *The Collected Writings of Willem de Kooning*, ed. George Scrivani (New York: Hanuman Books, 1988), 57.

100. Rosenberg, "The American Action Painters," 37.

101. See Doss, *Benton, Pollock and the Politics of Modernism.*

102. Betty Pepis, "Art at Home," *New York Times* (September 25, 1955): 50–51.

103. See Serge Guilbaut, *How New York Stole the Idea of Modern Art: Abstract Expressionism, Freedom, and the Cold War*, trans. Arthur Goldhammer (Chicago: Uni-

versity of Chicago Press, 1983); and Penny Von Eschen, *Satchmo Blows Up the World: Jazz Ambassadors Play the Cold War* (Cambridge, Mass.: Harvard University Press, 2004).

104. Quoted in Eva Cockcroft, "Abstract Expressionism, Weapon of the Cold War," in Frascina, *Pollock and After*, 153.

105. Harry Levin, "What Was Modernism?" in *Refractions: Essays in Comparative Literature* (New York: Oxford University Press, 1966), 276.

106. Lionel Trilling, "On the Teaching of Modern Literature," in *The Moral Obligation to Be Intelligent*, 398.

107. Allen Ginsberg, "A Blake Experience," in *On the Poetry of Allen Ginsberg*, ed. Lewis Hyde (Ann Arbor: University of Michigan Press, 1984), 122.

108. Barry Miles, *Ginsberg: A Biography* (New York: Simon and Schuster, 1989), 103.

109. Allen Ginsberg, *Composed on the Tongue*, ed. Donald Allen (Bolinas, Calif.: Grey Fox Press, 1980), 112..

110. Allen Ginsberg, "Notes for *Howl* and Other Poems," in *The New American Poetry: 1945-1960*, ed. Donald Allen (New York: Grove Press, 1960), 415.

111. Jack Selzer, *Kenneth Burke in Greenwich Village: Conversing with the Moderns, 1915–1931* (Madison: University of Wisconsin Press, 1996), 19.

112. Kenneth Burke, *Counter-Statement* (Berkeley: University of California Press, 1931), 31.

113. Burke, *Permanence and Change*, 74.

114. Quoted in "The Western Round Table on Modern Art," 33.

115. Quoted in "The Western Round Table on Modern Art," 32.

116. Kenneth Burke, *A Grammar of Motives* (Berkeley: University of California Press, 1945), 30.

117. Kenneth Burke, *A Rhetoric of Motives* (Berkeley: University of California Press, 1969), 28.

Chapter Two. Reconsidering the Authoritarian Personality in America

1. Clement Greenberg, "New York Painting Only Yesterday," in *Art and Culture* (Boston: Beacon Press, 1961), 230.

2. David Riesman, "Some Observations on the Limits of Totalitarian Power," in *Individualism Reconsidered and Other Essays* (Glencoe, Ill.: Free Press, 1954), 414–25.

3. William Barrett, "The Evils of Egalitarianism," *Saturday Review* 37, no. 50 (December 11, 1954): 14.

4. Erich Fromm, *Escape from Freedom* (New York: Holt, Rinehart, and Winston,1941), 104. See Wilfred McClay, *The Masterless: Self and Society in Modern America* (Chapel Hill: University of North Carolina Press, 1994).

5. Fromm, *Escape from Freedom*, 105.

6. Arthur Schlesinger, Jr., *The Vital Center: The Politics of Freedom* (Boston: Houghton Mifflin, 1949), 104.

7. Daniel Bell, "The Post-Industrial Society," in *Technology and Social Change*, ed. Eli Ginzberg (New York: Columbia University Press, 1964), 44.

8. Barbara Melosh, "Manly Work: Public Art and Masculinity in Depression America," in *Gender and American History Since 1890*, ed. Barbara Melosh (New York: Routledge, 1993), 177.

9. William Whyte, *The Organization Man* (New York: Simon and Schuster, 1956), 7.

10. Theodor Adorno, "On the Fetish Character in Music and the Regression of Listening," in *The Culture Industry* (New York: Routledge, 1991), 40.

11. Theodor Adorno, *Stars Down to Earth and Other Essays on the Irrational in Culture*, ed. Stephen Look (New York: Routledge, 1994), 57.

12. Besides the 900-page tome by Adorno and his collaborators, the series also published Bruno Bettelheim and Morris Janowitz's *Dynamics of Prejudice* (1950), Nathan Ackerman and Marie Jahoda's *Anti-Semitism and Emotional Disorder* (1950), Paul Massing's *Rehearsal for Destruction* (1949), and Leo Lowenthal and Norbert Guterman's *Prophets of Deceit* (1949).

13. T. W. Adorno, Else Frenkel-Brunswik, Daniel Levinson, and R. Nevitt Sanford, *The Authoritarian Personality* (New York: Harper and Brothers, 1950), 411.

14. Nathan Glazer, "The Authoritarian Personality in Profile," *Commentary* 9, no. 6 (June 1950): 583.

15. Edward Shils, "Authoritarianism: 'Right' and 'Left'" in *Studies in the Scope and Method of "The Authoritarian Personality,"* ed. Richard Christie and Marie Jahoda (Glencoe, Ill.: Free Press, 1954), 27.

16. Adorno et al., *The Authoritarian Personality*, 772.

17. See, for instance, Richard Pells, *The Liberal Mind in a Conservative Age: American Intellectuals in the 1940s and 1950s*, 2nd edition (Middletown, Conn.: Wesleyan University Press, 1989).

18. Nancy Jachec, "Adorno, Greenberg, and Modernist Politics," *Telos* 110 (Winter 1998): 105–18.

19. Nevitt Sanford, "The Approach of *The Authoritarian Personality*," in *Psychology of Personality: Six Modern Approaches*, ed. J. C. McCary (New York: Grove Press, 1956), 292.

20. Milton Rokeach, *The Open and Closed Mind* (New York: Basic Books, 1960), 109.

21. Daniel Bell, *Marxian Socialism in the United States* (Ithaca, N.Y.: Cornell University Press, 1996), 6.

22. Examples of such studies included Philip Selznick's *The Organizational Weapon* (1952), Morris Ernst and David Loth's *Report on the American Communist* (1952), Hadley Cantril's *The Politics of Despair* (1958), and Frank Meyer's *The Moulding of Communists* (1961).

23. Paul Lazarsfeld, "Problems in Methodology," in *Sociology Today: Problems and Prospects* (New York: Basic Books, 1959), 55.

24. Gabriel Almond, *The Appeals of Communism* (Princeton, N.J.: Princeton University Press, 1954), 272.

25. Irving Howe and Lewis Coser, *The American Communist Party: A Critical History* (Boston: Beacon Press, 1962), 522.

26. Arthur Schlesinger, Jr., "Whittaker Chambers and His 'Witness,'" *Saturday Review* 35, no. 21 (May 24, 1952): 9. On Chambers and the rise of McCarthyism, see Robert Genter, "Witnessing Whittaker Chambers: Communism, McCarthyism, and the Confessional Self," *Intellectual History Review* 18, no. 2 (July 2008): 243–58.

27. Horkheimer, *Eclipse of Reason,* 141.

28. Sigmund Freud, *The Ego and the Id*, trans. Joan Riviere, rev. and ed. James Strachey (New York: W. W. Norton, 1960), 24.

29. Lionel Trilling, "The Poet as Hero: Keats in His Letters," in *The Moral Obligation to Be Intelligent*, 245.

30. Lionel Trilling, "William Dean Howells and the Roots of Modern Taste," in *The Moral Obligation to Be Intelligent*, 220.

31. Ernst Simmel, "Introduction," *Anti-Semitism: A Social Disease*, ed. Ernst Simmel (New York: International Universities Press, 1946), xxiii.

32. Lionel Trilling, "Wordsworth and the Rabbis," in *The Moral Obligation to Be Intelligent*, 195.

33. Macdonald, *The Root Is Man*, 39.

34. Freud, *The Ego and the Id*, 59.

35. Theodor Adorno, "Sociology and Psychology," *New Left Review* 46 (November-December 1967): 88.

36. Horkheimer and Adorno, *Dialectic of Enlightenment*, 192.

37. Allen Tate, "The Man of Letters in the Modern World," in *Essays of Four Decades*, intro. Louise Cowan (Wilmington, Del.: ISI Books, 1999), 3.

38. Lionel Trilling, "The Princess Casamassima," in *The Moral Obligation to Be Intelligent*, 173.

39. Trilling, "The Poet as Hero," 240.

40. Theodor Adorno, "Toward a Portrait of Thomas Mann," in *Notes to Literature*, volume 2, trans. Shierry Weber Nicholsen (New York: Columbia University Press, 1992), 19, 16.

41. Macdonald, *The Root Is Man*, 95.

42. Clement Greenberg, "Jackson Pollock: 'Inspiration, Vision, Intuitive Decision,'" in *Jackson Pollock: Interviews, Articles, and Reviews* (New York: The Museum of Modern Art, 1999),113.

43. Max Horkheimer, "The Lessons of Fascism," in *The Tensions That Cause Wars*, ed. Hadley Cantril (Urbana: University of Illinois Press, 1950), 241.

44. Russell Davenport, "A *Life* Round Table on the Pursuit of Happiness," *Life* 25, no. 2 (July 12, 1948): 108. Other influential works including Harold Lasswell's *Power and Personality* (1948), Erik Erikson's *Childhood and Society* (1950), and Abraham Maslow's

Toward a Psychology of Being (1962) similarly linked the failures in man's personality to the failures in the educational system.

45. Lionel Trilling, "Manners, Morals, and the Novel," in *The Moral Obligation to Be Intelligent*, 118.

46. Lionel Trilling, "The Sense of the Past," in *The Liberal Imagination: Essays on Literature and Society* (New York: Viking Press, 1950), 183.

47. On Adorno's concept of mimesis, see Karla Schultz, *Mimesis on the Move: Theodor W. Adorno's Concept of Imitation* (Berne: Peter Lang, 1990).

48. Theodor Adorno, "Presuppositions: On the Occasion of a Reading by Hans G. Helms," in *Notes to Literature,* 2: 97.

49. Theodor Adorno, "The Essay as Form," in *Notes to Literature*, 1: 13.

50. Adorno, "Valery's Deviations," 138.

51. John Crowe Ransom, "The Mimetic Principle," in *The New Criticism*, 197.

52. Theodor Adorno, "The Artist as Deputy," in *Notes to Literature*, 1: 107.

53. Clement Greenberg, "The Missing Link: Review of *An Essay on Man* by Ernst Cassirer," in *Collected Essays*, 2: 26.

54. Adorno, *Minima Moralia*, 18.

55. On Riesman's background, see David Riesman, "Becoming an Academic Man," in *Authors of Their Own Lives: Intellectual Autobiographies by Twenty American Sociologists*, ed. Bennett M. Berger (Berkeley: University of California Press, 1990), 22–74.

56. Letter to Hannah Arendt, June 8, 1949, Hannah Arendt Papers, Library of Congress, correspondence file, 1938–1976.

57. Letter to Hannah Arendt, June 14, 1949, Arendt Papers.

58. David Riesman, "The Path to Total Terror," *Commentary* 11, no. 4 (April 1951): 393.

59. David Riesman, "Tensions, Optimism, and the Social Scientist," *Psychiatry* 13, no. 4 (November 1950): 520.

60. Horkheimer, "The Lessons of Fascism," 230.

61. Riesman, "Some Observations on the Limits of Totalitarian Power," 423.

62. Harris Dienstfrey, "'The Lonely Crowd' at Bay," *Commentary* 33, no. 3 (March 1962): 270.

63. David Riesman and Nathan Glazer, "*The Lonely Crowd*: A Reconsideration in 1960," in *Culture and Social Character: The Work of David Riesman Reviewed*, ed. Seymour Lipset and Leo Lowenthal (Glencoe, Ill.: Free Press, 1961), 434.

64. David Barboza, "An Interview with David Riesman," *Partisan Review* 61, no. 4 (April 1994): 575.

65. Fromm, *Escape from Freedom*, 278.

66. Riesman and Glazer, "*The Lonely Crowd*: A Reconsideration in 1960," 427.

67. David Riesman with Nathan Glazer and Reuel Denney, *The Lonely Crowd: A Study of the Changing American Character*, abridged edition (New Haven, Conn.: Yale University Press, 1961), 44, 42.

68. "Freedom—New Style," *Time* 64, no. 13 (September 27, 1954): 24.

69. Dennis H. Wrong, "Riesman and the Age of Sociology: Critic of 'Groupism' and the Zeitgeist," *Commentary* 21, no. 4 (April 1956): 331–38.

70. John Aldridge, "Gray New World," *Nation* 180, no. 26 (June 25, 1955): 585.

71. Lionel Trilling, "Two Notes on David Riesman," in *A Gathering of Fugitives* (Boston: Beacon Press, 1956), 92.

72. Riesman, *The Lonely Crowd*, xxxii.

73. David Riesman, "Some Observations on Intellectual Freedom," in *Individualism Reconsidered*, 137.

74. Reuel Denney and David Riesman, "Leisure in Urbanized America," in *Reader in Urban Sociology*, ed. Paul Hatt and Albert Reiss (Glencoe, Ill.: Free Press, 1951), 474.

75. David Riesman, *Faces in the Crowd*, abridged edition (New Haven, Conn.: Yale University Press, 1965), 206.

76. Barboza, "Interview with David Riesman," 579.

77. Riesman, *Faces in the Crowd*, 12.

78. Riesman, *The Lonely Crowd*, xiv.

79. David Riesman, "Psychological Types and National Character: An Informal Commentary," *American Quarterly* 5, no. 4 (Winter 1953): 332.

80. Riesman, *The Lonely Crowd*, 259.

81. For the most thoughtful reading of Riesman to date, see Eugene Lunn, "Beyond 'Mass Culture': *The Lonely Crowd*, the Uses of Literacy, and the Postwar Era," *Theory and Society* 19, no. 1 (February 1990): 63–86.

82. David Riesman, "Listening to Popular Music," in *Individualism Reconsidered*, 184.

83. Riesman, *The Lonely Crowd*, 295.

84. *America and the Intellectuals*, 97.

85. Riesman, *Faces in the Crowd*, 585.

86. Riesman, "Psychological Types and National Character," 334.

87. Riesman, *The Lonely Crowd*, 246.

88. Riesman, "Psychological Types and National Character," 330.

89. Riesman, *Faces in the Crowd*, 11.

90. Riesman and Glazer, "*The Lonely Crowd*: A Reconsideration in 1960," 427.

Chapter Three. Psychoanalysis and the Debate over the Democratic Personality

1. Lionel Trilling, *Freud and the Crisis of Our Culture* (Boston: Beacon Press, 1955), 12.

2. Eli Zaretsky, *Secrets of the Soul: A Social and Cultural History of Psychoanalysis* (New York: Vintage Books, 2004), ch. 11.

3. Simon Jarvis, *Adorno: A Critical Introduction* (New York: Routledge, 1998), 84.

4. Norman O. Brown, *Life Against Death: The Psychoanalytical Meaning of History* (Middletown, Conn.: Wesleyan University Press, 1959), 159.

5. "The Mind: Science's Search for a Guide to Sanity," *Newsweek* 46, no. 17 (October 24, 1955): 59.

6. Geoffrey Gorer, "Are We 'By Freud Obsessed?'" *New York Times Magazine* (July 30, 1961): 5.

7. See Gerald Grob, "The Forging of Mental Health Policy in America: World War II to New Frontier," *Journal of the History of Medicine and Applied Sciences* 42, no. 4 (October 1987): 410–46; and Nathan Hale, *The Rise and Crisis of Psychoanalysis in the United States: Freud and the Americans, 1917–1985* (New York: Oxford University Press, 1995).

8. Ellen Herman, *The Romance of American Psychology: Political Culture in the Age of Experts* (Berkeley: University of California Press, 1995), 88.

9. William Menninger, *Psychiatry in a Troubled World* (New York: Macmillan, 1948), 121.

10. Roy Grinker and John Spiegel, *Men Under Stress* (Philadelphia: Blakiston, 1945), 427.

11. William Menninger, "An Analysis of Psychoanalysis," *New York Times Magazine* (May 18, 1947): 50.

12. See Jeanne Brand, "The National Mental Health Act of 1946: A Retrospect," *Bulletin of the History of Medicine* 39, no. 3 (May–June 1965): 231–45.

13. "For the Psyche," *Time* 47, no. 10 (September 2, 1946): 73; and "The Mind," *Time* 46, no. 17 (October 24, 1955): 61.

14. Marie Nyswander, "Remaking Your Ideas About Psychiatry," *Vogue* 131, no. 2 (January 15, 1958): 90–91.

15. "Talking Doctors," *Newsweek* 28, no. 21 (November 18, 1946): 70.

16. Hale, *The Rise and Crisis of Psychoanalysis*, ch. 16.

17. Franz Alexander, "Wider Fields for Freud's Techniques," *New York Times Magazine* (May 15, 1949): 53.

18. Zaretsky, *Secrets of the Soul*, ch. 11.

19. Lawrence Frank, "Freedom for the Personality," in *Society as the Patient: Essays on Culture and Personality* (New Brunswick, N.J.: Rutgers University Press, 1948), 206.

20. On the history of the culture and personality school, see Milton Singer, "A Survey of Culture and Personality Theory and Research," in *Studying Personality Cross-Culturally*, ed. Bert Kaplan (New York: Harper and Row, 1961).

21. Abram Kardiner, *The Psychological Frontiers of Society* (New York: Columbia University Press, 1945), 24–25.

22. Erich Fromm, *The Sane Society* (New York: Rinehart, 1955), 69.

23. Abraham Maslow, *Toward a Psychology of Being* (Princeton, N.J.: Van Nostrand, 1962), 157.

24. Harold Lasswell, *Psychopathology and Politics* (Chicago: University of Chicago Press, 1930), reprinted in *The Political Writings of Harold D. Lasswell* (Glencoe, Ill.: Free Press, 1951), 173.

25. On Adorno's reversal, see Joel Whitebook, "The Marriage of Marx and Freud: Critical Theory and Psychoanalysis," in *Cambridge Companion to Critical Theory*, ed. Fred Rush (Cambridge: Cambridge University Press, 2004), 74–102.

26. Adorno, "Scientific Experiences of a European Scholar in America," 367.

27. Adorno et al., *The Authoritarian Personality*, 781.

28. Sanford "The Approach of *The Authoritarian Personality*," 290.

29. Adorno et al., *The Authoritarian Personality*, 5–6.

30. See Jessica Benjamin, "Authority and the Family Revisited: or, A World without Fathers?" *New German Critique* 13 (Winter 1978): 35–57; and Joel Whitebook, *Perversion and Utopia: A Study in Psychoanalysis and Critical Theory* (Cambridge, Mass.: MIT Press, 1995).

31. Sigmund Freud, *Inhibitions, Symptoms, and Anxiety*, trans. Alix Strachey (New York: W. W. Norton, 1959), 57.

32. Max Horkheimer, "Authoritarianism and the Family Today," in *The Family: Its Function and Destiny*, ed. Ruth Nanda Ashen (New York: Harper and Brothers, 1949), 365.

33. Herbert Marcuse, "The Obsolescence of the Freudian Concept of Man," in *Five Lectures*, trans. Jeremy J. Shapiro and Shierry M. Weber (Boston: Beacon Press, 1970), 44–61.

34. Horkheimer, "Authoritarianism and the Family Today," 365.

35. Elaine Tyler May, *Homeward Bound: American Families in the Cold War Era* (New York: Basic Books, 1988).

36. See, for example, "The American Family in Trouble," *Life* 25, no. 4 (July 26, 1948): 83–99; and "The Vanishing Family," *Time* 49, no. 7 (February 17, 1947): 56.

37. Erik Erikson, "The Legend of Hitler's Childhood," in *Childhood and Society* (New York: W. W. Norton, 1963), 326–58.

38. Adorno et al., *The Authoritarian Personality*, 759.

39. Horkheimer, "Authoritarianism and the Family Today," 366.

40. Theodor Adorno, "How to Look at Television," in *The Culture Industry*, 162–63.

41. Grace Palladino, *Teenagers: An American History* (New York: Basic Books, 1996), 52.

42. Bill Davidson, "18,000,000 Teen-agers Can't Be Wrong," *Collier's* 139, no. 1 (January 4, 1957): 13–25; and Edgar Friedenberg, *The Vanishing Adolescent* (New York: Dell, 1959).

43. Dwight Macdonald, "Profiles: A Caste, a Culture, a Market —Part I," *New Yorker* 34, no. 40 (November 22, 1958): 57–94; and Dwight Macdonald, "Profiles: A Caste, a Culture, a Market —Part II," *New Yorker* 34, no. 41 (November 29, 1958): 57–107.

44. Macdonald, "Profiles—Part I," 57.

45. See, for instance, the special issue "Youth: Change and Challenge," *Daedalus: Journal of the American Academy of Arts and Sciences* 91, no. 1 (Winter 1962). On postwar intellectuals and the problem of juvenile delinquency, see James Gilbert, *A Cycle of*

Outrage: America's Reaction to the Juvenile Delinquent in the 1950s ((New York: Oxford University Press, 1986).

46. H. H. Remmers and D. H. Radler, *The American Teenager* (Indianapolis: Bobbs-Merrill, 1957), 254–55.

47. Macdonald, "Profiles—Part I," 60.

48. Adorno, "Scientific Experiences of a European Scholar in America," 362.

49. See, for instance, Else Frenkel-Brunswik, "A Study of Prejudice in Children," *Human Relations* 1, no. 3 (1948): 295–306; and Else Frenkel-Brunswik, "Patterns of Social and Cognitive Outlook in Children and Parents," *American Journal of Orthopsychiatry* 21, no. 3 (July 1951): 543–58.

50. Else Frenkel-Brunswik, "Further Explorations by a Contributor to 'The Authoritarian Personality,'" in *Studies in the Scope and Method of "The Authoritarian Personality,"* 237.

51. Adorno, "Scientific Experiences of a European Scholar in America," 364.

52. William Graebner, "The Unstable World of Benjamin Spock: Social Engineering in a Democratic Culture, 1917–1950," *Journal of American History* 67, no. 3 (December 1980): 612–29.

53. Nathan Ackerman, *The Psychodynamics of Family Life: Diagnosis and Treatment of Family Relationships* (New York: Basic Books, 1958), 343.

54. Nancy Weiss, "Mother, the Invention of Necessity: Dr. Benjamin Spock's *Baby and Child Care*," *American Quarterly* 29, no. 5 (Winter 1977): 519–46.

55. Trilling, "The Poet as Hero," 239.

56. Trilling, *Freud and the Crisis of Our Culture*, 57.

57. Adorno, *Minima Moralia*, 46.

58. "Queer People," *Newsweek* 34, no. 15 (October 10, 1949): 52. On the problem of homosexuality in the early Cold War, see John D'Emilio, *Sexual Politics, Sexual Communities: The Making of a Homosexual Minority in the United States, 1940–1970* (Chicago: University of Chicago Press, 1983); and K. A. Cuordileone, *Manhood and American Political Culture in the Cold War* (New York: Routledge, 2005).

59. "Homosexuality in America," *Life* 56, no. 26 (June 26, 1964): 66–80. On homosexuality and the psychiatric community, see Ronald Bayer, *Homosexuality and American Psychiatry: The Politics of Diagnosis* (New York: Basic Books, 1981).

60. Irving Bieber et al., *Homosexuality: A Psychoanalytic Study* (New York: Basic Books, 1962), 42.

61. Horkheimer, "Authoritarianism and the Family Today," 370.

62. Lionel Trilling, "The Kinsey Report," in *The Liberal Imagination*, 240. On Trilling and the Kinsey Report, see Robert Corber, *In the Name of National Security: Hitchcock, Homophobia, and the Political Construction of Gender in Postwar America* (Durham, N.C.: Duke University Press, 1993).

63. On the Frankfurt school and reactionary images of homosexuality, see Andrew Hewitt, *Political Inversions: Homosexuality, Fascism, and the Modernist Imaginary* (Stanford, Calif.: Stanford University Press, 1996).

64. On Freud's different etiologies of homosexuality, see Kenneth Lewes, *The Psychoanalytic Theory of Male Homosexuality* (New York: New American Library, 1988).

65. Adorno, "Sociology and Psychology," 96.

66. Horkheimer and Adorno, *Dialectic of Enlightenment*, 192.

67. Adorno, *Minima Moralia*, 46.

68. Theodor Adorno, "Freudian Theory and the Pattern of Fascist Propaganda," in *The Culture Industry*, 152.

69. Margaret Mead, "Administrative Contributions to Democratic Character Formation at the Adolescent Level," in *Personality in Nature, Society, and Culture*, ed. Clyde Kluckhohn and Henry Murray (New York: Alfred A. Knopf, 1948), 524.

70. Horkheimer, "The Lessons of Fascism," 209.

71. Horkheimer and Adorno, *Dialectic of Enlightenment*, 87. See James Livingston, *Pragmatism and the Political Economy of Cultural Revolution* (Chapel Hill: University of North Carolina Press, 1994).

72. Horkheimer, *Eclipse of Reason*, 140.

73. Horkheimer and Adorno, *Dialectic of Enlightenment*, 87.

74. See Jancovich, *Cultural Politics of the New Criticism.*

75. Twelve Southerners, *I'll Take My Stand: The South and the Agrarian Tradition* (New York: P. Smith, 1930), 175.

76. Dwight Macdonald, *Memoirs of a Revolutionist* (New York: Farrar, Straus, and Cudahy, 1957), 57. See Gregory Sumner, *Dwight Macdonald and the* Politics *Circle: The Challenge of Cosmopolitan Democracy* (Ithaca, N.Y.: Cornell University Press, 1996).

77. Dwight Macdonald, "Our Golden Age," *Politics* (June 1944): 145.

78. Edgar Friedenberg, *The Vanishing Adolescent*, 2nd ed., intro. David Riesman (New York: Dell, 1962), 8.

79. David Riesman, "Oral Tradition, Written Word, Screen Image," in *Abundance for What?* (New Brunswick, N.J.: Transaction, 1993), 439.

80. David Riesman, "Continuities, Discontinuities in Education of Women," in *Abundance for What?* 333.

81. Denney and Riesman, "Leisure in Urbanized America," 476.

82. David Riesman, "The Themes of Work and Play in the Structure of Freud's Thought," in *Individualism Reconsidered*, 311.

83. David Riesman, "The Themes of Heroism and Weakness in the Structure of Freud's Thought," in *Individualism Reconsidered*, 370.

84. David Riesman, "Two Adolescents," *Psychiatry* 14, no. 2 (May 1951): 162.

85. Riesman, "Themes of Heroism and Weakness," 368.

86. David Riesman, "Authority and Liberty in the Structure of Freud's Thought," in *Individualism Reconsidered*, 359.

87. David Riesman, "The Ethics of We Happy Few," in *Individualism Reconsidered*, 42.

88. David Riesman, "The Study of National Character," in *Abundance for What?* 592.

89. "Norman O. Brown's Body: A Conversation Between Brown and Warren G. Bennis," *Psychology Today* 4, no. 3 (August 1970): 45.

90. "Freud's Disciple," *Time* (July 15, 1966): 82.

91. Norman Brown, *Hermes the Thief: The Evolution of a Myth* (Madison: University of Wisconsin Press, 1947), 110.

92. Hesoid, *Theogony*, trans. Norman O. Brown (New York: Liberal Arts Press, 1953), 48.

93. "Norman O. Brown's Body," 43.

94. Thomas Morgan, "How Hieronymous Bosch and Norman O. Brown Would Change the World," *Esquire* 59, no. 3 (March 1963): 102.

95. "Norman O. Brown's Body," 44.

96. Brown, *Life Against Death*, xvii.

97. Norman O. Brown, "Psychoanalysis and the Classics," *Classical Journal* 52, no. 6 (March 1957): 241.

98. Brown, *Life Against Death*, 7.

99. "Norman O. Brown's Body," 45.

100. Norman O. Brown, *Love's Body* (Berkeley: University of California Press, 1966), 82.

101. "Norman O. Brown's Body," 45.

102. Norman O. Brown, "Apocalypse: The Place of Mystery in the Life of the Mind," *Harper's Magazine* 222, no. 1332 (May 1961): 47.

Chapter Four. A Question of Character

1. William S. Burroughs, *Queer* (New York: Penguin Books, 1985), 50.

2. Mills, *The Sociological Imagination*, 158.

3. Harold Martin, "They Tried to Make Our Marines Love Stalin," *Saturday Evening Post* 224, no. 8 (August 25, 1951): 106–10.

4. On the Korean brainwashing scare, see Robert Genter, "'Hypnotizzy' in the Cold War: The American Fascination with Hypnotism in the 1950s," *Journal of American Culture* 29, no. 2 (June 2006): 154–69.

5. "Washed Brains of POWs: Can They Be Rewashed?" *Newsweek* 41, no. 14 (May 4, 1953): 37.

6. Tris Coffin, "Brain Rays: Russia's Secret Weapon," *Coronet* 38, no. 2 (June 1955): 120–25.

7. Emma Harrison, "New Evils Seen in Brainwashing," *New York Times* (September 4, 1956): 27.

8. Catherine Lutz, "Epistemology of the Bunker: The Brainwashed and Other New Subjects of Permanent War," in *Inventing the Psychological: Toward a Cultural History of Emotional Life in America*, ed. Joel Pfister and Nancy Schnog (New Haven, Conn.: Yale University Press, 1997), 245–67.

9. Joost A. M. Meerloo, *The Rape of the Mind: The Psychology of Thought Control, Menticide, and Brainwashing* (Cleveland: World Publishing, 1956).

10. "Psychiatrist Aids 'Germ' Confessor," *New York Times* (March 10, 1954): 3.

11. Norman Mailer, "Quickly: A Column for Slow Readers," in *Advertisements for Myself* (Cambridge, Mass.: Harvard University Press, 1992), 303.

12. Robert Lindner, *Must You Conform?* (New York: Holt, Rinehart, and Winston, 1956), 81.

13. Annette Cox, "Playing Cowboy: The Art Criticism of Harold Rosenberg," in *Art-as-Politics: The Abstract Expressionist Avant-Garde and Society* (Ann Arbor: UMI Research Press, 1982).

14. Harold Rosenberg, "The Heroes of Marxist Science," in *Tradition of the New*, 192.

15. Norman Mailer, *The Presidential Papers* (New York: G. P. Putnam's Sons, 1963), 184.

16. William Burroughs, *Letters* to *Allen Ginsberg, 1953–1957*, ed. Ron Padgett and Anne Waldman (New York: Full Court Press, 1982), 156.

17. William S. Burroughs, *The Soft Machine* (New York: Grove Press, 1961).

18. Daniel Odier, ed., *The Job: Interviews with William S. Burroughs* (New York: Penguin Books, 1974), 38.

19. William S. Burroughs, *Nova Express* (New York: Grove Press, 1964), 73.

20. William S. Burroughs, *Naked Lunch* (New York: Grove Press, 1959), 162.

21. Jack Kerouac, *Big Sur* (New York: Penguin Books, 1962), 203.

22. Allen Ginsberg, *Journals: Early Fifties, Early Sixties*, ed. Gordon Ball (New York: Grove Press, 1978), 158.

23. Lyle Stuart, "An Intimate Interview with Norman Mailer," in *Conversations with Norman Mailer*, ed. J. Michael Lennon (Jackson: University Press of Mississippi, 1988), 22.

24. Paul Goodman, *Nature Heals: The Psychological Essays of Paul Goodman*, ed. Taylor Stoehr (New York: Free Life Editions, 1977), 85.

25. Mildred Edie Brady, "The Strange Case of Wilhelm Reich," *New Republic* 116, no. 21 (May 26, 1947): 20.

26. "Boxed In," *Newsweek* 56, no. 10 (September 5, 1960): 66.

27. Wilhelm Reich, *The Function of the Orgasm: Sex-Economic Problems of Biological Energy*, trans. Vincent R. Carfagno (New York: Farrar, Straus and Giroux, 1973), 233.

28. Wilhelm Reich, *Character Analysis*, 3rd edition, trans. Vincent R. Carfagno (New York: Farrar, Straus and Giroux, 1945), 155.

29. James Atlas, *Bellow: A Biography* (New York: Random House, 2000), 112.

30. Saul Bellow, *Seize the Day* (New York: Penguin Books, 1956).

31. Norman Mailer, "Quickly: A Column for Slow Readers," 301.

32. Norman Mailer, *An American Dream* (New York: Vintage Books, 1965), 133. On Mailer's use of Reich, see Andrew Gordon, *An American Dreamer: A Psychoanalytic Study of the Fiction of Norman Mailer* (Cranbury, N.J.: Associated University Presses, 1980).

33. Mailer, *An American Dream*, 17.

34. Harold Rosenberg, "Missing Persons," in *Tradition of the New*, 200.

35. Harold Rosenberg, "Character Change and Drama," in *Tradition of the New*, 136.

36. Brady, "The Strange Case of Wilhelm Reich," 22.

37. Reich, *Function of the Orgasm*, 383.

38. Wilhelm Reich, *The Cancer Biopathy*, volume 2, *The Discovery of the Orgone*, trans. Andrew White (New York: Farrar, Straus and Giroux, 1948).

39. Norman Mailer, "The White Negro," in *Advertisements for Myself*, 339.

40. Mary Dearborn, *Mailer: A Biography* (Boston: Houghton Mifflin, 1999), 116.

41. Miles, *Ginsberg*, 95.

42. Jack Kerouac, *On the Road* (New York: Penguin, 1955), 152.

43. William Burroughs, *The Letters of William Burroughs*, ed. Oliver Harris (New York: Viking Press, 1993), 78.

44. William S. Burroughs, *Junky*, ed. Oliver Harris (New York: Penguin Books, 2003), 3.

45. Burroughs, *Nova Express*, 156.

46. Trilling, *Freud and the Crisis of Our Culture*, 53.

47. Michael Wreszin, *A Rebel in Defense of Tradition: The Life and Politics of Dwight Macdonald* (New York: Basic Books, 1994), 195.

48. Robert Lindner, "The Instinct of Rebellion," in *Must You Conform?* 127.

49. Burke, *Permanence and Change*, 33.

50. Burke, *A Grammar of Motives*, xv.

51. Kenneth Burke, "Twelve Propositions on the Relation Between Economics and Psychology," in *Philosophy of Literary Form: Studies in Symbolic Action*, 3rd edition (Berkeley: University of California Press, 1973), 310.

52. Erving Goffman, *Asylums: Essays on the Social Situation of Mental Patients and Other Inmates* (New York: Anchor Books, 1961), xiii.

53. Yves Winkin, "Erving Goffman: What Is a Life? The Uneasy Making of an Intellectual Biography," in *Goffman and Social Organization: Studies in a Sociological Legacy*, ed. Greg Smith (New York: Routledge, 1999), 24.

54. On Goffman's background, see A. Javier Trevino, "Introduction: Erving Goffman and the Interaction Order," in *Goffman's Legacy*, ed. A. Javier Trevino (Lanham, Md.: Rowman and Littlefield, 2003), 1–49.

55. Clifford Geertz, "Blurred Genres: The Reconfiguration of Social Thought," in *Local Knowledge: Further Essays in Interpretive Analysis* (New York: Basic Books,1983), 26.

56. Erving Goffman, *The Presentation of Self in Everyday Life* (New York: Anchor Books, 1959), 244.

57. Goffman, *The Presentation of Self in Everyday Life*, xi.

58. Erving Goffman, *Encounters: Two Studies in the Sociology of Interaction* (Indianapolis: Bobbs-Merrill, 1961), 88.

59. Goffman, *The Presentation of Self in Everyday Life*, 15.

60. Goffman, *Encounters*, 120.

61. Saul Bellow, "The Writer and His Audience," *Perspectives USA* 9 (Autumn 1954): 101.

62. Goffman, *The Presentation of Self in Everyday Life*, 81.

63. Erving Goffman, "Embarrassment and Social Organization," in *Interaction Ritual: Essays on Face-to-Face Behavior* (New York: Pantheon Books, 1967), 97–112.

64. See, for instance, Jürgen Habermas, *The Theory of Communicative Action*, volume 1, trans. Thomas McCarthy (Boston: Beacon Press, 1984), 85–94.

65. Goffman, *Encounters*, 52.

66. Goffman, *The Presentation of Self in Everyday Life*, 13.

67. Erving Goffman, "The Nature of Deference and Demeanor," in *Interaction Ritual*, 73.

68. Erving Goffman, "Mental Symptoms and Public Order," in *Interaction Ritual*, 138.

69. Goffman, *Asylums*, 154.

70. Erving Goffman, *Stigma: Notes on the Management of Spoiled Identity* (New York: Simon and Schuster, 1963), 62.

71. Goffman, *Asylums*, xiii.

72. Goffman, *Encounters*, 140.

73. Goffman, *Stigma*, 105.

74. Goffman, *Encounters*, 90.

75. Goffman, *Stigma*, 106.

76. Goffman, *Asylums*, 320.

77. Goffman, *Encounters*, 151.

78. Erving Goffman, "On Face-Work," in *Interaction Ritual*, 31.

79. Jim Miller, "Democracy and the Intellectual: C. Wright Mills Reconsidered," *Salmagundi* 70–71 (Spring–Summer 1986): 83.

80. C. Wright Mills, *C. Wright Mills: Letters and Autobiographical Writings*, ed. Kathryn Mills and Pamela Mills (Berkeley: University of California Press, 2000), 262.

81. On Mills's intellectual background, see Rick Tilman, *C. Wright Mills: A Native Radical and His American Intellectual Roots* (University Park: Pennsylvania State University Press, 1984).

82. Memorandum to Margaret Nicolson, Oxford University Press, October 15, 1945, box 4B389, Charles Wright Mills Papers, 1934–1965, Barker Texas History Center, University of Texas at Austin.

83. C. Wright Mills, "The Professional Ideology of Social Pathologists," in *Power, Politics, and People: The Collected Essays of C. Wright Mills*, ed. Irving Louis Horowitz (New York: Ballantine Books, 1963), 549.

84. Mills, *The Sociological Imagination*, 161.

85. C. Wright Mills, "Review of Karen Horney's *Our Inner Conflicts*," *Briarcliff Quarterly* 3, no. 9 (April 1946): 85.

86. Hans Gerth and C. Wright Mills, *Character and Social Structure: The Psychology of Social Institutions* (New York: Harcourt, Brace and World, 1953), 5.

87. C. Wright Mills, *White Collar: The American Middle Classes* (New York: Oxford University Press, 1951), 159.

88. Gerth and Mills, *Character and Social Structure*, 14.

89. Burke, *Permanence and Change*, 33.

90. Mills, *White Collar*, xvi.

91. Mills, *The Sociological Imagination*, 17.

92. Mills, *Letters and Autobiographical Writings*, 101.

93. Dwight Macdonald, "The Mills Method," in *Discriminations: Essays and Afterthoughts, 1938–1974* (New York: Grossman, 1974), 296.

94. Mills, *Letters and Autobiographical Writings*, 161.

95. C. Wright Mills, "This Is the Answer," box 4B389, Mills Papers.

96. Mills, *Letters and Autobiographical Writings*, 248.

97. Gerth and Mills, *Character and Social Structure*, 11.

98. Mills, *Letters and Autobiographical Writings*, 222.

99. Mills, *The Sociological Imagination*, 162.

100. Gerth and Mills, *Character and Social Structure*, 160.

101. Mills, *Letters and Autobiographical Writings*, 27.

102. Mills, *The Sociological Imagination*, 161.

103. Gerth and Mills, *Character and Social Structure*, 85.

Chapter Five. Beyond Primitivism and the Fellahin

1. Quoted in Richard Rhodes, *The Making of the Atomic Bomb* (New York: Simon and Schuster, 1986), 673–74.

2. Edmund Burke, *A Philosophical Inquiry into the Origin of Our Ideas of the Sublime and Beautiful*, ed. Adam Phillips (New York: Oxford University Press, 1990), 53. See Rob Wilson, *American Sublime: The Genealogy of a Poetic Genre* (Madison: University of Wisconsin Press, 1991).

3. Burke, *Philosophical Inquiry*, 54.

4. Mailer, "The White Negro," 338.

5. Quoted in Barry Miles, *William Burroughs: El Hombre Invisible* (London: Virgin Books, 2002), 29.

6. Barnett Newman, "Response to the Reverend Thomas F. Mathews," in *Barnett Newman: Selected Writings and Interviews*, ed. John P. O'Neill (New York: Alfred A. Knopf, 1990), 287.

7. See W. Jackson Rushing, "The Impact of Nietzsche and Northwest Coast Indian Art on Barnett Newman's Idea of Redemption in the Abstract Sublime," *Art Journal* 47, no. 3 (Autumn 1988): 187–95; Jeremy Strick, *The Sublime Is Now: The Early Work of Barnett Newman* (New York: PaceWildenstein, 1994); and Jeffrey Weiss, "Science and Primitivism: A Fearful Symmetry in the Early New York School," *Arts Magazine* 57, no. 7 (March 1983): 81–87.

8. Barnett Newman, "'Frontiers of Space': Interview with Dorothy Gees Seckler," in *Selected Writings*, 249.

9. Mark Rothko, *The Artist's Reality: Philosophies of Art*, ed. Christopher Rothko (New Haven, Conn.: Yale University Press, 2004), 8. See Stephen Polcari, "The Intellectual Roots of Abstract Expressionism: Mark Rothko," *Arts* 54, no. 1 (September 1979): 124–34; and Weiss, "Science and Primitivism."

10. Barnett Newman, "Interview with Lane Slate," in *Selected Writings*, 251. Later in life, Newman wrote the foreword to the published memoirs of Russian anarchist Peter Kropotkin, declaring Kropotkin's defense of personal freedom as one of the most powerful arguments "against the State, the police, central authority, and organization." See Barnett Newman, "'The True Revolution Is Anarchist!'" in *Selected Writings*, 45.

11. Clyfford Still, "Statement 1959," in *Theories of Modern Art*, ed. Herschel B. Chipp (Berkeley: University of California Press, 1970), 575. On abstract expressionism and anarchism, see David Craven, *Abstract Expressionism as Cultural Critique* (New York: Cambridge University Press, 1999).

12. Quoted in *Mark Rothko* (London: Tate Gallery, 1987), 81. On Rothko and mythology, see Dore Ashton, *About Rothko* (New York: Oxford University Press, 1983).

13. Quoted in *Mark Rothko*, 80.

14. Barnett Newman, "Art of the South Seas," in *Selected Writings*, 100.

15. James Baldwin, "The New Lost Generation," in *The Price of the Ticket: Collected Nonfiction, 1948–1985* (New York: St. Martin's Press, 1985), 306.

16. Barnett Newman, "The First Man Was an Artist," in *Selected Writings*, 157.

17. Thomas Weiskel, *The Romantic Sublime: Studies in the Structure and Psychology of Transcendence* (Baltimore: Johns Hopkins University Press, 1976), 98.

18. Reich, *Function of the Orgasm*, 230.

19. On romantic modernism and primitivism, see Kirk Varnedoe, "Abstract Expressionism," in *"Primitivism" in 20th-Century Art*, ed. William Rubin (New York: Museum of Modern Art, 1984), 615–59; and Robert Carleton Hobbs, "Early Abstract Expressionism: A Concern with the Unknown Within," in *Abstract Expressionism: The Formative Years*, ed. Robert Carleton Hobbs and Gail Levin (New York: Whitney Museum of American Art, 1978), 8–26.

20. W. Jackson Rushing, "Ritual and Myth: Native American Culture and Abstract Expressionism," in *The Spiritual in Art: Abstract Painting, 1890–1985* (New York: Abbeville Press, 1986), 275.

21. Barnett Newman, "Northwest Coast Indian Painting," in *Selected Writings*, 106.

22. See Rushing, "The Impact of Nietzsche and Northwest Coast Indian Art," 189.

23. Barnett Newman, "The Plasmic Image," in *Selected Writings*, 144–45.

24. Robert Rosenblum, "Notes on Rothko's Surrealist Years," in *Mark Rothko* (New York: Pace Gallery, 1981), 8.

25. Rushing, "Ritual and Myth," 285.

26. Elizabeth Langhorne, "Pollock, Picasso, and the Primitive," *Art History* 12, no. 1 (March 1989): 64–92.

27. Homi Bhabha, "The Other Question," in *The Location of Culture* (New York: Routledge, 1994), 94–120.

28. Polcari, "The Intellectual Roots of Abstract Expressionism."

29. Quoted in *Mark Rothko*, 78.

30. Diane Waldman, "Mark Rothko: The Farther Shore of Art," in *Mark Rothko, 1903–1970: A Retrospective* (New York: Harry N. Abrams,1978), 17–70.

31. Philip Wylie, *Generation of Vipers* (New York: Dalkay Archive Press, 1996), 8, 98.

32. Philip Wylie, *An Essay on Morals* (New York: Rinehart, 1947), 100.

33. Carl Jung, *The Basic Writings of C. G. Jung*, ed. Violet S. de Laszlo (Princeton, N.J.: Princeton University Press, 1990), 301.

34. Quoted in Irving Sandler, *The Triumph of American Painting: A History of Abstract Expressionism* (New York: Praeger, 1970), 65.

35. On Pollock and Jungian therapy, see Jeremy Lewison, *Interpreting Pollock* (London: Tate Gallery, 1999), 3–30.

36. Selden Rodman, *Conversations with Artists* (New York: Devin-Adair, 1957), 82.

37. B. H. Friedman, *Jackson Pollock: Energy Made Visible* (New York: Da Capo Press, 1995), 183.

38. John Graham, *System and Dialectics of Art* (New York: Delphic Studios, 1937), 15.

39. Quoted in Judith Wolfe, "Jungian Aspects of Jackson Pollock's Imagery," *Artforum* 11, no. 3 (November 1972): 67.

40. Newman, "The First Man Was an Artist," 159.

41. Quoted in Patricia Still, "Clyfford Still: Biography," in *Clyfford Still*, ed. Thomas Kellein (Munich: Prestel-Verlag, 1992), 147.

42. Stephen Polcari, *Abstract Expressionism and the Modern Experience* (Cambridge: Cambridge University Press, 1991), 378. See also David Anfram, "Clyfford Still's Art: Between the Quick and the Dead," in *Clyfford Still: Paintings, 1944–1960*, ed. James T. Demetrion (New Haven, Conn.: Yale University Press, 2001), 17–46.

43. Polcari, *Abstract Expressionism and the Modern Experience*, 95.

44. Other artists followed the lead of Still and equated the artistic act and shamanism. As art historian Elizabeth Langhorne has detailed, Jackson Pollock appropriated Native American myths, traditions, masks, and symbols not merely to express an affinity with non-Western cultures but to present his paintings as a parallel form of shamanistic self-discovery, a claim he reiterated to friends and family members throughout the 1940s. See Langhorne, "Pollock, Picasso, and the Primitive," 78.

45. Mailer, *An American Dream*, 7.

46. Mailer, "The White Negro," 363.

47. Barnett Newman, "Pre-Columbian Stone Sculpture," in *Selected Writings*, 61.

48. Quoted in Dennis McNally, *Desolate Angel: Jack Kerouac, the Beat Generation, and America* (Cambridge, Mass.: Da Capo Press, 2003), 77.

49. Oswald Spengler, *The Decline of the West* (New York: Alfred A. Knopf, 1937), 105, 169, 170.

50. Kerouac, *On the Road*, 277.

51. On surrogacy and American identity, see Carroll Smith-Rosenberg, "Surrogate Americans: Masculinity, Masquerade, and the Formation of a National Identity," *PMLA* 119, no. 5 (2004): 1325–35.

52. Gerald Nicosia, *Memory Babe: A Critical Biography of Jack Kerouac* (New York: Grove Press, 1983), 22.

53. Jack Kerouac, *Satori in Paris and Pic* (New York: Grove Press, 1985), 52.

54. See David Leeming, *James Baldwin: A Biography* (New York: Henry Holt, 1994), 38–41.

55. Baldwin, "The New Lost Generation," 308.

56. James Baldwin, "Notes for a Hypothetical Novel," in *The Price of the Ticket*, 243.

57. Baldwin, "The New Lost Generation," 308.

58. James Baldwin, "The Black Boy Looks at the White Boy," in *The Price of the Ticket*, 298.

59. James Baldwin, "A Question of Identity," in *The Price of the Ticket*, 98.

60. Mailer, "The White Negro," 340.

61. Baldwin, "The Black Boy Looks at the White Boy," 296.

62. James Baldwin, "Many Thousands Gone," in *The Price of the Ticket*, 66.

63. Studs Terkel, "An Interview with James Baldwin," in *Conversations with James Baldwin*, ed. Fred Standley and Louis Pratt (Jackson: University Press of Mississippi, 1989), 6.

64. James Baldwin, "Stranger in the Village," in *The Price of the Ticket*, 81.

65. James Baldwin, "In Search of a Majority," in *The Price of the Ticket*, 233.

66. James Baldwin, *Another Country* (New York: Vintage Books,1962), 42.

67. James Baldwin, "Encounter on the Seine: Black Meets Brown," in *The Price of the Ticket*, 36.

68. James Baldwin, "Mass Culture and the Creative Artist: Some Personal Notes," in *Culture for the Millions? Mass Media in Modern Society*, ed. Norman Jacobs (Princeton, N.J.: D. Van Nostrand, 1961), 121.

69. Baldwin, *Another Country*, 212.

70. James Baldwin, "The Fire Next Time," in *The Price of the Ticket*, 368.

71. Erich Fromm, *The Art of Loving* (New York: HarperCollins, 1956), 112.

72. Baldwin, "The Fire Next Time," 375.

73. Baldwin, "Notes for a Hypothetical Novel," 237.

74. Baldwin, *Another Country*, 296.

75. Terkel, "An Interview with James Baldwin," 21.

76. James Baldwin, "White Man's Guilt," in *The Price of the Ticket*, 410.

77. James Baldwin, "The Creative Process," in *The Price of the Ticket*, 317.

78. Baldwin, *Another Country*, 86.

79. James Baldwin, "East River, Downtown," in *The Price of the Ticket*, 264.

Chapter Six. Masculinity, Spontaneity, and the Act

1. Jasper Johns, *Jasper Johns: Writings, Sketchbook Notes, Interviews*, ed. Kirk Varnedoe (New York: Museum of Modern Art, 1996), 157. See also Rosalind Krauss, "Jasper Johns," *Lugano Review* 1, no. 2 (1965): 84–98.

2. Johns, *Writings, Sketchbook Notes,* 287.

3. Arthur Schlesinger, Jr., "The Crisis of American Masculinity," in *The Politics of Hope* (Boston: Houghton Mifflin, 1963), 242.

4. Cuordileone, *Manhood and American Political Culture in the Cold War.*

5. Schlesinger, *The Vital Center*, 40.

6. Betty Hoffman, "Masculinity: What Is It?" *American Mercury* 80, no. 1 (January 1963): 96, 123–24; Judson and Mary Landis, "The U.S. Male . . . Is He First-Class?" *Collier's* 130, no. 3 (July 19, 1952): 22–24; Elizabeth Dunn, "What Is a Man?" *Reader's Digest* 52, no. 314 (June 1948): 64–66; J. Robert Moskin, "The American Male: Why Do Women Dominate Him?" *Look* 22, no. 3 (February 4, 1958): 76-80;George B. Leonard, Jr., "The American Male: Why Is He Afraid to Be Different?" *Look* 22, no. 4 (February 18, 1958): 95–104; and William Attwood, "The American Male: Why Does He Work So Hard?" *Look* 22, no. 5 (March 4, 1958): 71–75.

7. Leonard, "The American Male," 98.

8. Richard Smith, "The Executive Crack-Up," *Fortune* 51, no. 5 (May 1955): 108–11, 172–79.

9. Russell Chappell, "Today's Jobs: The Killing Pace," *Newsweek* 47, no. 22 (May 28, 1956): 81–84; Maxine Davis, "How to Keep Your Husband Alive," *Look* 22, no. 17 (August 19, 1958): 35–36; "Measure of Neglect," *Time* 67, no. 16 (April 16, 1956): 80; and Raymond Schuessler, "Anatomy of Executive Health," *American Mercury* 89, no. 429 (October 1959): 43–45.

10. John Lagemann, "What's Eating Middle-Aged Men?" *Coronet* 41, no. 5 (March 1957): 73–77.

11. Grace Mayes, "The American Male Is Okay, But—," *New York Times Magazine* (May 12, 1946): 18.

12. Elaine Tyler May, *Homeward Bound: American Families in the Cold War Era* (New York: Basic Books, 1988).

13. Dorothy Barclay, "The Family—Center of Attention," *New York Times Magazine* (September 14, 1952): 48.

14. Edith Stern, "The Miserable Male," *American Mercury* 67, no. 299 (November 1948): 538.

15. John Sisk, "Enter the Man's Man," *Commonweal* 69, no. 12 (December 19, 1958): 311.

16. Schlesinger, "The Crisis of American Masculinity," 245.

17. Michael Kimmel, *Manhood in America: A Cultural History* (New York: Free Press, 1996).

18. Peter Biskind, *Seeing Is Believing: How Hollywood Taught Us to Stop Worrying and Love the Fifties* (New York: Pantheon Books, 1983).

19. Alfred Kinsey, Wardell Pomeroy, and Clyde Martin, *Sexual Behavior in the Human Male* (Philadelphia: W. B. Saunders, 1948), 235–38.

20. Albert Ellis, *Sex Without Guilt* (New York: Lyle Stuart, 1958), 134.

21. Morris Ernst and David Loth, *American Sexual Behavior and the Kinsey Report* (New York: Greystone Press, 1948), vii.

22. Pitirim Sorokin, *The American Sex Revolution* (Boston: Porter Sargent, 1956), 17.

23. Stern, "The Miserable Male," 538.

24. Quoted in "The Playboy Panel: The Womanization of America," *Playboy* 9, no. 6 (June 1962): 47.

25. Wylie, *Generation of Vipers*, 80–81.

26. Lindner, *Must You Conform?* 39.

27. Irving Howe, *Politics and the Novel* (New York: Horizon Books, 1957), 239.

28. Hugh Hefner, "The Playboy Philosophy," *Playboy* 10, no. 7 (July 1963): 45.

29. Kerouac, *On the Road*, 4.

30. Quoted in Tom Clark, *Jack Kerouac* (San Diego: Harcourt, Brace, Jovanovich, 1984), 126.

31. Atlas, *Bellow*, 164.

32. Lennon, *Conversations with Norman Mailer*, 41.

33. Reich, *The Function of the Orgasm*, 96.

34. Paul Goodman, "Sex and Revolution," in *Nature Heals*, 71.

35. Paul Goodman, "Great Pioneer But No Libertarian," in *Nature Heals*, 83.

36. Paul Goodman, "The Political Meaning Behind Some Recent Revisions of Freud," in *Nature Heals*, 55.

37. Lennon, *Conversations with Norman Mailer*, 191.

38. Mailer, "The White Negro," 347.

39. Norman Mailer, "The Man Who Studied Yoga," in *Advertisements for Myself*, 177.

40. Wilhelm Reich, *The Mass Psychology of Fascism*, 3rd edition, trans. Theodore Wolfe (New York: Orgone Institute Press, 1946), viii.

41. Harold Rosenberg, "Art and Work," in *Discovering the Present: Three Decades in Art, Culture, and Politics* (Chicago: University of Chicago Press, 1973): 65–67. See Sylvia Harrison, *Pop Art and the Origins of Post-Modernism* (Cambridge: Cambridge University Press, 2001), 68–95.

42. Harold Rosenberg, "The Herd of Independent Minds," in *Discovering the Present*, 16.

43. Rosenberg, "Art and Work," 67.

44. Daniel Belgrad, *The Culture of Spontaneity: Improvisation and the Arts in Postwar America* (Chicago: University of Chicago Press, 1998).

45. Meyer Schapiro, "Recent Abstract Painting," in *Modern Art, 19th and 20th Centuries: Selected Papers* (New York: George Braziller, 1978), 218.

46. Jack Kerouac, "Essentials of Spontaneous Prose," in *Good Blonde and Others*, ed. Donald Allen (San Francisco: Grey Fox Press, 1993), 70–71.

47. Clyfford Still, *Clyfford Still* (San Francisco: San Francisco Museum of Modern Art, 1976), 119.

48. "The Champ," *Time* 72, no. 24 (December 15, 1958): 58. On Pollock's masculine identity, see Amelia Jones, *Body Art / Performing the Subject* (Minneapolis: University of Minnesota Press, 1998); and Caroline Jones, *Machine in the Studio: Constructing the Postwar American Artist* (Chicago: University of Chicago Press, 1996).

49. "Baffling U.S. Art: What Is It About?" *Life* 47, no. 19 (November 9, 1959): 79; "Posh Pollock," *Time* 72, no. 24 (December 15, 1958): 58.

50. Quoted in Steven Naifeh and Gregory White Smith, *Jackson Pollock: An American Saga* (New York: Clarkson N. Potter, 1989), 541.

51. Jackson Pollock, "Interview with William Wright," in Karmel, *Jackson Pollock: Interviews, Articles, and Reviews*, 20–23.

52. James Coddington, "No Chaos Damn It," in *Jackson Pollock: New Approaches*, ed. Kirk Varnedoe and Pepe Karmel (New York: Museum of Modern Art, 1999), 103.

53. Jackson Pollock, "My Painting," 18. See Carol Mancusi-Ungaro, "Jackson Pollock: Response as Dialogue," in Varnedoe and Karmel, *Jackson Pollock: New Approaches*, 148–49.

54. Riesman, *Faces in the Crowd*, 621.

55. David Riesman, "An American Crisis," in *Abundance for What?*, 40.

56. Ralph Ellison to Albert Murray, September 28, 1958, in Murray and Callahan, *Trading Twelves: The Selected Letters of Ralph Ellison and Albert Murray*, 197.

57. C. Wright Mills and Patricia J. Slater, "The Barricade and the Bedroom," in *Nature Heals*, 63.

58. C. Wright Mills, "The Person," box 4B338, folder entitled "The Person," Mills Papers.

59. James H. East, ed., *The Humane Particulars: The Collected Letters of William Carlos Williams and Kenneth Burke* (Columbia: University of South Carolina Press, 2003), 104.

60. Burke, *A Grammar of Motives*, 15, 85.

61. Quoted in Andrew Decker, "Still Waiting," *Artnews* 94, no. 2 (February 1995): 115.

62. Still, *Clyfford Still*, 119.

63. Naifeh and Smith, *Jackson Pollock*, 651.

64. Jeffrey Potter, *To a Violent Grave: An Oral Biography of Jackson Pollock* (New York: G. P. Putnam, 1985), 130.

65. On the ambiguities of the male orgasm as a form of representation, see Linda Williams, *Hardcore: Power, Pleasure, and the "Frenzy of the Visible"* (Berkeley: University of California Press, 1989), 93–119.

66. Potter, *To a Violent Grave*, 187.

67. Quoted in Naifeh and Smith, *Jackson Pollock*, 467

68. The quote is from Fredric Taubes's *The Technique of Oil Painting*, a book in Pol-

lock's private collection. See Mancusi-Ungaro, "Jackson Pollock: Response as Dialogue," 146.

69. Clement Greenberg, "Review of the Exhibitions of Joan Miro, Fernand Leger, and Wassily Kandinsky," in *Collected Essays*, 1: 65.

70. Hal Foster, "The Expressive Fallacy," in *Recodings: Art, Spectacle, Cultural Politics* (Seattle: Bay Press, 1985): 59–73.

71. Barbara Rose, "Jackson Pollock at Work: An Interview with Lee Krasner," in Karmel, *Jackson Pollock: Interviews, Articles, and Reviews*, 41.

72. Quoted in Naifeh and Smith, *Jackson Pollock*, 539.

73. See Tania Modleski, *Feminism Without Women* (New York: Routledge, Chapman, and Hall, 1991), 90–111.

74. Jones, *Body Art*, 72.

75. Rosenberg, "The American Action Painters," 35.

76. Harold Rosenberg, *Barnett Newman* (New York: Harry N. Abrams, 1978), 70–71.

77. Barnett Newman, "The Plasmic Image," in *Selected Writings*, 145

78. Jonathan Fineberg, *Art Since 1940: Strategies of Being* (New York: Harry N. Abrams, 2000), 101.

79. Newman, "The Plasmic Image," 140.

80. Mailer, *The Presidential Papers*, 144.

81. Mailer, "The White Negro," 351.

82. Norman Mailer, "A Public Notice on Waiting for Godot," in *Advertisements for Myself*, 324.

83. Richard Stern and Robert Lucid, "Hip, Hell, and the Navigator," in Lennon, *Conversations with Norman Mailer*, 38.

84. Burroughs, *Naked Lunch*, 8.

85. Conrad Knickerbocker, "White Junk," in *Burroughs Live: The Collected Interviews of William S. Burroughs, 1960–1997*, ed. Slyvere Lotringer (Los Angeles: Semiotext(e), 2001), 80.

86. Burroughs, *Naked Lunch*, 200–203.

87. Barnett Newman, "The Sublime Is Now," in *Selected Writings*, 173. See John Golding, *Paths to the Absolute: Mondrian, Malevich, Kandinsky, Pollock, Newman, Rothko, and Still* (Princeton, N.J.: Princeton University Press, 2000).

88. Potter, *To a Violent Grave*, 154.

89. Quoted in Demetrion, *Clyfford Still: Paintings, 1944–1960*, 165.

90. Wylie, *An Essay on Morals*, 185.

91. Burke, *A Grammar of Motives*, 66.

92. Burke, *A Rhetoric of Motives*, 37.

93. Kenneth Burke, "George Herbert Mead," in *Philosophy of Literary Form*, 379.

94. Burke, *A Grammar of Motives*, 65.

95. MacAgy, "Western Round Table on Modern Art," 34.

96. Burke, "George Herbert Mead," 380.

97. Quoted in "The Western Round Table on Modern Art," 34.

98. Johns, *Writings, Sketchbook Notes,* 105.

99. "The Younger," *Newsweek* 66, no. 8 (February 24, 1964): 82.

100. Johns, *Writings, Sketchbook Notes,* 184.

101. Moira Roth, "The Aesthetics of Indifference," *Artforum* 16, no. 3 (November 1997): 50.

102. Johns, *Writings, Sketchbook Notes,* 59.

103. See John Yau, *The United States of Jasper Johns* (Cambridge, Mass.: Zoland Books, 1996).

104. Johns, *Writings, Sketchbook Notes,* 172.

105. Clement Greenberg, "After Abstract Expressionism," in *Collected Essays,* 4: 127.

106. Deborah Solomon, "The Unflagging Artistry of Jasper Johns," *New York Times Magazine* (June 19, 1988): 64.

107. Johns, *Writing, Sketchbook Notes,* 20.

108. Freud, *The Ego and the Id,* 20. See Kaja Silverman, *The Threshold of the Visible World* (New York: Routledge, 1996); and Elizabeth Grosz, *Volatile Bodies: Toward a Corporeal Feminism* (Bloomington: Indiana University Press, 1994).

109. Freud, *The Ego and the Id,* 20.

110. Johns, *Writings, Sketchbook Notes,* 56.

111. Joan Carpenter, "The Infra-Iconography of Jasper Johns," *Art Journal* 36, no. 3 (Spring 1977): 221–27.

112. Paul Taylor, "Jasper Johns," *Interview* 20, no. 7 (July 1990): 100.

113. Jill Johnston, *Jasper Johns: Privileged Information* (New York: Thames and Hudson, 1996), ch. 2.

114. Johns, *Writings, Sketchbook Notes,* 254.

115. Ludwig Wittgenstein, *Philosophical Investigations,* trans. G. E. M. Anscombe (Englewood Cliffs, N.J.: Prentice Hall, 1958), 85.

116. Johns, *Writings, Sketchbook Notes,* 113.

117. Wittgenstein, *Philosophical Investigations,* 48.

118. Johns, *Writings, Sketchbook Notes,* 89.

Chapter Seven. Rethinking the Feminine Within

1. Jack Kerouac, *Jack Kerouac: Selected Letters, 1940–1956,* ed. Ann Charters (New York: Penguin Books, 1995), 495.

2. Jack Kerouac, "cityCityCITY," in *Good Blonde and Others,* 194.

3. Kerouac, *Selected Letters,* 495.

4. Burroughs, *Nova Express,* 97.

5. James Baldwin, "The Preservation of Innocence," in *James Baldwin: Collected Essays,* ed. Toni Morrison (New York: Literary Classics of the United States, 1998), 596.

6. Philip Wylie, "The Womanization of America," *Playboy* 5, no. 9 (September 1958): 51–52, 77–79.

7. Joanne Meyerowitz, ed., *Not June Cleaver: Women and Gender in Postwar America, 1945–1960* (Philadelphia: Temple University Press, 1994).

8. *American Women*, Report of the President's Commission on the Status of Women (Washington, D.C.: U.S. Government Printing Office, 1963).

9. Helen Colton, "I Am a Selfish Mother," *Reader's Digest* 55, no. 33 (December 1949): 13–15; and Louise Rich, "I Can't Find My Apron Strings," *Reader's Digest* 71, no. 426 (October 1957): 51–53.

10. Dorothy Sue Cobble, "Recapturing Working-Class Feminism: Union Women in the Postwar Era," in Meyerowitz, *Not June Cleaver*, 57–83; and Nancy Gabin, *Feminism in the Labor Movement: Women and the United Auto Workers, 1935–1975* (Ithaca, N.Y.: Cornell University Press, 1990).

11. Daniel Horowitz, *Betty Friedan and the Making of the Feminine Mystique: The American Left, the Cold War, and Modern Feminism* (Amherst: University of Massachusetts Press, 1998); and Susan Lynn, "Gender and Progressive Politics: A Bridge to the Social Activism of the 1960s," in Meyerowitz, *Not June Cleaver*, 103–27.

12. John Willig, "Lament for the Male Sanctuary," *New York Times Magazine* (March 10, 1957): 19, 72–73.

13. Poppy Cannon, "It's a Man's World . . . Maybe,"*Reader's Digest* 50, no. 299 (March 1947): 4.

14. William Whyte, "The Wife Problem," *Life* 32, no. 1 (January 7, 1952): 32–48.

15. Moskin, "The American Male," 78.

16. Schlesinger, "The Crisis of American Masculinity," 237.

17. Ferdinand Lundberg and Marynia Farnham, *Modern Woman: The Lost Sex* (New York: Grosset and Dunlap, 1947), 235.

18. Helene Deutsch, *The Psychology of Women* (New York: Grune and Stratton, 1945), 289.

19. "Playboy Panel," 44.

20. Norman Mailer, *Deaths for the Ladies* (New York: Putnam Books, 1962), 44.

21. Jack Kerouac, *The Subterraneans* (New York: Grove Press, 1958), 76.

22. See Ann Gibson, *Abstract Expressionism: Other Politics* (New Haven, Conn.: Yale University Press, 1997).

23. Burroughs, *Letters of William S. Burroughs*, 79.

24. Burroughs, *Naked Lunch*, 75.

25. On the Orestes complex and modern culture, see Alice Jardine, *Gynesis: Configurations of Woman and Modernity* (Ithaca, N.Y.: Cornell University Press, 1985); Frederic Wertham, *Dark Legend* (Garden City, N.Y.: Doubleday, 1941); and Frederic Wertham, "The Matricidal Impulse: Critique of Freud's Interpretation of *Hamlet*," *Journal of Criminal Psychopathology* 2 (1941): 455–64.

26. Wylie, *Generation of Vipers*, 209.

27. Jung, *Basic Writings*, 323.

28. Wylie, *Essay on Morals*, xiv.

29. Wylie, *Generation of Vipers*, 123.

30. See Mari Jo Buhle, *Feminism and Its Discontents: A Century of Struggle with Psychoanalysis* (Cambridge, Mass.: Harvard University Press, 1998); and Michael Rogin, *Ronald Reagan, the Movie and Other Episodes in Political Demonology* (Berkeley: University of California Press, 1987).

31. See, for instance, June Bingham, "Can You Love a Child Too Much?" *Woman's Home Companion* 77, no. 7 (July 1950): 76–77; Herman Bundeson, "The Overprotective Mother," *Ladies Home Journal* 67, no. 3 (March 1950): 243–44; Geoffrey Gorer, "The American Character," *Life* 23, no. 7 (August 18, 1947): 94–112; and Amram Scheinfeld, "Are American Moms a Menace?" *Ladies Home Journal* 67, no. 11 (November 1945): 36, 138.

32. Edmund Bergler, *Neurotic Counterfeit-Sex* (New York: Grune and Stratton, 1951), 46.

33. Edmund Bergler, *Homosexuality: Disease or Way of Life?* (New York: Hill and Wang, 1956), 113.

34. "Playboy Panel," 45.

35. Robert Coughlan, "Changing Roles in Modern Marriage," *Life* 41, no. 26 (December 24, 1956): 109.

36. Burroughs, *The Soft Machine*, 105.

37. Burroughs, *Naked Lunch*, 149.

38. Potter, *To a Violent Grave*, 67, 203.

39. See David Freke, "Jackson Pollock: A Symbolic Self-Portrait," *Studio International* 184, no. 950 (December 1972): 217–21.

40. Potter, *To a Violent Grave*, 69.

41. Michael Leja, *Reframing Abstract Expressionism* (New Haven, Conn.: Yale University Press, 1993), 147–74. See also Judith Wolfe, "Jungian Aspects of Jackson Pollock's Imagery," *Artforum* 11, no. 3 (November 1972): 65–73.

42. Leja, *Reframing Abstract Expressionism*, 258.

43. Mailer, *An American Dream*, 7.

44. Andreas Huyssen, "Mass Culture as Woman: Modernism's Other," in *After the Great Divide: Modernism, Mass Culture, Postmodernism* (Bloomington: Indiana University Press, 1986), ch. 3.

45. Potter, *To a Violent Grave*, 214.

46. Mailer, *An American Dream*, 4.

47. Jardine, *Gynesis*, 230.

48. See Nicosia, *Memory Babe*.

49. Jack Kerouac, "What Am I Thinking About?" in *Good Blonde and Others*, 181.

50. Kerouac, *On the Road*, 7.

51. Jack Kerouac, "The Origins of the Beat Generation," in *The Good Blonde and Others*, 57.

52. Kerouac, *On the Road*, 132.

53. David Savran, *Taking It like a Man: White Masculinity, Masochism, and Contemporary American Culture* (Princeton, N.J.: Princeton University Press, 1998).

54. "Playboy Panel," 139.

55. Willem de Kooning, "Content Is a Glimpse," in *Collected Writings*, 77.

56. On the history of de Kooning's *Woman* series, see E. A. Carmean, Jr., "Willem de Kooning: The Women," in *American Art at Mid-Century: The Subjects of the Artist*, ed. E. A. Carmean, Jr., and Eliza Rathbone (Washington, D.C.: National Gallery of Art, 1978): 157–182.

57. Quoted in Mark Stevens and Annalyn Swan, *De Kooning: An American Master* (New York: Alfred A. Knopf, 2004), 314.

58. De Kooning, "Content Is a Glimpse," 82–83.

59. Quoted in Stevens and Swan, *De Kooning*, 338.

60. Quoted in Harold Rosenberg, *Willem de Kooning* (New York: Harry N. Abrams, 1968), 49.

61. Quoted in Curtis Bill Pepper, "The Indomitable De Kooning," *New York Times Magazine* (November 20, 1983): 70.

62. Quoted in Marla Prather, *Willem de Kooning: Paintings* (New Haven, Conn.: Yale University Press, 1994), 132.

63. Hubert Crehan, "Woman Trouble," *Art Digest* 27, no. 14 (April 15, 1953): 5; Alexander Eliot, "Under the Four Winds," *Time* 68, no. 26 (June 28, 1954): 77.

64. Rosenberg, *Willem de Kooning*, 20.

65. "Artists' Sessions at Studio 35" in *Modern Artists in America*, ed. Robert Motherwell and Ad Reinhardt (New York: Wittenborn Schultz, 1951), 12.

66. Willem De Kooning, "Film Script," in *Collected Writings*, 174.

67. Quoted in Selden Rodman, *Conversations with Artists* (New York: Devin-Adair, 1957), 102.

68. *Women: A Collaboration of Artists and Writers* (New York: Samuel N. Kootz Editions, 1948), n.p.

69. Norman Mailer, "Some Children of the Goddess," *Cannibals and Christians* (New York: Dial Press, 1966), 104.

70. Mailer, "The White Negro," 351.

71. "Playboy Panel," 142.

72. Keroauc, "Essentials of Spontaneous Prose," 69.

73. Hilton Kramer, "Month in Review," *Arts* 33, no. 5 (February 1959): 49.

74. Jasper Johns, "Collage," *Arts* 33, no. 6 (March 1959): 3.

75. "His Heart Belongs to Dada," *Time* 73, no. 18 (May 4, 1959): 58.

76. Paul Taylor, "Robert Rauschenberg: 'I Can't Even Afford My Works Anymore,'" *Interview* 20, no. 12 (December 1990): 147.

77. Johns, *Writings, Sketchbook Notes*, 50.

78. Karen Horney, *Feminine Psychology* (New York: W. W. Norton, 1967), 133–46.

79. Sigmund Freud, *Civilization and Its Discontents*, ed. James Strachey (New York: W. W. Norton, 1961), 21.

80. Johns, *Writings, Sketchbook Notes*, 59

81. Quoted in Michael Warner, "Homo-Narcissism; or, Heterosexuality," in *Engendering Men: The Question of Male Feminist Criticism*, ed. Joseph Boone and Michael Kadden (New York: Routledge, 1990), 204.

82. Horney, *Feminine Psychology*, 135.

83. James Baldwin, "Nothing Personal," in *The Price of the Ticket*, 391.

84. James Baldwin, "The Male Prison," in *The Price of the Ticket*, 102.

85. William Spurlin, "Culture, Rhetoric, and Queer Identity: James Baldwin and the Identity Politics of Race and Sexuality," in *James Baldwin Now*, ed. Dwight McBride (New York: New York University Press, 1999), 105.

86. Robert Kirsch, "Herd of Aloners in Novels Chided," *Los Angeles Times* (October 11, 1959): E7.

87. Baldwin, "The Black Boy Looks at the White Boy," 290.

88. Baldwin, "The Male Prison," 102.

89. See Leeming, *James Baldwin*, 44–45.

90. James Baldwin, "Here Be Dragons," in *The Price of the Ticket*, 688.

91. W. J. Weatherby, *James Baldwin: Artist on Fire* (New York: Dell, 1989), 119.

92. James Baldwin, *Giovanni's Room* (New York: Dell, 1956), 21.

93. On Freud and sexuality, see Jessica Benjamin, *Like Subjects, Love Objects: Essays on Recognition and Sexual Difference* (New Haven, Conn.: Yale University Press, 1995), 49–79.

94. Baldwin, "The New Lost Generation," 313.

95. Baldwin, *Giovanni's Room*, 16.

96. Judith Butler, *The Psychic Life of Power* (Stanford, Calif.: Stanford University Press, 1997), 134.

97. Baldwin, *Giovanni's Room*, 16.

98. Baldwin, "Here Be Dragons," 678.

99. Terkel, "An Interview with James Baldwin," 21.

100. Baldwin, "Here Be Dragons," 690.

101. Baldwin, "The Male Prison," 105.

Chapter Eight. Rhetoric and the Politics of Identification Writ Large

1. See Miles, *William Burroughs*, 182.

2. Burroughs, *The Job*, 49. On Burroughs and the avoidance of language, see Cary Nelson, *The Incarnate Word: Literature as Verbal Space* (Urbana: University of Illinois Press, 1973), ch. 9.

3. Burroughs, *Nova Express*, 28.

4. Burroughs, *The Soft Machine*, 92.

5. William S. Burroughs, *The Ticket That Exploded* (New York: Grove Press, 1962), 51.

6. Adorno, "Lyric Poetry and Society," 38.

7. Burke, "Definition of Man," 3.

8. Burke, *A Rhetoric of Motives*, xiv.

9. John Bender and David Wellbery, "Rhetoricality: On the Modernist Return of Rhetoric," in *The Ends of Rhetoric: History, Theory, Practice*, ed. John Bender and David Wellbery (Stanford, Calif.: Stanford University Press, 1990), 3–39.

10. Kant, *Critique of Judgment*, 171.

11. Calvin Schrag, "Rhetoric Resituated at the End of Philosophy," *Quarterly Journal of Speech* 71, no. 2 (1985): 164–74. See also Paul Jay, *Contingency Blues: The Search for Foundations in American Criticism* (Madison: University of Wisconsin Press, 1997).

12. Burke, *A Rhetoric of Motives*, xiv.

13. Kenneth Burke, "Rhetoric—Old and New," in *New Rhetorics*, ed. Martin Steinmann, Jr. (New York: Charles Schribner's Sons, 1967), 63.

14. Burke, *A Rhetoric of Motives*, 55.

15. Burke, "Rhetoric—Old and New," 62.

16. Burke, *A Rhetoric of Motives*, 23.

17. Burke, "Rhetoric—Old and New," 63.

18. See Roy Schafer, *Aspects of Internalization* (Madison, Wis.: International Universities Press, 1968).

19. Sigmund Freud, *Interpretation of Dreams*, trans. James Strachey (New York: Avon Books, 1965), 183.

20. Diana Fuss, *Identification Papers* (New York: Routledge, 1995), 41.

21. Kenneth Burke, *Attitudes Toward History*, 3rd ed. (Berkeley: University of California, 1959), 267.

22. Kenneth Burke, "Rhetoric and Poetics," in *Language as Symbolic Action*, 301.

23. Burke, *Attitudes Toward History*, 264.

24. Burke, *A Rhetoric of Motives*, 21.

25. Kenneth Burke, "The Philosophy of Literary Form," in *The Philosophy of Literary Form*, 39.

26. Burke, *Attitudes Toward History*, 318.

27. Burke, *A Rhetoric of Motives*, 39.

28. Burke, "Twelve Propositions," 307.

29. Burke, *A Rhetoric of Motives*, 177.

30. C. Wright Mills, "Situated Actions and Vocabularies of Motive," in *Power, Politics, and People*, 441.

31. Gerth and Mills, *Character and Social Structure*, 114.

32. Burke, *Permanence and Change*, 14.

33. Gerth and Mills, *Character and Social Structure*, 117.

34. Mills, *The Sociological Imagination*, 161.

35. Mills, "Situated Actions and Vocabularies of Motive," 443.

36. Mills and Mills, eds., *C. Wright Mills: Letters and Autobiographical Writings*, 291.

37. Mills, *The Sociological Imagination*, 36.

38. C. Wright Mills, "The Cultural Apparatus," in *Power, Politics, and People*, 406.

39. C. Wright Mills, "The Cultural Apparatus," box 4B380, notebook 11–12, Mills Papers.

40. C. Wright Mills, "Mass Media and Public Opinion," in *Power, Politics, and People*, 578.

41. Mills, "The Cultural Apparatus," Mills Papers.

42. Mills, *The Sociological Imagination*, 211.

43. Gerth and Mills, *Character and Social Structure*, 118.

44. Mills and Mills, *Letters and Autobiographical Writings*, 112. On Mills's notion of sociological poetry, see Patricia Cormack, *Sociology and Mass Culture: Durkheim, Mills, and Baudrillard* (Toronto: University of Toronto Press, 2002); and Christopher Shannon, *Conspicuous Criticism: Tradition, the Individual, and Culture in American Social Thought from Veblen to Mills* (Baltimore: Johns Hopkins University Press, 1996).

45. Mills, *The Sociological Imagination*, 196.

46. Mills, "The Cultural Apparatus," C. Wright Mills Papers.

47. Letter to Kenneth Burke, November 7, 1982, box 38, folder 9, Ralph Ellison Papers, Manuscript Division, Library of Congress, Washington, D.C.

48. Ishmael Reed, Quincy Troupe, and Steve Cannon, "The Essential Ellison," in *Conversations with Ralph Ellison*, ed. Maryemma Graham and Amritjit Singh (Jackson: University Press of Mississippi, 1995), 364.

49. Ralph Ellison, "Notes, Lectures," box 173, folder 1, Ellison Papers.

50. Ellison, "Notes, Lectures," box 173, folder 4, Ellison Papers.

51. John S. Wright, "The Conscious Hero and the Rites of Man: Ellison's War," in *New Essays on Invisible Man*, ed. Robert O'Meally (New York: Cambridge University Press, 1988), 185.

52. Robert G. O'Meally, *The Craft of Ralph Ellison* (Cambridge, Mass.: Harvard University Press, 1980).

53. Alfred Chester and Vilma Howard, "The Art of Fiction: An Interview," in *Conversations with Ralph Ellison*, 8.

54. Ralph Ellison, "Brave Words for a Startling Occasion," in *Collected Essays of Ralph Ellison*, 152.

55. Ellison, "The Little Man at Chehaw Station," 492.

56. Ralph Ellison, "Indivisible Man," in *The Collected Essays of Ralph Ellison*, 364.

57. Irving Howe, "Black Boys and Native Sons," *Dissent* (Autumn 1963): 354.

58. Ralph Ellison, "The World and the Jug," in *The Collected Essays of Ralph Ellison*, 172.

59. Ralph Ellison, "Harlem Is Nowhere," in *The Collected Essays of Ralph Ellison*, 321.

60. Ellison, "The World and the Jug," 170.

61. Ralph Ellison, "Speech to United States Military Academy, West Point, New York," March 26, 1969, box 173, folder 6, Ellison Papers.

62. Ellison, "The World and the Jug," 177.

63. Ralph Ellison, *Invisible Man* (New York: Random House, 1952), 471.

64. Ellison, "The World and the Jug," 170.

65. Burke, *Attitudes Toward History*, 225.

66. Ellison, "The World and the Jug," 177.

67. Burke, *Attitudes Toward History*, 289.

68. Ibid.

69. Ellison, "Drafts and Notes," box 152, folder on *Invisible Man*, Ellison Papers.

70. Ellison, *Invisible Man*, 580.

71. Burke, *Attitudes Toward History*, 341.

72. Ellison, *Invisible Man*, 580.

73. Burke, *Attitudes Toward History*, 39. My reading of Burke is taken from James Livingston, "The Politics of Pragmatism," *Social Text* 49 (Winter 1996): 149–72.

74. Ellison, *Invisible Man*, xviii.

75. Ralph Ellison, "Blues People," in *The Collected Essays of Ralph Ellison*, 286.

76. Ellison, *Invisible Man*, 153–54.

77. Albert Murray, *Stomping the Blues* (New York: McGraw-Hill, 1976), 25.

78. Lewis Mumford, *The Golden Day: A Study in American Experience and Culture* (New York: Horace Liveright, 1926), 30. On the relationship between Ellison's novel and Mumford's work, see Alan Nadel, *Invisible Criticism: Ralph Ellison and the American Canon* (Iowa City: University of Iowa Press, 1988).

79. Mumford, *The Golden Day*, 41.

80. Ralph Ellison, "Invisible Man," Lecture at Hunter College, May 27, 1953, box 170, folder 9, Ellison Papers.

81. Ellison, *Invisible Man*, 41.

82. Ellison, "Drafts and Notes," box 152, folder on *Invisible Man*, Ellison Papers.

83. Ellison, *Invisible Man*, 485.

84. Chester and Howard, "The Art of Fiction," 18.

85. Ellison, *Invisible Man*, 575.

86. Burke, *Attitudes Toward History*, 210.

87. Ellison, *Invisible Man*, 507–8.

88. Ralph Ellison, "That Same Pain, That Same Pleasure," in *The Collected Essays of Ralph Ellison*, 76.

89. John O'Brien, "Interview with Ralph Ellison," in *Conversations with Ralph Ellison*, 232.

90. Ellison, "Drafts and Notes," box 152, folder on *Invisible Man*, Ellison Papers.

91. Ralph Ellison, "Hidden Name and Complex Fate," in *The Collected Essays of Ralph Ellison*, 208.

92. Ralph Ellison, "An American Dilemma: A Review," in *The Collected Essays of Ralph Ellison*, 335.

93. Ellison, "The World and the Jug," 158.

Conclusion

1. Victor Bockris, *Warhol* (New York: Da Capo Press, 1997), 198–99.

2. Irving Howe, "Mass Society and Post-Modern Fiction" (1969), in *Decline of the New*, 203.

3. Howe, "The Culture of Modernism," 33.

4. Levin, "What Was Modernism?" 276.

5. Frank O'Hara, "Personal Poem," in *Lunch Poems* (San Francisco: City Light Books, 1964), 33.

6. Daniel Bell, *The Cultural Contradictions of Capitalism* (New York: Basic Books, 1976), 145.

7. Herbert Marcuse, *An Essay on Liberation* (Boston: Beacon Press, 1969), 45.

8. Kerouac, "Origins of the Beat Generation," 64.

9. On the origins of postmodernism, see Margaret Rose, *The Post-Modern and the Post-Industrial* (Cambridge: Cambridge University Press, 1991); Steven Best and Douglas Kellner, *The Postmodern Turn* (New York: Guilford Press, 1997); and Perry Anderson, *The Origins of Postmodernity* (New York: Verso, 1998).

10. Leslie Fiedler, "The New Mutants," in *The Collected Essays of Leslie Fiedler*, volume 2 (New York: Stein and Day, 1971), 383.

11. Susan Sontag, "One Culture and the New Sensibility," in *Against Interpretation and Other Essays* (New York: Anchor Books, 1966), 303.

12. Ihab Hassan, *The Dismemberment of Orpheus: Toward a Postmodern Literature* (New York: Oxford University Press, 1971).

13. Stanley Aronowitz, "A Mills Revival?" *Logos* 2, no. 3 (Summer 2003): 1.

14. Kevin Mattson, *Intellectuals in America: The Origins of the New Left and Radical Liberalism, 1945–1970* (University Park: Pennsylvania State University Press, 2002), 48.

15. James Gilbert, *Men in the Middle: Searching for Masculinity in the 1950s* (Chicago: University of Chicago Press, 2005), 46.

16. Richard Noland, "The Apocalypse of Norman O. Brown," *American Scholar* 38, no. 1 (Winter 1968): 59–68.

17. Eldridge Cleaver, *Soul on Ice* (New York: Dell, 1991), 136.

18. Jerry Watts, *Heroism and the Black Intellectual: Ralph Ellison, Politics, and Afro-American Intellectual Life* (Chapel Hill: University of North Carolina Press, 1994), 108.

19. Irving Howe, "This Age of Conformity," in *A World More Attractive: A View of Modern Literature and Politics* (New York: Horizon Press, 1963), 275.

20. David Hopkins, *After Modern Art, 1945–2000* (New York: Oxford University Press, 2000), 111.

21. Ellison, "The Little Man at Chehaw Station," 499.

22. John Hersey, "'A Completion of Personality': A Talk with Ralph Ellison," in *Conversations with Ralph Ellison*, 286.

23. Ellison, "The Little Man at Chehaw Station," 496.
24. Mills, *The Sociological Imagination*, 164.
25. Burke, "Rhetoric and Poetics," 301.
26. Gerth and Mills, *Character and Social Structure*, 160.
27. Mills, *The Sociological Imagination*, 166.

INDEX

ACKNOWLEDGMENTS

LIKE MOST ACADEMIC works, this book took much too long to write. In many ways, I should offer an apology to everyone in my life for having spent so much time completing this. I have been very lucky that a seemingly endless number of people have stood by me over the years, and I am grateful to have this opportunity to thank them. My first debt goes to my undergraduate history advisor, Jim Livingston, who not only introduced me to the field of intellectual history but also taught me how to think outside disciplinary boundaries. His example is more than obvious throughout my work. At Columbia University, Alan Brinkley and Elizabeth Blackmar were incredibly supportive and generous with their time and willing to entertain my odd research interests. Ann Douglas graciously read an early version of this manuscript and helped to improve it immensely. More than anyone else at Columbia, Casey Blake understands the difficulties young scholars face, and he has helped me on numerous occasions, most recently with finding a home for this work.

I could not have written this book without generous financial and professional support from several institutions. My early academic career was supported by Columbia University's History Department, and the initial stages of this project were begun with financial assistance from the Lane Cooper Foundation. I was also lucky enough to spend three engaging years at the Institute for Social and Economic Research and Policy at Columbia University, and I would like to thank Peter Bearman and Bill McAllister for their generosity and their belief in this project. I was an Andrew Mellon Postdoctoral Fellow at the University of Michigan, and I owe thanks to everyone who made my two-year stay in Ann Arbor so memorable. Fordham University provided me with a home for several years, and thanks go to Doron Ben-Atar, Nancy Curtin, and Barry Goldberg for their generosity. I would also like to thank Phil Nicholson and my other colleagues at Nassau Community College for their continuing support.

Some of the arguments in these pages were tried out in earlier forms. Portions of Chapter 1 previously appeared as "'I'm Not His Father': Lionel Trilling, Allen Ginsberg, and the Contours of Literary Modernism," *College Literature* 31, no. 2 (Spring 2004): 22–52, and portions of Chapter 8 previously appeared as "Toward a Theory of Rhetoric: Ralph Ellison, Kenneth Burke, and the Problem of Modernism," *Twentieth-Century Literature* 48, no. 2 (Summer 2002): 191–214. I thank both journals for permission to reproduce revised versions here. The research for this book was helped by access to several archives. I would like to thank Nik Mills for permission to quote from the C. Wright Mills Papers at the Center for American History at the University of Texas at Austin. I would also like to thank John Callahan for permission to quote from the Ralph Ellison Papers at the Library of Congress. For helping to make this book more readable and more accessible, I would like to thank Bob Lockhart and his staff at the University of Pennsylvania Press for their suggestions, interest, and encouragement.

I also owe an enormous debt to all of my friends—old and new—who carried me through not just the writing of this book but the past several years in general, friends who read drafts of each chapter, who listened to me cry and complain, who went with me to baseball games, and who graciously helped to carry endless boxes of books from one apartment to the next. For that and so much more, I would like to thank Joel Allen, Paul Anderson, Emily Axel, Matt and Miriam Backes, Andy Campbell, Chris Capozzola, John Carson, Kristen Cerelli, Henry Chen, Pauline Chow, Jen Dunfee, Martha Jones, Kevin Lalli, Archana LaPollo, Mike and Monica Liggio, Amy Marsman, Peter McElvanna, Andy McStay, Keith O'Brien, Stephanie Sapiie, Ellen Stroud, and Michelle Trehy. This book would never have been completed without the help of all these wonderful people.

Similarly, I owe an enormous debt to my family—old and new—who have helped me through a litany of changes over the years and who have provided me time and time again with a wonderful respite from everything. I would like to thank the entire D'Aquanno family—John, Lisa, Johnny, Nick, Craig, Christine, Andrew, Nathan, and Julia—for welcoming me into their lives. My family in Florida—Nancy Byrd, Dana Troian, and Michael Dreggors—and my family in North Carolina—Charles, Laura, and Caroline Genter—have stood by me over the years, and I thank them deeply for that. More than anyone else, Phyllis Genter has helped to hold this growing family together, and I thank her for everything she has done for me and our family. Finally, this book would not have been possible without help from my parents. When I was a young boy, my father would frequently take my brother and me to the local newsstand where he would buy the latest comic books for us. He always said it was important for us to appreciate reading, regardless of the material. As an adult, I have of course exchanged the Incredible Hulk for more esoteric books, but the point remains the same. I thank him for everything he has taught me. I dedicate this book to him and to the memory of my mother. I hope I have captured some of her spirit in these pages.